CITY CO

FLAUBERT THE MASTER

Gustave Flaubert in middle age: a photograph from life by Nadar.

FLAUBERT
THE MASTER

A CRITICAL AND BIOGRAPHICAL STUDY (1856-1880)

Enid Starkie

WEIDENFELD AND NICOLSON
5 Winsley Street London W 1

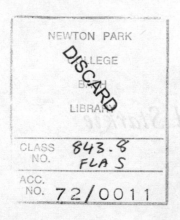

ISBN 0 297 00226 0

Printed in England by C. Tinling and Co. Ltd, London and Prescot

For
DAVID CECIL
because he shares
the author's love and admiration
for Flaubert

CONTENTS

ILLUSTRATIONS

The medallion illustrated on the jacket is reproduced by permission of the Radio Times Hulton Picture Library.

PUBLISHER'S NOTE

At the time of her death in April 1970, Enid Starkie
had handed the completed manuscript of *Flaubert the
Master* to the publishers, but there were still many
inconsistencies to be rectified, and many of the
source-notes were incomplete. The publishers have
made a few minor changes which they felt would in
any case have been made at proof-stage, but the book
is fundamentally as Enid Starkie submitted it. Most
of the missing source-notes have been added but a
very few proved impossible to trace.

INTRODUCTION

This study of Gustave Flaubert and his work, when planned in 1961, was intended to be in two volumes. Circumstances prevented its being finished as one consecutive whole, and, as it seemed possible, at one time, that only Volume One would be written – if at all – more was included in the Conclusion of that volume than would normally have been the case or was advisable. This is regrettable, as it has destroyed the unity of the complete work, and some aspects were touched upon, but not fully studied or investigated, which should have gone into Volume Two. These will have to be amplified in the present book and will lead to some repetition.

This volume, entitled *The Master*, is intended to show Flaubert in full possession of his art and craft, and how he used them in different ways, without repeating himself; each novel being intended to solve a separate problem and to treat it in a different way, with a different style.

Salammbô is a historical novel, a return to one of his earliest strands of inspiration when, as a boy, he was more interested in history than in any other subject. It is however a newer form of historical novel than that practised before him in the nineteenth century.

L'Éducation Sentimentale is a psychological study of character and as well of contemporary life; it also continues a trend from his youth, exemplified for instance in *Passion et Vertu* and the first *Éducation Sentimentale*.

La Tentation de Saint Antoine investigates religious and philosophical thought, as was done earlier in *Smarh* and in the first *Tentation de Saint Antoine*.

These three novels exemplify the main aspects of Flaubert's genius, the historical, the contemporary and the legendary. *Trois Contes* treats all three in a miniature form, and draws them all together in one single strand.

Bouvard et Pécuchet shows human intellectual failure, and the incapacity of man to reach any certainty.

The book is intended also to give a picture of Flaubert as a man, as a human being, not only as an artist. The longer the reader is acquainted with him, the fonder he becomes of him. All his friends – even the most casual – felt this and he had very many of them, men and women, who loved him and enjoyed his company. The reputation he has had – especially in books – of being gloomy, pessimistic and bear-like, was completely unfounded. It is true that his work, taken as a whole, is pessimistic and sad; that theoretically, he did not think much of human nature but, in practice, his friends could do no wrong and he was a gay member of any society, whose energy wore out his companions and who delighted in childish jokes and pranks, and in lewd stories. He was generally sad in his correspondence, but one must not take what an author says in his letters as a statement of fact, but only as an effort to clarify a temporary state of mind, to make it concrete. On the contrary, his excitement and pleasure in company continued, through illness, unhappiness and disaster, until a few weeks before he died, as one can see from his behaviour at the last Saint Polycarp festivities which took place a fortnight before his death in 1880.

He was also a devoted friend who spared himself no pain on the behalf of those he loved. There were few who met him, men or women, who did not fall for his charm and surrender to it. It is hoped that this will become apparent in this book.

The manuscripts of all the novels are now available to the reader. We have seen, in Volume One, that the manuscripts, drafts and all the notes for *Madame Bovary* are preserved in the Bibliothèque Municipale at Rouen. The manuscript of *Salammbô*, with all the notes, plans and drafts, are in the Bibliothèque Nationale in Paris. Two copies of the finished manuscript of *L'Éducation Sentimentale* are in the Bibliothèque Historique de la Ville de Paris. Unfortunately the notes used for its composition were not bequeathed to any library after the death of his niece in 1931, but were sold and bought by the actor Sacha Guitry, and they have not been available

2

since then. This is a grievous loss for Flaubert's greatest work. However there are the documents in connection with the work which are preserved amongst the *Bouvard et Pécuchet* papers in the Bibliothèque Municipale at Rouen.

All the drafts, notes and plans which went to the composition of the three versions of *La Tentation de Saint Antoine* are in the Bibliothèque Nationale in Paris, as well as all those for *Trois Contes*. The manuscripts, notes, plans and fair copies of *Bouvard et Pécuchet* are all in the Bibliothèque Municipale at Rouen, a truly gigantic and terrifying 'dossier'.

A great deal of Flaubert's correspondence – but not all – is in the Spoelberch de Lovenjoul Collection belonging to the Institut at Chantilly; but there are some letters scattered in various other places, as for instance in the Bibliothèque Nationale, but all have not yet been collected. There is, for instance, a letter from Flaubert to George Sand, in the Spoelberch de Lovenjoul Collection, dated 18 October 1871, which for some unknown reason has not been published in the collected *Correspondance*, as it is neither blasphemous nor obscene, and it is still unpublished.[1] There are two letters from him to Jane de Tourbey, of May and June 1865, which have been printed by Auriant in his *Les Secrets de la Comtesse de Castiglione*.[2] As far as I know these have been published nowhere else. There are further letters to her, extracts from which are printed by Suffel in his *Flaubert*, though not the entire letters.

There are also in the Spoelberch de Lovenjoul Collection letters addressed to Flaubert, some of which should be published, especially Louis Bouilhet's correspondence with him; his letters to Louise Colet have been published, but not those to Flaubert, which are more interesting and more significant.

As has been remarked in the Introduction to *The Making of the Master*, Flaubert's correspondence has been hitherto very imperfectly published and it is hoped that the edition being prepared by Jean Bruneau, for the Bibliothèque de la Pléiade, will be more satisfactory. Even in the four supplementary volumes of letters in the standard edition of Conard, published since the end of the last war, there are many omissions and excisions, largely for the sake of decency, which should no longer be necessary. Some of the passages have been merely crossed out in the originals and these can easily be replaced in subsequent editions. Some others, however, have been so much scored out and obliterated that it is impossible now to decipher them, which is a pity. One wonders whether they were really more indecent than the passages merely crossed out. It was thought that the early bowdlerization was due to Flaubert's niece, but she has been dead now nearly forty years.

The omissions are particularly frequent in the letters addressed to Duplan, to whom Flaubert seems to have written more freely and more pornographically than to his other friends. They may have shared a homosexual relationship, as Flaubert frequently addresses him as 'vieux pédéraste', and he describes to him, with vivid details, a school for young pederasts, either imagined or real.[3] In a passage in another letter he says:[4] 'Lâche ta vieille ce samedi-là. Préviens-la donc. Il me tarde d'embrasser ta binette. Moi je délaisserais pour toi *celles dont tu es jaloux.*' Two examples of his pornographic style, crossed out by whoever was editing the letters, are given in the notes.[5] Where passages have been crossed out in the originals, there are sometimes notes in the margin of the text, saying: 'Begin after this.' A portrait of Flaubert is incomplete if one omits his love of salacious stories and lewd situations. This is an aspect of his character which he kept out of his printed works.

There are many letters which it would have been illuminating to possess and which have not been preserved. Louise Colet's letters to him were burnt by her daughter; we do not know what has become of Jane de Tourbey's and very few of his letters to her have reached us; Princesse Mathilde probably insisted on her letters being returned to her after his death – as she had done with Sainte-Beuve's correspondence after his death in 1869, as we know from the acrimonious correspondence between herself and the critic's secretary, Troubat. No letters from either side have come down to us from Flaubert and the second English governess of his niece, Juliet Herbert, although it is known that he cherished a great affection for her and used to go to visit her in London. There must have been some correspondence between them, but this problem will be discussed in a later chapter.

The sources of each book have not been thoroughly investigated, except when it was essential for an understanding of the novel – this would have overweighted the book still further. Also, in each case, the sources have been thoroughly investigated by others and published. The search for possible sources leads to exaggeration, as every vague similarity between Flaubert and another author is seized upon and hailed as a source. In any case the sources of a creative artist are not very important, but only the use that he makes of them in his work, and not their accuracy. Sometimes, however, the sources of an author do tell us something about him. J. J. Seznec has shown how much Flaubert's fantastic imagination – especially in *La Tentation de Saint Antoine* – comes from the works of art – paintings, drawings and statuary – which he knew and admired. These are sources important psychologically. Also only Flaubert would have pursued the minute research which he carried out for *Bouvard et Pécuchet*, a great deal of which was unnecessary for the novel, but which reveals the author's gratuitous love of knowledge for its own sake, without thought of the use he might put it to, and this is significant in him as a person.

Each of Flaubert's books has some works which are useful for its understanding:

For *Salammbô*: P. B. Fay: *Sources and Structure of Flaubert's Salammbô*; A. Hamilton: *Sources of the Religious Element in Flaubert's Salammbô*; L. Benedetto: *Le Origini di Salammbô*.
For *L'Éducation Sentimentale*: P. Castex: *Flaubert, L'Éducation Sentimentale*; M. J. Durry: *Flaubert et ses Projets Inédits*.
For *La Tentation de Saint Antoine*: J. J. Seznec: *Nouvelles Études sur la Tentation de Saint Antoine*; A. Lombard: *Flaubert et Saint Antoine*.
For *Trois Contes*: C. Duckworth: *Trois Contes*; G. Michaut: *Trois Contes*.
For *Bouvard et Pécuchet*: M. J. Durry: *op. cit.*; A. Cento: *Flaubert, Bouvard et Pécuchet*; D. L. Demorest: *À travers les Plans, Messages et Dossiers de Bouvard et Pécuchet*.

For Flaubert as a writer and a stylist, there are two valuable books, D. L. Demorest: *L'Expression Figurée et Symbolique dans l'Œuvre de Gustave Flaubert,* which is perfect of its kind; and E. L. Ferrère: *L'Esthétique de Flaubert.*
The books listed in the Bibliography of this volume are those which are important for Flaubert's life and works after 1857, after the publication of *Madame Bovary*; those treating that novel were listed in the Bibliography of Volume One.
The books and articles on Flaubert multiply each year, but

there is one from the United States, especially, which is indispensable, as it is the only full *étude d'ensemble* in any language – Benjamin Bart's *Flaubert*. Bart has seen all the documents – published and unpublished – and is thus able to build up a complete picture of the author. His method will not, however, commend itself to everyone. He does not always give his references and it is therefore difficult to investigate his sources. Also he often uses Flaubert's correspondence, as well as his works, without quotation marks, as if they were part of his narrative and written by himself, so that it is impossible to disentangle whether it is Flaubert or Bart writing; all goes into the biographical text, written in the third person. He is also inclined to use the fictional material of the novels as if they were true fact and thus evidence, which is always dangerous. He tends too to rely too much on the psycho-analytical method, which may often lead to false conclusions, as it does not allow sufficiently for creative activity, which is very important in a writer such as Flaubert.

Except when otherwise stated, the edition used for the works and correspondence is that published by Conard in twenty-nine volumes. The passages quoted from the Spoelberch de Lovenjoul Collection of the letters are unpublished, except when otherwise stated. All translations from the French are my own.

I would like to thank the following for their aid: Mademoiselle Jeanne Dupic, Librarian at the Bibliothèque Municipale at Rouen, for her help and for having opened the library for me when it would otherwise have been closed; Monsieur de Saint Rémy, Librarian at the Bibliothèque Historique de la Ville de Paris, for permission to consult the *Carnets* and the manuscripts of *L'Éducation Sentimentale*; Monsieur Pommier, Monsieur Pierrot and Monsieur Josserand, for their valuable help when I was working on the Spoelberch de Lovenjoul Collection at Chantilly; Monsieur Julien Cain, former Administrateur of the Bibliothèque Nationale in Paris, who has done so much to collect the large number of Flaubert manuscripts and documents at the library, and for his invaluable advice and help; Miss Joanna Richardson, especially for communicating to me certain unpublished portions from the Primoli and Popelin papers, particularly the last letter which Flaubert wrote, which she published in *The Times Literary Supplement,* on 15 June 1968, and which, hitherto, was unknown. I would also like to thank my former student, Sonia Spurdle, for help in

Introduction

checking references in Paris which I was prevented from investigating myself.

I would also like to thank the British Academy for their generous help in awarding me grants to carry out the research for this book, and without which it would not have been completed.

And finally I would like to thank my publishers, Weidenfeld and Nicolson, for help and advice in producing this book, and also the first volume, and for their patience and devoted service.

Oxford, December 1969   ENID STARKIE

Part One

The Second Empire

CHAPTER ONE

AFTER MADAME BOVARY

Flaubert's life greatly changed after the publication of *Madame Bovary*. He now ceased being the provincial who came to the capital only for odd nights, staying in a hotel. He became almost a Parisian, remaining in Paris for a large part of the year – most of the winter – though he always returned to his country house at Croisset, near Rouen, when he was occupied in writing his books. He collected his material in Paris but used it at Croisset, where he kept his books and his notes.

Since 1856, when *Madame Bovary* was being serialized in *La Revue de Paris* and he was correcting his proofs, he had rented an apartment at 42 Boulevard du Temple, a modest apartment on the third floor consisting of an entrance hall; two reception rooms looking out on to the boulevard; a dining-room and a bedroom looking on to the courtyard; and a lavatory. These he furnished himself. Taine, who visited it, has described it.[1] It faced south, he said, with a good view. It was profusely furnished with carpets and hangings; with divans and arm-chairs upholstered in red leather; there were medallions everywhere, cupboards of carved wood and an Indian god on the mantelpiece. Flaubert seemed to have had a great liking for carved oak, as all the bookcases at Croisset also were of the same dark wood. Later on, when he was more settled, his mother joined him in Paris to look after him, and she rented an apartment in the same building, of the same size, but on the second floor.

At this time in Paris Flaubert made a new set of acquaintances. Up to the publication of *Madame Bovary*, Du Camp and Bouilhet seem to have been his only friends and he saw neither of them now very often, as both were living in Paris and in Rouen.

But a coldness had arisen temporarily between himself and Du Camp on account of the difficulties which had arisen in connection with the publication of *Madame Bovary* in *La Revue de Paris*.[2]

In the meantime, however, Bouilhet was no longer in Paris. He had never liked the capital – in this he was unlike Flaubert – even in his early days when he had gone there to seek fame and fortune and to meet literary men. Even in those days, he had written to Flaubert:[3]

Paris bores me to death, I don't quite know why. But I'm suffering like a wretched man. I regret Rouen!!! You'll laugh at that. But it's quite true I assure you, and literature bores me excessively. It disgusts me to dive into that mud. Stupidity is at its height; there is radically no place there for an honest man. I've had more than enough of it. I see no end to it all and the game isn't worth the candle. I've done one foolish thing in my life, a fundamental foolish thing; and that is to have come to Paris.

He hated the sordid struggle of the literary life in Paris, without private means. In 1857 the librarianship in the little town of Mantes, half way between Paris and Rouen, where Flaubert had so often gone to meet Louise Colet, became vacant. He was appointed and so Flaubert, who was now in Paris, could again see him only intermittently.

At Mantes Bouilhet lived quietly in peace for ten years, with his humble mistress, Léonie Leparfait, and her illegitimate son. She was the daughter of a farmer who had been abandoned by her lover, with a bastard, when Bouilhet met her. She was his mistress for fifteen years and looked after him with great devotion, especially during his last twelve years when he was librarian at Mantes and later at Rouen. It was a very different life from the one he had led in Paris, when he was a member of the literary world and was the lover of Louise Colet and Madame Roger des Genettes. However he willingly gave up his fashionable life in Paris and his intelligent mistresses, and settled down in bourgeois happiness in Mantes. This was the happiest time of his life. He now had a fixed salary for the first time in his life, and living was cheap in Mantes. He had a nice little house and garden near the river, was well looked after by his faithful mistress and had a ready-made family in her son, of whom he was very fond. He did not care that he was not received by the conventional bourgeois society, on account of the irregularity of his home life. He was left in peace to carry on his professional duties and he had some leisure for his literary pursuits. These years at Mantes and at Rouen, as librarian, were his years as a dramatist. It had begun with the comparative success of *Mademoiselle de Montarcy* in 1856, for which Flaubert had worked so hard. Then there was *Hélène Peyron* in 1858, which had eight performances at the Odéon. Next there were the fiascos of *L'Oncle Million* and *Dolores* in 1862. Then, as we shall see, he collaborated unsuccessfully with Flaubert in the composition of *Le Château des Cœurs* in 1863. Next *Faustine* was put on by Marc Fournier very luxuriously at the Théâtre de la Porte Saint Martin, but it lasted only a month. Then he wrote a historical play, *La Conjuration d'Amboise*, which was produced in 1866 and reached its hundredth performance in March 1867. All these, except the first, were written while he was at Mantes.

In Paris Flaubert's new friends in the literary world were Sainte-Beuve, Gautier, the two Goncourt brothers, the Russian novelist Turgenev, and the popular writer Ernest Feydeau, who cashed in on literary successes. There was also Jules Duplan, who became his closest friend after Louis Bouilhet. Duplan collected material for him, for his documentation, but he could not criticize his friend's work as Bouilhet did.

After his trial, in January 1857, for offences against morality and religion, in which he was acquitted but not awarded costs, Flaubert remained very much cast down and depressed. He began, at first, to work at his *Tentation de Saint Antoine* and he intended that it should be his next published work, as fragments from it had appeared in *L'Artiste* the previous December. These had not been well received and mention of them had been made at his trial as a proof of his anti-religious sentiments. He was now afraid of continuing with the plan of publication, in case another law-suit should be instigated against him for blasphemy. He wrote to Madame Pradier in February 1857:[4]

I had intended to publish immediately another book which had taken several years to write, composed from the Fathers of the Church, full of mythology and antiquity – I must now sacrifice this pleasure, for it would certainly take me to the courts – two or three other plans which I had in prospect are postponed for the same reason. How powerful is social hypocrisy! At the present time every portrait is considered satire, and history an accusation. That is why I am so tired and so sad.

At the same time he was collecting material for the story which was to become *Saint Julien l'Hospitalier* in *Trois Contes* in 1877. It is not known why he chose to embark on this topic at this time.

He seems to have been toying with another project in 1857, which appears to have worried Bouilhet, though no title is mentioned, though it may have been *Salammbô*, which he certainly began in 1857. Bouilhet wrote to him:[5]

Either you misunderstood me, or else I expressed myself badly, about my feelings concerning your future book. Like you, not only do I think it possible, but I hope that it will be very beautiful – only it is of an appalling difficulty which horrifies me – and I was surprised at seeing you throwing yourself with such light-heartedness into such a scabrous subject – that's all! Next, which is less important, and which has not the shadow of importance with regard to art – is, in my opinion, the untimeliness of the book in the present crisis of your reputation; I may be wrong, but it would seem to me wiser for you to embark on another work of observation with the resolve never to return to the same sort of thing again.

Later in the year Bouilhet wrote again and, this time, he must be referring to the future *Salammbô*, as Flaubert had written to Feydeau in April,[6] 'I'm having a lot of trouble with *Carthage*.' He also wrote several times, in May, to Duplan, who had been trying to persuade him to return to *Saint Antoine*.[7] 'No, my dear boy, in spite of your advice I'm not going to abandon *Carthage* to take up *Saint Antoine* again, because I am no longer in that climate of ideas, and I'd have to re-do it completely which wouldn't be a small job . . . I'm in the midst of *Carthage* and I'm going to try to bury myself in it as much as possible and to be inspired.'

He went on working at the book, which continued to be called *Carthage*. He was doing a great deal of research for it and, by the end of July 1857, he told Duplan that he had read over a hundred books.[8] In August he told Bouilhet that his reading was almost completed.[9] He began writing in September and, at the end of the month, he told Duplan that he had written fifteen pages.[10] The following month he describes his heroine;[11] the book is still called *Carthage*, but he wrote to Charles Edmond in October saying that it was to be called *Salammbô* – she is the heroine, a character invented by him, the daughter of Hamilcar.[12]

He was, however, becoming very much discouraged as he was

making no headway, and, in September, Bouilhet, trying to encourage him, wrote to him, in simulated medical terms: 'Come on now! Have you forgotten the tortures of *Madame Bovary*? The stronger the child the more painful the gripes. I assure you that your child is developing well – I already see its head – it is viable. The book cannot be as "living" as *Madame Bovary*. That would be impossible – I'll even go as far as to say that it would be a mistake – over distant objects there must be a certain mistiness, some blurring is better than a clear outline – real life must only appear at intervals, as lightning flashes on the horizon, in the distance – the danger is the beauty of the subject.'[13]

His work was also interrupted because he was much occupied with Bouilhet's theatrical ventures. In 1856 he had all the excitement of the production of his *Mademoiselle de Montarcy* at the Odéon theatre, which was a success.[14] In 1857 he was trying, in vain, to get *Hélène Peyron* produced but, after prolonged efforts, succeeded in getting it put on only in November 1858, when it had a comparative success. It was kept on until 12 January 1859, and put on again from 27 January to 7 February 1859. The Emperor and the Empress attended a performance on 9 January 1859. But the following play, *L'Oncle Million*, produced in December 1860, was a complete failure, as Flaubert related to Duplan.[15] All this took up a great deal of his precious time which could, more profitably, have been spent on his own work, which was going badly. He had a bad winter that year, as he was ill with influenza and he was anxious also on his mother's behalf – she had pleurisy.

Finally he decided, in February 1858, that he must get away from France and he determined to leave in April.[16] He believed that he was on the wrong track, that he could not see his characters nor their surroundings clearly and that he must go to North Africa to be able to see things in perspective, on the spot. He wrote to Mademoiselle Leroyer de Chantepie to say goodbye,[17] saying:

I must absolutely pay a visit to Africa, so, at the end of March, I'll go back to the land of dates. I'm very happy at the thought of it. I'll live on horseback, sleep in tents. What good gulps of air I'll swallow at Marseilles on the steamboat. I only need to go to Kheff, thirty leagues from Tunis, and wander about in the neighbourhood of Carthage, in a circumference of a radius of ninety leagues, to know deeply the country which I'm claiming to study. My plan is done and I'm a third of the way through the second chapter – the book will have fifteen. You see that I'm not very far on! Even with all the luck in the world I can't be finished before two years.

He started on his trip on 12 April 1858, he was away for six weeks, and he was back in Paris on 6 June.

He stopped, on the way to Africa, at Marseilles and tried, once more, to discover the whereabouts of Eulalie Foucaud, the creole woman with whom he had a brief affair, when he was eighteen, on his first trip abroad, after his *baccalauréat* in 1840.[18] He had never forgotten her and every time that he passed through Marseilles he looked for traces of her. He wrote to Bouilhet:[19]

I saw the house in Marseilles again where, ten years ago, I knew Madame Foucaud. Everything is very much changed! The ground floor, which was the drawing-room, is now a bazaar and, on the first floor, there is a barber's establishment. I went there twice to be shaved. I'll spare you any comment and the Chateaubriand-like reflections on the flight of the days and the shedding of leaves and hair. No matter! it was a long time since I had thought or felt so deeply – I don't know! Philoxène would say 'I've read the stones of the staircase and the walls of the house.'
I found myself very lonely in Marseilles for the two days. I went to the museum, to the theatre. I visited the old quarters of the town; I smoked in outlying pubs, in the midst of the sailors, gazing at the sea.

Flaubert was in Algeria when Petrus Borel was at Mostaganem, living like a peasant tilling his own land. He had gone there after the Revolution of 1848, when he despaired of ever making a living at literature in Paris. He had first been an Inspecteur de la Colonisation, but through various misfortunes and inefficiency he had lost his appointment.[20] He was to die in 1859. It is a pity that he and Flaubert did not meet, as he had been one of the famous revolutionary writers in the thirties in Paris, and Flaubert had, in those days, greatly admired his writings. Later, in 1860, he was to ask Feydeau to procure for him all the works of Petrus Borel. He does not seem to have realized that he might have met him in 1858 in Africa.

Although he had gone to Africa to visit Carthage he saw it only four times – on 27 April and on three days from 4 to 7 May. He seemed more interested, surprisingly, in the modern life and the clash of civilizations which he saw in North Africa. He became acquainted with the local residents of different nationalities, mostly occupied with archaeological research. He met the Englishman Wood and the Frenchman Léon Roches, both of them working on the ruins of Carthage, and the famous Father Bourgade, who was also active in the excavations of Carthage. Father Bourgade had become chaplain to the French residents and he had many other functions as well. In 1842 he had been nominated as chaplain to the Chapelle Saint Louis de Carthage. He also opened a hospital and a school for boys of all nationalities. Flaubert, who got on easily with people, became friendly with all of them and they greatly helped him to see what he wanted.[21]

He visited a courtesan in Tunis, but this had none of the luxury and glamour of his visit to Kuschiuk Hânem in Egypt when he was young. He has described his visit in his *Carnet No. 10*, preserved in the Bibliothèque Historique de la Ville de Paris. It is not printed in his *Notes de Voyages* and is unpublished. The brothel was very dirty and sordid as he describes it.[22] 'Près du Souk aux cuirs – escalier merde . . . une chambre au fond une à gauche. Ces dames au salon.' He chose his girl called Rahel,

petite, maigre, museau allongé, les sourcils complètement rejoints par la peinture noire-rouge . . . Dans le patio, flambeaux d'argile verts, au milieu sur une table, poissons dans un bocal, l'au de vie [*sic*], les deux chambres ouvertes, un grand flambeau par terre, au milieu comme un candelabre d'église . . . Ma chambre: pierres. On cale la porte avec deux pierres, portière en mince calicot au fond. Gueulades des Juifs. On bouche la fenêtre avec un oreiller. Gd. lit à moustiquaire, horribles draps, couvertures à bandes rouges. Un matelas brun de crasse. On voit le jour par les murs et on a peur de faire s'écrouler la maison en limont. Mouvement de poële à frire continu.

To balance the 'danse de l'abeille' of Kuschiuk Hânem there was a 'dense du crapaud, le cul plus haut que tout le reste, gde liberté de manière. Le valet de Marsan cumule les deux goûts. Sortis à deux heures du matin.'

The most precious thing which Flaubert gained from his visit to North Africa was a living feeling for the country and the various scenes it offered. He thought that none of it could have altered very much in appearance since the time of Hamilcar. This gives a vividness to his descriptions which he would not have been able to convey before seeing them in reality. One day he noticed a dromedary on a terrace working a well, and he imagined that it must have been so in the time of Carthage.[23] He noticed all the different colours of the local stone at various hours of the day according to the light.

On 5 June Flaubert was back again in Paris. He spent the first few days seeing all his friends, and particularly his women friends, of whom he had a great many since he was living in Paris, and of whom mention will be made in the following chapter – Madame Pradier, Jane de Tourbey, Madame Sabatier, all well known in the demi-monde in the heyday of the Second Empire. Jane de Tourbey, one of his favourites, he saw every day and sometimes several times a day. On 9 June he was back at Croisset and he spent four days sleeping to recover from the fatigues of the journey and also from the rioting in Paris. Then he took out the manuscript of *Salammbô* and realized, as he said to Feydeau, that he would be obliged to rewrite the whole thing.[24] He worked hard for a week with Bouilhet but came to the conclusion that little could be salvaged of his previous work. He felt full of energy and ready to embark on the book again. He was nevertheless appalled at what had still to be done and, as he said to Mademoiselle Leroyer de Chantepie, he would not be able to finish it within three years. It was then that he composed the prayer which figures at the end of the Carthage section of *Notes de Voyages*, and which he dates 'Saturday 12 to Sunday 13 June, midnight':[25]

Que toutes les énergies de la nature que j'ai aspirées me pénètrent et qu'elles s'exhalent dans mon livre. A moi, puissances de l'émotion plastique! résurrection du passé, à moi! à moi! Il faut faire, à travers le Beau, vivant et vrai quand même. Pitié pour ma volonté, Dieu, des âmes! donne-moi la Force – et l'Espoir.

Nevertheless, in spite of all his hopes and hard work, he was finding it very difficult to make progress with *Salammbô* and he was much tempted to abandon it altogether. It seemed beyond his powers and he thought of starting on something else. Bouilhet was trying to encourage him and wrote to him in August 1860:[26] 'You seem to me very low, my poor friend, but I don't understand that for a mere question of detail – big despairs I understand, but they are concerned with the work as a whole – you are no longer at that stage.'

He wrote again the following March:[27] 'You'll go back to

your Giscon' – one of the characters from *Salammbô* – 'you're too much on the right path to be seriously impeded. Your book is rising, be sure of that, it is developing in interest, in strength. That doesn't mean that the first chapters are inferior but the book proves that it is based on a good plan since it rises progressively.' By September, however, Flaubert seemed more cheerful and Bouilhet was able to say to him:[28] 'Well done! my dear old fellow, you seem to me pleased with your work.'

When Flaubert had been in North Africa, it had not been the past as much as the present there which had occupied his thoughts, the contrast between the static and unchanging past and the contemporary world. When he could not make any progress with *Salammbô* he toyed with the idea of writing a novel dealing with the clash between East and West. In one of his *Carnets*, dated 1859, there is the plan of such a book.[29] 'Le grand roman social à écrire (maintenant que les rangs et les castes sont perdus) doit représenter la lutte ou plutôt la fusion de la Barbarie et de la civilisation. La scène doit se passer en Orient et en Occident. Oppositions de mœurs, de paysages et de caractères. Tout y paraît, le héros principal devait être un Barbare qui se civilise près d'un civilisé qui se barbarise.'

However, the following year he abandoned the plan when he was seriously working at *Salammbô*, even though he was still in difficulties. At the same time he was spending a lot of time on the works of his friends. He squandered months of precious time on Ernest Feydeau's wretched novel *Daniel*, almost rewriting it. It was eventually dedicated to him. Feydeau had cashed in on the notoriety of *Madame Bovary* by producing *Fanny* in 1858. A critic had said that *Madame Bovary* was immoral but that *Fanny* was indecent. Now that he thought it safe he thought of publishing a still more daring novel, one of the scenes of which described the hero looking through a hole in a hotel partition wall at the girl undressing next door. Flaubert was very envious of the ten thousand francs for which Feydeau had sold the rights, considering that Michel Lévy had paid him only five hundred for the rights on *Madame Bovary* for five years, most of which had gone on his lawsuit.[30] It is hard to think that Flaubert could have had any good opinion of *Daniel*.

The coldness between Flaubert and Du Camp, which had arisen during the publication of *Madame Bovary* in *La Revue de*

Paris, had somewhat abated during the past three years, and they were now seeing one another again. After the suppression of the review in 1859 on account of its too liberal ideas, Du Camp went to the *Revue des Deux Mondes,* and later, in 1864, to the *Débats,* where he remained until his death. He also wrote for *La Revue Nationale* and *Le Moniteur Universel.* In 1860 he separated from Madame Delessert, the fashionable woman of the world who had been his mistress since he returned from the East in 1851. Then he decided to go to Italy to fight for Garibaldi's cause. Flaubert was very anxious on his behalf and wrote to him in August 1860:[31] 'If you've five minutes to spare, my dear Max, then send me a word only so that I should know what is happening to you, damn it all, if you're dead, alive or wounded. I'm doing my utmost not to think about you, but the thought of you obsesses me and comes back to me a hundred times an hour. I imagine you in the most dreadful situations, and you know that I have a lively imagination visually, and I build up pictures which aren't gay and which wrench my heart. I don't ask for any details but only what has become of you.'

Du Camp remained only four months in Italy and did not see very much fighting. He returned safely to France and wrote a book entitled *Expédition des Deux Siciles* to recount his exploits. It was published in 1861. Like all his previous books it is colourless and factual. He merely recounts the fighting and the conditions, but nothing seems to have struck his imagination or to have stirred him personally. He returned to Paris and took up his fashionable life of parties and visits to such houses as that of Princesse Mathilde. He then adopted the life which was to be his until his death. He lived now with a humbler mistress than Madame Delessert, carried on fashionable journalism and went to Baden every autumn for his very bad arthritis, which was said to be due to syphilis. He soon embarked on a novel dealing with contemporary life – a subject similar to that of Flaubert's *Éducation Sentimentale* – which appeared in *La Revue Nationale* in 1865 and 1866 and, in book form, in 1867. It was *Les Forces Perdues.* He eventually abandoned purely literary creative work and became the historian of Paris, but he did not lose his ambition and he was elected a member of the French Academy in 1880.

A friendship which Flaubert greatly valued during the time of composition of *Salammbô* was that with Charles Baudelaire. Of all the writers in France during the nineteenth century, they had most in common. They had the same ideals of literature, the same view of beauty, and both were out of sympathy with the material-istic standards of the age. Baudelaire had been much moved by *Madame Bovary*, and was horrified by Flaubert's trial in January 1857. His review of the book was one of the most acute and sensitive, but its publication had been delayed on account of his own trial, in which he was less fortunate than Flaubert, for he was convicted and fined and several of his poems were banned. In July 1857 he sent his *Fleurs du Mal* to Flaubert, who wrote to thank him for it and was enthusiastic in his praise.[32] His letter ends: 'In short, what pleases me above everything in your book is that Art is predominant in it. And then you sing of flesh without liking it, in a sad and detached way which I find sympathetic. You are unyielding like marble and penetrating like an English mist.'

Flaubert read him his *Novembre* in July 1860, which was a great mark of consideration as he did not often show his work to others – especially not a work which he had discarded. When it appeared in 1860, Baudelaire sent him his *Paradis Artificiels*, in which Flaubert was much interested, but he made the objection that the poet had taken sides and had not remained scientifically detached.[33]

It seems to me that, in a subject treated from so high a point of view, in a work which is the beginning of science, in a work of natural observation and induction, you have – and several times – stressed too much the *Spirit of Evil*. One feels a sort of Catholic leaven, here and there. I would have preferred it if you had not *blamed* hashish, opium, excess, but do you know what will come of it later? But note that this is only a personal opinion which I do not value greatly. I do not recognize the right of criticism to substitute its thought for that of another.

Baudelaire answered:[34] 'I was struck by your remark and, having gone very severely into the memory of my dreams, I noticed that, at all times, I have been obsessed by the impossibility of realizing certain actions or sudden thoughts of man, without the hypothesis of the intervention of an evil force external to him. Here is a weighty admission which the whole nineteenth century leagued against me will not make me blush for.' At the busiest time of the composition of *Salammbô*, when he was trying to finish the book, in January and February 1862, Flaubert took time off to support Baudelaire's ill-fated candidature for the French Academy, although he did not approve of the venture and thought it useless. He did not spare himself on Baudelaire's behalf and wrote many letters to recommend him. In fact he did more for him than most of his closest friends.

In the meantime Flaubert was working desperately hard on his novel. On 6 May 1861 he thought that he had virtually finished the book. He is alleged not to have spoken to anyone for weeks except on Sundays, and his servant Narcisse was told to inform him when that day had arrived.[35] Early in May he wrote to the Goncourt brothers asking them to come to a reading of the book:[36]

The solemn occasion is on Monday. Influenza or not, no matter! 'Merde!'
Please forgive me for having made you wait so long. Here's the programme.
1. I begin to shout at 4 o'clock punctually, so come about 3 o'clock.
2. At 7 o'clock, eastern dinner. You'll be served human flesh, bourgeois brains, tigresses' clitoris fried in rhinoceros butter.
3. After the coffee a resumption of the punic bawling until the listeners croak.
Does this suit you?
Punctuality and mystery. Yours ever.

The Goncourts have described the reading in their *Journal*.[37] It lasted from four o'clock until six o'clock and Flaubert read in his bellowing sonorous voice. Then, at seven o'clock, they had dinner. When dinner was over and they had smoked a pipe, the reading continued, with Flaubert summarizing what he did not read, and it went on until two o'clock in the morning. He favoured these marathons, and this reading resembles that of the first *Tentation de Saint Antoine*, in 1849, to Bouilhet and Du Camp. The Goncourts were not impressed, but they say that they will give their honest opinion of the work of a man whom they like, and whose first work they had admired:

Salammbô is beneath what I expected from him. His personality, so well hidden, even absent, in that very impersonal work *Madame Bovary*, bursts out here, inflated, melodramatic, declamatory, rolling in bombast, loud colours. Flaubert sees antiquity, oriental antiquity, in the shape of Algerian bric-à-brac. Some of the effects are childish, others ridiculous. Then a great weariness comes from these eternal descriptions, from these lists button by button, in this minute description of each costume. His Mathô is fundamentally only an operatic tenor in a barbarian poem.

Du Camp was also guarded in his opinion. He considered that the book could not be as successful as *Madame Bovary*, and that it contained too many battles. He thought it powerful but perhaps too luxurious.[38]

In June 1861, Flaubert went on business with his mother to Trouville, where the family had property. He then returned to Croisset and declared that he would not stir from there until he had finished the book. In September he wrote to Madame Sandeau to say that he was embarking on the final chapter and that he expected to have completed the book by the end of the year.[39]

But still the novel dragged on and it was only on 30 June 1862 that it was finally completed, although he had told Mademoiselle Leroyer de Chantepie, in April, that it was already finished.[40]

Flaubert had, at first, not wanted to give the book to the publisher of *Madame Bovary*, Michel Lévy, with whom he had not been satisfied and of whose meanness he had complained. Finally, weary of all the disputations, he let him have it, but he would not negotiate the contract himself and entrusted Ernest Duplan, a lawyer, with the business. Flaubert had wanted thirty thousand francs, which, although a large sum, was small compared to the three hundred thousand which Hugo had received, the same year, for *Les Misérables*. But the latter was a longer book and Hugo's reputation was far greater than Flaubert's. It was finally decided that he was to receive ten thousand francs, but on condition that he would allow Lévy to have his next modern novel at the same price.

Then the publisher tried to insist on illustrations, as he considered that the book needed them, but Flaubert was adamant in his refusal. Writing to Duplan he said.[41]

The persistence with which Lévy insists on demanding illustrations puts me into a rage impossible to describe . . . There was no point in expending so much art, in an effort to leave everything vague, for an old fool to come along and destroy my dream with his inept precision.

He wrote again two days later:[42]

Never as long as I live shall I allow myself to be illustrated ... A woman who is drawn is like one woman, that's all. The idea is then fixed, closed, complete and all writing is then useless; whilst a woman who is described in writing makes one dream of a thousand women. Thus, this being a question of aesthetics, I absolutely refuse any sort of illustration.

Finally all the conditions were decided on and the contract signed.[43]

Salammbô appeared on 24 November 1862 and it was, contrary to all expectations, an immediate success with the general public. The two great literary successes of 1862 were Flaubert's *Salammbô* and Hugo's *Les Misérables*. Flaubert was disgusted at the popularity of Hugo's novel, as he had always hitherto greatly admired him. He wrote to Madame des Genettes:[44]

To you I can say everything. Well! our God is in decline! *Les Misérables* exasperates me, and it is impossible to attack it as one might be taken for a police spy. The position of the author is impregnable, unassailable. I, who have spent the whole of my life adoring him, I am, at the moment, *indignant*. I must, however, burst out! I find, in this book, neither truth nor grandeur. As for the style, it seems to me deliberately inaccurate and low. It is a way of flattering the populace. Hugo is obliging and has kind attention for everyone.

Salammbô was also a fashionable success with the Court. The Empress asked for particulars of the costumes, to use them at a fancy dress ball. Sainte-Beuve wrote to Matthew Arnold on 25 January 1863:[45] '*Salammbô* is our great event! The Empress is so much impressed that she wants to dress up as Salammbô for some palace mask, and she wishes to meet the author.'

Salammbô appeared at various fashionable balls that winter. Madame Rimsky-Korsakov impersonated her at Prince Walewski's ball on 23 February 1863, and the famous courtesan Jane de Tourbey appeared as her at a ball at the Théâtre de la Porte Saint Martin. Princesse Mathilde also asked for drawings of the costumes,[46] while Du Camp wrote to Flaubert to tell him of a 'petit four' called 'des Salammbô', and later sent him a photograph of the Queen of Spain dressed as Salammbô.[47]

There was also, greatest flattery of all, a parody put on at the

Théâtre du Palais Royal, on 1 May 1863, entitled *Folammbô ou les Cocasseries Carthaginoises.*[48]

But what pleased Flaubert especially was a letter which he received from Berlioz, immediately after the publication of the book; although he did not know a great deal about music, he had always admired his romantic genius.[49]

I wanted to rush to your house today, but that was impossible for me; however I cannot wait any longer to tell you that your book has filled me with admiration, astonishment and even terror – I am frightened by it and I have dreamt of it the last few nights. What a style! What archaeological knowledge, what an imagination! Oh! your mysterious Salammbô and her involuntary passion, full of horror for the enemy who has ravished her, is an invention of the highest poetry, while, at the same time, remaining the truest of truth.

Let me shake you by your mighty hand and sign myself your devoted admirer.

                                        Hector Berlioz.

Let no one now dare abuse our language.

So great a success was *Salammbô* that plans were made to make an opera from it.[50] Flaubert was not averse to this, as he had always had a passion for the theatre. Théophile Gautier was to produce the libretto and Verdi was first thought of for the music but the negotiations do not seem to have progressed very far. It is said that Berlioz was next approached, but he was busy at the time with his own *Les Troyens à Carthage* and he turned down the offer. Gautier, in the meantime, was not progressing very quickly with the libretto and Flaubert, at his request, produced a scenario himself. This has been published by Descharmes and Dumesnil,[51] but it is very different from the novel – more vulgar and obvious – and it is impossible to believe that it would have made a great work.

The matter seemed to be at a standstill when the Franco-Prussian war began, but Flaubert was still thinking of the opera after the war and the Commune, in 1872, when Victor Massé was to compose the music.[52] He was eventually discarded and the task entrusted to Ernest Reyer, a pupil of Berlioz. Théophile Gautier was now dying and the libretto was entrusted to his son-in-law, Catulle Mendès.[53] Flaubert, however, quarrelled with him and chose Jules Barbier for the work, but his scenario did not please him and he was replaced by Camille du Loche.[54] Matters had now dragged on to 1879. Flaubert was delighted with du Loche's libretto, and Reyer had begun composing the music, but in May 1880 Flaubert died and this put matters still further back. At the time when he was working with Reyer, Flaubert altered the plot of his novel for the purposes of the opera. He toyed with the idea of making Salammbô's old servant Taanach much younger, the rival of Salammbô for Mathô's love, who did not want her. At the end she stabs Mathô to death. Another plan was that Salammbô should stab Mathô to death in front of the statue of Tanit. But she kills herself instead of Mathô and he seizes the same dagger and uses it on himself. Taanach, by this time, has disappeared. The battle scenes have been cut out and there is nothing left of the struggles of Carthage.[55] What curious things artists do when they abandon their own parts! It is strange that Flaubert, who prided himself on his historical accuracy, should have lent himself to such a distortion of known fact. Mathô was a historical character, and it is a recorded fact that, after he was captured by the Carthaginians, he was tortured to death by them.

All the vicissitudes through which the work then went need not concern us here, nor the attempts with other librettists and musicians. However Ernest Reyer's and Camille du Loche's work was finally put on in Brussels on 10 February 1890 and in Paris on 16 May 1892. It was said to have been a success, but by that time there was little left of the original work.[56]

A fragment from the opera, *Le Conseil des Anciens,* was played at Reyer's funeral in 1909.[57]

It appears that the novel was later turned into a film called *Salammbô,* and produced in 1916, in which the heroine, with the consent of her father Hamilcar, marries Mathô and lives happily thereafter with him.[58] Perhaps Flaubert, had he known of this film, might not have been as outraged as one would have imagined, for his own changes in the story were quite as monstrous.

Although *Salammbô* was a great success with the general public, Flaubert continued to be attacked and abused by the Church on the score of the relationship of Mathô and Salammbô, which was considered immoral and indecent. He wrote to Jules Duplan:[59]

As for attacks, do you know that I was denounced as a corruptor of morals in two churches? (1) In Sainte Clothilde and (2) in La Trinité, rue de Clichy. There the preacher was Father Bercel – I don't know the name of the other. Both fulminated against the lewdness of the masquerades, against the costumes of Salammbô. The said Bercel recalled Bovary and claims that, this time, I want to bring back paganism. And so the Academy and the clergy loathe me. That *flatters* and excites me.

The success of *Salammbô* changed Flaubert's life. It brought him the friendship of Princesse Mathilde, the cousin of the Emperor, and gave him an entry to Court and to the highest society. It is then that, for seven or eight years, until the Franco-Prussian war, he became a fashionable man about town, intimate with Prince Napoleon and Princesse Mathilde; also with the Emperor and Empress, being invited to the Imperial Court and to the most fashionable *salons* of the day.

CHAPTER TWO

BLUE STOCKINGS AND COURTESANS

One of the striking features of Flaubert's life, after the publication of *Madame Bovary,* was the number of women who became close friends of his. It was astonishing how many women liked him and sought out his company, and it is difficult to explain the charm he had for them. He looked old for his age and, at first sight, seemed unattractive physically and lacking personal glamour. But they knew that he was infinitely kind in spite of his gruff exterior, was interested in others, listened with sympathy and patience to all that they said to him and gave them good advice to the best of his ability. Then he looked at them from out of his very beautiful, gentle and kind eyes – his one remaining fine feature. He never left their letters unanswered, and however busy he was he gave them all his attention. He may have expressed a low opinion of women but that was before he had made a large number of feminine friends. He wrote to Feydeau in 1859:[1]

No! my dear fellow, I do not accept the fact that women understand sentiment. They perceive it only in a personal and *relative* manner. They are the hardest and most cruel of beings. 'Woman is the desolation of the just man.' Proudhon said this. I don't admire this gentleman very much, but this aphorism is a thought of genius, frankly.

One must not trust women (in the matter of literature) except in matters of delicacy and nervous tension. But what is really noble and high escapes them. The toleration that we have for them is one of the causes of the moral degeneration in which we wallow. Towards our mothers, our sisters, our daughters, our wives, we all of us act with inconceivable cowardice.

Many of these women friends had read *Madame Bovary,* when it was published in 1857, and found themselves in his heroine.

This did not wholly surprise him and when he was writing the book he wrote to Louise Colet:[2] 'If my book is good it will gently caress many a feminine wound, and many a woman will smile as she recognizes herself.'

Between coming to live in Paris, before he was thirty-five, and his illness, when he was twenty-one, he had lived quietly with his mother at Croisset. There had been his stormy affair with Louise Colet, but, besides her, he had met or known few women. When Louise Colet wished to be jealous of him and of his past, as a victim, she could find only Eulalie Foucaud, whom he had known for a couple of days at Marseilles. He was then eighteen and had a fleeting relationship with her but had never seen again.[3] There had also been Louise Pradier, the unfaithful wife of the sculptor, who had known him as a boy and whose brother was one of his schoolmates. There is no evidence that Flaubert had any relations but those of friendship with her, but he was interested in her as a character, and she was one of the models for Emma Bovary.

After the break with Louise Colet, early in 1855, he was left without any woman confidante and he felt the loss keenly. He was starved for feminine companionship. However, when he settled in Paris in 1856 and had a home of his own there, away from his mother's vigilant eye, he began to collect a large circle of women friends, most of them after the publication of *Madame Bovary*; but more came later after the great popular success of *Salammbô* in 1862.

The first of these women friends whom his first novel brought him was Mademoiselle Leroyer de Chantepie. Her unpublished and lengthy correspondence to him is preserved in the Bibliothèque Nationale in Paris.[4] She was twenty-one years older than he – though he does not seem to have known that at first – and, although he corresponded with her for twenty years, he never met her. Her first letter to him is dated 18 December 1856, when she had just finished reading *Madame Bovary*, the last instalment of which had appeared in *La Revue de Paris* on 15 December. She told him that no book had ever made such a profound impression on her. She does not refrain from telling him that she too was a novelist and she offered to send him her books.[5] She was a spinster who lived alone in the provincial town of Angers, a woman of some means and education, though pathologically self-centred and introverted. Flaubert was as yet too inexperienced as a published writer to realize the nature of fan-mail and he did not see that her letter was the typical letter of the self-centred author, wishing to draw attention to herself and to talk about herself. He was much touched and, although he could not answer immediately – he was at the time in the throes of his law-suit – he wrote on 18 February 1857. She had sent him two of her novels, which he promised to read when he had more leisure. Here began a long correspondence which he must often have wished that he could break. At first he took her very seriously and tried to answer all her questions, and to explain to her how it was that he had gained his knowledge of feminine psychology. He realized that she was morbidly egotistical and he tried to encourage her to forget herself and to lose herself in her art. He took all her scruples very seriously and discussed them with her. He said to her:[6]

> Write to me everything you want, lengthily and often, even if I have to be a long time in answering, for since yesterday we are old friends, I know you now and I love you. What you have experienced I have felt personally.

She confessed her age to him, and if he was disappointed he did not show it, but thanked her for her frankness and said that they would now be able to talk like two men together. She probably did not realize what a compliment this was from him.[7]

> Your letter is so honest, so true and so *intense*; it moved me so greatly that I cannot refrain from answering it immediately. I thank you first for having told me your age. That puts me at my ease. We can now talk together as two *men*. The trust which you put in me honours me. I don't think I'm unworthy of it.

She certainly took advantage of his suggestion that she should write lengthily and tell him everything. She wrote enormously long letters, page after page, about herself, her isolation, and her sacrifice of self for others; of the unsympathetic milieu in which she was obliged to live, with no one with whom she could talk, and everyone taking advantage of her. She said that her only consolation was in literature and art. Then she talked about her unhappiness and her soul.[8] She wrote:

> And now I am going to talk to you about my soul. Do not believe that I am occupied with myself [this after pages about herself]. My life has been spent and is spent in continual devotion to others, often to indifferent people.

Flaubert realized that a great deal of her unhappiness came from brooding on herself. He told her to think less of herself, to read and to study. He wrote her long letters, often six printed pages, to try to encourage her and to help her to find something worth living for. But her answers were full of self-pity and she wrote once:[9]

What use has my youth been to me, or my fortune; my devotion to everyone, nothing. Those who have loved me have done me more harm than those who have hated me. I do not love them any more, for it was not them whom I loved, but only the creations of my imagination.

She was often touchy with him and, although he wrote her long letters of sympathy and advice, she wrote when perhaps he had been prevented from replying immediately, on account of pressure of work.[10] 'Even if, dear Monsieur, you had completely forgotten me, I would have no reason for astonishment. I have no claim to occupy your thoughts. It is natural that you should forget me and that I should think of you.' And the following year she wrote in a similar vein. 'I have often thought about you and, although I am only an atom in your life, perhaps you have said sometimes, "What is she doing? What has become of that poor suffering soul?" ' Time and again he had to reassure her that he had not forgotten her.[11]

She tried to persuade him to use his influence to obtain contracts for her book. No one, she said, would be able to refuse him anything. 'Your name is a sure guarantee of all acceptance.'

The close and affectionate friendship lasted, on his side, for twelve years, and then diminished when she tried to use him for her own ends and was offended when he would not agree. She told him then of her admiration for *Madame Bovary* as if this was a claim she had on his attention and service.[12]

In 1865 the theatre in Angers had been burnt to the ground. She was much upset by this, as she liked going to the operas. She organized a subscription for rebuilding, which went on for years with little result, as the town did not want to spend the large sum necessary. She then wrote to Flaubert that Angers was now only a village, without a theatre. 'I have a nostalgia for opera,' she said, 'and I am afraid that I may die without having seen the theatre again.' She asked him for help and compared herself to

Lazarus begging for crumbs from the rich man's table. 'They must be very hard-hearted,' she said, 'to refuse this, those who have everything. Dear Monsieur, if you could advise me you will do it, as, to please you, I would do the impossible.'[13]

She next thought of asking him to intervene with the Emperor to ask him to order the theatre to be rebuilt. Flaubert was reluctant to do this, as he did not know the Emperor very well and had not known him very long, and he did not believe in the cause. He replied advising her to do nothing, saying that one could not force a town to have a theatre if it did not want one, that, moreover, there were no funds available, and that the Emperor was powerless in the matter.[14] She answered him in disgust and anger, addressing him now merely as 'Cher Monsieur':[15]

Your answer is harsh and it hurt me very much indeed ... You're invited to Court, your personal worth, your intellect, your connection with those in high places in literary and political circles, must surely give you great influence. I've never asked anyone for a service which might be disagreeable or burdensome to them, but the kindly interest, the friendship even, which you have shown me made me feel that you would be the first person to offer me your support, to assure the success of my modest request. Don't tell me that the Emperor can do nothing, he is the absolute master of all wills, he rules the destiny of Europe, he can do everything, one word from his mouth, one sign from his hand, would be more than enough to make all the mayors and municipal councils of France obey. The Emperor is great by his genius and his heart, and I'm sure that if I could implore him myself, in person, he would grant me my poor little request.

He answered:[16]

I am very much distressed that you misunderstood my last letter so much. I did not think that you would see in the frank expression of my thought the slightest harshness. You have taken for egoism what is only the truth. ... I took no steps to be agreeable to you because they would have laughed in my face. *I give you my word of honour.* Besides, I do not possess the authority with which you credit me. For instance, last Friday, I had the greatest difficulty in obtaining permission to visit Fontainebleau, and they were on the point of turning me out, very politely, it is true, and, without Octave Feuillet, who is the librarian there, I would have had to return to Paris like a simple mortal. I assure you, dear Mademoiselle, you have got a totally false idea of the facts ... Do not believe that there was, on my part, any lack of goodwill, and remain assured of the affection which I bear you.

She answered him again in September:[17] 'I'm not accustomed to be refused, probably because I'm not accustomed to ask.'

Although he wrote later to send her his New Year's greetings, the episode marked the end of their warm friendship. He sent her a copy of *L'Éducation Sentimentale* and she acknowledged it. She wrote after the death of George Sand, in 1876, when she asked for information on her last days – Sand had been one of the great admirations of her life – and she surmised that he had forgotten her. This after all the letters that he had written her! She also suggested that he must have forgotten even her name! She added that, in her will, she had left George Sand, as well as a precious work of art, her memoirs. 'It was a kind of admission of confidence in her, and now I am embarrassed as to what to do with them and I think that I shall confine these memoirs to the flames.' Perhaps she hoped that Flaubert would ask for them. He answered her immediately.[18]

No! I have not forgotten you, because I do not forget those whom I love. I was, however, astonished at your long silence, not knowing to what to attribute it . . .

Poor Madame Sand often spoke to me of you, or rather we often spoke of you together; you used to interest her so much. One had to know her as I knew her to realize how much there was that was feminine in that great 'man', the immense depths of tenderness that there were in this genius. She will remain one of the greatest examples of France, a unique glory.

How is your mind? Do you still read philosophy? I recommend to you the latest book by Renan. It will please you. And do not be so long again without writing to me, for I am always yours.

There were no further letters and the friendship petered out after twenty years. Flaubert had been – at first, at all events – full of compassion for her loneliness, her unhappiness, her frustrations, and did all he could to alleviate them. She was, in many ways, like one of his own creations, like the Flemish virgin whom he thought of as a subject for a novel while on his trip to the East. He was always considerate and affectionate to her. She was one of the few people to whom he wrote before he went on his journey to North Africa in 1858. It was a strange friendship which cannot have brought him much satisfaction, except in sympathy.

In spite of all the immensely long letters that she wrote him, filled mostly with lamentations about herself, he wrote to her once:[19]

Write me very long letters. They are all charming in the most intimate sense of the word. I am not astonished that you once gained a prize in epistolary style. But the public does not know what you write to me. What would it say? Keep for me always a good place in your heart and believe in the lively affection of the man who kisses your hands.

It is astonishing how Flaubert, in the midst of his gruelling work on *Salammbô*, was able to carry on this long correspondence with Mademoiselle Leroyer de Chantepie, a similarly full one with Mademoiselle Amélie Bosquet, and another with Madame Roger des Genettes. Also, after 1863, with Princesse Mathilde and George Sand.

Amélie Bosquet was very different from Mademoiselle Leroyer de Chantepie and Flaubert's sentiments for her were very much more passionate. They were somewhat similar to those he had cherished earlier for Louise Colet – Amélie Bosquet was also a writer – and she occupied for about ten years a position that was very like Louise's, except that he never became her lover. But this was not from want of asking her, and her unpublished letters to him show that it was she who refused.[20] She bequeathed Flaubert's letters to the Bibliothèque Municipale at Rouen, and appended a note to them which is not absolutely true to the facts:[21]

In spite of the expressions of fondness in the letters which G. Flaubert addressed to me, and of their freedom of expression, to tell the truth he never, according to the old-fashioned expression, 'paid court to me', and I never wanted it. Moreover all his friends knew that, from the day when he gave himself up entirely to literature, from the moment of the publication of *Madame Bovary*, he would have feared to the utmost degree any bond which would have put any hindrance in the way of his work. Nevertheless our conversations were very lively, and it happened frequently that we remained talking for two or three hours alone together. But the intoxication which took hold of us then was entirely intellectual and, if I judge what was happening to him by what I was experiencing myself, I would say that the fire which flared up in our minds absorbed completely all the powers of our being.

Amélie Bosquet was illegitimate but was later recognized by her father.[22] She had a half-brother, Aimé Bosquet, who had been at the Collège de Rouen with Flaubert but, they do not seem to have known one another. He composed rather undistinguished poetry. She was six years older than Flaubert, being born during the Hundred Days, and she died in 1904, at the age of eighty-nine. It has generally been said that she was governess to Flaubert's niece, but this is not correct – he met her first, in 1858, at a picture exhibition at the Library, when he was already the notorious author of *Madame Bovary*.

Amélie Bosquet was well known as a local writer under the name of Émile Bosquet. She began publishing in *La Revue de Rouen* when she was twenty-four. In 1845 she published *La Normandie Romanesque et Merveilleuse,* which can still be read today on account of its folklore. She knew the working-class quarters of Rouen very well and described them vividly in *Le Roman des Ouvrières.* Shortly after Flaubert got to know her she wrote *Une Femme bien élevée* and, very much later, in 1897, *Une Écolière sous la Restauration,* which is a historical document for the time. In 1862, after the death of her mother, she migrated to Paris to take her place in its literary life.

Flaubert liked discussing literary problems with her – in fact she, Louise Colet and George Sand were the only women with whom he discussed literary topics, probably because they were all writers.

There may have been something coarse-grained in her and tactless, for she once made some reference to him about his relationship with Louise Colet which either hurt or irritated him so that he responded roughly. She apologized and he answered her:[23]

You were mistaken about the meaning of my last letter, since you make me excuses. What is certain is that the reparation has given me more pleasure than the offence hurt me. Only women know how to wound and to caress at the same time! My liaison with Madame Colet left no wound in me, in the ordinary sentimental and deep acceptance of the word. It is rather the memory (and still now the feeling) of a long irritation.

Then he went on to speak of the gossip, allusions and jokes of which he was the object since her novel *Lui,* in which he had been treated unfavourably. And he was hurt when he heard that she too was taking part in the campaign. He said:

Flaubert the Master

Don't imagine that I bear you any grudge for it, no! I embrace you very tenderly for all the nice things that you say to me. That is the truth.

But why do you too joke about it? Why do you follow all the others, for they have a ready-made opinion of me that nothing will eradicate (I don't try, it is true, to undeceive people) that I'm devoid of sentimen. . . .

They are always mistaken about me. Whose fault is it? Mine no doubt. I'm more lyrical that they believe, but I bear the punishment of my height and my red face.

I'm still as shy as a youth and I'm capable of keeping in my drawers faded bouquets. In my youth, I loved beyond measure, loved without return, deeply, silently. I spent nights gazing at the moon, dreaming of elopements, of journeys to Italy, dreams of glory for *her*, tortures of body and soul, spasms at the perfume of a shoulder, and sudden pallor beneath a gaze; I've known all that, and known it very well. Each of us has in his heart a royal room; I've walled up mine, but it isn't destroyed.

There is no doubt that Flaubert wished to become her lover. In an unpublished portion of a letter, he says to her:[24] 'I kiss both your hands since decency prevents me from going any further.' Later, in another unpublished letter,[25] 'I dream about your eyes and I kiss your beautiful neck, on the right, then on the left, holding your two hands tightly, more affectionately than respectfully,' and again:[26] 'I kiss both sides of your charming neck, since that is all that you give me. You have, nevertheless, such delightful eyelids, brown like . . .' Flaubert puts dots in his letters to indicate that he has gone off into a dream. Then he continues: 'But I'm becoming improper.'

After she had refused to become his mistress she said to him:[27]

No! I'm not so proud of my virtue as you believe because I'm sure that it is not virtue for virtue's sake, in a word, pure virtue. At my age there are a thousand reasons for a woman to be virtuous, and not one for her not to be so. Unfortunately I've the misfortune of being reasonable, but I agree that a woman with good sense is a failed human being. Goodbye my very dear friend, write me a few of your little notes which give me much pleasure, even when you kiss me.

She begs him for a note to prove that they are reconciled and asks him to come and see her, but she was disappointed when he did not:[28]

I longed avidly for that visit which would have confirmed our reconciliation, of which I assure you I'm very happy. For want of a visit write me a letter of souvenir, I beg you, however short. In my solitary life in the country it would be a most agreeable incident. But it would not be diversion that I would be seeking, but the assurance of your regained friendship to which I give the best of my heart.

Flaubert eventually wrote:[29]

If you had a little less of that virtue of which you seem so proud, you would be stronger in masculine psychology, and you would know, my beautiful friend, that my faculties are not at command, and that literature does not replace everything else, that is to say does not take the place of the rest ...
Goodbye, I kiss your beautiful eyes (if you permit it, naturally, don't be angry) and the two sides of your charming neck.

She wrote again:[30] 'Must I now, my dear friend, make a woman's confession. Well! I was very much flattered that you should still think of kissing me.'
Although their friendship was renewed it no longer possessed the same warmth. She was jealous of George Sand and expressed her feelings to him:[31]

I was afraid that George Sand might have banished me completely from your heart. They say that you kept her for a fortnight at Croisset and imagination embroiders on that! They imagine that things occurred!

She added that she had heard that George Sand had returned home worn out and exhausted. As we shall see later, if George Sand returned tired out, it was because Flaubert had kept her talking of literature until 4 o'clock in the morning.
He continued to discuss literature with Amélie Bosquet and to criticize her work. He was always sincere with her, sometimes even severe. Perhaps he would have been less harsh if she had yielded to him – he never wrote as severely to Louise Colet, but then he probably admired Amélie Bosquet more as a writer.[32] It must be admitted that she took his criticism very well, as he agreed. He told her that he had written to her as to a man:[33]

One is right to love you for you're a good woman and a fine mind. How many others, who are not worthy of cleaning your boots, would have borne me a grudge for the hard things in my last letter! I wrote to you as to a man and I was right. In the meantime, I love you more than ever and I embrace you.

The friendship lasted until 1869, when she wrote an unkind and unsympathetic review of his *Éducation Sentimentale*, which was probably due to disillusionment in him. In the unpublished memoir which she wrote after his death,[34] she said that the fashionable life which he led in Paris, after the success of *Salammbô*, had separated them and that she did not care for his worldly phase. She said that his friendship with Princesse Mathilde and the Emperor and Empress had dug a gulf between them. 'During the last years of the Empire,' she wrote, 'Gustave Flaubert had become completely the friend of Sainte-Beuve and of George Sand, the guest of Princesse Mathilde and the Empress, which did not attract me to him, especially as those whom I frequented were very different.'

The unfavourable review of *L'Éducation Sentimentale* which ended the friendship was published in *La Voix des Femmes,* from 11 to 18 December 1869. She had been offended because she imagined that she saw a caricature of herself in the character of La Vatnaz in the novel. She sent Flaubert the review with a covering letter:[35]

The article isn't very pleasant, I agree, but I couldn't do it otherwise; my thought, as it developed, imposed its will on me. Through the duty of friendship, I should have abstained, but I thought that you would tax me with ingratitude if I wrote this criticism, and with cowardice if I didn't write it. The alternative was embarrassing. It's for you to say if I've chosen ill or well.

Flaubert was deeply hurt by the unfairness of her criticism, but what he minded most of all was that she had published her unfavourable opinion in the press – he would not have done this to her, nor to any of his friends – and especially that she should do so after all he had done for her writings.

She revenged herself in the memoir, in which she shows herself spiteful, small-minded and unfair. She claimed that a mutual friend in Rouen had once asked him why he did nothing to further her interests, that this was evident to anyone who approached him, and that he had answered, 'she is too democratic!' This is, however, manifestly untrue, as her unpublished letters show that she had frequently to thank him for what he had done for her. She said that the only person over whom he ever took any trouble was his friend Bouilhet, who, many people claimed, was his brother. Amélie Bosquet came from Rouen and must have known – indeed probably did know – that this was not true.

One of the great and close friends of his later years was Madame Roger des Genettes. She too became his friend through *Madame Bovary*, though he had met her five years before, in February 1852, at the party in the house of Louise Colet where she had read a canto from Bouilhet's poem *Melaenis*. Bouilhet had just arrived in Paris and this was his first taste of success. He was much flattered at the way that Madame des Genettes read his verse and he addressed a poem to her to commemorate the occasion. Bouilhet, the provincial, was much gratified by her attentions; he was also much attracted by her beauty. He had never met anyone like her before, anyone of a class so much above his, and he felt that he had really reached fame when she became his mistress.

Madame Roger des Genettes came of a cultivated military family. An uncle and her brother both became generals, and she was also the niece of a well-known army surgeon, during the First Empire, whose grandson she married. Although she came of a well-established and well-to-do family, she seems to have been a woman of somewhat easy virtue, and many were her known lovers.

Flaubert had, at first, a low opinion of her, but then he knew her only through what Louise Colet said of her and she would never accept that he should be interested in anyone but herself. He did not meet her again until later but enjoyed all the scurrilous stories which Louise told him about her. He used contemptuously to call her 'la Mère Roger'. He thought her 'une infâme coquette' and an intellectual 'poseuse'. He thought that she had thrown herself at Bouilhet's head in a disgraceful manner, that she was only playing with him, would take someone else soon instead of him, and had already done so, although Bouilhet did not yet know anything about it – he would tell him when he saw him. 'Qu'elle s'amuse avec son beau Énault, cette pauvre petite Mère R. Qu'elle jouisse, triple jouisse, et fasse monter au gars R. des cornes grandes comme des cèdres tant mieux.'[36] He made fun of Bouilhet's passion for her:[37] 'Edma and Bouilhet are still writing to one another letters full of pose and "Pôhésie".' But he was glad when their relationship seemed to be cooling off.[38] 'You must know that Bouilhet and La Sylphide aren't writing to one another any more. Everything seems to have foundered and he has definitely sent her packing to be (fucked) by someone else.' He said: 'That Edma disgusts me even from afar.' But the most cruel indictment against her was in 1854:[39]

> Je reviens à . . . Bouilhet. C'est bien beau son histoire avec la Sylphide! . . . Cette Sylphide est une grande femme! Je l'estime, je la trouve très forte, pleine d'un bon petit chic, tout à fait Pompadour, talon rouge, Fort-l'Évêque, etc. Je suis effrayé quand je pense à la quantité . . . Si à chaque amant nouveau il pousse un andouiller aux cornes du mari, ce brave homme doit être non un cerf à dix-cors, mais un cerf cent-cors! Pendant qu'il lui pousse des andouillers, sa femme se repasse des andouilles! Farce, calembour! Ne faut-il pas avoir le petit mot pour rire.

He came to the conclusion that the husband, in spite of his blindness and non-poetic exterior, was really better than his wife.

But all this was some years before Flaubert met Madame Roger des Genettes, apart from the one meeting at Louise Colet's party. He did not get to know her intimately until after the publication of *Madame Bovary*. Thereafter he became a close friend of hers and a most faithful correspondent until the day of his death. It is not only that the number of letters is great, but that he seems to have written more intimately about himself than to any of his women correspondents, except George Sand. She was the confidante particularly of his last sad years, and she herself made few emotional demands on him. She was only three years older than he, but their relationship certainly remained platonic. It was to her that he confided the most intimate details of his life, particularly after the death of George Sand, who had been a mother figure in his life, and he asked her for advice and comfort.

His first letter to her was written when *Madame Bovary* was appearing in *La Revue de Paris,* and he thanked her for all the nice things that she said about the novel. Then, some days later, she wrote to ask him for tickets for the production of Bouilhet's play, *Mademoiselle de Montarcy* – it is curious that she did not write to Bouilhet himself. In January 1857 he wrote to thank her for her sympathy over his trial and told her that he had counted on that as a mark of her affection. She must have changed very much during the years since Flaubert had met her first, but, as has been already mentioned, he knew her then only through the scurrilous stories of Louise Colet. In the meantime she had become serious and religious and was interested largely in questions of philosophy and morals. Affectionate intimacy soon developed between them and they saw a great deal of one another when he was in Paris, for she lived very near him, on the Boulevard Beaumarchais. Every Thursday when he was composing *Salammbô* he would go to her apartment to read to her what he had written – this was the time when Bouilhet was at Mantes and not available.[40] He used to invite her to Croisset so that he could introduce her to his mother.

Deep affection and trust soon developed between them, but he would have liked to have known her better, really known her:[41]

I don't know you, you say; but you don't know what I'd give to live with you for two days, alone, entirely alone. There are a thousand things that would occur to me, that would occur to you. It seems to me that we are like two ghosts running after one another, whereas we could become two beings blended together.

She, on her part, told him that she did not know him, and he answered:[42]

You don't know me, you say, any more than a language of which one knows only a few words. But, nevertheless, I've hidden nothing from you. It seems to me that I'm naturally an open book. But the world and Catholicism have spoilt you. You are full of sophistries and confused feelings which prevent you from seeing the Truth. God has made you better than that, and it is because of that that I love you, for you must have greatly suffered and still suffer, poor dear friend. For my part I have the presumption to think that I know you. Well! I perceive, in your life and in your soul, depths of boredom and unhappiness, an eternal Sahara through which you wander endlessly. I don't know anyone as deeply sceptical as you and yet you torture yourself in every direction, trying to believe. I know that I often irritate you horribly and it is perhaps on that account that you like me. I blame you for treating me like everyone else, when I love you as no one will ever love you.

But he said that he could not understand her fully:[43]

You escape me often; you have aspects which evade me, ambiguities where I get lost. I can't reconcile your intellectual realism and your attachment for the Catholic tradition. There have been in your life, in your past which I don't know, pressures, constraints, as if from a long illness you haven't yet got over. You say that I sometimes look at you ironically; never, I swear, but only with astonishment, and let us not mince matters, with a little mistrust. You frighten me sometimes. You leave me suddenly just when my heart is about to melt, when I wish to absorb yours completely.

She was often sad, as he was too, and he confided to her his depression when he was beginning to compose *L'Éducation Sentimentale*:[44]

If you only knew how bored I am and how weary! The leaves are falling, I hear the knell of a bell; the wind is gentle but enervating. I have a longing to go off to the ends of the world, that is to say to you, to rest my poor aching head on your heart and to die there. Have you ever thought of the sadness of my life, and the will-power that I need in order to live? I spend my days absolutely alone, with no more company than in the depths of Africa. In the evening, having flogged myself all day, I succeed in writing a few lines which, next day, seem to me frightful. There are definitely gayer people than I. I'm crushed by the difficulties of my book. Have I grown old? Am I worn out? I believe it and believe that that is the root of the trouble. Then what I'm doing isn't easy, and I've become timid. During the last seven weeks I've written fifteen pages and they aren't worth much. How badly arranged the world is! What use are ugliness, suffering, sadness? Why are all our dreams so vain? Why everything? . . . At the moment I'm worn out! I'd need to enjoy myself a lot. How I think of you and I long for your wit and your grace.

After the war and the Commune, when her health failed and she was partially paralysed, she lived in the country and he did not see her so often, but he wrote to her constantly and she was his most intimate correspondent at the end of his life, when his mother and George Sand were dead. He told her then:[45] 'Are you not bound up with what is best in my past! Your memory recalls to my mind only charming things.' After his death, she wrote to Madame Neveu:[46]

It is now, today, eight years since death took away my poor Flaubert . . . He went, my poor faithful friend, and, from that intimacy of sixteen years, I keep only charming memories, wonderful letters and an inconsolable grief. He gave me a taste for living, the wish to work. I read carefully in order to be able to discuss with him what I was reading . . . Then he lit his pipe, and, when he was at Croisset, he used to take my letter away to read on the terrace which ran along the Seine.

Flaubert left her, in his will, the little writing desk he used every day, which had belonged to his sister Caroline; and she bequeathed it to her nephew, Pol Neveu, or rather, a few months before she herself died, she sent it to his mother in trust for him:[47]

Everything feels like a departure. The sky is weeping. I'm returning you your reviews and your thoughts, and I send you also, for your son, Flaubert's desk. From *Salammbô* to *Bouvard et Pécuchet* inclusive, he wrote everything on this desk. It has witnessed his rages, his discouragements – no discouragement was more terrible than when he was composing *L'Éducation Sentimentale*. On that mahogany ledge there's more than ink – I personally have seen tears.

She also wrote to her nephew:[48]

I've entrusted your mother with the task of giving you Flaubert's desk. I wanted that relic to fall into pious hands, and I chose you, my dear child. I want you, in your turn, to write beautiful pages on this mahogany ledge. I'm sure that this warm-hearted soul would have loved you and it would have been sweet for me to have been able to introduce you to one another.

These letters, published in 1894, after her death in 1891, are full of thoughts of Flaubert and affection for him:[49]

You see, my child, in that intimacy of sixteen years, I never heard him utter a discordant word, his violence was arrogant but his heart never jarred . . . With his air of a policeman, he had a delicacy which was quite feminine, and I've seen him bending out of my window at Villenauxe to fondle a flower which he did not want to pick.

Mademoiselle Leroyer de Chantepie, Mademoiselle Amélie Bosquet and Madame Roger des Genettes were women of his own class; all had pretensions towards a literary and intellectual life, and he could talk to them of his artistic preoccupations and ambitions. These were not, however, his only women friends. He was particularly happy with women who were on the fringe of society, the members of the demi-monde, largely actresses whom he got to know when he was preoccupied with the production of Bouilhet's plays – actresses such as Béatrice Pierson and Suzanne

Lagier. He liked their good humour, their freedom of speech and the fact that he could say anything to them – of which he took ample advantage. Suzanne Lagier particularly had the talent of keeping him amused and he even invited her to Croisset – a signal mark of favour not accorded to everyone. She would confide in him and she said to him once: 'Toi tu es le panier à ordures de mon cœur, je te confie tout.'(50)

At this time also he used to frequent one of the most famous courtesans of the Second Empire, Apollonie Sabatier, generally called La Présidente. Her eternal claim to fame is in having been Baudelaire's 'Vénus Blanche' and in having inspired some of his most beautiful poems. She was also notorious in having been the model for Clésinger's *La Femme piquée par un serpent*, which created a sensation and a scandal when it was shown at the Salon in 1847.

Madame Sabatier was one of the famous beauties of the Second Empire and she was known by everyone in the artistic and literary world. She was celebrated not only for her beauty and the elegance of her clothes but also for the kindness of her heart. Her Sunday luncheon parties were well known and one met there, as well as Baudelaire and Gautier, Barbey d'Aurevilly, Clésinger, Meissonier, the ubiquitous Ernest Feydeau and many others as well. These parties were celebrated for their freedom of conversation, and there was often much coarse – even lewd – talk, especially if Gautier were present, for the licence of his conversation was proverbial. In everything written about her, Madame Sabatier appears as a large-hearted woman who succeeded in making her friends feel at home by her warm sympathy. When Flaubert knew her first she was kept by the rich banker, Mosselmann, but in 1866 Richard Wallace made her his mistress and when, in 1870, he inherited his mother's immense fortune of over sixty million francs, he settled a large sum of money on her. Flaubert must have got to know her when he went to live in Paris and made his new literary friends. He certainly gave her a copy of *Madame Bovary* in 1857 on which he wrote:(51)

À l'esprit charmant, à la ravissante femme, à l'excellente amie, à notre belle, bonne, insensible Présidente, Madame Aglaé Sabatier, mince hommage de son tout dévoué Gve Flaubert.

He was anxious to be thought well of by her and he once asked Feydeau: 'Tell me what la Présidente said about me, I am anxious to know it.'[52] He used to attend her luncheon parties and he once told the Goncourts that his only pleasures were his visits to her.

He had a kind tender feeling for her and permitted himself a mild familiarity with her, as in this letter, his only letter to her – or at least the only one which has come down to us:[53]

Adorable Président, I put my hand to the pen to write to you, but *between ourselves* it is not to the pen that I would like to put my hand. I write to you, I say, this little note, to find out how is your dear health – which makes my own . . . Let me then know how you are, and believe in the sincere affection of the man who, alas, only kisses your hands.

This is very different from the spiritual feelings expressed by Baudelaire in his letters; different also from Gautier's, which are so pornographic and bawdy that they are impossible to quote without the risk of prosecution for obscenity.

With none of these was he very intimate, but there was also 'La Dame aux Violettes', one of the most famous members of the demi-monde in Paris at the time when it was most brilliant and highly considered, and there were accounts of their doings in the daily press just under the Court Circular. She was one of the most extraordinary phenomena of the Second Empire. She was called 'La Dame aux Violettes' because she usually carried a bunch of violets and she sent a large bunch to Sainte-Beuve's secretary to put on his coffin, for his funeral.

Her name was Marie-Anne Detourbey, the illegitimate daughter of an illegitimate woman, and it was said that the Mayor of Rheims was her father. He was an aristocrat, Monsieur de Saint Marceaux, and it is probably from him that she inherited her refinement and good manners. Her mother worked in a café and she too began her working life as a dish-washer. She did well at school and easily passed her leaving certificate at thirteen. The authorities then thought that she could be trained as an elementary school-teacher, but she had other ambitions and hoped eventually to get to Paris. When she left school at fifteen she was already a kept woman and gave birth to a stillborn child. At sixteen, having collected twenty-five francs, she left her bottle-washing and went to Paris. This was in 1853. One evening, at a café, she was noticed by Marc Fournier, the Director of Le Théâtre de la Porte Saint Martin. He was struck by her extraordinary beauty and thought that she was exactly suitable for the play which he was about to put on, *Les Sept Merveilles du Monde*.[54] He had been Director only since 1851 and this was the first of his fairy plays which were to make his fame.

She told Marc Fournier a very fanciful story of her background and he pretended to believe her. He took her up, made her his mistress and put her in an apartment in the rue Vendôme in the Marais. Through Marc Fournier she met many of the most interesting men of the day, especially Sainte-Beuve, who undertook her education. She was an apt pupil and she quickly learned to hold her own in the most intellectual and sophisticated society, and also the most aristocratic. Her position was quite different from that of the usual courtesan or kept woman. She changed her first name from Marie-Anne to Jeanne and eventually to Jane, and she ennobled her second name by the simple expedient of splitting it up and calling herself De Tourbey.

She reigned in Marc Fournier's house in the rue Vendôme and soon began to give herself airs and to behave like royalty. Her *salon* became one of the most brilliant and literary of the day and rivalled that of Princesse Mathilde – indeed some of the same people attended both.[55] She was naturally more intelligent and cultivated than the other courtesans of the time. She bought books and pictures and possessed several beautiful Delacroix and Corots, and she attracted many famous people to her *salon* – Dumas *père*, Offenbach, Sainte-Beuve, Flaubert and so forth. Renan gave her an autographed copy of his *Vie de Jésus*, and she told him how much she admired him. He wrote to her:[56]

Charming friend, each time that you tell me that this book touched your heart, it is for me a great joy ... When you tell me that you are moved I am happy, because I say to myself then that I have not done too badly. Your good friend Ernest Renan.

There is a beautiful picture of her painted by Amaury Duval when she was twenty-six, which was shown at the *salon* of 1863 and which now hangs in the Louvre.

The journalist Yriarte wrote a sketch of her in *Le Figaro* in 1868, entitled *La Dame aux Yeux Gris,* and, although he did not mention her name, there was no doubt who it was intended to be. He said that the secret of her charm for men was that she could listen and smile at the right moment. 'She has belonged to an artist, to a prince of letters, to a journalist, to a dramatist, to a musician, to one of the great of this world – you can add the names for yourself as you know them all.' The public had no difficulty in guessing who they were. 'She is dark, of medium height,' said Yriarte, 'elegant and fine boned, at the same time white and pale, somewhat elegaic and sentimental – she walks well and one senses that she is a thoroughbred. Her hand is perfect, long and narrow, psychic, her teeth are exquisite. Her mouth is somewhat thin and unyielding to kisses. Her complexion is matt with a shade of tea-rose. Her forehead is smooth and her eyebrows thick, and seem drawn with a paintbrush. Her eyes are famous; they are grey and the shadow cast by her lids softens their brightness.'

Marc Fournier was a very complaisant lover and she became the mistress of many famous men in Paris. Prince Napoleon, the Emperor's cousin and the brother of Princesse Mathilde, was madly in love with her and remained her lover for about ten years, until he eventually fell in love with the notorious courtesan Cora Pearl, who had just arrived from England. Amongst her many lovers was the journalist Émile de Girardin, who was said to have become her lover when Prince Napoleon separated from her, and he remained so until his death in 1881. Another lover was Khalil Bey, the Ottoman ambassador. He came to Paris in 1855, bringing with him the sum of £500,000, which he proceeded to spend. He bought a luxurious house, although he could have lived at the Turkish Embassy, to which he added stables and large cellars. During his tenure of office he gave lavish parties especially for Jane de Tourbey, and he showered diamonds and other presents on her. Then he returned to Constantinople ruined by his extravagance in Paris and died soon afterwards in a mad-house.[57] He had said to her once as he sent her a box for the theatre: 'My dear, here is the box for this evening. I beg you to keep me a place in it which, however big it might be, can never have the dimensions which you occupy in my heart.'[58]

The Goncourt brothers, with their usual spite, have described an evening at Jane de Tourbey's house:[59]

A rich and commonplace apartment, like these furnished apartments which are let to provincials for the marriage of a rich daughter. A regular carnival of guests – Paradol, Flaubert, Gautier, Girardin, lugubrious and bent, with his death's head, and his lock plastered, like a kiss-curl, on his skull. The mistress of the house, full of coquettish grace, but a little too anxious to make her drawing-room a miniature nineteenth-century Hôtel de Rambouillet. They play at innocent and erotic witty games.

It was probably through Sainte-Beuve that Flaubert met Jane de Tourbey. Unfortunately her letters to him have not come down to us, and very few of his to her. Jacques Suffel claims that he has seen them, that most of them belong to Madame André Maurois, and he has published, without dates, some extracts from them in his little book on Flaubert.[60] Flaubert certainly knew her in 1857, when *Madame Bovary* was published, for he sent her a copy of the book with this inscription:[61]

> À la très belle et très cruelle
> Jane de Tourbey
> Le plus soupirant
> De tous ses adorateurs

And, another time, he wrote for her one of the few pieces of poetry which we have from his pen, but whether it enhances his fame is another question:[62]

> Jane, tes mains sont de glace,
> Sur mes genoux, prends ta place,
> Chauffons-nous, chauffons-nous bien!
> L'ombre s'avance, et la nuit
> Roule son char sur la neige.
> Jane l'amour nous protège.

Flaubert treated her with tender gallantry, paid her compliments and felt romantic about her. She obviously enjoyed his company and confided in him as she did in no one else. She allowed him some intimacy and he was able to go to visit her in her room:[63]

I can still see your large eyes, full of laughter, and your little feet in their slippers. I see you in your dressing-room, standing beside your marble-topped table, beside all your darling implements, in that charming setting full of your habits.

Although, replying to someone who had asserted that he had not been her lover, Edmond About said that it was impossible to dine with her without sleeping with her,[64] it is very unlikely that she and Flaubert ever became lovers; but he wrote to her as if with deep love:[65]

I love you . . . I love only you. For three years my heart has lain at your feet, like a faithful dog, and you don't take it. There are days, like today, when I think of you enough to scream of it and to die of it. Let me, dear Jane, kiss both your hands, right up to your shoulders – and your two feet as high up as you like.

Once she asked Bouilhet to send him two big kisses on her behalf and Bouilhet did it in the form of a poem, which is unpublished.[66] He wrote to Flaubert:

> Il les aura demain matin,
> Ces deux baisers dont on l'accoste;
> Mais qu'il maudira son destin
> De n'être heureux que par la poste.
>
> A moins que cet échantillon
> D'une ardeur un peu trop mystique
> Ne donne à son cœur frénétique
> L'espoir d'un vague postillon.

Naturally I did not send these verses to the beautiful lady!

When he was in Africa in 1858 she was one of the few people to whom he wrote:[67]

It isn't to keep my promise that I write to you, dear and beautiful neighbour, but because I think of you incessantly, and I've only that to say, I swear by your beautiful eyes. In a week I am leaving. How my heart will beat when I ring your bell.

How is your honour? If you could only know how much I think about your apartment, which contains you and your furniture which surrounds you. Have you not, since I left, felt sometimes as if a breath were passing over you? It was something of me which was escaping from my heart, was going through space, invisibly, and reached over there. I have lived for five weeks with this memory, which is also a desire. Your image kept me company incessantly in my solitude. I have heard your voice through the noise of the waves and your charming face hovers around me . . . It seems to me that I have carried from your dear person, a sort of emanation which penetrates me. When I want to dream of Carthage, it is the rue Vendôme that comes to my mind. And I thought that I had got over all that. What pride! The heart is like a palm tree, it grows again as soon as it is stripped.

I've had no adventure, either tragic or amorous. I saw this morning, at the Bey's palace, all the dignitaries of the Regency kissing the big paw of that man. I know two others that I prefer! Let me take them and cover them with kisses. Yours, yours.

If you were kind you would write to me immediately. A drop of water in the desert, for pity's sake.

We know that she was one of the first people whom he visited on his return to Paris.

There are two further letters from Flaubert addressed to her (published apparently only by Auriant), letters which he wrote to congratulate her on a speech which Prince Napoleon had made for the opening of the Suez Canal.[68] One of them ends:

Think of me sometimes. When you've nothing better to do write to me. You know that I love you. So be kind to your unworthy slave, who kisses you on both cheeks, and holds both your hands tightly and tenderly, saying, your devoted friend Gustave Flaubert.

Marc Fournier had become famous for the magnificence of the settings of his plays. This, at first, brought him great riches, but eventually it ruined him, so that he went bankrupt in 1868. Jane de Tourbey saw this coming – she was a good business woman; she managed to extricate herself before the crash came, but she had put by a great deal of money by then, so she left him. The unfortunate Marc Fournier lived in great poverty for the rest of his life, and he died ten years later, in 1879, at a convalescent home run by Madame Brière de Boismont, the wife of the psychiatrist. He was well cared for by everyone in the home and did not regret his former fame and glory. Jane did not even attend his funeral.

At the end of the Second Empire Jane de Tourbey had, as one of her lovers, a very rich young man called Ernest Baroche. He was very much in love with her and proposed marriage to her, which none of her lovers had thought of doing. However, at the same time, she was having an affair with the Comte Edgar de Loynes and she was hoping to marry him, as she would have liked a title. Baroche was an officer, a member of the select Jockey Club, and the most beautiful man in Jane's entourage. Then the Franco-Prussian war broke out in 1870 and Baroche had to go to the front. He was killed very soon and then it was discovered that he had bequeathed his immense fortune to Jane de Tourbey. She was now rich enough to be a catch for de Loynes, who had only wanted money. In 1871, ten months after the death of Baroche, she married Count Edgar de Loynes. She was married in church, in Paris, with great pomp. (The priests who officiated were Father Lucciano and Monseigneur de Inganio, and the secretary of the

Papal Nuncio, Monseigneur Chigi.) It was a religious marriage, but she did not take the precaution of being married civilly as well, and so the marriage was not legal. Jane invested money on her husband's behalf in a factory, but he had no capacity for business and it failed. Then he fell in love with the widow of a Sicilian Prince, and he took advantage of the illegality of his marriage to have it annulled.

Flaubert had not seen anything of her during the war, as she had been in England, but he renewed his friendship with her when events became quiet again, and he was able to write to her with sympathy over her troubles.

After her husband left her Madame de Loynes changed her ambitions. She had been one of the most famous courtesans in the Second Empire but, as Madame la Comtesse de Loynes, she wanted another reputation – as a figure in the literary and political life of the Third Republic. She succeeded in this and managed to attract to her *salon* such men as Clemenceau and General Boulanger.

At the end of her life she dyed her hair blond, as she imagined that it made her look younger. She now had an apartment in the Avenue des Champs-Élysées, not far from the house of another famous literary and political hostess, Madame Armand de Caillavet, who was her rival. Madame de Caillavet had Anatole France as her chief lion and so Jane enticed to her *salon* the famous critic Jules Lemaître. It was at a fancy-dress ball when she was masked and he was bewitched by her lovely voice, that he fell in love with her. When he afterwards saw her unmasked and looked at her aged face, she seemed to him like the mother of La Dame aux Violettes in the beautiful picture. He was kind and did not like to show his disappointment and they became lovers for a time. She found him an apartment near hers, but he eventually left her as he grew tired of her trying to run his life for him. She eventually died on 15 January 1908 at the age of seventy-one.

But all this was many years after Flaubert had known her. Now it was still the Second Empire, Flaubert's fame was rising and Jane de Tourbey was still at the height of her beauty.

The most mysterious of Flaubert's alleged lovers was the second English governess of his niece, Juliet Herbert, who arrived in 1853 and probably remained with the family until Caroline married in 1864. Many critics assume that she became Flaubert's mistress, but they are able to bring no evidence whatsoever to support this theory. It is true that after she left the family to return to England, Flaubert went on several occasions to London to see her, and she came to France to visit the family. He would not have taken this trouble, when he was so busy, if he had not been attached to her; but one cannot say any more than that. What he had for her, probably, was the tender affection he had for so many women. There are few references to her in Flaubert's correspondence, and these are innocent, merely information about arrivals and departures. He did not even mention her to his friends, except on one occasion to Louis Bouilhet in, an unpublished letter, when she had been for two years with the family, and then not by name:[69]

> Since I saw you excited by the governess, I was also excited myself at table. My eyes willingly follow the gentle slope of her breast. I believe that she notices this for, five or six times per meal, she looks as if she had caught the sun. What a pretty comparison one could make between that slope of the breast and the glacis of a fortress. The cupids tumble about on it, as they storm the fortress.

This is the kind of letter which Flaubert often wrote to his male friends and it has little significance.

It is said that all her letters to Flaubert were destroyed by the niece and all mention of her erased from his correspondence. This last statement is untrue in the letters of his which have come down to us – there are no such erasures. As for her letters to him they would have been, according to custom, returned to her on his death, and she may then have destroyed them. As for his letters to her, it is virtually impossible that there had not been any – perhaps she did not keep them and so could not return them to his heirs after he died. If any had come back it is inconceivable that his niece would have destroyed them. She was an acute business-woman – no one knew better than she the value of every line that Flaubert had written, and she made money out of every note. She kept his letters to Louise Colet, outspoken though they were, but sold them for profit and published them – with cuts it is true – so why should she destroy his correspondence with Juliet Herbert? She did not destroy his obscene letters to Duplan, though she bowdlerized them on publication, but there is no line anywhere addressed to Juliet. What is strange is that we know nothing at all about her, neither her family, nor what she looked like, nor what she did after she left the family. There is no description of her anywhere and none of Flaubert's friends thought of mentioning her after his death, when so much was written about the other women in his life. It is impossible to know what she was like and anything that is written about her can only be invented. Philip Spencer quotes a certain Edmond Ledoux of Rouen as saying that he had seen a copy of *La Tentation de Saint Antoine*, which he alleges that Flaubert sent to Juliet Herbert, inscribed 'À ma fiancée'.[70] We shall however see later that Ledoux' testimony is not always above suspicion.

It is said that Caroline stayed with her in London during the Franco-Prussian war. However, a note in the correspondence states that she lodged with a Miss Farmer, her former governess.[71] One of these statements is not true. Miss Farmer had never been her governess, but a Mrs Farmer was a friend of Madame Flaubert who, when Hugo was in exile and his mail to France opened, used to receive his letters to send them on to Flaubert, who was to transmit them to Louise Colet. Perhaps Juliet Herbert did not have room for Caroline in her lodgings, with the maid who accompanied her. We know nothing about her circumstances.

Bart writes at great length about the visits which Flaubert paid to Juliet Herbert in London and Paris, and their passionate behaviour together, but he gives no proof of this. He refers to allusions to her on pages 406 to 421 in Volume Six of the *Correspondance*.[72] There are however no references to her on these pages, but only three, very innocent, to a Mademoiselle Julie – he may have misread the name – who is Flaubert's old servant, and was always called Mademoiselle Julie in the family. He declares that Flaubert spent a hectic fortnight with Juliet in Paris in September 1872. But the only proof of this which he gives is a letter to Madame Brainne, where he says that he is spending two weeks in Paris to work in libraries.[73] However, he often went to Paris for research work and he tells his niece what he had read during his stay.[74] Bart also declares that Flaubert spent three orgiastic weeks with her in Paris in September 1874, and that he had boasted to Laporte of his Herculean sexual prowess with her.[75] It is true that Flaubert was in Paris then, *veneris causa*, as he says, and that he boasted to Laporte of his powers and prowess, but there is no proof that it was with Juliet. It is well known that, when he went to Paris, he usually indulged in sexual debauch in some brothel, and used to describe his exploits to his closest male friend of the moment – accounts either boastful or sincere. There are many other allusions in Bart's book to wild meetings between Flaubert and Juliet in Paris, but, as no references are given, it is impossible to check the statements. What the imagination boggles at is the vision of a middle-aged English governess, a Victorian spinster, indulging in 'nameless' sexual orgies with Flaubert.

Bart also gives as proof of Flaubert's love for Juliet Herbert the fact that he called his dog Julio, but this seems somewhat far-fetched.

All these women, except Juliet Herbert, came to him as the result of the publication of *Madame Bovary*, but there were to be others, after the success of *Salammbô*, and also at the end of his life, during his poverty and unhappiness. They will be studied in a later chapter.

CHAPTER THREE

SALAMMBÔ

Salammbô appeared on 25 November 1862, and, as we have seen, it was an immediate success. The manuscript and rough notes are preserved at the Bibliothèque Nationale in Paris.[1] There are four copies of the book, at various stages, and four volumes of notes.[2] The final fair copy consists of 340 pages and is dated 'September 1857–April 1862'.[3] As in the manuscript of *Madame Bovary*, the chapters have not yet been given their titles, but only have numbers, and these were added only in proof. The final copy is neat, with few corrections.

Why did Flaubert think of writing *Salammbô*? It does not seem to have been amongst his earliest or later preoccupations, and it is not mentioned in his correspondence before he began working on it. It is true that, the year after he had seen the Breughel picture of Saint Anthony in Genoa in 1845, which was to inspire *La Tentation de Saint Antoine*, he read in Michelet's *Histoire Romaine* an account of the war between Carthage and the Mercenaries, and took notes on it which he kept for the rest of his life. (They were sold, after his death, by his niece.)[4] Perhaps he re-read the notes when he was at a loose end, after publishing *Madame Bovary*, when he gave up the plan of bringing out a version of *La Tentation de Saint Antoine* in 1857.

It seems that, when he was fifteen, he was reading Michelet, as he said to Chevalier.[5] He had had as a teacher Michelet's pupil Chéruel. Also he mentions Carthage, when he was seventeen, in *Arts de Commerce*, a paper which he was editing when he was at school.[6] But he obviously did not know much about it then, and he mentions it with Venice, merely as a town important in commerce. He talks about there being something monstrous and cruel in their richness and says that the name of Carthage is full of horror.

Houssaye tells us that it was Gautier who, in 1857, gave Flaubert the idea of writing *Salammbô*.[7] This does not, however, seem very likely, as Carthage at the time of the Punic War was not one of Gautier's interests. Perhaps it was the passion for early history at the time, fostered by the works of Renan, which had inspired Ernest Feydeau's popular work *Histoire des Usages Funépultures des Peuples Anciens*, published in 1856, the inspiration of many of the poems in *La Légende des Siècles,* published in 1859.

In the nineteenth century, there was a very great interest in historical fiction, and some of the most successful works were in this form. It was not, however, accurate history that the writers favoured – they cared less about truth than about having highly coloured historical detail. It was what one might call fancy-dress history rather than true history. *Salammbô* is very different indeed from the usual nineteenth-century historical novel. Flaubert wanted to study the past with the same accuracy and detachment as the *réaliste* used in the depiction of contemporary life and as he had done in *Madame Bovary*.[8]

Towards the middle of the century, however, interest in history became more scholarly and there was a leaning towards a more learned study of the past. Nevertheless many considered that *Salammbô*, on account of its deviation from normal Romantic fiction, could not possibly be a success, that it could not have interest for anyone, as the period was too little known to the general reader, and that Flaubert could not make any point of contact, as it had no connection with his own experience of life. That was also the opinion of a later critic, Émile Faguet.[9] 'The historical novel,' he said, 'can only interest us in so far as the period in which it takes place is already known to us, and in so far as the events developed involve one of our passions and carry it away very strongly.' Judged by such a standard *Salammbô* would have very little chance of success, as so little of the period was known even to scholars, and it had, in its first conception at all events, little to touch the emotions.

Flaubert had always been interested in history and when he was at school it had been his best subject. Many of his earliest works dealt with historical themes.

On his journey to the East, from 1849 to 1851, he had become much interested in the large number of different races living in the same country, and the clashes that arose from that. He did not want, in his historical novel, to study merely one country or one race. Where better could he study the diversity of races and customs than in a mercenary army, the members of which came from many different countries and civilizations. He wanted to show this against an unchanging background. We can see his interest in the clash of races in his *Notes de Voyages* which he composed on his return from the East and in the letters which he wrote to his friends from abroad. In the mercenary armies there were men – and even women – from every kind of country: the Gauls and the Celts from the north, the various African peoples, Libyans and Numidians and so forth; there were Greeks, people from the East, all with different customs and beliefs, different food and dress; many were primitive and barbarous, others were more civilized. Flaubert wanted to give a picture of Africa as he had seen it and known it, and he believed that it had altered very little since prehistoric times. These were the aspects which had moved him on his journey to the East and on his visit to North Africa in 1858. Even today there are many aspects of North Africa which have not changed. Flaubert considered that the landscape had not altered since the days of Hamilcar.

Flaubert realized all the different elements in Carthage at the time of Hamilcar. On the one hand there were the rich patricians, the merchants and landowners, thinking only of their own money, miserly and arid and very little preoccupied with winning the war, which was why they kept Hamilcar at a distance. They were mostly Phoenicians, but there were, as well, the mixed masses of Berbers, who had been in the country before the Phoenicians but had been dispossessed by them. Then there were the Nomads, the slaves and other people from many different places, not vastly different from the mercenaries who had been brought in to help to win the war and who were outside the town. The slaves and the Nomads were inclined to sympathize with the mercenaries.

Carthage, blinded by wealth, greed and avarice, had allowed the arrears of pay of the mercenaries to pile up and they were beginning to revolt. At the banquet given by the town in an effort to appease them, they are brought face to face with the richness of the city; they see the piled-up wealth, and they determine to seize it for themselves.

All these struggles and strife seem to have fascinated Flaubert and at first they were intended to be the subject of his novel. He called it *Carthage*. He did not yet consider the psychological differences of the characters. All his early plans and notes show that he was interested in the town of Carthage itself, in all its problems, and political manifestations. That was to be the main interest.

He was, however, primarily a novelist rather than a historian and he eventually added what we would call a love interest which is not historical and which became finally the most important part of the novel. The heroine, when she first appeared, was a woman called Pyrrha, the daughter of a rich senator who was in opposition to Hamilcar. But eventually Flaubert made her the daughter of Hamilcar himself, called her Salammbô and gave her name to the whole novel, indicating by this that she was more important than Carthage. It is a historical fact that Hamilcar had a daughter, but nothing is known about her, not even her name. At the banquet one of the mercenaries catches sight of her and falls passionately in love with her. This episode is invented. Flaubert understood personally such a phenomenon as it had happened to himself when he had fallen in love with Élisa Schlésinger, at the age of fourteen. He used the scene when he was sixteen in *Mémoires d'un Fou*, now in *Salammbô*, some years later in *L'Éducation Sentimentale*, and later still in *Hérodias*, from *Trois Contes*, when Herod catches sight of Salome and falls in love with her before he has even met her.

A great deal has been written about the sources of *Salammbô*. Ferrère has given the main works in his *L'Esthétique de Flaubert*.[10] We know from Flaubert's correspondence that he read the best part of a couple of hundred books to obtain his material. The largest number of these, however, were used to obtain practical details of background and setting and did not concern the main narrative descriptions of battles from Xenophon; he read Arabic books for details of diseases and medical treatment; he read the Cabala for the religious atmosphere, Apuleius for the conditions of the slaves. He used the Bible extensively; the Carthaginians were a semitic people and he considered that there would be much resemblance between them and the Jews. Some critics have even claimed that the book is too biblical. Flaubert himself said, in the section of his notes entitled 'Sources et Méthodes':[11]

'Where I lacked precise details, I took them from the Bible. When I had no ancient texts, I resorted to modern travellers and to my own personal memories.'

He obtained the main events of his novel from Polybius, Book I, where he found the historical material. He is unlikely to have read him in the original as his Greek was not sufficiently proficient. P. B. Fay believes that he used the translation by Dom Vincent Thuillier, with a commentary by Chevalier Forlar, published between 1727 and 1730.[12] But he might just as easily have found his material in the translation by Bouchot published in 1847 – in fact this seems more likely.

From Polybius he obtained the main story of the war, and he probably re-read Michelet's *Histoire Romaine*; he does not mention this, probably because Michelet got his material from Polybius, and so was not necessary to him. Michelet, however, gives an episode which is not in Polybius – the sacrifice of the children to Moloch to save Carthage. Flaubert was severely criticized for this episode and was accused of inventing it. Instead of answering that he had found the detail in Michelet[13] – which he had perhaps forgotten – he declared that the sacrifice of children was frequent in those days and mentioned by many writers. Michelet states that King Moab sacrificed hundreds of children to Baal and quotes Diodorus to that effect.

All the events which Flaubert uses in his novel – barring some which will be mentioned later – come from Polybius, as do all the characters except the heroine – Narr'Havas, Mathô, Spendius, Hannon, Giscon, Hamilcar and so forth. But the characters, the scenes and events which he borrows from Polybius have no depth – not even line or colour – there are only statements about them. For instance Polybius tells us, at the end, when Mathô is captured by the Carthaginians, only that he was tortured, but Flaubert describes his death vividly, in full. In the scene of the Défilé de la Hache, Polybius states only the fact that the mercenaries perished there; in the novel it becomes one of the most terrible scenes. Flaubert did a great deal of research on what happened to men who died of hunger and thirst. He consulted his brother the doctor, and Louis Bouilhet, who had taken a degree in medicine. He consulted the survivors from the shipwreck of *La Méduse*, most of whose shipmates had died on a raft in the open sea.

Flaubert has filled out the characters and the events with his novelist's talent, he has brought the scenes to life and has peopled them with real human beings.

He also used his freedom as a novelist to invent certain episodes. He invented the love story between Salammbô, Narr'Havas and Mathô, and few readers will regret this, as it is the most dramatic part of the novel, and it has verisimilitude. Flaubert said that his aim was not necessarily to use only historical facts, but he wanted to avoid the danger of being proved in the wrong. He does not however completely succeed in this. The siege of Carthage was a historical fact and it is known that Hamilcar did not come back there at that time, for Polybius makes it clear that he was busy outside the town besieging other cities. The novel also describes the rape of the veil of Tanit by Mathô, which had such an important influence on events and made it necessary for Salammbô to go to the mercenary camp to retrieve it. Tanit, the moon goddess, was the patron of Carthage, and Salammbô was her priestess. The stealing of the veil is a very important part of the action, both practically and psychologically. Yet, if the veil was really stolen and jeopardized the fate of Carthage, it would be an important historical fact and would be known to the historians of the time. Polybius has recorded the important historical facts but he is silent about this.

Some historians have also blamed Flaubert for recounting the actions of Hamilcar in Carthage and the youth of his little son Hannibal, saying that nothing was known about this. However, nothing is known against it either, and it does not impair the historical accuracy of the story. Flaubert needed the episodes to reveal the human and gentler side of Hamilcar's character, his love for his little son and his inhuman cruelty in being willing to dress a poor man's son as his own child to sacrifice him to Moloch. Another invention by Flaubert, which does not seem a very heinous crime, is that of the aqueduct in Carthage. One of the dramatic scenes in the novel describes Mathô and Spendius climbing into the town at night and cutting the aqueduct, thus threatening the inhabitants with death by thirst. Before he published the book Flaubert discovered that there had not, in fact, been an aqueduct in Carthage at the time of Hamilcar – it was a very much later Roman construction – but he decided to leave it and the reader is not sorry at this decision.

He also changed the character of Hannon and his adventures.

There was a general called Hannibal – not Hamilcar's son – one of the leaders in the Carthaginian army. Flaubert admits that it would have been very muddling to have two Hannibals and so he turned General Hannibal into Hannon and attributed to him Hannibal's actions. The exploits of the two generals were very similar and, in any case, what he wanted in the novel was the character of Hannon. The real Hannon was crucified in Sardinia, but Flaubert explains why he needed him to die near Carthage.

The action in *Salammbô* starts in the middle, without any preparation, as it was later to do in *Un Cœur Simple* in *Trois Contes*. We are brought right into the midst of the banquet given by Carthage for the mercenaries to divert them from the fact of the non-payment of the arrears in their pay. The mercenary troops have been sent back from Sicily and they have outraged the citizens of Carthage by their disorderly and dissolute conduct. Beginning thus with the banquet gives Flaubert the opportunity for the description of the rich surroundings and the luxurious food at the feast. We know what a part banquets play in his novels – all of them describe some kind of orgy:[14]

D'abord on leur servit des oiseaux à la sauce verte, dans des assiettes d'argile rouge rehaussée de dessins noirs, puis toutes les espèces de coquillages que l'on ramasse sur les côtes puniques, des bouillies de froment, de fève et d'orge, et des escargots au cumin, sur des plats d'ambre jaune.

Ensuite les tables furent couvertes de viandes: antilope avec leurs cornes, paons avec leurs plumes, moutons entiers cuits au vin doux, gigots de chamelles et de buffles, hérissons au garum, cigales frites et loirs confits. Dans des gamelles en bois de Tamrapanni flottaient, au milieu du safran, de grands morceaux de graisse. Tout débordait de saumure, de truffes et d'assa foetida. Les pyramides de fruits s'éboulaient sur les gâteaux de miel, et l'on n'avait pas oublié quelques-uns de ces petits chiens à gros ventre et à soies roses que l'on engraissait avec du marc d'olives, mets carthaginois en abomination aux autres peuples.

The feast becomes a great orgy and seems to be getting out of hand, until Salammbô descends from her apartments at the summit of the palace. The Libyan Mathô catches sight of her; he is immediately infatuated and falls passionately in love with her. But the Numidian prince, Narr'Havas, has also seen her. He is not one of the mercenaries, but has been sent to Carthage, a rich and civilized city, as if to a finishing school, so that he can become better educated and more polished and also in the hope that he may make a fine marriage by wedding the daughter of Hamilcar.

Narr'Havas considers that Salammbô is his; he is suddenly seized with rage against the negro, and he runs at him and wounds him.[15]

Il n'avait pas fini que Narr'Havas, en bondissant, tira un javelot de sa ceinture, et appuyé du pied droit sur le bord de la table, il le lança contre Mathô.

Le javelot siffla entre les coupes, et, traversant le bras du Libyen, le cloua sur la nappe si fortement, que la poignée en tremblait dans l'air.

Mathô l'arracha vite; mais il n'avait pas d'armes, il était nu; enfin, levant à deux bras la table surchargée, il la jeta contre Narr'Havas tout au milieu de la foule qui se précipitait entre eux. Les soldats et les Numides se serraient à ne pouvoir tirer leurs glaives. Mathô avançait en donnant de grands coups avec sa tête. Quand il la releva, Narr'Havas avait disparu. Il le chercha des yeux. Salammbô aussi était partie.

This is an important scene; we now know that there will be bitter rivalry between the two men Mathô and Narr'Havas.

In the meantime Mathô has thoughts for nothing except for Salammbô. Later, at dawn, just as the feast is ending, he watches, transfigured, the carriage disappearing in the distance, bearing Salammbô away.[16]

L'immobilité de Mathô étonnait Spendius; il était encore plus pâle que tout à l'heure, et, les prunelles fixes, il suivait quelque chose à l'horizon, appuyé des deux poings sur le bord de la terrasse, Spendius, en se courbant, finit par découvrir ce qu'il contemplait. Un point d'or tournait au loin dans la poussière sur la route d'Utique; c'était le moyeu d'un char attelé de deux mulets; un esclave courait à la tête du timon, en les tenant par la bride. Il y avait dans le char deux femmes assises. Les crinières des bêtes bouffaient entre leurs oreilles à la mode persique, sous un réseau de perles bleues. Spendius les reconnut; il retint un cri.

Un grand voile, par derrière, flottait au vent.

Finally the mercenaries are persuaded to leave Carthage, each having been given a piece of gold on account of their arrears of pay, and being promised that the balance will follow. They retire to Sicca and there, in idleness, frustration and rage, have murderous thoughts and plans for revenge, and decide to march back to Carthage.

Hannon, the main leader in Carthage in the absence of Hamilcar, and also his rival and enemy, goes to the camp of the mercenaries to explain to them why they have not been paid, saying that the coffers of the city are empty. The mercenaries are furious; they reject Hannon and determine to march on Carthage. The Carthaginians try to appease them and send to them, this time, Giscon, an honest man, with money. He says that he will pay them according to their nationalities. But Spendius the Greek, the only one of them who knows all the languages, mistranslates Giscon's words. They try to seize the money bags and demand food. Giscon tells them to ask Mathô for it. At this reply the mercenaries take hold of the money bags, fling Giscon into the most frightful prison and decide to delay their attack on Carthage no longer.

Then the battles ebb and flow, and surge round and round, with great similarity and monotony, whichever side is winning or losing, while the reader has difficulty in keeping them distinct – and, moreover, cares very little about the result. The war lasted for a great length of time, three years and four months, and Flaubert, as a historian, tries to give the impression of the lapse of time and of all the different battles which took place during the period.

One of the cleverest and most astute of the mercenaries is the Greek slave Spendius, who has been freed by Mathô and has attached himself to him. All the most intelligent plans are of his devising and Mathô would have been able to do nothing without him. He realizes that the Carthaginians believe that the fate of their city is linked with the possession of the veil of Tanit, the Zaïmph, and he determines to go with Mathô to steal it. Mathô's only interest in the expedition is the hope that he might see Salammbô again. In scenes of great drama Flaubert describes the two men climbing the walls of the city, entering the palace and finally the shrine where the goddess is housed. This episode, invented by Flaubert, gave him opportunity for the description of the riches of the temple. When, after many difficulties, they obtain the veil, Spendius's only idea is to get back as soon as possible to their camp; but Mathô wishes to see Salammbô again and to offer her the veil. Against Spendius's advice and better judgement they go to the room where she is sleeping.[17]

Elle dormait, la joue dans une main et l'autre bras déplié. Les anneaux de sa chevelure se répandaient autour d'elle si abondamment qu'elle paraissait couchée sur des plumes noires, et sa large tunique blanche se courbait en molles draperies, jusqu'à ses pieds, suivant les inflexions de sa taille. On apercevait un peu ses yeux, sous ses paupières entrecloses. Les courtines, perpendiculairement tendues, l'enveloppaient d'une atmosphère bleuâtre, et le mouvement de sa respiration, en se communiquant aux cordes, semblait la balancer dans l'air. Un long moustique bourdonnait.

Mathô tells her that he loves her, that for her he would leave the army, and that for her he had gone through all the dangers to steal the veil. He asks her to flee with him:

Je tâchais de venir jusqu'à toi!... Partons! il faut me suivre! ou, si tu ne veux pas, je vais rester. Que m'importe... Noie mon âme dans le souffle de ton haleine! Que mes lèvres s'écrasent à baiser tes mains!

She is however horrified at the sight of the veil, which she should never have seen or touched, and she cries for help.

With great difficulty Spendius and Mathô escape and return to camp. But Mathô's one regret is that he had not taken Salammbô as well as the veil.

Then Narr'Havas, who had formerly favoured Carthage, now thinks that the Republic cannot win and, always the opportunist, joins the mercenaries, in spite of his antagonism to Mathô. He thinks that they are bound to be victorious as they possess the sacred veil of Tanit.

In the meantime Hannon, in the absence of Hamilcar from Carthage, is elected chief of the army. He sets out to relieve the siege of Utica, which the mercenaries are besieging. The two armies clash in bloody combat, and Flaubert describes the battle in great detail, with one of his many elephant charges:[18]

Aussitôt la terre s'ébranla, et les Barbares virent accourir, sur une seule ligne, tous les éléphants de Carthage avec leurs défenses dorées, les oreilles peintes en bleu, revêtus de bronze, et secouant par-dessus leurs caparaçons d'écarlate des tours de cuir, où dans chacune trois archers tenaient un grand arc ouvert ...

Déjà du haut des tours on leur jetait des javelots, des flèches, des phalariques, des masses de plomb; quelques-uns, pour y monter, se

cramponnaient aux franges des caparaçons. Avec des coutelas on leur
abattait les mains, et ils tombaient à la renverse sur les glaives tendus.
Les piques trop faibles se rompaient, les éléphants passaient dans les
phalanges comme des sangliers dans des touffes d'herbes; ils arrachèrent
les pieux du camp avec leurs trompes, le traversèrent d'un bout à
l'autre en renversant les tentes sous leurs poitrails; tous les Barbares
avaient fui. Ils se cachaient dans les collines qui bordent la vallée par
où les Carthaginois étaient venus.

The mercenaries having fled in great disorder, Hannon enters
Utica, but he does not think of consolidating his victory, nor
does he consider it important enough to pursue them and to
finish them off. The mercenaries regroup themselves, fall upon the
Punic camp and destroy it by sending a lot of pigs covered with
burning pitch against it. Hannon returns to Carthage, in great
shame, but minding most of all the loss of his elephants.

Next, in its hour of need, and because Hannon had failed,
Carthage thinks of its one strong man, Hamilcar, who had been
kept from power by the spite of the Elders of the city. Now they
recall him from exile to lead them. He returns, organizes a powerful army and wins the battle of Macar, in the absence of Mathô.
But here again the Carthaginians are too sure of their victory and
do not consolidate it. Mathô and Spendius arrive and decide that
an attack against Carthage could be attempted. After many skir-
mishes, three armies under Mathô, Spendius and Narr'Havas
manage to join forces and to surround Hamilcar's army. It looks as
if it might be defeated and there is great anger in Carthage against
Hamilcar. The town then comes to the conclusion that there could
be no victory as long as it was deprived of the veil of Tanit, and it is
decided that Salammbô should be sent to get it back. The High
Priest plans that she should be dispatched to the mercenaries'
camp and it is clear that, in his mind, he considers that she should
use her beauty and her feminine wiles to achieve this end. The
scene of preparation is described with subtle sexual symbolism
in the episode with her serpent.[19]

La lourde tapisserie trembla, et par-dessus la corde qui la supportait,
la tête du python apparut. Il descendit lentement, comme une goutte
d'eau qui coule le long d'un mur, rampa entre les étoffes épandues,
puis, la queue collée contre le sol, il se leva tout droit; et ses yeux,
plus brillants que des escarboucles, se dardaient sur Salammbô.
L'horreur du froid ou une pudeur, peut-être, la fit d'abord hésiter.

Mais elle se rappela les ordres de Schahabarim, elle s'avança le python se rabattit et lui posant sur la nuque le milieu de son corps, il laissait pendre sa tête et sa queue, comme un collier rompu dont les deux bouts traînent jusqu'à terre. Salammbô l'entoura autour de ses flancs, sous ses bras, entre ses genoux; puis le prenant à la mâchoire, elle approcha cette petite gueule triangulaire jusqu'au bord de ses dents, et, en fermant à demi les yeux, elle se renversait sous les rayons de la lune. La blanche lumière semblait l'envelopper d'un brouillard d'argent, la forme de ses pas humides brillait sur les dalles, des étoiles palpitaient dans la profondeur de l'eau; il serrait contre elle ses noirs anneaux tigrés de plaques d'or. Salammbô haletait sous ce poids trop lourd, ses reins pliaient, elle se sentait mourir; et du bout de sa queue il lui battait la cuisse tout doucement; puis la musique se taisant, il retomba.

Then she is dressed for the expedition.[20]

D'après les recommandations de Schahabarim, Salammbô lui avait ordonné de la rendre magnifique; et elle l'accommodait dans un goût barbare, plein à la fois de recherche et d'ingénuité.

Sur une première tunique, mince, et de couleur vineuse, elle en passa une seconde, brodée en plumes d'oiseaux. Des écailles d'or se collaient à ses hanches, et de cette large ceinture descendaient les flots de ses caleçons bleus, étoilés d'argent. Ensuite Taanach lui emmancha une grande robe, faite avec la toile du pays des Sères, blanche et bariolée de lignes vertes. Elle attacha au bord de son épaule un carré de pourpre, appesanti dans le bas par des grains de sandrastrum; et par-dessus tous ces vêtements, elle posa un manteau noir à queue traînante; puis elle la contempla, et, fière de son œuvre, ne put s'empêcher de dire:
'Tu ne seras pas plus belle le jour de tes noces!'

Salammbô reaches Mathô's tent, and then follows the love scene, the finest in the novel, a scene of great beauty achieved, as were the love scenes in *Madame Bovary*, with great discretion and decency. Mathô tells Salammbô that he loves her and describes all that they will do together. He becomes a poet in the intensity of his passion.[21]

Salammbô était envahie par une mollesse où elle perdait toute conscience d'elle-même. Quelque chose à la fois d'intime et de supérieur, un ordre des dieux la forçait à s'y abandonner; des nuages la soulevaient; en défaillant, elle se renversa sur le lit dans les poils du lion. Mathô lui saisit les talons, la chaînette d'or éclata, et les deux bouts, en s'envolant, frappèrent la toile comme deux vipères rebondissantes. Le zaïmph tomba, l'enveloppait; elle aperçut la figure de Mathô se courbant sur sa poitrine ...

66

... et les baisers du soldat, plus dévorateurs que des flammes, la par
couraient; elle était comme enlevée dans un ouragan, prise dans la force
du soleil.

Then he lies with his head on her breast and weeps. She thinks,
'Is this really the mighty man who has made Carthage tremble?'
He then falls asleep and she disengages herself and leaves with the
veil.

In this scene we realize what has occurred only from the fact
that the little gold chain which loosely bound the ankles of
virgins in Carthage had snapped; and because the old prisoner
Giscon overhears what has been going on in the tent, considers
that she has betrayed her native town of Carthage, and curses
her:[22]

'Pas un seul jour je n'ai désespéré de Carthage! Quand même j'aurais
vu contre elle toutes les armées de la terre, et les flammes du siège
dépasser la hauteur des temples, j'aurais cru encore à son éternité! Mais,
à présent, tout est fini! tout est perdu! Les Dieux l'exècrent! Malédiction
sur toi qui as précipité sa ruine par ton ignominie.

'Ah! j'étais là,' s'écria-t-il. 'Je t'ai entendue râler d'amour comme une
prostituée; puis il te racontait son désir, et tu te laissais baiser les mains!
Mais, si la fureur de ton impudicité te poussait, tu devais faire au moins
comme les bêtes fauves qui se cachent dans leurs accouplements, et ne
pas étaler ta honte jusque sous les yeux de ton père!'

One does not know what might have happened later, but there is a
mighty thunder-storm and lightning sets fire to the mercenary
camp. In the ensuing excitement and disorder, Salammbô makes
her way to her father's camp, bringing with her the veil of Tanit.

The notes for the novel are more explicit and leave no doubt
about what has really happened in the tent.[23] 'Hamilcar charmé
reçoit Naravas [*sic*] et lui fiance sa fille – il faut qu'on voie cette
scène, et la balle de Pyrrha dont le cu est encore barbouillé du
foutre mercenaire. Elle consent cependant, elle cède, n'est-elle
pas destinée à mourir.'

In the midst of the fire in the camp Hamilcar attacks the mercenaries and routs them. Narr'Havas, always with his eye to the
main chance, now that Carthage had taken possession of the veil
again, sees what is happening and goes to Hamilcar, saying to him,
pointing to his army: 'Barca! je te les amène. Ils sont à toi!'[24]
Hamilcar delighted, and seeing the importance of this defection,

embraces him and promises him his daughter's hand in marriage, as soon as the war is over.

In the meantime the war was continuing, and neither side seemed to be winning. Then Spendius has the idea of climbing up to the aqueduct and of cutting it, thus depriving the town of water. In order to save the town the sacrifice of the children to Moloch is planned in an effort to appease him. Hannon, knowing of the presence of Hamilcar's little son Hannibal, hidden away in the palace, is determined that he should be amongst the children sacrificed. There follows the gruesome scene where Hamilcar dresses up a poor man's son in his own child's clothes and sacrifices him, pretending to feel overwhelming grief in order to divert the attention of the onlookers, so that many admit that they did not know that the chief had so much humanity. The children are burnt alive in a horrible machine divided into compartments to take a victim each:[25]

Les bras d'airain allaient plus vite. Ils ne s'arrêtaient plus. Chaque fois que l'on y posait un enfant, les prêtres de Moloch étendaient la main sur lui, pour le charger des crimes du peuple. . . . Les dévots criaient: 'Seigneur! mange!' et les prêtres de Proserpine, se conformant par la terreur au besoin de Carthage, marmottaient la formule éleusiaque: 'Verse la pluie! enfant!'

Les victimes à peine au bord de l'ouverture disparaissaient comme une goutte d'eau sur une plaque rougie, et une fumée blanche montait dans la grande couleur écarlate.

Cependant l'appétit du Dieu ne s'apaisait pas. Il en voulait toujours. Afin de lui en fournir davantage, on les empila sur ses mains avec une grosse chaîne par-dessus, qui les retenait. Des dévots au commencement avaient voulu les compter, pour voir si le nombre correspondait aux jours de l'année solaire; mais on en mit d'autres, et il était impossible de les distinguer dans le mouvement vertigineux des horribles bras. Cela dura longtemps, indéfiniment jusqu'au soir. Puis les parois intérieures prirent un éclat plus sombre. Alors on aperçut des chairs qui brûlaient. Quelques-uns même croyaient reconnaître des cheveux, des membres, des corps entiers.

Evening falls and the fires in the machine die down. But still citizens come, dragging children with them, in case the God was not yet appeased. One hears the instruments sounding in the distance, the cries of the mothers as their children are torn from

68

their arms, and the sound of flesh as it sizzles on the hot coals. The Barbarians come to the foot of the walls and gaze in amazed horror at the scene before them.

However, scarcely have the people returned to their homes than the rain begins to fall in torrents. It is Moloch answering the prayers of his faithful. All the water tanks are soon filled; past misery is forgotten as the city comes to life again.

The mercenaries are now in a bad way. The largest part of their army is trapped in the Défilé de la Hache, from which they cannot extricate themselves. It is only a question of time when they will all be exterminated. Hamilcar now thinks that the war is virtually over, and he sends Narr'Havas to bring the news to Salammbô and to say that he was ready to give him her hand. Salammbô, who imagines that she now hates Mathô on account of the way he has treated her in his tent, can nevertheless not understand how this rather effeminate young man can ever be her master. She receives him in her garden, so different from the rough battle-fields:[26]

Les colombes, sur les palmiers autour d'eux, roucoulaient douce-ment, et d'autres oiseaux voletaient parmi les herbes: des galéoles à collier, des cailles de Tartessus et des pintades puniques. Le jardin, depuis longtemps inculte, avait multiplié ses verdures; des colo-quintes montaient dans le branchage des canéficiers, des asclépias parsemaient les champs de roses, toutes sortes de végétations formaient des entrelacements, des berceaux; et des rayons de soleil, qui des-cendaient obliquement, marquaient çà et là, comme dans les bois, l'ombre d'une feuille sur la terre. Les bêtes domestiques redevenaient sauvages, s'enfuyaient au moindre bruit. Parfois on apercevait une gazelle traînant à ses petits sabots noirs des plumes de paon dis-persées. Les clameurs de la ville, au loin, se perdaient dans le murmure des flots. Le ciel était tout bleu; pas une voile n'apparaissait sur la mer.

At last Narr'Havas ceases speaking and Salammbô gazes silently at him. He is beautifully dressed in a white linen robe embroidered in gold, and he is covered with jewels. He looks every inch a young king. But, as Salammbô gazes at him, she cannot help the memory of Mathô rising to her mind and she feels that she must ask about him. Narr'Havas answers that he will soon be captured and he promises to kill him. To which she answers: 'Yes! kill him! kill him!' Then Narr'Havas tells her all that he will do for her when the war is over and they are married. She does not, however, feel deep passionate love for him; she cannot forget Mathô and her body remembers his caresses in the tent, even though she thinks that she hates him and desires his death.

In the meantime the men trapped in the Défilé de la Hache are in a desperate plight and are driven, through starvation, to cannibalism; some do not even wait for the death of their comrades but kill those who are too weak to defend themselves and eat their flesh.

Then they decide to send emissaries to Hamilcar to beg for peace and mercy. Ten men are chosen, amongst them the leader Autharite and Spendius, and the latter, as the most intelligent and astute man, is to be the spokesman for the group. They arrive at Hamilcar's camp, a horrible starving band:[27]

Ils avaient les pupilles extraordinairement dilatées, avec un grand cercle noir autour des yeux, qui se prolongeait jusqu'au bas de leurs oreilles; leurs nez bleuâtres saillissaient entre leurs joues creuses, fendillées pear des rides profondes; la pau de leur corps, trop large pour leur muscles, disparaissait sous une poussière de couleur ardoise; leurs lèvres se collaient contre leurs dents jaunes; ils exhalaient une infecte odeur; on aurait dit des tombeaux entr'ouverts, des sépulcres vivants.

There is a dish of pumpkins cooking in Hamilcar's tent and, when he turns away for a moment, the prisoners throw themselves upon the pot and plunging their faces into it they finish it like ravenous animals.

Hamilcar says that he will spare the men in the Défilé if they will send him ten unharmed hostages. 'Twenty if you like, Master,' answers the cowardly Spendius, glad to think that he will escape, but Hamilcar insists on keeping the ten who have come to him as emissaries. Spendius faints at this news and all his companions draw away from him but none of them utters a word of complaint. They are mercilessly crucified:[28]

Quelques-uns, évanouis d'abord, venaient de se ranimer sous la fraîcheur du vent; mais ils restaient le menton sur la poitrine, et leur corps descendait un peur malgré les clous de leurs bras fixés plus haut que leur tête; de leurs talons et de leurs mains, du sang tombait par grosses gouttes, lentement, comme des branches d'un arbre tombent des fruits mûrs, et Carthage, le golfe, les montagnes et les plaines, tout leur paraissait tourner, tel qu'une immense roue; quelquefois,

un nuage de poussière montant du sol les enveloppait dans ses tour-
billons; ils étaient brûlés parure soif horrible, leur langue se retournait
dans leur bouche, et ils sentaient sur eux une sueur glaciale couler, avec
leur âme qui s'en allait.

All die courageously, even Spendius, who, at the last moment,
when everything is hopeless, finds the fortitude to face death with
impassibility.

Mathô is not in the Défilé de la Hache with the bulk of the
army, but with his own men outside. Hannon decides for his
own glory to try to conquer him – one must never forget his
rivalry with Hamilcar and his hatred of him. Hannon is captured
and then tries to buy his freedom by treachery. He tells Mathô
that he is rich and could pay him well; he offers to hand Hamilcar
over to him and to divide Carthage with him. But Mathô does
not believe him and thinks he is only trying to buy time and that
he will act treacherously to him as he has done to Hamilcar. The
army condemn him to death and crucify him in one of the most
terrible scenes in the book:[29]

Ils arrachèrent ce qui lui restait de vêtements – et l'horreur de sa
personne apparut. Des ulcères couvraient cette masse sans nom; la
graisse de ses jambes lui cachait les ongles des pieds; il pendait à ses
doigts comme des lambeaux verdâtres; et les larmes qui ruisselaient
entre les tubercules de ses joues donnaient à son visage quelque chose
d'effroyablement triste, ayant l'air d'occuper plus de place que sur
un autre visage humain. Son bandeau royal, à demi dénoué, traînait
avec ses cheveux blancs dans la poussière.

Ils crurent n'avoir pas de cordes assez fortes pour le grimper
jusqu'au haut de la croix, et ils le clouèrent dessus, avant qu'elle fût
dressée, à la mode punique.

When Hamilcar finds him later, he has difficulty in recognizing
him:[30]

Au faîte de la plus grande, un large ruban d'or brillait; il pendait sur
l'épaule; le bras manquait de ce côté-là ... Ses os spongieux ne tenant
pas sous les fiches de fer, des portions de ses membres s'étaient
détachées, et il ne restait à la croix que d'informes débris, pareils à
ces fragments d'animaux suspendus contre la porte des chasseurs.

The last remnants of the mercenary army are dying in the Défilé.
There is no need now to send any soldiers against them, as the

wild animals, which have been turned into the gorge, are finishing the work of destruction:[31]

Les bêtes féroces, les lions surtout, depuis trois ans que la guerre durait, s'étaient multipliés. Narr'Havas avait fait une grande battue, puis courant sur eux, après avoir attaché les chèvres de distance en distance, il les avaient poussés vers le Défilé de la Hache; et tous maintenant y vivaient, quand arriva l'homme envoyé par les Anciens pour savoir ce qui restait des Barbares.

Sur l'étendue de la plaine, les dions et des cadavres étaient couchés, et les morts se confondaient avec des vêtements et des armures. À presque tous le visage ou bien un bras manquait; quelques-uns paraissaient intacts encore; d'autres étaient desséchés complètement et des crânes poudreux emplissaient des casques; des pieds qui n'avaient plus de chair sortaient tout droit des cnémides, des squelettes gardaient leurs manteaux; des ossements, nettoyés par le soleil, faisaient des taches luisantes au milieu du sable.

Les lions reposaient, la poitrine contre le sol et les deux pattes allongées, tout en clignant leurs paupières sous l'éclat du jour, exagéré par la réverbération des roches blanches. D'autres, assis sur leur croupe, regardaient fixement devant eux; ou bien, à demi perdus dans leurs grosses crinières, ils dormaient roulés en boule, et tous avaient l'air repus, las, ennuyés. Ils étaient immobiles comme la montagne et comme les morts. La nuit descendait; de larges bandes rouges rayaient le ciel à l'occident.

Dans un de ces amas qui bosselaient irrégulièrement la plaine, quelque chose de plus vague qu'un spectre se leva. Alors un des lions se mit à marcher, découpant avec sa forme monstrueuse une ombre noire sur le fond du ciel pourpre; quand il fut tout près de l'homme, il le renversa, d'un seul coup de patte.

Puis étalé dessus à plat ventre, du bout de ses crocs, lentement, il étirait les entrailles.

Ensuite il ouvrit sa gueule toute grande, et durant quelques minutes il poussa un long rugissement, que les échos de la montagne répétèrent, et qui se perdit enfin dans la solitude.

Tout à coup, de petits graviers roulèrent d'en haut. On entendit un frôlement de pas rapides, et du côté de la herse, du côté de la gorge, des museaux pointus, des oreilles droites parurent; des prunelles fauves brillaient. C'étaient les chacals arrivant pour manger les restes.

This wonderfully evocative piece of prose is entirely of Flaubert's inspiration and there is no hint or similar suggestion in Polybius.

Mathô is finally captured by Narr'Havas. He is bending down to pick up a sword, when his enemy comes up behind and throws a net over him, catching him like a wild animal. He is tied to an elephant, with his limbs outstretched, as if crucified, and brought back to Carthage. The capture of Mathô marks the end of the war between Carthage and the Mercenaries, as there is no one left now to carry on the struggle. Carthage finally wins what Michelet called 'la guerre inexpiable.'[32] There are to be great celebrations for the end of the war and also for the marriage of the chief's daughter, Salammbô. She is also to be fêted for having saved the city by risking her life to bring back the veil of Tanit. Mathô's death is to be the centre of attraction of the celebrations. Many suggestions are made for the manner of carrying out his execution. It is suggested that he should be skinned alive, have molten lead poured into his entrails, or be starved to death. One plan is to tie him to a tree and to train a monkey to stand behind him and hit him on the head with a piece of rock. Another plan is to drive him round tied to a dromedary, another to put burning wicks of oil under his skin – they imagine him like a burning candelabrum waving in the wind. But all these plans would only involve a small number of people and one is evolved which would allow the whole population to take part in it. The Ancients decided that he would go from his prison to the square, without any kind of escort, with his hands bound behind his back. It is forbidden to strike at his heart or to injure his eyes, so that he should be able to realize his martyrdom to the end.[33]

At the start of the festivities Mathô is released from his subterranean dungeon, and he stands, at first bewildered by the sudden full daylight, like a wild animal abruptly freed from captivity. Then begins his long calvary. He runs the gauntlet of the whole town, through the streets, and the entire population wounds him, as he passes, in every possible place, but they are held back by chains so that he should not be finished off too soon. He is soon one large bleeding mass; one of his ears has been torn off by a child; one cheek split from top to bottom by a maiden with her spindle; pieces of his skin have been torn off; buckets of filth are thrown over him; and above it all obscene curses are shouted at him. Some women have sharpened their nails into long points the better to be able to tear off his skin as he staggers by. Finally he reaches the central square of the town. It is time to hand him over to the priests, now that the populace have had their fun. Salammbô is gazing at him and she sees nothing but him, but she feels now that she does not want him to die:[34]

Cet homme, qui marchait vers elle, l'attirait.

Il n'avait plus, sauf les yeux, d'apparence humaine; c'était une longue forme complètement rouge; ses liens rompus pendaient le long de ses cuisses, mais on ne les distinguait pas des tendons de ses poignets tout dénudés; sa bouche restait grande ouverte; de ses orbites sortaient deux flammes qui avaient l'air de monter jusqu'à ses cheveux; et le misérable marchait toujours!

Il arriva juste au pied de la terrasse. Salammbô était penchée sur la balustrade; ces effroyables prunelles la contemplaient, et la conscience lui surgit de tout ce qu'il avait souffert pour elle. Bien qu'il agonisât, elle le revoyait dans sa tente, à genoux, lui entourant la taille de ses bras, balbutiant des paroles douces; elle avait soif de les sentir encore, de les entendre; . . . elle allait crier. Il s'abattit à la renverse et ne bougea plus.

Salammbô, presque évanouie, fut rapportée sur son trône par les prêtres s'empressant autour d'elle. Ils la félicitaient: c'était son œuvre.

The High Priest splits open Mathô's breast with his knife, cuts the heart out and offers it to the setting sun. Narr'Havas then comes forward to claim his bride.[35]

Narr'Havas, enivré d'orgueil, passa son bras gauche sous la taille de Salammbô, en signe de possession; et, de la droite, prenant une patère d'or, il but au génie de Carthage.

Salammbô se leva comme son époux, avec une coupe à la main, afin de boire aussi. Elle retomba, la tête en arrière, par-dessus le dossier du trône, blême, raidie, les lèvres ouvertes, et ses cheveux dénoués pendaient jusqu'à terre.

Ainsi mourut la fille d'Hamilcar pour avoir touché au manteau de Tanit.

That is what the crowd believed, but Flaubert knew better – that she had died like any Romantic heroine of love. With Mathô dead, she could not endure life with Narr'Havas. In the notes he says:[36] 'Regard de la jeune fille sur le corps déchiré de Mathô – elle l'aime – c'est lui l'époux – ils ont été mariés par la mort – elle pâlit et tombe dans le sang de Mathô.'

Told concisely like this, with many omissions – especially of the long and monotonous battle scenes and sieges – the story sounds logical and coherent, like a real novel. It must not be forgotten that *Salammbô* is a novel and intended to be so; it is not, as Flaubert points out, a historical text or an archaeological treatise. In a novel the characters play an important part – if not the most important part. It is true that the main characters – except Salammbô herself – are all genuine historical people. Salammbô, as Flaubert's own invention, allowed him great freedom and scope. She is like most of his women characters, and she has something of Emma Bovary in her make-up, with her vague dreaming and her constant dissatisfaction. She also resembles the character Flaubert conceived when thinking of the books that he would write on his return from his journey to the East – Anubis, who dreamed of being loved by a God. Salammbô is a mystical character, the priestess dedicated to Tanit, and she has spent all her youth in the precincts of the temple. In the tent with Mathô she imagines that she is being possessed by the God Moloch and she cries out: 'Moloch tu me brûles!'[37]

At first Flaubert had given her a more decisive character and had attributed to her more energy and independence. We see in his notes that he had first intended her, on her own initiative, to decide to save Carthage by going by herself to Mathô's camp to bring back Tanit's veil.[38] However, he changed his mind afterwards. His idea of the oriental woman was that she had no power of free action on her own, that she was without individuality, and he places her under the domination of the High Priest, who uses her for his own ends. She is also subservient to Narr'Havas and accepts him without question as her husband because she has been ordered to do so by her father. What raises her above being a mere tool in the hands of others is her passion for Mathô and, as we have seen, she dies for love of him. Her feelings for him are very mixed, as Flaubert explains in his notes for the novel.[39] 'Du reste Mathô lui inspire plus de peur que d'amour. Malgré cela Mathô ne lui est pas indifférent – curiosité de la femme civilisée – attrait du Barbare – elle ne s'en rend pas compte.' She hates him and wants his death, yet she is moved by his brutal strength, and afterwards cannot forget his embraces in the tent.

The other two members of the triangle, Narr'Havas and Mathô, are very well drawn and contrasted. Narr'Havas is a delicate and nobly born prince, almost like a girl with his sensitiveness and love of fine clothes, minutely described by Flaubert. He is somewhat devious in character and what he gains is through underhand tricks rather than through personal courage. He is ready to change sides when he thinks that it suits his convenience. His support of

Hamilcar, his later defection to Mathô and his final return to Hamilcar are not in Polybius, but are true to his character. It is somewhat typical of him that he conquers Mathô by a trick and not through combat.

The negro Mathô is a fine physical specimen, a rough brute proud of his muscular strength, with great sexual powers and courage, but of limited intelligence. He needs someone with more intellect to advise him and to lead him, so he allows himself to be guided by the clever, astute and unscrupulous Spendius. He is all passion and feeling, but he has a fatal weakness and allows himself to be governed by his emotions. He catches sight of Salammbô at the banquet and thereafter can think of nothing else, thereby wrecking his life. Flaubert manages to convey the physical attraction.

Hamilcar is very different and is a real leader. In Flaubert's novel, he is very like what we know of him in history – intelligent, brave, cruel and ruthless and confident in his authority. Flaubert brings all this out in the few scenes in which he appears. He shows his ruthless cruelty when he sacrifices a poor man's son instead of his own to Moloch. He reveals his gentle and human side in the scenes with Hannibal, his little son, who has been brought up in secret in the palace. Hamilcar's love for his son and pride in him are very movingly described.

Spendius is the Greek slave, freed by Mathô at the banquet, who has attached himself to him out of gratitude. He is astute and intelligent, far cleverer than Mathô, and all the ingenious plans for the conquest of Carthage originate with him. He is very like the Greeks of ancient literature and he has something of Ulysses in his make-up. Flaubert has cleverly shown that he is nevertheless a slave and that this has coloured his mentality. The effect is particularly seen when the mercenaries, who had gone to Hamilcar as emissaries, hear that they must die. Spendius, who is one of them, breaks down, to the great disgust of his companions, though he recovers eventually when he realizes that there is no further hope of reprieve.

Hannon, Hamilcar's rival for power in Carthage, is the symbol of all that is evil and one of the most repulsive characters, physically and mentally, that Flaubert ever described. He suffers from leprosy and elephantiasis and the author has obviously enjoyed depicting the foulness of his body. He is false and treacherous. He tries to cheat the mercenaries out of their arrears of pay. When he is captured by Mathô, he offers to defect to him, to conquer Hamilcar and to divide Carthage with him. He dies horribly crucified, a just retribution for all his crimes.

All these characters are well differentiated and psychologically subtly drawn. We believe in them, understand their motives and are concerned in their fate. Hamilcar, used to power and confident in himself; Narr'Havas, the nobly born nomad and a free man; Mathô, the big negro brute; Spendius, the clever crafty Greek, with the mentality of a slave. They are all in Polybius, but they have character which they do not possess in the Greek historian's account and they reveal Flaubert's talent as a novelist.

Today the chief interest in *Salammbô* lies in the love story depicted against the background of history, and the historical events are necessary, as they affect the action and the characters. Flaubert hoped to place Carthage in a bright light and illuminate the whole period, as Michelet illuminated everything which he studied. He hoped to link together painstaking scholarship and imaginative insight.

Nevertheless, in spite of the accuracy and vividness of his description, the historical aspect is much less interesting to the reader today than the sentimental. He finds it difficult to be interested in either side, as both seem to him equally cruel, distasteful and barbarous. In the end he no longer cares who is victorious in this struggle to death, but only in the fate of the individuals. In the battles there is great monotony, whichever side is described, and Flaubert realized this himself. It is impossible to keep one battle distinct from the other, they are all so similar. There are endless elephant charges on both sides. Whether it is the mercenaries or the Carthaginians, there are the same entrails being spilt out, the same blood flowing. The subject also encouraged Flaubert's leaning towards sadism, which had been apparent in his earliest works. He had not had the opportunity for this in *Madame Bovary,* though some critics – Sainte-Beuve for instance – had accused him of cruelty in that book. But even the death of Emma is described with great discretion and moderation – remarkably so if it is compared with scenes in other novels at the time. There is, however, no restraint in *Salammbô,* witness the terrible crucifixion of Hannon, the torture and death of Mathô, the barbarous treatment of the prisoners by the mercenaries and the killing of the hostages by the Carthaginians. Each side is as cruel as the other. There is the terrible description of the extermination of the mercenaries in the Défilé de la Hache, where they die of hunger and thirst, become cannibals and are finally finished off by the wild beasts. There is the gruesome scene where the Barbarian drinks the blood of his vanquished foe:[40]

Un des gardes de la Légion, resté en dehors, trébuchait parmi les pierres. Zarxas accourut, et, le terrassant, il lui enfonça un poignard dans la gorge; il l'en retira, se jeta sur la blessure, et, la bouche collée contre elle, avec des grondements de joie et des soubresauts qui le secouaient jusqu'aux talons, il pompait le sang à pleine poitrine; puis tranquillement, il s'assit sur le cadavre, releva son visage en se renversant le cou pour mieux humer l'air, comme fait une biche qui vient de boire à un torrent, et, d'une voix aiguë, il entonna une chanson des Baléares.

Flaubert would have defended himself by saying that all sides were equally cruel at that time, that it was the general colour of the period and that he depicted it in both camps.

Nevertheless all is not cruelty in the novel. In the midst of all the horrors which made Flaubert seem so hard, his characteristic compassion could not help breaking through at times. He describes movingly the comradeship between the mercenaries coming from all quarters of the world. Their shared memories and dreams of home. He had great feeling and sympathy for small humble people, and this quality is seen in all his books. He depicted movingly the friendship of the ordinary soldiers, their love and support of one another, in the long companionship of the battlefields:[41]

La communauté de leur existence avait établi entre ces hommes des amitiés profondes. Le camp, pour la plupart, remplaçait la patrie; vivant sans famille, ils reportaient sur un compagnon leur besoin de tendresse, et l'on s'endormait côte à côte, sous le même manteau, à la clarté des étoiles. Dans ce vagabondage perpétuel à travers toutes sortes de pays, de meurtres et d'aventures, il s'était formé d'étranges amours, unions obscènes aussi sérieuses que des mariages, où le plus fort défendait le plus jeune au milieu des batailles, l'aidait à franchir les précipices, épongeait sur son front la sueur des fièvres, volait pour lui de la nourriture; et l'autre, enfant ramassé au bord d'une route, puis devenu Mercenaire, payait ce dévouement par mille soins délicats et des complaisances d'épouse.

Hamilcar had decided that those who had escaped from the Défilé de la Hache should fight, in twos against one another, and that the victors would have their lives spared, but the men could not strike one another.[42]

Tous demandaient à mourir, et aucun ne voulait frapper. On en voyait un jeune, çà et là, qui disait à un autre dont la barbe était grise: 'Non! non, tu es le plus robuste! Tu nous vengeras, tue-moi!' et l'homme répondait: 'J'ai moins d'années à vivre! Frappe au cœur, et n'y pense plus!' Les frères se contemplaient les deux mains serrées, et l'amant faisait à son amant des adieux éternels, debout, en pleurant sur son épaule . . .
Parfois deux hommes s'arrêtaient tout sanglants, tombaient dans les bras l'un de l'autre et mouraient en se donnant des baisers. Aucun ne reculait. Ils se ruaient contre les lames tendues.

It is not only in the description of horrors that there is excess, but also in the depiction of palaces and temples, so that one cannot see the place for the detail, and the picture makes no final impact. We see this in the picture of the temple, of the palace of Hamilcar and the apartments of Salammbô.

However, one can skip many of these passages and forget them, and return to the lovely descriptions of the local scenes which Flaubert remembered from his journey to the East in his twenties, and later when he visited North Africa. One of the outstanding successes in this style is the picture of the sun rising over Carthage, in the dawn after the feast in Hamilcar's palace. Quite rightly Sainte-Beuve considered this one of the finest passages in the book:[43]

Mais une barre lumineuse s'éleva du côté de l'Orient. À gauche, tout en bas, les canaux de Mégara commençaient à rayer de leurs sinuosités blanches les verdures des jardins. Les toits coniques des temples heptagones, les escaliers, les terrasses, les remparts, peu à peu, se découpaient sur la pâleur de l'aube; et tout autour de la péninsule carthaginoise une ceinture d'écume blanche oscillait tandis que la mer couleur d'émeraude semblait comme figée dans la fraîcheur du matin. Puis à mesure que le ciel rose allait s'élargissant, les hautes maisons inclinées sur les pentes du terrain se haussaient se tassaient, telles qu'un troupeau de chèvres noires qui descend des montagnes. Les rues désertes s'allongeaient; les palmiers, çà et là sortant des murs, ne bougeaient pas; les citernes remplies avaient l'air de boucliers d'argent perdus dans les cours, le phare du promontoire Hermaeum commençait à pâlir. Tout au haut de l'Acropole, dans le bois de cyprès, les chevaux d'Eschmoûn, sentant venir la lumière, posaient leurs sabots sur le parapet de marbre et hennissaient du côté du soleil.

The two main reviews of *Salammbô* were the one by Sainte-Beuve which appeared in *Le Constitutionnel* on 8, 15 and 22 December 1862; and the one by a German scholar, Guillaume Froehner, which was published in *La Revue Contemporaine* on 31 December 1862. These reviews are important because Flaubert took the trouble to answer them, and his answers are significant for an understanding of what he had wanted to achieve in the novel. The two articles are of very different nature and scope. Froehner was not a literary man and he was not even a Frenchman. It is alleged that his review was inspired by the spite and malevolence of Louise Colet.[44] She had been trying to get in touch with Flaubert, in spite of all the harm she had done him in her novel *Lui*. She wrote in a condescending but favourable way about *Salammbô* to Madame Roger des Genettes, asking her to pass the remarks on to Flaubert, as she said 'not for him, for whom I care very little, but for myself, as I am anxious never to commit an injustice'. Flaubert made no attempt to pick up the olive branch or to see her and so enraged was she that she abused him like a fishwife to Madame Roger des Genettes. 'A sense of justice,' she said, 'which I never abandon made me recognize what talent there was in *Salammbô*. But, if you have said it or written it to the author, you ought also to have acquainted him with the absolute contempt which his character inspires in me and the horrible repulsion that I feel for his anticipated decrepitude.'

It is said that, after this, she worked against him and prompted Froehner's malicious attack.

Sainte-Beuve's article was of a very different kind from Froehner's. He was a literary man, sophisticated, with cultured tastes. In 1862, when *Salammbô* appeared, he was fifty-eight and was inclined to be timid and to lack adventurousness. He was now very cautious of what he wrote about contemporary authors, as there was always the danger of a law-suit, and he felt on surer ground when he discussed the past, and works of the past. In 1857, he had been only half-hearted in his praise of *Madame Bovary* and also, in the same year, of Baudelaire's *Fleurs du Mal* – both Baudelaire and Flaubert were dangerous characters, with the eyes of the authorities on them – so as not to shock susceptibilities and to endanger his own position. Both of them had been taken to the courts on the grounds of obscenity and immorality. Baudelaire had been condemned and, although Flaubert had been acquitted, he had been cautioned by the judge, and there were many who considered that he too should also have been condemned. Sainte-Beuve, with his need of the support of the authorities, was often in a critical position in this difficult time for literature, with the strict censorship under the Second Empire, and he did not want to fall into disfavour with the government, for he depended, for his living, on the official papers in which he published his *Lundis* and later his *Nouveaux Lundis*. He genuinely would have liked to praise *Salammbô* unreservedly, for he had no animosity against Flaubert and, in fact, the two men liked and admired each other. Flaubert answered him in a very different way from the way that he answered Froehner. It is also however clear that Sainte-Beuve, who was a sophisticated man of the world, did not really like the novel. Even at the height of Romanticism – he was of the same generation as Hugo, being two years younger – he had not favoured the highly coloured form of the movement, but preferred the more realistic, of which his own *Poésies de Joseph Delorme*, his first collection of poems, is one of the best examples. In his opinion of *Salammbô* he was inclined to exaggerate the flamboyant side of Flaubert's work, and did not see how different it was. Also, quite genuinely, he could not take all the barbarity and cruelty – sadism he called it – in the novel. He himself preferred the sophistication of the seventeenth and eighteenth centuries, the life of the *salon* to the life of the camp.

What is remarkable in both articles is that neither critic discusses the book as the novel it was intended to be, and neither deals with its literary merits – though it is true that Sainte-Beuve praises certain descriptive passages. Both the critics apply a totally different standard to the book than they would have applied to a historical novel by Alfred de Vigny, Alexandre Dumas or Victor Hugo. They expected it to reveal the most advanced research and knowledge of history and archaeology, but they did not think of the necessary attributes of fiction. It is true that Sainte-Beuve does make some criticism of Salammbô's character, and considered that she was too much like Emma Bovary, or like a sentimental Elvire – the heroine of Lamartine's *Méditations*

Poétiques published in 1820. Flaubert defends his portrayal by saying that no one knows the oriental woman as no one has been near enough to her to study her.

It must be admitted that Sainte-Beuve's criticism often deals with very minor and insignificant points, for instance the use of bitch's milk as a remedy for leprosy, but Flaubert answered that he had often seen it used for this purpose on his visit to the East in 1849. Sainte-Beuve also objected to the richness of the accessories and questioned whether they were true to history. Flaubert assured him that there were many such descriptions in the Bible and that the Carthaginians, as a semitic people, were very like the Jews.

Finally Flaubert declared that there were no documents to prove him in the wrong and to avoid this had been the height of his ambition.

Sainte-Beuve declared that the storm which ended Mathô's and Salammbô's lovemaking in the tent had no grounds in history. Flaubert answered that there were frequent thunderstorms in North Africa, so why not this storm, which, in any case, occupied only three lines. It is hard to be sympathetic with this objection considering that the whole scene in the tent was invented by Flaubert.

Sainte-Beuve also accused him of portraying a very untypical Greek in Spendius, and he said that he should have been a philosopher who might have pointed the moral. Spendius was, however, a freed slave, a mercenary, and Sainte-Beuve does not ask himself what a philosopher would be doing in an army of mercenaries and fighting in a foreign land. The critic also took exception to the invention of the episode of the veil of Tanit. Here he is on surer ground critically and historically; as has been previously stated, if this important event had occurred in the Punic War, it would have been recorded by Polybius or some other historian.

What hurt Flaubert most bitterly, and what he most resented, was Sainte-Beuve's justified criticism of the sadism of the book. Knowing what his reputation was, he thought that, if the most famous critic of the day made this charge, the public would believe that he was a disciple of the Marquis de Sade and this would do him a great deal of harm with the general public.

Flaubert tried to answer him reasonably and sincerely. He agreed that, as he was writing the novel, he discovered that there was no aqueduct in Carthage at the time of Hamilcar; but he wanted the scene as a vivid part of the plot and so he left it. He also admitted, as has been previously stated, that he had joined together in one person Hannon and the Hannibal who was not Hamilcar's son.

His own view of his book was that the pedestal was too heavy for the superstructure, and that he needed another hundred pages or so to fill out the person of Salammbô; he admitted that there were too many battles, but he thought that these were necessary for the true history of the book, since they existed in Polybius, and the Punic War could not be described without them. The modern reader cannot help regretting that some of the battle scenes were not omitted and the space given to the human side of the characters.

Flaubert ended by thanking him for devoting three instalments of his articles to his one book alone, in a letter which has hitherto remained unpublished except in a review:[45]

> I thank you very much, cher Maître, you have treated me as kindly as possible. Your preamble *touched* me very much indeed. I did not need that to know that you loved me, but such pledges of esteem are always very flattering – even for cannibals.

Sainte-Beuve was afraid that Flaubert might be offended at what he had said, but the latter answered him in a letter which has also remained unpublished except in a review:[46]

> Less good friends than before, Oh! cher Maître, what nonsense! Better friends! What a charming man you are! This time I do not only shake you by the hand, I embrace you!

They ended better friends than ever and Flaubert took umbrage at nothing that he said.

He was, however, very much more angry in his reply to Froehner. He declared that his novel had not been written as a work of archaeology and should not have been judged as such. It was fiction and there were no footnotes, or preface. This was worth saying, as no critic seemed to be aware of the fact. Froehner's remarks are largely those of the ignorant and pedantic critic, which so enrage any author – the picking of small points which have very little connection with the action or the subject, while seeing nothing of the main argument. He objected, for instance, to the choice of certain names of streets in Carthage and demanded what was the evidence for their existence. Flaubert answered, very reasonably, that a rue des Tanneurs and a rue des Teinturiers were found in most towns of antiquity and there was no reason to suppose that they would not exist in Carthage.

Flaubert's answers to Froehner were, in many cases, the same as those that he gave to Sainte-Beuve, on questions of fact, but he was much more bitter in his reply. It must be admitted that most of Froehner's criticisms were not worth making and were of extreme triviality. Flaubert's final remarks show how angry he was :[47]

Amongst your inaccuracies, I have only pointed out the grossest, which touched special points. As for your vague criticism, your personal opinions, and the literary analysis of my book, I did not refer to it at all. I kept to your domain, that of science, and I repeat to you once more, that I am only fairly strong in it. I do not know Hebrew, nor Arabic, nor German, nor Greek, nor Latin, but I do pride myself on knowing French. I often used translations, but also sometimes originals. In my doubts I consulted the men who, in France, pass as the most competent and, if I was not better guided, it was because I did not have the honour, the advantage, of knowing you. Please forgive me. If I had taken your advice, would I have succeeded any better? I doubt it. In any case I would have been deprived of the expressions of goodwill which you give me here and there in your article and I would have spared you the kind of regret which ends it. But be reassured, Monsieur, although you seem, yourself, terrified of your strength, and although you seriously think that you have 'torn my book piece by piece', do not be afraid, be easy in your mind, you have not been cruel . . . but only slight.

As far as the truth of *Salammbô* is concerned, most ancient historians, given the paucity of the existing documents, are of the opinion that the description of Carthage and the surrounding countryside and towns is true and that Flaubert cannot be proved in the wrong; also that most of the events are correct, with a few inventions which have verisimilitude. The most serious criticism which can be levelled against the book is on the score of its length and of the monotony of the battle scenes. As a novel it is very readable and marks a new departure in historical fiction. It would also be a valuable document for anyone studying that phase of the Punic War, as it gives a vivid picture of the time, and of many of the main figures connected with it. Henry James thought that 'it displays in the highest degree what is called the historical imagination. There are passages in it in which literary expression, of that refined, subtilized and erudite sense of the picturesque which recent years have brought to so high a development, seems to have reached its highest level.'[48]

Benjamin Bart quotes Bryher as saying that she understood why Colette preferred *Salammbô* to Flaubert's other novels:[49] 'Perhaps his study of Carthage and the mercenaries (how one can smell the lions), is nearer to us now with our memory of blitzes and invasions than his greater but narrower studies of French provincial life.'

Salammbô did Flaubert a great deal of good in society and raised him from an almost unknown writer – except for a *succès de scandale* – to being one of the best-known men of letters of the day. The success of *Salammbô* changed his life and for seven or eight years, until the Franco-Prussian war, he became a fashionable man about town, frequenting princes and emperors, being invited to Court and to the most fashionable *salons* of the day. It was then too that he was decorated with the cross of the Légion-d'Honneur.

CHAPTER FOUR

PRINCESSE MATHILDE AND GEORGE SAND

Flaubert's women friends, mentioned in an earlier chapter, came to him as the result of the publication of *Madame Bovary* in 1857, but *Salammbô*, published in 1862, brought him two further close friends, Princesse Mathilde and George Sand. Princesse Mathilde, nearly two years his senior, remained his friend until his death in 1880, and his feelings for her seem to have been warmer than those of mere friendship. His love for George Sand, who was seventeen years older than he, was almost that of a son for a mother and, when she died in 1876, he said that he felt as if he had lost his mother a second time – she had died in 1872.

Princesse Mathilde was the daughter of Lucien Bonaparte, the former King of Westphalia, brother of the Emperor Napoleon. Since the fall of the Empire, her father had lived in exile. She was sister to Prince Napoleon, nicknamed Plon-Plon. She was the niece of two emperors and the cousin of a third, for she was the cousin of Louis Bonaparte, who was to become Napoleon III. When she and her cousin were very young they were betrothed, but he became involved in political plots and had to flee to England. She then married a multi-millionaire Russian and in 1841 came to Paris. Her husband, Prince Demidoff, was a profligate and suffered from venereal disease. At a public function in his house in Paris, in the rue Saint Dominique, he struck her in the face before two hundred people. She withdrew to her apartments and, the following day, went to Russia, to Saint Petersburg, where her uncle the Tsar arranged a separation for her from her husband and insisted on alimony of about eight thousand pounds a year. Demidoff could do nothing against this, as the bulk of his fortune was in Russia and it could have been confiscated by order of the

Tsar. Princesse Mathilde then settled in Paris, for, although she had not a drop of French blood in her veins, she always felt excessively French. She was warmly received by Louis-Philippe and his family – had he not brought back the ashes of Napoleon to be buried in the Invalides? – and she became warmly attached to them. She never lost her friendship for them, even in their adversity, after their overthrow in the Revolution of 1848.

When Louis Bonaparte came to France and was elected Prince President, there were rumours of a marriage between him and Princesse Mathilde, but the prince's notorious affairs with Miss Howard, with the Comtesse de Castiglione and many others, made this delicate. In any case she was still married to Demidoff and only separated from him. There was also her notorious affair with Alfred-Émilien Nieuwerkerke, a magnificent-looking man whom she had first met in Italy in the early days of her marriage, and with whom she was passionately in love. He eventually owed his career and his promotion to her, when she was the power behind the throne. He was an important person in the Second Republic and the Empire, becoming Directeur Général of all the museums in 1848 and Surintendant des Beaux Arts in 1863, but he fell from favour at the fall of the Empire. Most of the artists of the time had the greatest contempt for him and knew that he owed what success he had to the favour of the Princess.

Princesse Mathilde was the official hostess for her cousin while he was President and Emperor until he married Eugénie de Montijo. He gave her the magnificent house in the rue de Courcelles where she held her *salon*, and also a large grant from the Civil List.

Princesse Mathilde became one of the most famous hostesses of the Second Empire. She was handsome in an imperious way, she was immensely rich, she had a beautiful town house and also a country estate near Enghien. She gave a variety of parties in the rue de Courcelles. On Sundays there were the royal guests and the family. On Tuesdays she invited official personages, ministers and ambassadors. But on Wednesdays she invited those she thought of as her special friends, mostly artists, musicians and men of letters. These are the parties by which she is best known – they were her *salon*, of which she was so proud. She does not seem to have had any natural taste for literature and was more anxious to attract well-known names than to make discoveries on her own. Nevertheless some of the best-known people of the Second Empire were to be found at her *salon*, and they seemed to enjoy her company and hospitality – or to be flattered by it. They included Sainte-Beuve, Renan, Mérimée, Littré, Dumas *père* and *fils*, Ary Scheffer, Flaubert and so forth. The poets were somewhat thin on the ground, for Hugo was in exile, Musset had died in 1857 – he was once invited but arrived drunk at the party – and Vigny was to die in 1863. Leconte de Lisle was not invited, nor Baudelaire. The former had done a prison sentence in 1848 as a revolutionary and was a well-known republican; while the latter had been convicted at his trial in 1857. The main poet was Théophile Gautier, and later, with François Coppée, he was the only one; he was called 'le poète mathildien', and he was a member of her *salon* until the day of his death in 1872.

Sainte-Beuve was considered the greatest writer of the Second Empire, with Balzac and Stendhal dead and Hugo in exile, and he was probably the biggest lion in her *salon* – he was certainly the one for whom she did most. He had begun his imperial connection with Princesse Julie, Marquise Roccagiovini, the sister of Princesse Primoli, the cousin of Princesse Mathilde. At her Friday evenings in the rue de Grenelle, she invited many of the same people as her cousin, but her *salon* was less literary and Sainte-Beuve was glad to be a member of the other, where he remained until his quarrel with the Princess in the last year of the Empire, in 1869.

Princesse Mathilde's artistic parties were often thought by the conventional members of society to be too liberal, too bohemian and too advanced; yet in the opposition she was never considered anything but a Bonaparte and a supporter of the régime. In severe circles her bazaar – as her *salon* was often called – aroused a great deal of criticism. The spiteful Horace de Viel-Castel quotes from a certain Abbé Coquereau:[1]

The *salon* of Princesse Mathilde has become impossible . . . The society which gathers there is of the strangest; it is a society of petty socialists, low flatterers, and atheists even lower and more sycophantic: Sainte-Beuve, Littré, Renan . . . The Princess is Russian and Italian, she mumbles prayers in her chapel in the morning and, in the evening, considers wonderful the impious socialistic remarks of Littré, or the hatred of priests of the ex-seminarist, Renan. Sainte-Beuve, that fat and rotund journalist, who resembles a bald ortolan, is the choir-boy, incense-burner, of the *salon*, and burns before the Princess the over-refined perfumes of his shop, in the hope of being appointed to the Senate . . . Poor Princesse Mathilde imagines that she has a *salon*, but she has only a bazaar, where *every flatterer* lives at the expense of the man who is listening to him. The frequentation of people with vulgar manners is vulgarizing her; and she has reached the point of taking for *majestic ease*, the commonest familiarity.

Viel Castel's remarks may be due to pique as, in the early sixties, he was no longer received by Princesse Mathilde, for it was rumoured that he had stolen pictures from the Louvre.

Flaubert's *Salammbô* appeared in November 1862 and its success was remarked by Princesse Mathilde. Always on the look-out for lions for her *salon*, she invited him to dinner on 21 January 1863, so she did not lose very much time.[2] Flaubert asked Jules de Goncourt what he should do. He answered:[3] 'I'm much inclined to advise you to appear there once or twice, so that I can see you there and dine with you.' So he accepted her invitation.

What did the Princess really think of Flaubert? We do not know. Did she consider him more than a lion at her parties, or did she consider him ludicrous? We know that she called him Mathô, after the hero of *Salammbô*, which indicates that she thought him wild, strong and passionate. The only thing which we know that she said is quoted by Marcello Spaziani in *Gli Amici della Principessa Matilde*.[4] 'The truth is that he was a simple man, trusting, demonstrative and not at all envious. The illness from which he suffered must have influenced and modified his mind and his spirit, but it never impaired his honesty, his kindness and the charm of his heart.'

Flaubert soon grew very much attached to her and there was something emotional and more than mere friendship in his attitude to her, and in his relationship with her. Very soon he was signing his letters to her 'Your affectionate' and 'Your humble and very sincerely devoted and affectionate'. He tells her constantly that he is lonely for her presence, and counts the days until he can see her again. He thought of all sorts of little attentions for her, and once, when she had a cold, he made his niece buy pastilles for her, to the extent of a dozen boxes.[5]

Affection was not only on his side and, from her actions, she seems to have had affection for him. In the early days of their relationship, on 30 March 1874, with her brother and his wife, she went to Rouen to see him, and he escorted them round the town, showing them the beauty and historical spots. She presented him with some of her water-colours, which was a great honour, and, another time, with a little Indian knife, for which he thanked her profusely:[6]

> This afternoon, at six o'clock, they brought me from Rouen your charming present, Princess. I find it so pretty and it gives me so much pleasure that I am keeping it on my table, in the midst of my papers, and I gaze at it without tiring, like the big child that I am . . . But what flatters me even more than the gift is the remembrance. I had forgotten the promise that you made me at Saint-Gratien, in those good days that I spent with you. I imagine that the time is coming when you will leave for Compiègne. I shall not move until you return, naturally, as my trip to Paris has really no other cause than to see you, I am anxious not to miss you . . .
>
> I kiss both your hands, Princess, and I am entirely yours.

Later she sent him her likeness, which touched him greatly:[7]

> I do not know, Princess, in what terms once more to thank you for the week I spent with you. My visit to Saint-Gratien seems to me like an exquisite dream. It seems to me that something of your person floats in the air there, and I like everything there, there is so much charm everywhere. I shall live for two months on these memories and they will keep me company in my solitude. And how often I shall go over, one by one, all the happy moments that I spent with you. The first thing that I shall do, when I get back to Rouen, the day after tomorrow, will be to have your portrait framed, and I shall put it on the mantelpiece, in the place where the pious put their relics.
>
> Think of me some time, Princess, that is to say send me your news from time to time, and allow me to place myself at your feet and to kiss both your hands.

She frequently invited him to Saint-Gratien and he always spent a week or a fortnight there. In their *Journal*, the Goncourt brothers describe Saint-Gratien as a comfortable house with no elegance, with no works of art, and flowers in holders affixed to the walls.[8] Flaubert used to say that his days at Saint-Gratien were amongst the happiest of his life. It was there, one evening, that he read a passage from his recent great success, *Salammbô*, to the assembled company. Primoli has described the evening, and one can realize here Flaubert's histrionic talents:[9]

He has just read at the top of his voice, declaimed, fragments from *Salammbô*, the scene of the serpent, the meeting of the daughter of Hamilcar with Mathô. It is Mathô himself who is speaking, or rather it is Frédéric Lemaître.[10] But that great artist would not be able to give the impression of Flaubert reading, shouting, intoning his work. His sea-green eyes flash from under black brows, which overshadow them; his moustache stands on end, his chest swells, his hand trembles, and the book which he is clutching seems agitated by a wave.

Through Princesse Mathilde Flaubert was to meet the Emperor and the Empress, but of that later.

She realized that the surest way of pleasing him was to favour Louis Bouilhet. She went to the first night of Bouilhet's play *La Conjuration d'Amboise*, at the Odéon Theatre on 29 October 1866, and brought with her many members of her household.[11] To please Flaubert she once invited Bouilhet to Saint-Gratien, but, by some wretched accident, the unfortunate poet had eaten garlic for lunch. Nieuwerkerke, with his usual arrogance, went upstairs and said to the Princess: 'There is a poet downstairs stinking of garlic.'[12] The scene is very typical of Louis Bouilhet.

In spite of her broadmindedness and her tolerant attitude to her friends, Princesse Mathilde objected to Flaubert seeing so much of Jane de Tourbey and she scolded him for this.[13] She complained to the Goncourts about having to share with such women the society and the thoughts of her friends such as Taine, Renan and Flaubert, who robbed her of twenty minutes when they were dining with her to go and spend them 'chez ces filles'. She vituperated against such examples of the domination of women, honoured by the company of philosophers, men of letters and science, of these 'fillasses' who had not even the excuse of an art, a talent, a name, or the genius of a Rachel.

It was at Saint-Gratien that a curious event occurred which seems to have caused much private amusement amongst the Princess's friends. Primoli has recounted the story, and he must have obtained the material from the Princess herself, whom he called his aunt, though his mother was only her cousin. He relates that once when Flaubert was staying at Saint-Gratien, he requested a private interview with the Princess when everyone else had gone. She agreed, and when all the other guests had retired for the night Flaubert came back. Primoli continues:[14]

The door opens a crack, Mathô enters slyly, more like a timid school-boy than a conquering hero. With a suspicious gaze he looks round the room, he assures himself that all the guests have disappeared. He slips then in between the table and the sofa, he lets himself fall into an upholstered armchair near the Princess. Without saying a word he watches her working ... The Princess feels this burning gaze which wanders over her neck, over her shoulders, on her hand ... She waits ... Somewhat irritated by these eyes fixed on her, she suddenly lifts her head and says: 'Well! what have you to say to me that is so urgent? We are alone as you wished, and I am ready to listen to everything.'

Then Flaubert, uttering a few incoherent words, jumped up and ran away. A few days later he wrote in the autograph album of Princesse Charlotte Primoli, dating it '20 February 1865': 'Women will never know how timid men are.'[15]

Flaubert also told the Princess some years later. 'I was so upset when I left you on Thursday evening, I was no longer clear in my mind. Princesse Charlotte [Primoli] will have told you of my grotesque embarrassment in the train. No one will ever know how much weakness there is hidden beneath my policeman's exterior.'[16] He also told her that he wished she was a simple bourgeoise so that he could talk to her more easily.[17]

Flaubert wanted to write a book which would please the Princess, and it was for her that he composed *L'Éducation Sentimentale,* as he told her. He wrote it, he said, 'to inspire pity for these poor men so misunderstood, and to prove to women how shy they are'.[18] It was to her that he had read the whole of the book while he was writing it, and she had seemed very much moved by it.[19] When it was published in November 1869, he sent her the book with a letter of dedication.[20]

Princess, here is the book which you have deigned to listen to from beginning to end. I have been unable to append a suitable dedication; too many things stirred in my heart as I offered it to you. What matter! When your eyes rest on these two volumes you will think a little about a man who loves you very much, Princess, and who is wholly yours.

Princesse Mathilde enjoyed being a patron to her friends and was ready to serve them. She was able to obtain for Flaubert from the Emperor the cross of Chevalier de la Légion-d'Honneur, in August 1866. The Minister of Education, Victor Duruy, informed the Princess immediately:[21]

I have the honour to announce to you that His Majesty has just signed the nomination of M. Flaubert to the order of the Légion d'Honneur. I am very happy to have been able thus to accede to the wishes of your Imperial Highness in proposing the author of Salambe [*sic*] to the Emperor's choice.

Please accept, Princess, the homage of my respectful devotion.

Flaubert wrote also to thank the Princess for her kind efforts on his behalf:[22]

How kind of you to write to me immediately. I recognize in this the excellence of your heart. I have no doubts about the goodwill of M. Duruy, but I imagine that the idea was somewhat suggested to him by someone else. And so the red ribbon, is more than a favour for me, it is almost a souvenir. I did not need that to think often of Princesse Mathilde . . .

In the meantime while awaiting the pleasure and the honour of seeing you again, Princess, I kiss your hands and beg you to believe that I am your very grateful, devoted and affectionate, G. Flaubert.

Princesse Mathilde also gave Flaubert the little miniature model of the cross.[23]

On the last New Year's Eve of the Empire Flaubert wrote to the Princess to send her his best wishes for 1870:[24]

I wish you then, Princess, a *good year*. May each of your wishes be realized and may nothing unfortunate befall you, in a word may everything please you, from the political resolutions to the temperature from heaven! Be as happy as possible. When this period of the year arrives, one sums up the twelve months, as shopkeepers carry out their inventory. As for me, I find your name on all the pages of my big ledger, on the credit side, naturally . . .

What matter, amongst all expressions of homage which will be rendered to you, and the wishes that will be uttered to you, there are none more deep or more sincere than mine, Princess, for I am wholly yours.

Then, nine months later, the war came and Princesse Mathilde went, for a time, into exile. As we shall see later, Flaubert did much to facilitate her escape and went to see her in Belgium, where she had taken refuge. When the war and the Commune were over, she returned to France and they resumed their friendship, which lasted until his death. However there was then a small cloud over it, as Flaubert had not approved of the manner of her return.

Flaubert had met George Sand, though only casually, after he published *Madame Bovary*, but his real friendship with her dated from the publication of *Salammbô*, when she reviewed the book favourably. He wrote to thank her:[25]

> Dear Madame, I am not grateful to you for having fulfilled what you call a duty. The kindness of your heart has touched me, and your sympathy has made me proud, that is all. Your letter, which I have just received, adds to your article and surpasses it, and I do not know what to say to you, except that *I frankly like you very much* ... As for your warm invitation, as a true Norman, I reply neither yes nor no. I shall perhaps go one day, to surprise you, for I have a great longing to see you, and to converse with you. It would be sweet for me to have your likeness, to hang it on the wall of my study in the country, where I often spend long months quite alone. Is this request indiscreet? If not, a thousand thanks in anticipation. Receive these with the earlier ones which I repeat.

George Sand was seventeen years older than Flaubert. Now a woman of fifty-nine, she had settled down comfortably into middle age, in the country. She had become a lady bountiful, stout and plain, living in her château with her son and his wife. She looked like a comfortable grannie, though her son's children, in 1863, were not yet born. There was now nothing left of the dashing, boyish girl, of the eighteen-thirties in Paris, in the little masculine suit and top hat, as she was painted by Delacroix.

After the letter of January 1863, there is no further letter from Flaubert to her until 1866, but there may have been others which have not come down to us, as there is one from her to him, in February 1863, which is probably an answer to his of the previous month. Flaubert, however, rarely left a letter unanswered. It is, unfortunately, only a fragment in her published letter, but it is unlikely to have been an isolated example.[26] This is the first of their discussions on literature:

> To put nothing of one's heart into what one writes? I don't understand at all, no not at all. As for me, it seems to me that one can't put anything else. Can one separate one's mind from one's body? Is it something different? Can sensation ever be limited? Can the human being be cut in two? Finally, not to give oneself entirely in one's work

94

seems to me as impossible as to weep with anything else but one's own eyes, and to think with anything else but one's own brain. What did you mean? Answer me when you have the time.

They also met in Paris, and were certainly at the Magny dinner on 12 February 1866. The Magny dinners were founded in December 1862 by Sainte-Beuve, Gavarni and the two Goncourts. They were mostly literary and artistic men who attended and they met at the Restaurant Magny, where Sainte-Beuve used normally to dine. The meetings took place twice a month and were at first called the Dîners Gavarni. George Sand wrote an account of the dinner in her *Journal*, which is quoted by Suffel.[27] Women were normally not allowed to the dinners, but an exception was made in the case of George Sand at the request of Flaubert. It is interesting to note that Princesse Mathilde tried to get Sainte-Beuve to invite her in 1863 and he was somewhat shocked by the suggestion.[28] The dinners, at that time, were only a year old and her Imperial Highness might have cramped the other members at a gathering where speech was very free. George Sand said:

First dinner at Magny's with my little friends. They received me as well as possible. They were very brilliant. Gautier always sparkling and paradoxical. Saint-Victor charming and distinguished. Flaubert passionate and more sympathetic to me than the others, why I do not yet know ... One pays ten francs per head, the dinner is mediocre, they smoke a lot, speak shouting at the top of their voices, and everyone leaves when he wants to. I got home at half past ten.

George Sand knew Mademoiselle Leroyer de Chantepie, who was one of her admirers, and it is interesting that she gave her advice very similar to that given to her by Flaubert. She advised her to go about more, to think less about herself and her unhappiness and to work more. She seemed better able than Flaubert to save herself from being devoured.

The friendship between Flaubert and George Sand grew and he was soon confiding everything to her. He used to call her 'chère Maître' or 'chère Maître adorée' or again 'chère amie du bon Dieu'.

The friendship was not, however, solely on his side and she soon grew very much attached to him. She called him 'cher ami de mon cœur'. She tells him that she is constantly thinking of him as she works. His letters are, she assures him, like the blessed rain which makes everything in her fructify. And she wrote to him once:[29] 'I have received your letter this morning, my dear friend. Why do I love you more than most of the others, even more than old tried friends? I'm looking for the reason.' She was particularly touched when, after the death of Alexandre Manceau, he went to Palaiseau to be with her. Alexandre Manceau, a steel engraver, was a young friend of her son Maurice Sand and he often came to Nohant to stay with the family as early as the Second Republic. He soon became a great favourite with his hostess. She was then not far off fifty and he was thirteen years younger. She used on him her well-developed maternal feelings, and perhaps others as well – her maternal feelings had always been very mixed. He first became her secretary and then took charge of everything at Nohant. He was very delicate, being consumptive, and this moved her still more. He had great influence on her and soon she could not do without him.

This had gone on for more than ten years and Maurice Sand came to resent Manceau's presence at Nohant: he, the son, seeing a stranger not much older than himself occupying the chief place. To save unpleasantness, George Sand bought a little house at Palaiseau, and she went there with Manceau, who was now desperately ill, in 1864. His health deteriorated further and he died on 21 August 1865. By some irony he left the whole of his fortune to Maurice Sand, who disliked him and who annotated his mother's *Journal* ironically wherever Manceau's name was mentioned.

Flaubert won George Sand's heart by going to see her at Palaiseau after the death of Manceau. She kept on Palaiseau, which was full of her young friend's memories. She wrote to Flaubert from there in November 1865:[30]

It seems to me that it will bring me luck if I say goodnight to my dear friend, before beginning work. Here am I all alone in my little house. The gardener and his family live in the little house in the garden. We are the last house, at the end of the village, quite isolated, in the open country, which is a lovely oasis . . . I am sad nevertheless. This absolute solitude, which has always been for me holiday and recreation, is now shared by a dead man, who vanished as a lamp goes out and is still here. I do not consider him unhappy in the region he now inhabits, but the image he has left near me, which is only a reflection, seems to lament at not being able to speak to me. No matter! Sadness is not unhealthy as it prevents us from drying up.

You are probably hard at work, alone also, as your mother must be in Rouen. You are not obliged to write to me if you're not in the mood. No real friendship without *absolute* liberty.

I'll see you in Paris next week, then again at Palaiseau, and then at Nohant.

One of the highest points in Flaubert's friendship with George Sand was the occasion of her two visits to Croisset in August and November 1866. He very rarely invited his women friends to his home, but these visits were a great success. George Sand and Madame Flaubert found that they had very much in common, and the mother was very much touched by the love and interest shown by the famous author for her son.

The visit in August, the first visit, was very carefully planned. Flaubert met her in Rouen with a carriage and showed her the town before going out to Croisset.

The kindest and most vivid picture of Croisset is the one she wrote in her *Journal* (unpublished passages from which are printed by Maurois in his life of George Sand entitled *Lélia*). It is very different from what the Goncourts had said when they had complained that there had only been silver on the table and no gold.[31] 'There is no other metal on the table but silver, and that has a cold effect.' George Sand had written:[32]

Flaubert's mother is an old lady of great charm. The situation is quite delicious, the house, comfortably and well arranged; attentive servants, cleanliness, water and one's every want *anticipated* . . . I live like a fighting cock! . . . In the evening Flaubert read me his magnificent *Tentation de Saint Antoine*. We chatted away in his study until two in the morning. *Wednesday 29 August*. We got back at one o'clock, a fire was lit; we dried ourselves and drank tea . . . Then I started out with Flaubert, and made the round of the estate; garden, terraces, orchard, kitchen-garden, farm and the *citadel*, a curious old wooden house which he uses as a store room. View across the Seine . . . a beautifully sheltered spot on rising ground . . . Dressed. Excellent dinner. I played cards with the two old ladies. Later I had some talk with Flaubert, and went to bed at two. Bed very comfortable.

She stayed only for three days this time, but they were very happy days and she wrote to him on her return home:[33]

Please embrace for me your dear mother and your charming niece. I am really touched by the kind welcome I received in your 'canonical' setting, where a wandering animal of my kind is an anomaly which might be awkward. Instead of that I was received as if I was a member of the family, and I experienced that good breeding which comes from the heart. Remember me to all these kind friends. I was really very happy in your house.

And then you are a kind and good fellow, even though you are a great man, and I love you with all my heart. My head is full of Rouen, of its public buildings, of its strange houses. All that seen with you struck me with redoubled force. But your house, your *citadel*, that is like a dream and it seems to me that I am still there. Paris seemed to me small as I crossed its bridges, and I wanted to leave. I have not seen all of you enough yet, and your background . . . I embrace you all and I bless you all.

Two days later she wrote again:[34]

I was very happy after the week I spent with you; no cares, a good rest, beautiful country, affectionate hearts and your good and frank face in which there is something paternal. Age has nothing to do with it, one feels in you the protection of infinite kindness, and one evening, when you called your mother 'my child', tears rose to my eyes. It cost me a lot to leave you, but I was preventing you from working, and then – a disease of old age is to be unable to stay put. I am afraid to become too much attached and to weary people. Old people must show extreme discretion. From afar I can tell you how much I love you, without the danger of tiresome repetition. You are one of the rare spirits who has remained open to impressions, and a lover of art but not corrupted by ambition or intoxicated by success. In short you'll always be twenty-five years old by all sorts of ideas which are out of date, as certain senile young men claim nowadays . . . I embrace you tenderly and your mother too, and the charming niece.

Flaubert wrote immediately:[35]

How nice and kind your letter of this morning was, chère Maître. It continues for me the farewell look that you gave me yesterday at the train. Everybody speaks of you since your departure. You pleased everybody here very much. That is how it is! One does not take into account the irresistible and involuntary seduction of your person. You must come back again, if not now, and for much longer.

I am always yours. I need not tell you that everyone asks me to give you everything I can think of that is most friendly.

As a result of her visit to Croisset in August 1866, George Sand presented Flaubert with a complete edition of her works. One wonders what he really thought of her writings in his heart of hearts, as they went against everything which he admired in literature. But he was incapable of thinking ill of anything which anyone of whom he was fond ever wrote. We have no evidence, from his correspondence, that he ever read the whole of her collected works. George Sand, however, was always very modest about her own achievements in literature, in spite of her fame at this time. She realized perfectly well why she was a success and never took any pride in it, and she always declared that Flaubert was far the greater writer. She admired him sincerely and always said that he was the only person with whom she could discuss literature. She wrote to him once:[36] 'You are the only person with whom I have been able to exchange any ideas except those of the trade.'

In 1866, as a result of their intimacy at Croisset, she asked his permission to dedicate a book to him. This was *Le Dernier Amour*.

George Sand went back to Croisset in November, where this time she stayed a week, and it seems to have been a happy time for both writers. She wrote of it in her *Journal*:[37]

Left Paris at one o'clock with Gustave. The express travelled very fast. Lovely weather, charming country, good conversation. At Rouen station we found Madame Flaubert and her other son, the doctor. At Croisset went round the garden. Talked, dined, and then more talk and reading, until half past one. Comfortable bed, slept like a log ...
4 November 1866: Wonderful day! Walked round the garden, as far as the orchard. Worked. I am deliciously snug in my little attic room, which is very warm. The niece, her husband, and the old Crépet lady came to dinner ... Puzzles. Gustave read me his fairy story. It is full of admirable and charming things, but is too long, too richly orchestrated, too full. We had another talk which lasted until half past two. I felt hungry and we went down to the kitchen in search of cold chicken. We poked our noses into the yard, just long enough to get some water from the pump. It was as mild as a spring night. We ate. Retired upstairs again. We smoked, we went on with our talk. We separated at four o'clock in the morning.

This is the visit which Amélie Bosquet had described, alleging that many people had surmised that 'things had happened', since George Sand had returned to Nohant looking exhausted and worn out. It never occurred to her that the debauches between the two authors had been literary and not physical.

Flaubert wrote to her after she had left:[38]

> I am quite *'unnerved'* since you have left; it seems to me that I haven't seen you for ten years. My sole subject of conversation with my mother is to speak of you. Everybody here adores you. Under what star were you born to be able to unite in your person such diverse qualities, so many and so rare?
>
> I don't know what kind of feeling I bear you, but I feel for you a particular affection, that I have never felt for anyone else hitherto. We get on very well together, don't we? That is very pleasant . . .
>
> To love you 'more' is difficult for me, but I embrace you most tenderly. Your letter of this morning, so sad, moved me deeply. We separated at a moment when many things were going to rise to our lips! All the doors between us are not yet open. You inspire in me a great respect and I dare not ask you questions.

The letters which Flaubert wrote to George Sand on literature are the most interesting that he wrote, more significant than those he had written to Louise Colet when he had been composing *Madame Bovary*, because he could discuss matters with her from the professional point of view. Although they did not agree on literary matters they could always discuss and argue their varying points of view. She wrote:[39]

> Your letters fall on me like rain which moistens and brings to growth immediately what is germinating in the ground; they make me want to answer your reasons because your reasons are strong and demand replies.
>
> I don't claim that my answers are strong also; but they are sincere and they come from my roots, like the plants above mentioned . . . *My roots* can't be dug up and I'm surprised that you ask me to make them bear tulips when they can only answer you with potatoes! . . . Amongst artists and men of letters I have found no depth. You are the only one with whom I could exchange ideas besides those relating to the trade . . . They said that one must not write for the ignorant, and they scorned me because I only wanted to write for them, since they needed something. The masters are well provided for, rich and satisfied. The fools need everything and I pity them. Love and pity can't be separated and that is the uncomplicated mainspring of my thought . . . I pity humanity and I would like it to be good, because I can't separate myself from it; because it is me; because the harm that it does strikes me to the heart; because its shame makes me blush; because its crimes twist my entrails; because I cannot understand heaven in the sky or on earth for myself alone.

You ought to be able to understand me, who are kindness from top to toe.

Their ideas on literature were diametrically opposite. She thought that one should write to express one's personality, to get in touch personally with one's readers, and she could not understand Flaubert's attitude.[40]

Who asks you to put your personality on the stage? Indeed that is no use unless it is done frankly as a story. But to remove one's soul from what one is doing, what is the meaning of this morbid fancy? To hide one's opinion of the people one is describing, and consequently to leave the reader uncertain on the opinion he should have, that is asking to be misunderstood, and then the reader leaves you, for, if he wants to hear the story which you are telling him, it is on condition that you show him clearly that one is strong and the other weak.

She thought that literature should point the way, give some guidance; and that the reader likes to know whom he should admire and whom blame. She thought it impossible to keep the author's personality away from the reader:[41]

You cannot withdraw from this contemplation; for man is you, and man is the reader. Whatever you may do your story is a conversation between you and him. If you show him evil coldly, without showing him goodness, he gets angry. He asks himself whether it is he who is evil or you. You are however working to move him and to attach him to you; you will never succeed in that if you are not moved yourself, or if you hide it so well that he believes you are indifferent. He is right. Perfect impartiality is anti-human, and a novel must be human before anything else. If it is not you will not be thanked if it is well written, well composed, well observed in detail. An essential quality is lacking, interest.

She thought that literature should raise up humanity and bring it consolation. Flaubert,[42] on the contrary, thought that the author should be invisible in his creation as God in His, and that the public should know nothing about him. He considered that the novelist had not the right to express his opinion on anything. George Sand found this disconcerting and inhuman.

Flaubert thought that one should not earn money from one's pen. He tactlessly wrote this to George Sand, who had worked all her life since she was little more than a girl to earn her living and that of her family – indeed she could not have lived without it. It was easy for Flaubert to talk in this way, as he had private means and could live without anything extra. She wrote to him:[43]

I live like a proletarian on my day's wages; when I am no longer able to do my day's work then I'll be despatched off to the next world, and I'll need nothing more.

She was always distressed at the sadness and pessimism of what he wrote, for she did not think that this was his real nature, and she considered that he hid his true feelings as if on principle, but, in so doing, he made people more unhappy than he need.[44]

Flaubert answered that the world deserved nothing but contempt.[45] He wrote to her:

Why are you so sad? Humanity offers nothing new. Its incurable wretchedness has filled me with bitterness from my youth. And so now I have no disillusionment. I think that the crowd, the herd will always be loathsome . . .

Ah! dear good Maître, if only you could hate! That is what you lack, hatred. In spite of your large sphinx-like eyes, you have always seen the world through a golden colour. It came from the sun of your heart; but so much darkness has arisen that you can no longer recognize the things. Come on! shriek, thunder. Seize your big lyre and pluck the bronze strings; the monsters will flee. Water us with the drops of blood of wounded Thémis.

We shall see later that, through the years, the influence of George Sand softened Flaubert.

The friendship between Flaubert and George Sand was to develop during the few years that were left to her after the war, and especially during the years after his mother's death in 1872. Later it was for her that he was to write *Un Cœur Simple* in *Trois Contes*, to show her that he was not completely cold and devoid of sentiment. She herself had no doubt of this and knew the softness and the kindness of his heart.[46] Indeed she was one of the people who realized most fully the warmheartedness of his nature beneath his gruff exterior.

CHAPTER FIVE

THE MAN ABOUT TOWN

Flaubert had published *Salammbô* in 1862 and, although he toyed with many plans – amongst them what he called his novel of modern Paris, which was to become *L'Éducation Sentimentale* – the first work which he undertook was a fairy play, rather like a pantomime, written in collaboration with Louis Bouilhet and d'Osmoy and entitled *Le Château des Cœurs*. According to Du Camp neither of the other two authors was very enthusiastic about the play. Flaubert never lost his passion for the stage and, when he was a boy, he and his friends frequently put on plays in the Hôtel Dieu at Rouen. Later, when he was a man, many of his companions described his histrionic talents and called him 'un saltimbanque manqué'. The Goncourt brothers relate how, one evening at Gautier's house at Neuilly,[1] 'They request Flaubert to dance *L'Idiot des Salons*. He asks for Gautier's frock coat, pulls up his collar, I do not know what he does with his hair, his face, his whole appearance, but there he is suddenly transformed into a fantastic caricature of gross stupidity.'

The play was finished in October 1863, and then Flaubert tried to get it produced. He offered it first to Marc Fournier, for the Théâtre de la Porte Saint Martin, but Fournier did not think that it had any chance of success and he refused it. One of the difficulties of its production would be the expense of the frequent scene changes.

Flaubert made further efforts to have it performed in 1864, in 1866 and 1869; and, after the war, in 1872, 1873, 1874 and 1877. It was never produced and was only published a few months before he died, in 1879, in a periodical called *La Vie Moderne*.

It is strange that Flaubert, with his meticulous standards in novel writing, should have been far less particular for the theatre, and he never took the trouble to master stagecraft.

Le Château des Cœurs is certainly not a good play, for it has far too many disjointed plots. Moreover this kind of fairy atmosphere needs a very special sort of poetic writing, such as is found in Musset and Shakespeare, a light touch which Flaubert and Bouilhet were incapable of providing.

The characters are also weak psychologically and they are too much the mouthpiece of Flaubert's ideas; they are not always in character and they express his cynical view of life, as the play is intended to be a satire of the bourgeoisie. The psychology may also owe something to *L'Éducation Sentimentale*. Paul, the hero, bears some resemblance to Frédéric, Kloeker has something of the banker Dambreuse and Madame Kloeker of Madame Dambreuse.

There are many idiotic ballets in the play and a ridiculous ending when all the characters, having swallowed a heart – they had, previously, been completely devoid of this organ – are totally transformed. The play ends with a pantomime apotheosis and a grand finale with the ironic lines:

> La vertu étant récompensée
> On n'a rien à dire.

Drama was, however, not Flaubert's only interest at the time, though the play came first. He had many plans in his mind. He was certainly thinking of the modern novel dealing with Paris. He was also pondering over the material which was later to become *Bouvard et Pécuchet*.

The years after the success of *Salammbô* until the war, or rather until the death of Louis Bouilhet in July 1869, were the happiest and most successful of Flaubert's life. He was famous and appreciated, he was received everywhere and he enjoyed it. His health was good and it was noticed that during the years of success he had no recurrence of his nervous complaint, which returned only with financial worry after the war.

This was the gayest period of the Second Empire, the sixties, when a regular frenzy of amusement seemed to seize on everyone. It was the period of Offenbach and 'la Foire Impériale', the time of Hortense Schneider.

But, behind all this glitter and luxury, there was corruption and extravagance, and a terrible contrast between richness and poverty. Flaubert was studying all this when he was writing *L'Éducation Sentimentale*, though he applied it to an earlier period, the last years of the reign of Louis-Philippe.

This was also the gayest and most frivolous period of Flaubert's life, when he frequented the highest in the land. As we have seen, in 1863 he became acquainted with Princesse Mathilde and became one of her close friends. Through her he soon met the Emperor and the Empress and Prince Napoleon. Although Princesse Mathilde did not get on very well with the Empress, Flaubert was attracted to her – or perhaps only dazzled by her rank and beauty. He was always very anxious to know what she thought of him and he gave her flowers, white camellias. He asked his friend Jules Duplan to get them for him:[2]

Please will you, immediately, do me the following service? Go to the Passage de l'Opéra and order from Madame Prévost a bunch of white camellias, the finest you can find, I insist that it must be specially smart. (One must give a good opinion of oneself if one belongs to the inferior classes of society.) The box must arrive on Monday morning so that I can present it Monday evening. The shopkeeper can either forward the bill to the station, or you can pay it, whichever you prefer.

Don't forget, I'm counting on you. An immediate reply if you please.

What may seem strange is that Flaubert seems to have become a close friend of Prince Napoleon, as one would not have imagined that there could have been much in common between the two men. In the Spoelberch de Lovenjoul Collection at Chantilly there are many letters from him to Flaubert which show considerable intimacy.[3] Flaubert wrote once to Jane de Tourbey that he was proud that such a man should shake him by the hand.[4] They went out to balls and to the theatre together, and the Prince once wrote to him:[5]

Here, dear Monsieur Flaubert, is the ticket for this evening. You need only go straight to my box, and we'll have supper together afterwards, *but without a word to anyone.*

Robert Mitchell and Comte Fleury have told of the Prince's entertainments:[6]

Once a week on Wednesday, the Prince used to entertain to dinner some friends: Flaubert, Renan, Sainte-Beuve, Émile de Girardin, etc., and others who have made no mark in history, and whose names I do not remember. Flaubert, with his immense height, his enormous head of a Gaullish warrior, used to frighten a little Princess Clotilde [the wife of the Prince] who had difficulty in getting accustomed to his excessive paradoxes.

He was proud of being invited to the Prince's parties and, naïvely, did not disguise his pleasure from his niece:[7]

What account can I give you of the Prince's ball? The rooms were very numerous and luxurious in decoration. What surprised me most was the quantity of drawing-rooms, twenty-four, leading one into the other, without counting the little passage rooms. 'Monseigneur' was very much surprised at the number of people whom I knew. I must have spoken to a couple of hundred people. In the midst of this brilliant gathering, what did I see but a few Rouen mugs . . . I kept away from the group with horror, and I went to sit on the steps of the throne, beside Princess Primoli.

Flaubert always used to call Bouilhet by the nickname 'Monseigneur'.

Flaubert was soon invited to most of the royal parties, even to Compiègne, which was a great honour, and he could not restrain his pride when he wrote to his niece:[8]

The bourgeois of Rouen would be still more flabbergasted if they only knew my success at Compiègne! I speak without exaggeration. In a word, instead of being bored, I enjoyed myself very much. The only thing that is hard is the constant change of clothes, and the punctuality of the hours. I'll tell you all that later. I'm still half asleep, and I'm going to take a bath.

He was very anxious always to be correctly dressed on all occasions and he asked Duplan what it meant, for a civilian, when the invitation stated 'en uniforme'.[9] François Coppée says that he wore smart clothes of a somewhat old-fashioned cut, with a 'soupçon de jabot', and patent-leather boots.[10] As Flaubert said to his niece, it was a far cry from their old provincial life:[11]

I dined on Saturday with Princesse Mathilde, I went to the ball at the Opera, until five o'clock this morning, with Prince Napoleon, and the Ambassador from Turin, in the grand imperial box. There it is! . . . Ah! how far all this from our comfortable little provincial life!

However, the height of Flaubert's social life occurred during the festivities for the International Exhibition of 1867, which was almost the last flicker of the glory of the Second Empire. That was the year also when Hortense Schneider, who was the symbol of the Second Empire, reached the pinnacle of her fame when she created the part of the Grande Duchesse de Gérolstein in Offenbach's operetta of the same name.

The Exhibition took place in an enormous construction of glass and iron, in the Champ de Mars, and was opened by the Emperor in April. The first night of the *Grande Duchesse de Gérolstein* took place on the day of the opening and was a delirious success for Hortense Schneider. All the smartest members of the Court and the Diplomatic Corps were present at the Théâtre des Variétés for the performance. The public appreciated the inverted satire against the military cast. Napoleon was present but no one knew, as he twirled his moustache, what he thought of this denigration of the army, though it is said that Thiers, who was an enemy of the Emperor, enjoyed it very much. He was not sorry to see the régime attacked.

Many foreign royal visitors came to Paris to see Hortense Schneider, and not the Exhibition. Edward Prince of Wales was assiduous in his attentions to her and spent more time with her than on his duties in the exhibition. The Tsar of Russia had his box ordered from Moscow, and, shortly after his arrival in Paris, was at the Variétés. Emperor William of Germany and his son Frederick were there, and Von Moltke and Bismarck, and it is said that they were more impressed by the army reviewed by the Grande Duchesse de Gérolstein than by that reviewed by the Emperor.

There came to Hortense Schneider's dressing room at the theatre three emperors, seven kings, twenty-two princes and many more. It was at this time that a jealous rival called her 'le Passage des Princes'.

The great event of the Exhibition season, however, was the grand ball given at the Tuileries Palace on 10 June 1867 for all the foreign royal guests, to which Flaubert was invited. He mentions it with assumed irony to his niece:[12]

The sovereigns wish to see me as one of the splendid curiosities of France, and so I'm invited to spend the evening with them on Monday next.

For the occasion he borrowed his niece's little 'tigre', that is to say the diminutive groom who was to sit at the back of his carriage so that he could arrive in style at the palace. Nevertheless, he was very proud and he said to George Sand:[13]

I spent thirty-six hours in Paris this week to attend the ball at the Tuileries. Without joking it was wonderful. Paris moreover is becoming tremendous. It is going mad and becoming colossal. We are perhaps returning to the Orient and the idols are reappearing. We are threatened with a new Babylon.

He said to Princess Mathilde:[14]

The ball at the Tuileries remains in my memory as a fairy-like event, like a dream. The only thing I lacked was to see you from nearer and to be able to speak to you. Isn't this like Madame Bovary impressed by her first ball?

Flaubert's old friends did not look with favour on this worldly phase of his life. We have seen that Amélie Bosquet was somewhat shocked at the change in him, which she considered separated them. Bouilhet also did not approve of his friend spending so much time at parties and considered that he was wasting himself.[15] He talked disparagingly of his too fashionable life, and he accused him of allowing his tastes and aspirations to incline more towards society than they had at that glorious time when he sent Du Camp to the devil, after he had tried to persuade him to come and live in Paris. This incident occurred when Du Camp and Flaubert had returned from their Eastern trip, and the former was seeking success in a fashionable and ambitious life in Paris, while the latter remained quietly at Croisset, working on *Madame Bovary*, and would not be drawn into the fashionable and literary life of the capital.

During this period Flaubert's beloved niece reached womanhood. She was the daughter of his only sister, who had died in childbirth in 1846 at the age of twenty-one. She had lived all her life with him and his mother and he had brought her up, educating her himself. He loved her as dearly as if she had been his own child. Now that she was growing up, he hoped that she might be a companion to him and fill his life with gaiety and light. She reached the age of seventeen in January 1863, and then, unfortunately for him, she fell in love with a young timber merchant in Rouen who went by the name of Commanville, or sometimes de Commanville. Flaubert, whose instincts were usually sound and whose profession made it possible for him to evaluate character psychologically, was very doubtful at first of the suitability of the young man, but Caroline wept when he tried to persuade her not to hurry with her decision and he was not proof against her tears. She was obstinate and would not yield, and she snobbishly thought that Commanville was vaguely noble. However, when investigations for the marriage were undertaken, it was discovered, as Gérard-Gailly proves,[16] that the young man had no right to the name of Commanville, much less to de Commanville, that he came from a couple of generations of illegitimacy. This was not generally known in Rouen, as he seemed well established and to be doing well in his business. After this Caroline seems to have been in a state of uncertainty and unable to make up her mind definitely. Her uncle also was in a quandary – he continued to be doubtful about the young man but, at the same time, he wanted his niece to have everything that she desired even if he did not think her choice ideal. He had to leave Croisset before any decision was reached, but he wrote to her from Paris:[17]

And now let's speak of the important matter. Well! my poor Caro, you are still in a state of doubt, and perhaps even now, after a third interview, you are no further advanced. It is a serious decision to make and I'd be exactly in the same condition if I was in your pretty shoes. You must ponder seriously, study your whole nature (heart and soul) to see if the gentleman has in him chances of happiness. Human life is fed on other things than practical considerations and exalted sentiments. But, on the other hand, if bourgeois life makes you die of boredom what can you decide? Your poor grandmother wants to marry you in the fear she has of leaving you alone, and I too, my dear Caro, I'd like to see you united to an honest fellow who would make you as happy as possible! When I saw you the other evening, weeping so bitterly, your unhappiness tore my heart to pieces. We love you, my darling, and the day of your wedding will not be a joyful day for your two old comrades. Although I am not jealous by nature, the fellow who will become your husband, whoever he may be, will displease me at first; but that isn't the question. I shall forgive him later and I shall love him and cherish him, if he makes you happy.

He tells her that she might find more brilliant people in Paris, as wit and accomplishments are normally the appurtenance of Bohemians. But they are usually poor and he could not, for one single instant, countenance the idea that she should marry a poor man. He said that he would rather see her wed a millionaire grocer than a needy great man. We shall see later how he was paid out for wishing to marry his niece in the most bourgeois manner possible.

Caroline had said that she wished to get away from Rouen. She had lived there all her life except for visits to Paris, which had given her the taste for the lights of the capital. Her uncle answered that if business turned out well she could eventually come and live in Paris, but that it was better to live in Rouen with money than in Paris without a penny. He ended:

I'm like you, as you can see, I lose my head and I decide alternately one thing and then the other. It is very difficult to see clearly in questions which involve one too much. It would be difficult for you to find a husband above you in intelligence and education; if I knew of one who fulfilled these conditions and had, moreover, everything else necessary, I'd go and fetch him for you quickly. You're then forced to accept an inferior man. But could you love a man you looked down on? Could you live happily with him? That is the whole question! They'll no doubt badger you to give a quick answer. Don't do anything hastily, whatever happens, my darling, and count on the affection of your old uncle who embraces you.

He returned from Paris to Croisset to discuss the matter with her. She, however, remained obstinate in her resolve and her uncle wanted her to have anything that she wished. Everything must have been decided by 29 February, for on that day Flaubert sent his greetings to his 'future nephew'.

She finally married Ernest Commanville on 6 April 1864, when she was eighteen. Maxime Du Camp, who was one of Flaubert's oldest friends and had known Caroline since the day of her birth, understood that his friend would remain lonely without her and he wrote him a letter to reach him on the morning of the wedding:[18]

I imagine, my dear old friend, that you won't be gay tomorrow, and that the house will seem to you very sad, when you get back to it in the evening with your mother – and so I'm writing to tell you that I embrace you both. Tibi.

An unpleasing picture of the young woman emerges from Flaubert's letters to her, and none of his friends liked her. He had

sacrificed very much for her, thinking only of pleasing her and
made no demands on her, but she repaid him with very little
warmth of affection and what she wanted personally seems always
to have come first with her. She was ambitious and snobbish,
seeking out people in high places and royalty, and thinking only
of improving her social status. 'I am flattered by the fine acquaintances you are making,' he wrote to her once.[19] 'The members of
the royal family of Sweden are, from what I hear, the kindest in the
world, and those around them must be like them.' She thought
at one time of buying the Château de Miromesnil, where Guy de
Maupassant was born, and negotiated for it, but the negotiations
fell through. She soon owned a town house in the rue de Clichy
in Paris and a country house and estate, near Dieppe. She
abandoned Rouen as soon as possible. She attended fashionable
balls, gave smart receptions and cultivated important people.

What was unkindest of all was her complete indifference to her
uncle's feelings. She often hurt him deeply by leaving unanswered
his long letters to her. She hardly ever came to see him and did
not take advantage of the fact of her husband being away on
business to visit him and her grandmother at Croisset. He asked
her once to forgo a holiday in the Pyrenees to go and stay with her
grandmother so that she should not be alone. She refused. Yet
the old lady had looked after her since the day of her birth. She
did not often invite Flaubert to her house and indeed sometimes
deliberately stayed away when she knew that he was coming.
He once complained to her:[20]

And so, not only do you refuse my invitations, and don't come to
see me at Croisset, but you avoid my presence by taking refuge at the
borders of the Ocean the days you know that I am to appear.
Oh! Oh! Oh!

She often made her health an excuse for not seeing him, and
he worried about her like an anxious father; but there is no proof
that she was ever anything but strong and she was to live to the
age of eighty-five, and to bury two husbands.

Towards Commanville he behaved with respect and deference.
He himself had no capacity for business and he considered his
nephew an honest and efficient businessman. This was, eventually,
to lead to his undoing.

Up to the time of his fashionable life in Paris, Flaubert had lived frugally and economically, making only a few short visits in Paris, when he stayed at an hotel. But after the success of *Salammbô*, when he began to attend Court, his expenses grew very heavy and he got into financial difficulties. He was spending a great deal of money in an effort to keep up with his rich and noble friends. It is true that he had a comfortable income, inherited from his father, but it was no longer sufficient to provide for his increased needs and obligations. He was also making very little money from his writings. All that he had gained from *Madame Bovary* had gone to pay the legal expenses of his trial in 1857. The amount he had made on *Salammbô* – quite a considerable amount for the time – had not been sufficient to keep up with the increased extravagance of his life: being entertained at Court, staying at Compiègne, and visiting Princesse Mathilde's country house at Saint-Gratien for weeks at a time.

Madame Flaubert, who had administered her husband's income and savings economically during his lifetime, had also husbanded his inheritance after his death and had invested her son's money carefully. For twenty years this had gone very well, but towards 1865 she began to grow anxious at his debts, and land had to be sold to extricate him from the worst difficulties, for she discovered that he owed several thousands of francs. He owed nearly two thousand francs to his tailor, five hundred for gloves and three thousand for the redecoration of his study at Croisset. He had also had to furnish his apartment in Paris.

To meet his obligations he borrowed money from his faithful friend Jules Duplan and five thousand francs from his publisher, but still he could not get straight. He confessed to his mother his difficulties and she sold up a farm and divided the amount between her two children. However, she remained very anxious and wrote to her lawyer to complain:[21]

The financial affairs of Gustave put me in a state of great embarrassment ... He knows perfectly well, however, that his extravagant expenses come on to me, and that it is only by living with an extreme economy to which I was not accustomed, that I can reach the end of the year.

Flaubert, feeling that his mother was delaying too long, wrote himself to the lawyer, saying that he believed that she did not realize how urgent the matter was:[22]

I beg you to undeceive her. Nothing irritates me more than to be in
the position in which I find myself. Do what you think suitable, so
long as I have as soon as possible some effigies of the monarch, so that
I can pay my debts, live in peace for some time, without having to
think of that devil of money . . .

Yes! Settle all that, I beg you, so that I'm rid of these matters, which
madden me, irritate me and stupefy me.

Nothing is more painful to me than to have constantly to ask my
mother for money. Try to persuade her that I'm not indulging in mad
debauch. Alas! I wish I was, and I'd be a bit more gay! And since she
has decided to pay my debts, let her do it thoroughly and without too
many recriminations.

The following year he was again in difficulties and, having tried
without success to get a large loan through the lawyer, at any
rate of interest, approached his friend Jules Duplan to try to
obtain it for him from anywhere:[23]

Here is the reason for my letter. You know that, last winter, I asked
Fovard to find six thousand francs for me, to borrow, which I would
return at my convenience, capital and interest together. The rate of
interest was a matter of indifference to me, I would have accepted the
most advantageous conditions for the lender. I've been to the said
Fovard several times, and I wrote him four or five urgent letters,
without his taking the slightest notice. At the end I seemed im-
portunate, or a scoundrel of no importance. I admit, *inter nos*, that it was
very disagreeable to me, and that I am not keen to begin again. But, as I
am anxious that my family, my mother particularly, should not know of
my excesses, I do not know to whom to apply.

Will you ask your brother, if he can (answering informally for my
probity) find amongst his clients a good fellow who would lend me six
or seven thousand francs; it is probable (without wishing to promise
anything) that I would return them in three years after the publication
of my book . . . I don't know what has prevented Fovard from doing
me this service . . . If your brother found that for me, it would be kind;
if not I must turn elsewhere, but I can't see where.

It does not seem that Flaubert succeeded in this plan, but in
1867 he made the great mistake of allowing his nephew to take
charge of his affairs, to pay his debts, to sell out capital and to pay
him the interest on his investments. He asked him not to say
anything to his mother about the arrangement:[24] 'And, naturally,
don't tell my mother anything about it. She would imagine that

I am bankrupting myself and that would cause her distress. It is no use worrying her.'

Henceforth Flaubert was never to know where he stood, nor what he possessed, nor what he owed. When he tried to obtain money to pay his debts of honour to Duplan, who was in financial embarrassment and wanted to be repaid, he had great difficulty in obtaining money from Commanville. When Commanville received a demand from his uncle, he did not answer himself but told his wife what to reply:[25]

Answer your uncle that the money he asks for will be paid to him if necessary, but, at the present moment, the cleverness of a dealer consists in getting paid what is owed to him and in postponing his own payments. That is to say to pay only what is absolutely necessary ... Moreover tell him simply that, as I was leaving for Rouen, I could not answer him.

Eventually Flaubert lost all his money, largely owing to his nephew, either on account of his dishonesty or his incompetence.

In the meantime Flaubert's friends, seeing him extravagant and careless with money and never thinking of economy, were anxious on his behalf. Once he asked Duplan to rent him a bedroom and sitting-room in a nearby hotel because repairs were being carried on in his apartment and the noise was disturbing his work.

In 1856 he had taken an apartment in Boulevard du Temple for the publication of *Madame Bovary* and, in 1869, he moved to the rue Murillo for the publication of *L'Éducation Sentimentale*. This added greatly to his debts.

However, the Franco-Prussian war, which broke out in July 1870, put an end to his extravagant social life.

CHAPTER SIX

THE END OF AN ERA

The last book which Flaubert wrote during the Second Empire was *L'Éducation Sentimentale*. He began writing it on 1 September 1864 and finished it on 16 May 1869, but he was already thinking of it in 1862, when he finished *Salammbô* and allowed himself to be diverted by the stage.

In 1861, when he thought of writing the book to enshrine the great love of his life, it was thirteen years since he had seen the Schlésingers, as they had gone to Baden when he was on his journey to the East, between 1849 and 1851.

When he was thirteen he had fallen romantically in love with Élisa Schlésinger, a young married woman many years his senior, whom he had seen on the beach when he was on holiday with his family at Trouville. It was a 'coup de foudre' from which he never recovered, and she set permanently the pattern of his emotional life, so that he was never able to love another woman fully. Her husband was a shady German businessman in Paris who was eventually obliged to leave the country and return to Germany.

Flaubert had written to Élisa in 1856 to say that he could not go to Baden for the wedding of her daughter, as he was in process of bringing out *Madame Bovary* in *La Revue de Paris*; he had written to her again in 1859 to commiserate with her on the death of her mother.[1] He was then composing *Salammbô* and said that he knew nothing about her or her family. It was after this that he wrote to Amélie Bosquet that we each had, in our heart, a royal chamber, but that he had walled up his.[2]

Why, in 1862, did Flaubert particularly think of writing *L'Éducation Sentimentale*? It was probably because circumstances brought the memory of Élisa Schlésinger vividly to his mind. In January 1862 he wrote to Maurice Schlésinger to say that his mother had heard that Madame Schlésinger was ill with some nervous complaint and he wanted news.[3] Maurice Schlésinger answered Flaubert on 16 December 1862 to give him the sad news of his wife.[4] He told him that she had been in a mental home for the past ten months. He wrote again a few days later, on 21 December: 'As I said to you, my poor Za [Élisa] has been for ten months in a mental home and I am not allowed to see her. For six months she hasn't written to us a word – she says that it hurts her to write and puts her in a state of emotion which must be avoided.'

Madame Schlésinger had been interned in a home at Emmedingen near Baden, and the specialist had said that she was suffering from acute melancholia, the chief cause of which lay in the ordeals suffered by a woman of noble character who had always sacrificed herself.[5] In *L'Éducation Sentimentale* we can see, in the conduct of Arnoux to his wife, what Élisa Schlésinger must have endured and which brought on her mental trouble.

Du Camp, who went to Baden every summer and autumn for several months, wrote to Flaubert on 20 August 1863:[6] 'Talking of childhood, did I tell you that Mother Schlésinger was mad, suffering from extreme melancholia, and is shut up in a nursing-home? They keep this carefully dark, but I heard it from her doctor himself.' On 10 September he wrote again:[7] 'Mother Schlésinger has come out of her nursing-home and has returned to Baden. I saw her recently in the Avenue Lichtenthal, leaning on the arm of her son; she was magnificent; thin, pale, hair quite white, and enormous wild eyes, she looked like a Guanhunara' (the old heroine of Hugo's play *Les Burgraves*). Du Camp adds: 'I thought again of you, of all that you had told me about her, and that put me in a state of indescribable sadness.'

Flaubert had, however, now known of her condition for nearly a year, but delicacy probably prevented him from mentioning it.

Steinhardt-Leins, the son of Élisa's granddaughter, has written about his great-grandmother, but what he says must be taken with caution, as he is often wrong.[8] He had heard of the events only through his grandmother, who was only a year old at the time.

We know then that in 1862 and 1863 Flaubert knew of the
illness of Élisa Schlésinger and this coloured the plan which he
made of the future novel. He made a plan in 1863, in his *Carnet 19*
(preserved at the Bibliothèque Historique de la Ville de Paris,
and published by M. J. Durry).[9] The novel was then entitled
Madame Moreau, and it was only later that he took over the name
for the hero. It is clear that the novel was intended to be autobiographical, for it is indicated 'Mme Sch – M. Sch – et moi'.
The early part follows the final novel in most details. But the
ending is very different, and many episodes are not yet included.
There is nothing yet about the events of the age which are so
important a part of the finished book. Flaubert writes: 'Adultère,
mêlé de remords' . . . 'fin en queue de rat' . . . 'le sentiment finit
de soi-même – on se sépare. Fin! on se revoit de temps à autre –
puis on meurt.'

Next some other episodes are added. Mme Moreau yields, she
comes once or twice to appointments, 'elle l'aime quand il ne
l'aime plus, c'est à ce moment-là qu'il la possède ou qu'elle
s'offre.' Then he had a change of idea. 'Il serait plus fort de ne
pas faire baiser Mme Moreau qui, chaste d'action, se rongeait
d'amour. Elle aurait eu son moment de faiblesse que l'amant
n'aurait pas vu dont il n'aurait pas profité.'

Next he thought of using her mental state, and to make her die
mad in hospital. 'Elle finit folle, hystérique – le mari devenu bon
la soigne. Fr. les a abandonnés.'

At last we get the idea of the final great scene. 'Dernière entrevue
de Mme – elle s'offre. Mais elle ne l'excite plus et il a peur des
dégoûts futurs, ne pas la rendre ridicule – il en a pitié; elle s'en
va – il la voit monter en fiacre – et tout fut fini.' The final scene
can here be seen in embryo. There is however a great difference,
that here it is cold and detached, with much less concern on the
part of the hero. When writing this scene Flaubert had not seen
Élisa for fourteen years; his love had probably grown cold,
covered over with the dust of years. He may even have forgotten
what his feelings had been. He had not then thought of the
emotion of the scene but only of the facts. He had thought
of it in the abstract, as one who might not love again. But everything was altered when he saw Élisa again.

He began writing the book in September 1864 and he probably
felt the desire to see her once more before he could continue. He

had certainly never previously planned to go to Baden, but it is known that he went there in July 1865, ten months after he had begun writing. The *Badenblatt* mentions, amongst famous visitors to the town, that he was there on 15 July, and again the following week, but not thereafter, so that he must have been there for a fortnight.[10] It seems impossible that he should have visited Baden and not have seen Élisa Schlésinger, who had been released from hospital and lived near the centre of the town, only ten minutes from where Flaubert was staying. He would hardly have gone to Baden to see Maxime Du Camp, whom he could entertain at any time in Paris. At this time, in July 1865, Flaubert would have become aware how changed Élisa was since he had seen her, and since her illness. He would have discovered that her hair had gone white, which will be an important fact in the novel.

Gérard-Gailly is of the opinion that the reunion occurred in October 1864,[11] and he gives the not very convincing testimony of a boy of fourteen. He says that Élisa had gone to Mantes to stay with her old school friend, Madame Lefort, that she went with this boy, Georges Mercier, to Croisset, to see Flaubert, and that the boy remembered it afterwards. If she was indeed at Mantes it would certainly not have been difficult for her to go to Croisset, but there is no evidence of it and Flaubert has not mentioned it. Gérard-Gailly also thinks that the atmosphere of the scene is more true to Croisset than to Paris, but not everyone will agree with this.

The reason for the insistence on dates is that there is a scene in *L'Éducation Sentimentale* which seems to have been drawn from real life. That is the final meeting of Marie Arnoux and Frédéric Moreau, seventeen years after the main events of the novel, when they have grown old. Frédéric notices, with a stab of pain, that her hair has grown quite white. There is considerable controversy as to when this meeting could have taken place. As has just been seen, Gérard-Gailly thinks that it was in October 1864. However, Flaubert, in the novel, states that the meeting took place in March 1867 and in Paris, and he was usually accurate about such matters. It is possible, and very likely, that a meeting between Élisa Schlésinger and Flaubert did, in fact, take place in Paris in March 1867. Flaubert was there then and he wrote to Bouilhet, who was librarian at Mantes, on 27 March 1867, to find out how long Élisa was to be there.[12] It is most likely that she went to

Jane de Tourbey, the famous
courtesan who held brilliant
literary *salons*. She and Flaubert
became great friends. Painting
by Armand Duval.

Madame Roger des Genettes.
She was for many years a
confidante of Flaubert's,
especially after the death of
George Sand.

Princesse Mathilde.
Patroness of the arts and
letters, she was an
admirer of Flaubert's
work.

The *salon* of Princesse
Mathilde where Flaubert
was so often received.

Paris to meet him. If he saw her then – as is probable – he would already have known that her hair was white, from the previous meeting at Baden, which seems just as likely as the one in Paris. But *L'Éducation Sentimentale* is a novel and not a record of real life. It was artistically more satisfying for there to be only one meeting, after the long separation, and for this to be the last meeting and the final scene. He wanted, in the novel, the scene to be unique and as beautiful as possible, and a great deal of its beauty came from its finality. The atmosphere, in the novel, seems more true to Paris than to Croisset or to Baden.

This final scene in the novel was not, however, the end of the long story of Flaubert and Élisa Schlésinger. They met again after the war, as will be related in a later chapter.

What did Maurice and Élisa Schlésinger think of *L'Éducation Sentimentale*? Did Flaubert send them a copy? Autographed copies of all his books, save this one, were found amongst Élisa's effects after her death. If they had seen it, they would certainly have recognized themselves in the characters in the novel. Helmuth Steinhardt-Leins declared that his mother, Élisa Schlésinger's granddaughter, remembered the book arriving in September 1869, a beautiful copy bound in gold brocade and inscribed 'À Madame Élisa Schlésinger'.[13] She was, however, as we know, only a year old at the time. Moreover the book was published in November and Flaubert was correcting proofs still at the end of August, so it is unlikely that a bound copy could have been sent to Germany in September. Steinhardt-Leins said that the book was subsequently burnt with a large number of Flaubert's letters to Élisa. All this is very mysterious and does not ring true, and there is no proof that any of it occurred. Perhaps Flaubert gave her a copy – or showed her the book – after the war, when she stayed with him at Croisset when her husband was dead; but perhaps he did not want her either to know what he had written about her. Perhaps it was her daughter who burned it after her death. The daughter Maria never forgave her mother for having allowed her to be registered as of an unknown mother. Later, when she lived in Germany, she became very Germanophile and, although she was born French, she applauded the Prussian victory. Her brother, on the contrary, was Francophile and fought on the side of the French during the war. Élisa Schlésinger remained very French and her situation in Germany, during the war, was very painful for her. The daughter, who hated her mother, would resent anything that Flaubert had to do with her.

In the meantime Flaubert was working very hard on the research and documentation for his novel, badgering all his friends for information on various topics, both political and social, which had taken place during the years which led to the Revolution of 1848. He tried to find out everything about all the movements of the time – what the people were reading and saying; the conditions of the poorer classes, the workers in the factories, the shops and the offices; the appearance of the city at the time – and the results are seen in the notes preserved in the Municipal Library at Rouen. It was amazing that he found the energy and the strength to do so much when he was living his engrossing and busy fashionable life, and also carrying on the enormous correspondence with so many friends, both men and women.

When Flaubert was writing *L'Éducation Sentimentale*, Du Camp was composing a novel with a very similar theme entitled *Les Forces Perdues*. It is not intended to suggest that either author owed anything to the other, or copied him. Both authors shared the opinion of many thinkers of the time, that the generation had wasted itself. Both authors believed that they belonged to a generation that had squandered its strength and its spiritual resources. Flaubert wrote to Mademoiselle Leroyer de Chantepie about it:[14]

Read a new novel by an intimate friend of mine, Maxime Du Camp. It appeared in *La Revue Nationale* and its title is *Les Forces Perdues*. That is exactly how we were in our youth; all the men of my generation find themselves there.

I'd like to have your personal opinion on this work.

Les Forces Perdues is not a very good novel – Du Camp had not a great deal of talent for fiction, and he did not know how to create character. But it is certainly better, and more significant because of its theme, than anything he had written hitherto. It is only in the theme that it resembles Flaubert's novel – the hero, Horace, has some family likeness to Flaubert's Frédéric, in that they both waste their lives and talents. Horace is described on his death bed:[15] 'Horace avait renoncé. Il ne demandait plus rien à la vie comme si, d'avance, il eût épuisé ce qu'elle contenait.' And, as he lies dying, he says: 'Il y a de l'amertume en moi plutôt que de la douleur. Quelle vie manquée, que de facultés restées stériles, que d'efforts avortés, que de forces perdues.'

However, we do not know why he has failed, or what his potentialities are, or what he might have achieved. Both heroes make nothing of their lives, but Horace eventually dies, whereas Frédéric lives on in his failure.

Les Forces Perdues was published in 1867, two years before Flaubert's novel. Du Camp declared that this would be his last novel and he kept to this resolve.[16] In the meantime the Empire was sliding towards its close, though few seemed to be aware of this fact. The régime was becoming more unpopular and one felt opposition on all sides. As we have seen, the last flash was in the year 1867, with the wonderful pageant for the International Exhibition, with the review of the troops and the magnificent ball at the Tuileries Palace. But even here there were some unpleasant undercurrents and there was an attempt at the assassination of the Tsar.

It was the intellectuals who were turning most against the Empire, against the strong Catholic party and against censorship. Men of letters, and the great Sainte-Beuve especially, were becoming more dissatisfied with the restrictions of the Empire and the conventional clerical party. He did not however think that his political opinions should have any effect on his relations with Princesse Mathilde. More and more he was supporting the free-thinkers such as Littré and Renan – these had been members of the *salon* of Princesse Mathilde – and he considered himself the spokesman for freedom of speech and thought. In 1867, at a meeting of the Senate, the Comte de Ségur made a speech to object to what he called the scandalous appointment of Renan to the Collège de France. Sainte-Beuve rose to protest against such treatment meted out to an honest man and a great scholar, whose friend he was proud to be.

Next there was the question of the removal of certain books from public libraries, works by Rousseau, Voltaire, Proudhon, Michelet, Renan, Balzac and so forth, and, on 25 June 1867, Sainte-Beuve spoke in opposition to this. His speech was published in *Le Moniteur* and Flaubert wrote to Princesse Mathilde in praise of it and in favour of Sainte-Beuve. He thought that, with her liberal views, she would approve of what he had said, for she was not as prudish as the Empress:[17]

What do you think of Sainte-Beuve? I thought him very fine! He valiantly defended the 'troops' and in good terms. His opponents seem to me despairingly mediocre. Where does that hate against literature come from? Is it envy or stupidity? Both doubtless, with, over and above, a strong dose of hypocrisy.

Princesse Mathilde did not agree with him – she thought that Sainte-Beuve had gone too far. Flaubert wrote again:[17]

What you tell me about Sainte-Beuve is perhaps true. Perhaps he went beyond the limits (from a certain point of view which incidentally is not mine). But his opponents had shown him the way, and then it is difficult to remain within limits! One is cowardly on one side, brave on the other. What is one to do?

Flaubert wrote to Sainte-Beuve in praise of what he had said:[18]

Cher Maître, all those who are not sunk in the lowest stupidity, all those who love Art, all those who think, all those who write, owe you infinite gratitude – for you pleaded their cause, and defended their God – our nameless God, who is being abused. In such a place there was only that to say. The *moderation* and the precision of your language only brings out the more clearly the vagueness of their ineptitude – they are not strong definitely – not at all strong.

What a sorry thing is humanity! Here is the highest political assembly of the first country in the world. All the same you have politely spat the truth at them. It will stick to them. I wish that my arms could be thirty-five leagues long, to be able to embrace you. That is what I am counting on doing in a month.

He also told him that he should give up his journalism and write a book on the subject. He said to him: '*You alone* have sufficient authority to be heard. If you were gone who would defend us? You must live then for us. I embrace you tenderly.'

More and more Sainte-Beuve was being considered dangerous. There was the matter of the Good Friday dinner-party in 1869, at which various meats were served, which was used as an argument to prove that he was an atheist. It was called 'une orgie'. At the dinner there were, amongst other guests, Taine, Renan and Flaubert. It was generally considered that this was a deliberate insult to the Church. Now it is known from Sainte-Beuve's secretary, Troubat, that the fixing of the dinner for that particular day was purely by chance.

Then *Le Moniteur* tried to insist on Sainte-Beuve removing

from an article a remark against the Bishop of Montpellier. He refused and brought the article to *Le Temps*, which accepted it with alacrity, for it was in opposition to the Empire. Princesse Mathilde considered that this action of Sainte-Beuve was treachery and disloyalty against herself, and she begged him not to go to *Le Temps*. He refused, believing that his action had nothing to do with friendship, and that freedom of speech was essential in all relationships. The article appeared and the Princess went round immediately to Sainte-Beuve's house. We have, in the memoirs of Jules Troubat, an account of the lamentable and distressing scene.[19]

Sainte-Beuve and Troubat were surprised when they heard the carriage draw up outside the house, as it was not the Princess's day to visit him. She entered in a tearing rage. Schérer, who was calling on Sainte-Beuve at the time, left the room discreetly and Troubat followed him. Some time later Sainte-Beuve came to ask Troubat to come to his study and keep the Princess company while he retired to deal with his physical complaint. She was waving her muff about frantically and looked like an enraged version of Napoleon.

'It is my brother and I,' she shrieked at Troubat, 'who made Sainte-Beuve a Senator.' Troubat answered that he did not see in what way Sainte-Beuve had deserved ill from the Empire.

'Monsieur Sainte-Beuve was a vassal of the Empire,' she shouted. Troubat was shocked at this and could not stand it, and – although he was no braver than anyone else and he had, before him, her Imperial Highness acting like an infuriated tigress – he answered: 'There are no vassals nowadays, only citizens.' The shouting now became so vehement that Sainte-Beuve came in and told his secretary that he was talking too loudly.

After the Princess had departed, Troubat repeated to his master what she had said about his being a vassal of the Empire. Sainte-Beuve grew pale and answered: 'They'll see if I'm a vassal.'

The following day the Princess went to see the Goncourt brothers, and walking up and down in anger she burst out against Sainte-Beuve.[20] She said that she would never see him again, never again. 'He! It is on his account,' she shrieked, 'that I quarrelled with the Empress. And remember all he got from me!

At my last visit to Compiègne, he asked me for three things, and I obtained two of them from the Emperor. And what was I asking him to do? Not to abandon his convictions; I only asked him not to sign a contract with *Le Temps* . . . He might have gone to *La Liberté*, with Girardin, that was possible, that was his world . . . Oh! he's a bad man. Only six months ago I wrote to Flaubert, "I fear that in a short time he'll do us a bad turn." He wrote to me for New Year's Day, expressing gratitude for all the comfort and ease which surrounded his illness and which he owed to me. No! one can't behave like that!'

She was almost choking, and beating her breast. 'I'm not speaking of the Princess,' she cried, 'but of the woman!' Then, shaking Goncourt by the lapels of his coat, she cried: 'Come! Goncourt, isn't it infamous? To go to *Le Temps*, our personal enemies, where we are insulted every day.'

Then she told Goncourt what she had said to Sainte-Beuve: 'Your house is a house of whores, a house of ill-fame, and I went there for your sake. Oh yes, I was hard on him! What are you but a feeble old man, who can't even attend to his own physical needs?[21] But what ambition can you still have? I wish that you had died last year, you would then at least have left me with the memory of a friend.'

A few days later she again vituperated against the critic: 'He said that nothing obliged him to resign from the Senate and that, in any case, his resolve was not to serve the little Prince Imperial.' Then she suddenly burst out, irrelevantly: 'You see finally, with a woman like me, there can really never exist a friendship with an incomplete man.'

It is hard to forgive the Princess for her outburst against Sainte-Beuve. It was not only that she had lost control of herself and was in a rage, but what she said should not have been said by anyone of fine feelings, and especially not to a desperately sick old man, virtually dying of a most painful prostate complaint. It was not merely that she lost her temper and abused him like a fishwife, but a sensitive person could not have said such things, whatever the circumstance, and one is profoundly shocked that someone who was called 'la bonne Princesse', the kind Princess, could behave in such a way. It is true that Goncourt was not completely convinced of her benevolence the first time he met her, and he described her as 'a stout woman, with the remains of a good-looking woman . . . with an air of bonhomie which does not completely disguise her fundamental hardness'.[22] It is true also that he somewhat altered this opinion later when he got to know her. Yet he recounts that her butler once said that the Princess loved no one, only her furniture.[23] And he relates her shocking and insensitive behaviour on one occasion with a hunchback:[24] 'Yesterday in the hall of the railway station, she suddenly cried out: "There's a hunchback! They say it's lucky to touch her hump".' And, in spite of the remonstrances of those who were with her, she ran over and touched it. They hastily dragged her away before the hunchback's friends should lynch her.

Sainte-Beuve was bewildered and could not understand what had happened; he thought that when she had got over her rage, and had come to her senses, she would return again and that they would be friends as before. When, after a fortnight, she had not written nor come to see him, he wrote her a dignified letter, which is deeply moving:[25]

Princess, a fortnight has gone by. In vain I look for the reason and question myself, but I cannot discover that I was in any way personally in the wrong with regard to your Highness. You had accustomed me, Princess, to a quite different kind of friendship – so different that I could consider the interview of Monday only as an out of the ordinary accident, something which did not come from you, but from someone else.

As for me, I have put the marker after Sunday's visit. The book closes that day for me at half past five in the afternoon. Will it be opened again one day? I know well how much I owe to so many acts of kindness, to so many memories, to so many offers of friendship, the pledges of which surround me and will never cease to surround me. The amazement which seized hold of me on Monday and which I have found it difficult to get over will pass. Everything which preceded it lives and will live. And in this, at least, I shall keep the faith which I so often lack elsewhere. Even when I can no longer hope, I shall still wait, and an inner voice will continue to murmur deep in me: No! it cannot be!

I lay at your feet, Princess, the homage of my respectful and unalterable affection.

She replied next day,[26] telling him that the man who had refused her so stubbornly what she had asked him was not the man she had known and loved. She said that her violence was the result of the shock which she had felt, as a friend, at his refusal, which she could only regard as going over to the enemy. The other side, she declared, was now celebrating her defeat and its victory. The letter was inflexible and there was nothing he could do about it.

Later, hearing that his health was deteriorating rapidly, she sent a friend to suggest a reconciliation, but this time Sainte-Beuve refused her advances and, according to Troubat, said that he had now sailed too far away to disembark at Saint-Gratien.

When she heard that he lay dying, she sent a letter of renewed friendship and, with failing breath, he dictated a reply:[27] 'Princess, it is a profound satisfaction to have found again what one had ceased to believe in. Respect and affection. Sainte-Beuve.'

Troubat said that Princesse Mathilde, who never forgot anything, could not forgive what Sainte-Beuve had said to her about her cousin Princesse Julie.[28] Although she had no particular affection for her, and there was rivalry between them, she did not want her to be abused by a commoner. The event which gave rise to Sainte-Beuve's letter was comic and it was very much talked of in smart circles in Paris in the summer of 1868 – there was even a paragraph about it in *Le Figaro*.

Princesse Julie, who was proud of her *salon* and her literary gifts, used to keep a diary where she recorded her impressions of her guests. She once sent Sainte-Beuve one of these note-books, but, by an unfortunate mishap, it was one in which she had recorded, wittily and spitefully, what she thought of him. He pretended to be amused and wrote to Princesse Mathilde to tell her of it, copying out the worst things which Princesse Julie had said of him:[29]

He leads, in spite of his age, a debauched life; he lives with three women at the same time who are in his home. Sainte-Beuve has left cards on me, has written to me, but he has never set foot in my drawing-room. He is admired as a writer, esteemed as a critic; and, when he speaks of a book, his judgement is accepted; but, as far as personal consideration is concerned, he has none. He moved heaven and earth to get into the Senate, of which he, nevertheless, made fun – he speaks evil of those who have done him a lot of good – he passes as being very greedy and, as I have mentioned above, his private life is very immoral. Monsieur Sainte-Beuve has only one God, pleasure. He is devoid of religious convictions, and, one day, he said, speaking of a working man and of himself: 'The man without education is a field flower whereas I am a hot-house bloom.'

Sainte-Beuve also sent Princesse Mathilde a copy of his own reply to the Princess.

Princess, I have the honour to return you your manuscript note-book which you did me the honour of showing me. Chance is sometimes mischievous and witty. It has been so this time, you will agree yourself, in giving me the opportunity of reading, through your own action, Princess, a note concerning myself, and I am tempted to thank you for it. This circumstance, in fact, permits me to tell you that, if I have never set foot in your drawing-room, it is certainly not for want of being invited by you. And so it is not through my lack of consideration, as you say, that I owe the fact of not being admitted, but through discretion on my part, and a feeling of withdrawal of which I can flatter myself today.

As for the other grave accusations with which you did not fear to soil your pen, there are many which refute themselves. As for my religious convictions, you yourself, Princess, have often brought up the subject when I had the honour of meeting you. I can say that the coarseness with which you expressed yourself would have given me the chance to judge you as being far more irreligious than I would ever ask a woman to appear.

My private life has one advantage – if it has its weaknesses, it is open to all, in full daylight. As for the story of the three women at home that is a Herculean legend on which I cannot pride myself . . . But what shocks me most in the paragraph unworthy of your pen is the saying which you attribute to me. What! could I have said that a man without education was a field flower, whereas I am a hot-house bloom? No, no believe me, Princess, I could never have said, nor thought, that a man was a flower. I keep these images for another sex.

Deign, Princess, to accept the final homage of a respect which will never again have the chance of expressing itself.

Princesse Mathilde told Flaubert what Saint-Beuve had done to her, but she probably did not tell him all that she had said. With his kind heart, his hatred of cruelty and of hurting anyone, Flaubert would certainly have been outraged by her conduct. He told her that he thought that she was making a mountain out of a molehill, and that it did not matter if Sainte-Beuve wrote for *Le Temps* so long as he wrote only literary articles. He was very conciliatory to her and, on the whole, took her part against Sainte-Beuve, for he was afraid that she might think that he was being disloyal to her. It does however come as a shock that he could have considered that Sainte-Beuve should have yielded and given up his contract with *Le Temps*, for the sake of gratitude to a benefactor, for this would have been tantamount to admitting that he owed his position solely to patronage and not to his suitability for the post. He wrote to her:[30]

> To return to Sainte-Beuve; his greatest wrong, in my opinion, is to have done something which displeases you, and since you ask him not to write in that paper, he should have pleased you ... What I would not excuse is a break with the government which loaded him with benefits ... I reread your letter as I write, and I am distressed, enough to have tears in my eyes, for it seems to me that this affair has wounded you to the heart, and you are suffering as if from a betrayal ... But, once more, what displeases me, and what I do not forgive him, is for having distressed you. You, you, Princess, who have been particularly good to him, more than good, devoted.

He wrote to George Sand a few days later:[31]

> I have seen Sainte-Beuve and Princesse Mathilde, and I know fully the story of their break, which I think irrevocable. Sainte-Beuve was indignant with Dalloz and he went over to *Le Temps*. The Princess begged him not to do it. He didn't listen to her, that's all! My opinion on all this, if you'd like to know it, is this. The first mistake was that of the Princess, who was too excited; but the second, and the worst, was old Beuve's, who did not behave like a gentleman. When one has as a friend, someone so kind, and when this friend has given you thirty thousand francs' income, one owes her deference. It seems to me that if I'd been Sainte-Beuve I'd have said: 'That displeases you. Don't let's mention it again.' He lacked manners and comportment.

Princesse Mathilde considered that she owned those whom she obliged. She showed here her love of power and how false and shallow a thing was her patronage of the arts. She showed also what is regarded as a woman's trait of character, but, if that is so, it does not do her credit. She said to the Goncourts that it was not the insult to the Princess that she resented most, but to the woman.

Where the opposition to the Empire was most evident was in the matter of the Princess's attempts to get Théophile Gautier elected a member of the Academy. He was her very special author and she worked very hard for him. She could obtain orders and decorations from her cousin the Emperor for her protégés, but she could not sway the Academy, which was opposed to the

Empire. She thought that she had succeeded and she drove down to the Institut to hear of Gautier's victory, but what she heard was the election of Auguste Barbier.[32] She was furious and called the Academicians pigs, but what angered her most of all was that it was an anti-Bonaparte poet who was chosen.

Gautier liked to think that he was not elected on account of the reactionary opinions of some of the Academicians, because of the reputation he had gained at the Bataille d'Hernani, when he had sported a red velvet doublet. But this is not true – that incident was forgotten. In 1869 he was known as the leader of the Art for Art's Sake movement, the writer under whose banner most poets placed themselves. He was one of the best-considered authors in Paris. He was known as the poet of *Émaux et Camées*, the most characteristic collection of poems of the day, and for his articles on art in *L'Artiste*, of which he had been the venerated editor in 1856. His failure was a political one and the Academy showed its disapproval of the Empire by rejecting him. He was known for his friendship with the Imperial family, especially with Princesse Mathilde – was he not her poet: 'le poète mathildien'? To oppose him the Academy chose a poet forgotten since 1830, Auguste Barbier, who had been then known for his anti-Napoleonic sentiments, expressed in his *Ïambes*, at a moment, before the death of L'Aiglon, when there might be a Napoleonic revival. Barbier considered that Napoleon had wrecked the work of the Revolution, as he said in *L'Idole*:

> Ô Corse aux cheveux plats! que ta France était belle
> Au grand soleil de messidor!
> C'était ine cavale indomptable et rebelle,
> Sans frein d'acier ni rênes d'or;
> Une jument sauvage à la croupe rustique,
> Fumante encor du sang des rois,
> Mais fière, et d'un pied fort heurtant le sol antique,
> Libre pour la première fois.
> Jamais aucune main n'avait passé sur elle
> Pour la flétrir et l'outrager;
> Jamais ses larges flancs n'avaient porté de selle
> Et le harnais de l'étranger;
> Tout son poil était vierge, et, belle vagabonde,
> L'œil haut, la croupe en mouvement,
> Sur ses jarrets dressés, elle effrayait le monde
> Du haut de son hennissement.

Tu parus, et sitôt que tu vis son allure,
Ses reins si souples et dispos,
Centaure impétueux, tu pris sa chevelure,
Tu montas botté sur son dos.

If the election had been impartial, Théophile Gautier would undoubtedly have been chosen, for he had more claims for the Chair than Barbier, and in many forms of literature – in poetry, in fiction, in criticism, in the essay and also in ballet. But this must not blind us to the qualities of Barbier, who was a very fine poet. The election was, however, a purely political affair, which had very little to do with literature. It was a manifestation of anti-Empire feeling.

Did Princesse Mathilde really admire and value her 'poète mathildien', or was he, in his lifetime, only an ornament of her *salon* and a flatterer of her person? Goncourt relates how, one day, when she was writing her memoirs, she came to him to show him what she had written about Gautier.[33] 'Goncourt,' she said, 'I am going to read you my Gautier,' and she produced four or five sheets of paper. 'The Princess,' said Goncourt, 'is devoid of any kind of literary talent ... You have, I said to her, the right not to like Gautier's literature, and to say it; that is to admit your tastes in full sincerity, and to reveal yourself truly in your memoirs. But I consider that you really speak of Gautier as if he were a nobody. One does not feel sufficiently, Princess, that you are speaking of a considerable personality in literature.'

Then the Princess gathered up her papers and flounced out of the room in a temper.

In the meantime Louis Bouilhet was living quietly and happily in Mantes and writing his plays. It looked then as if fortune was going to smile on him when, through the kind offices of Princesse Mathilde, he was offered the librarianship of the Bibliothèque Municipale at Rouen, his native town, and he accepted it. He was returning to his homeland, which he had told Flaubert he had always regretted. This was promotion for him, for he now had a decent competence and a pleasant house, with not very onerous duties. He had complete security, yet the only thing that he wrote while he was at Rouen was his play *Aïssé*, which he never saw produced.

The truth is that his luck was not so good, for his appointment at Rouen came too late and, in 1868, he was already beginning to be ill. Flaubert began to feel anxious about him, especially as he was always in a state of deep depression. Writing to Jules Duplan, he said:[34]

I'm not at all pleased with 'Monseigneur'; he seems to me really ill, without being able to say exactly what it is. He coughs a lot, and pants like a whale. Add to that invincible sadness. 'Monseigneur' is becoming a hypochondriac, and yet the fool has as much talent as ever. He composes magnificent isolated lines of poetry but he can't find the subject of a play. That is what makes him despair, and hate the whole human race. He disparages everyone.

All through 1868, he seemed to be growing weaker. Flaubert obviously thought that a great deal of it was due to imagination, and that he was suffering from hypochondria. He thought that he should pull himself together and react against his depression. He wrote to George Sand:[35] 'My poor Bouilhet worries me very much. He's in such a nervous state that they've advised him to take a little trip to the south of France. He is overcome by invincible hypochondria. Isn't it queer, he who was once so gay?'

Bouilhet always answered him: 'There's really a physical cause; I assure you that I'm very ill sometimes.'[36]

He eventually decided to try a cure at Vichy, but this was not the treatment that he needed and he was sent home again. He then decided to consult Flaubert's brother, Achille, who discovered that his case was hopeless and that he could do nothing for him. After he had seen Achille Flaubert, he seemed somewhat better, and Flaubert felt that he could go to Paris one Saturday, but on the Sunday, at five o'clock, Bouilhet was seized with delirium, and began composing a new play, which he declared that he wanted to read to Flaubert. Then he began to tremble and murmured: 'Adieu, adieu!', leaned his head on Léonie's bosom, and quietly died.

Flaubert heard the news only on the Monday in Paris, but he could not leave immediately, as there was no train until one o'clock, and he wandered about the streets, distraught, in the tropical heat. In the train there was a prostitute who kept singing at the top of her voice and smoking cigarette after cigarette. When he passed through Mantes and saw the spire of the church, he thought that he would faint. It was there that Bouilhet had been happy and well, and more creative than elsewhere.

When Flaubert reached Bouilhet's house he rolled, with despair, in a nervous crisis on the lawn.[37] He then discovered many things. Bouilhet had wanted to marry Léonie to regularize their situation before he died, but she, fearing that he might then discover that he was dying, refused. Towards the end two bigotted and prudish sisters had arrived and made religious scenes around the dying man's bed, trying to bring him back to the faith; they were so violent in their behaviour that they had shocked even the Canon of the Cathedral. Bouilhet had dismissed them summarily and refused to allow any priest to enter the house. His anger had kept up his spirits to the end, when he died alone with Léonie. The sisters had also been counting on his furniture but, by his will, he left all his possessions to Léonie Leparfait and all his manuscripts and papers to her son.[38]

Flaubert was shattered by this death. He had not felt such grief since Alfred Le Poittevin had died twenty years before. As usual, in moments of great suffering, he thought of Maxime Du Camp. He had written to him as he watched beside his dead sister in 1846, also at the death of Le Poittevin in 1848, and now, after the death of Louis Bouilhet. Du Camp had known Bouilhet almost as long as he had known Flaubert, and had often been helpful to him at various stages in his literary career. In spite of their differences Flaubert and Du Camp were still what they had been in their twenties, 'Solus ad Solum'. It was then that they had exchanged rings inscribed with these words. There was no one else to whom Flaubert wished to write in the same way:[39]

My dear old Max, I feel the need to write you a long letter; I don't know whether I'll have the strength, but I'll try. Since he came back to Rouen, after his appointment as librarian, in August 1867, our poor Bouilhet was convinced that he'd lay his bones there. Everyone – I like the others – joked with him about his melancholy. He was no longer the man he had formerly been; he was completely changed except for his literary intelligence, which had remained the same. In short when I got back from Paris, at the beginning of June, I thought that he looked desperately ill ...

D'Osmoy and I were chief mourners; there were a great many people at the funeral. At least two thousand people ... Well! believe me that, as I followed his coffin, I was able to savour very clearly the grotesque side of the ceremony. I imagined that I heard the remarks he was making to me about it; he was speaking in me, it seemed to me that he was there at my side, and that we were following the funeral of someone else. It was atrociously hot, thundery weather. I was dripping with sweat, and the rise to the Cimetière Monumental finished me off. His friend Caudron had chosen a plot near that of my father. I leant on the rail to breathe. The coffin was on sticks above the grave. The speeches were going to begin – there were three – then I sobbed and my brother led me away . . . Yesterday I went to Rouen to collect all his papers; today I read all the letters that were written to me; and that is all. Oh! dear Max! it is very hard! . . .

My head is too painful to continue and besides what could I say to you? Goodbye. I embrace you ardently. You are the only one left, only you! Do you remember when we used to write 'Solus ad Solum'?

Bouilhet left an immense void in Flaubert's life, after a close friendship of more than twenty years. He had been his literary mentor and guide, and Flaubert never wrote anything without his advice. He might never have become the pure artist he did become if it had not been for Bouilhet's advice and help. Flaubert asked himself what was the point of writing now that he was no longer there. A few months later he wrote: 'When I lost my poor Bouilhet, I lost my midwife, the man who saw more clearly into my mind than I did myself. His death left a void in my life which I notice more and more each day.'[(40)]

Most people who saw Flaubert and Bouilhet together thought that it was the former who was the leader, but Du Camp claims that the contrary was true:[(41)]

To see Bouilhet, very gentle, and humble enough in appearance, very ironical, and answering reproofs by a joke, one would have imagined that Flaubert was the tyrant and Bouilhet a defeated man. But it was not at all like that; it was Bouilhet who was the master, in the matter of literature at least, and it was Flaubert who obeyed. Flaubert objected, moaned and groaned, but he had to yield in the end, to give in, although he said that he would not alter a word.

Du Camp thought that Bouilhet withdrew too much from life and that he would have done more, achieved more, if he had been willing to take more part in the life of his time. However, he thought the same of Flaubert:[(42)] 'They only looked at human things through art . . . The larger interests were a matter of indifference to them. In antiquity, in the Middle Ages, in the Renaissance, in modern times, they only admired form, that is the appearance of things, and the foundations were to be despised, and good only for the bourgeois.'

Du Camp thought Bouilhet a failure and it must be admitted that, from the point of view of the world, he was in fact a failure, for no one really wanted what he had to offer. He had a mild success with two of his plays, and his poetry was a somewhat weak *succès d'estime*. As far as prosperity was concerned, he reached financial ease too late to enjoy it, and the happiest time of his life was when he lived modestly in his little house at Mantes, with his simple mistress, and without much ambition. It is doubtful whether he would have had any ambition at all if it had not been for Flaubert.

Bouilhet had no doubt himself that his life had not been a success and he had as much pessimism with regard to humanity as Flaubert. In the month before he died he wrote *Abrutissement,* which begins: [43]

> Les hommes sont si mauvais
> Que, sans pleurer, je m'en vais
> Du monde.
> Pour la haine ou l'amitié
> Je n'ai plus qu'une pitié
> Profonde.

He had no hope that his name would remain – indeed it would not have remained as long as it did if it had not been for Flaubert's efforts on his behalf – and, a few days before he died, he composed *La Dernière Nuit*, expressing his complete disillusionment. [44]

> Toute ma lampe a brûlé goutte à goutte,
> Mon feu s'éteint avec un dernier bruit.
> Sans un ami, sans un chien qui m'écoute,
> Je pleure seul dans la profonde nuit.
>
> Derrière moi – si je tournais la tête
> Je le verrais – un fantôme est placé:
> Témoin fatal apparu dans ma fête,
> Spectre en lambeaux de mon bonheur passé.
>
> Mon rêve est mort, sans espoir qu'il renaisse.
> Le temps m'échappe, et l'orgueil imposteur
> Pousse au néant les jours de ma jeunesse,
> Comme un troupeau dont il fut le pasteur.

Pareil au flux d'une mer inféconde,
Sur mon cadavre au sépulcre endormi
Je sens déjà monter l'oubli du monde,
Qui, tout vivant, m'a couvert à demi.

Oh! la nuit froide! Oh! la nuit douloureuse!
Ma main bondit sur mon sein palpitant.
Qui frappe ainsi dans ma poitrine creuse?
Quels sont ces coups sinistres qu'on entend?

Qu'es-tu? qu'es-tu? parle ô monstre indomptable
Qui te débats, en des flancs enfermé?
Une voix dit, une voix lamentable,
'Je suis ton cœur, et je n'ai pas aimé!'

In the meantime Flaubert was working very hard at the last stages of *L'Éducation Sentimentale*. He had hoped that Bouilhet would go over the manuscript with him, as he had done for all his other books, but Bouilhet was now dead, and he asked Maxime Du Camp to undertake this task for him. Du Camp wrote that he spent three weeks working at the manuscript with Flaubert, fourteen or fifteen hours a day.[45] The trial obviously got on Flaubert's nerves, for he thought that his friend was too pernickety and that many of his observations were not worth making; he adopted only part of them – obstinacy prevented him from accepting the rest. For instance, Du Camp took exception to Flaubert writing 'Une heure sonna lentement' as he said that this was impossible. He was, of course, right, but Flaubert was describing the hero's mood rather than making an accurate statement, and he was irritated by the objection, refusing to alter it, so that it appears in the book. Yet it did not matter whether the hour was twelve, one or two o'clock and he could have changed it without altering the quality of his text.

In the midst of Bouilhet's death, and the correction of proofs, Flaubert moved to the rue Murillo, a pleasant little apartment of three rooms looking out on the Parc Monceau, which was nearer to Princesse Mathilde's house than his previous apartment.

L'Éducation Sentimentale appeared in November 1869 and Flaubert sent a copy to his mother inscribed:[46] 'À ma bonne vieille Maman, son poulot Gve Flaubert 17 9bre 69.'

It was a bad time to publish, as the political situation was very disturbed. Otherwise, as well, the book was not a success and few people appreciated it. Of the hundred and fifty copies which he sent to friends and acquaintances only thirty were even acknowledged. Popelin, poet and critic, the more than friend of Princesse Mathilde, was amongst those who did not thank Flaubert for his book and kept silent about it. Flaubert was very much disappointed at the reception of his novel. He set great store by it and hoped for very much from it. The press was generally hostile, especially the big press, such as *Le Temps* and *La Revue des Deux Mondes*. Particularly virulent was Barbey d'Aurevilly's article in *Le Constitutionnel* on 19 November 1869. He said that with *L'Éducation Sentimentale* it was the same as with Flaubert's other books, it was hailed as a masterpiece before publication. He then poked fun at the fact that Flaubert had had a large box made to contain the manuscript, and he said that he would henceforth be known as the man with the box. He added that, if one gives birth only once in seven years, one has time to decorate the cradle in which one lays the child. He declared that he had known women afflicted with scirrhosity who imagined that their tumour was a child, and grew fond of it. It was the same with the idolatrous maternal feeling of Flaubert for his literary offspring. He was a Murger, without the grace of Murger, a man of few thoughts and when, by chance he had one, he cooked it again and again, though not in its own juice, for it had none. *L'Éducation Sentimentale*, he opined, confirmed the opinion which had been formed of *Salammbô*.

Flaubert had, however, many kind letters from friends and admirers, such as Renan, Taine, Leconte de Lisle and Zola, which should have made up to him for the ignorant and scurrilous abuse. Banville wrote a very favourable review on 29 November in *Le National,* but what pleased Flaubert more was the warm letter he received from him:[(47)]

I have only just been able to procure your present address and I hasten to express to you all my enthusiasm for your book. Before you gave me the great plesaure of receiving it from you, I had already read it with admiration for your growing genius, and I spoke of it in the article on theatres in *Le National*, but in a shorter form than I would have wished, for, officially, I have the right only to deal with vaudevilles. If *L'Éducation Sentimentale* is a beautiful book, one must have lived, as we did, in 1840, to understand with what evocative power you have made that transitionary period live again, with its weaknesses and its vain aspirations. All that is true to the very marrow of the bone, and expressed in an immortal form.

Ever most faithfully yours, my dear friend.

Flaubert acknowledged his disappointment to George Sand, mentioning particularly Barbey d'Aurevilly's article and also all the friends to whom he had sent the book, who had remained silent for fear of compromising themselves.[48] Some 'bourgeois' in Rouen had even said that he should be prevented from writing such things. Sarcey had also compared him to the Marquis de Sade, whom, he admitted, he had never read. Flaubert thanked her particularly for her kind article published in *La Liberté* on 22 December 1869. However what hurt him most of all – he mentions it on several occasions in his correspondence – was the unfavourable review by Amélie Bosquet in *La Voix des Femmes*, which, as we have seen, was the cause of the ending of his friendship with her. He wrote to George Sand:[49]

A friend, Mlle Bosquet (who has received real services from me), has written two very bitter letters to me, and the second was accompanied by an article from *La Voix des Femmes*, in which she tore me to pieces. I prefer the conduct of de Saint-Victor, who, at least, abstained from writing.

None of this pains me but greatly astonishes me.

At the end of that sad year, in which he had lost his dearest friend, Flaubert spent Christmas with George Sand at Nohant. He was seemingly gay, but it was a hectic gaiety in which he tried to forget his sorrows. He was back in Paris on 28 December and his most immediate task was to prepare a posthumous volume of Bouilhet's poetry for publication and also to try to negotiate the production of his last play, *Aïssé*. This was to take years and he only succeeded after the war and the Commune, in 1872. He was also busy collecting subscriptions for a monument to the poet at Rouen and trying to gain the consent of the town council. The monument was finally erected only after Flaubert had died.

Flaubert remained sad and depressed, and found it difficult to react against his disappointment in *L'Éducation Sentimentale*. He also felt the emptiness of his life without Louis Bouilhet. He wrote to George Sand:[50]

No! chère Maître! I'm not ill but I've been very busy moving from Paris and settling in again at Croisset. Then my mother has been fairly ill – she's better now – and then I had to unravel the rest of my poor Bouilhet's papers, the essay on whom I've already begun. I wrote this week nearly six pages, which, for me, is very good. This work is very painful to me, in every way. The difficulty is to know what not to say . . . You say very beautiful and good things to me, to try to give me back my courage. I've none, but I act as if I had, which is perhaps the same thing.

I don't feel any need to write, because I wrote especially for one person, who is no longer there. That's the truth, but, nevertheless, I'll continue to write. But I've no taste left for it and the excitement has gone. There are so few people who like what I like, who are interested in what preoccupies me. Do you know, in the whole of Paris, which is so vast, one *single* house where they discuss literature? . . .

I ask for nothing better than to escape into a new relationship. But how? Nearly all my old friends are married, or are officials, or think of their business the whole year long, or shoot during the holidays, and play whist after dinner. I don't know a single one who would be capable of spending an afternoon with me reading a poet. They've their businesses and I've none. I'm in the same position as I was at eighteen. My niece, whom I love as a daughter, does not live with me; and my poor old mother is becoming so old that all conversation – save that of health – is impossible with her.

His mother also, at this time, had become extremely deaf, which made conversation still more painful.

The last year of the Empire was full of sadness and loss for Flaubert. There was Bouilhet's death in July 1869 and then Sainte-Beuve died in October. He had not been a very close friend of Flaubert's, but they admired one another and met with pleasure. Next, in March 1870, occurred the death of Flaubert's closest remaining friend, now that Bouilhet was gone, Jules Duplan. Flaubert wrote to Turgenev.[51]

The great grief that I suffered this winter was the death of my most intimate friend after Bouilhet, a good fellow who loved me like a dog, called Jules Duplan. These two deaths, happening one after the other, have crushed me. Add to that the desperate state of two other friends, less friends it is true, but they were, none the less, members of my immediate circle. I mean the paralysis of Feydeau, and the madness of Jules de Goncourt; also the death of Sainte-Beuve.

Jules de Goncourt died of a distressing illness, general paralysis of the insane, due to the tertiary stage of syphilis, on 20 June 1870.

However, what continued to affect Flaubert most bitterly, what he could not get over, was his grief for the loss of Louis Bouilhet, especially when he was at Croisset as he had seen him so frequently at Rouen. He felt that he had now no one with whom he could speak, and writing the memoir of his friend brought him back to him still more vividly. As he said to Edmond de Goncourt,[52] he saw him everywhere; his letters made him rise before him; he found his ghost behind every tree in the garden, on the divan in his study, and even in his own clothes, in the dressing-gown which he used to borrow when he came to Croisset for the night.

In the midst of his sadness, while he was working on his memoir of Bouilhet, the Franco-Prussian war broke out on 19 July, and took Flaubert, as well as many others, by surprise. He was, at first, disgusted by the bellicose state of mind of his compatriots. He had never liked the Empire but he hated disorder even more and, at the beginning of the war, he thought that it should be defended to the end. As he said to his nephew Commanville:[53]

Well! we're indeed in a fine state! The Empire is now only a question of days, but it must be defended to the bitter end!

Flaubert's feelings and ideas were to alter considerably during the course of the war.

CHAPTER SEVEN

L'ÉDUCATION SENTIMENTALE

L'Éducation Sentimentale, Flaubert's third printed novel, was published at the height of his powers, when he was forty-eight. It is generally nowadays considered as his greatest work, in form and style, characterization and thought. It was the last work composed during his period of hope and belief in himself and in the future, after the *succès de scandale* of *Madame Bovary* and his great popular success with *Salammbô*, when he was fêted and admired in the highest society in Paris. This was before the tragedy of the war and the Commune; before the death of his most dearly loved friend since Alfred Le Poittevin, Louis Bouilhet; and before the death of a large number of other close friends, Sainte-Beuve, and especially Jules Duplan, and finally, just as the war was breaking out, Jules de Goncourt, in June 1870. There was also the death of his mother, just after the Commune, in April 1872; and the death of someone who was a second mother to him, George Sand, in 1876. Then in 1875, there was his impoverishment, when, to save his niece's husband from bankruptcy, he sacrificed his private fortune, to live in penury for the rest of his life. He had never had a profession, had never been obliged to earn his living, and had no idea of how to do it – he could not, at close on fifty, adapt himself to new circumstances. All these misfortunes ruined the last ten years of his life, and robbed him of happiness and hope. *L'Éducation Sentimentale* marks the height of his literary career; it also marks the end of the happy, prosperous and successful period of his life. It was for him a very important date in his life.

The completed manuscript of *L'Éducation Sentimentale*, the fair copy of 498 pages, is preserved at the Bibliothèque Historique de la

Ville de Paris. There had also once been 2,355 foolscap sheets of notes, written on both sides of the paper, which had served for the composition of the book. The notes for *Madame Bovary* are preserved in the Municipal Library at Rouen but, unfortunately, the notes for *L'Éducation Sentimentale* were not bequeathed to a library on the death of Flaubert's niece and heir, but were sold, when she died, and as we have seen acquired by the actor and playwright Sacha Guitry, who has not made them available. This is a serious loss for such an important work.

However, Louis Biernawski, who prepared the edition of *L'Éducation Sentimentale* published by Conard in 1922, declares that, for his work, he consulted and used these notes, but that a great many of them were illegible.[1] However, the modern student would like to refer to the papers for himself.

There is, however, some material in the nature of documentation at the Bibliothèque Municipale at Rouen – notes on various specialized subjects which he collected as he was working; but he has not added any of his own reflections. These concern such topics as the fabrication of ceramics, the Revolution of 1848 and so forth, and are, naturally, not as interesting or as illuminating as the notes which served for *Madame Bovary*. There are also some notes, plans and suggestions in the *Carnets* preserved at the Bibliothèque Historique de la Ville de Paris, the most interesting of which were published by M. J. Durry in 1950.

We have seen that Flaubert had been thinking of the novel since 1862, but began writing it only when he had abandoned all hope of getting *Le Château des Cœurs* produced. He began composing the novel in September 1864. The manuscript is dated '1 September 1864 – 16 May 1869', and Flaubert was usually correct in the dating of his manuscripts. He took to complete it the five years which he usually seemed to need for a novel.

We have seen, in the previous chapter, why he chose to write this book at this particular juncture, rather than the one which was later to become *Bouvard et Pécuchet*.

The novel is divided into three comparatively even parts. Each has six chapters, except the third which has seven. It runs from 15 December 1840 to 2 December 1851, with two chapters forming an epilogue and taking place sixteen years later, in 1867. Flaubert, like Maxime Du Camp, believed that this generation, the generation of the age of Louis-Philippe, was a lost generation that had squandered its strength and its talents. The novel is an indictment of the whole of that generation, which he considered had achieved nothing. It runs from the Réforme to the *coup d'état* of 1851, and it is a capital document for the understanding of the time.

When Flaubert was in his twenties he wrote a book entitled *L'Éducation Sentimentale*, but the present author does not believe that it has any connection with the later novel, except title. As he never published the first novel, the title was free for him to use for the second.

What might be called the main theme of the novel, its heart and core, goes back, as we have seen, very far into Flaubert's life: to his romantic love for Élisa Schlésinger. His love for her was very like that of Baudelaire for Madame Sabatier, the 'Vénus Blanche' of *Les Fleurs du Mal*, a mixture of adoration, admiration and respect. Flaubert enclosed his worship for Élisa Schlésinger in what he was to call his 'chambre murée', his walled-up chamber, which he did not dare to enter, but he never forgot her and eventually enshrined her in the pages of *L'Éducation Sentimentale*.

The significant episode occurred during this holiday at Trouville when Flaubert saw a cloak in danger of being swept away by the incoming tide. He moved it out of the path of the waves and later, in the hotel, at lunchtime, he was thanked by its owner. She looked at him, as he says in *Mémoires d'un Fou*, and he lowered his eyes, blushing. She repeated her thanks and the words sank into his mind never to be forgotten; nor was the vision of her face ever to be effaced from his mind.

This is the first version, in *Mémoires d'un Fou*, written later when he was sixteen, and is probably true, but he altered it in *L'Éducation Sentimentale*. A similar episode occurs there but, more suitably for a novel, the young man is an adult of eighteen and not a youth of fourteen; also it is no longer a cloak that is in question, but a scarf. And, moreover, the scene takes place, not on the sea-shore, but on a paddle-steamer between Paris and Nogent, in which Frédéric, the hero, is returning after successfully passing his *baccalauréat* in the capital. The choice of the river instead of the sea is not chance, for it runs like a thread right through the novel and is the symbol of the hero's passage through life, with all its varieties and vicissitudes. The

Seine, in the same way, ran through Flaubert's existence, both at Croisset and in Paris, and he was never far from it.

Part One, from 15 September 1840 to 14 December 1843, establishes the hero Frédéric as a poor student in Paris. The first chapter deals with his journey to his home town of Nogent, after he has passed his *baccalauréat*. In chapter two we see together the two old friends, Frédéric and Deslauriers, who, in spite of vicissitudes, remain friends all through the novel. We see the people in Nogent, the milieu of Frédéric's mother, well-born but poor, and the rich vulgar local called Roque who has always hoped that his daughter will marry the handsome young man who, though without fortune, is the most aristocratic bachelor in the neighbourhood; he considers that he has sufficient money for all. He is the local agent for a banker in Paris called Dambreuse and he offers to introduce Frédéric to him.

Chapter three deals with Frédéric's first year as a student in Paris. He visits Dambreuse, who takes no notice of him as he considers him a nobody. After great difficulty he discovers the whereabouts of his lady of the steamer. Her husband, called Arnoux, is the editor of an art paper in Paris, but Frédéric's relationship with the family develops very slowly.

There are here some fine descriptions of student life in Paris at the time, poor and grey, and Frédéric meets the main students in the story – the hard-working Martinon, bound to succeed, the future fascist Sénécal and the aristocrat Cisy. He does not receive any invitation from the banker Dambreuse and feels himself falling out of love with Marie Arnoux through lack of seeing her.

Chapter four deals with the beginning of the unrest which will culminate in the Revolution of 1848, and there is fighting in the streets. Further acquaintances and friends appear who will be important in the narrative, especially Dussardier and Hussonnet. The former is the only idealistic and disinterested character in the book. Hussonnet, a journalist, is intimate with Arnoux and his wife and it is through him that Frédéric, at last, is enabled to enter their intimacy. He becomes one of the closest friends of the family – indeed Arnoux frequently uses him as a cloak for his own underhand dealings and his sordid love affairs.

Frédéric's old friend Deslauriers joins him in Paris in chapter five and we have glimpses of their life together. Frédéric, like

Flaubert before him, fails in his law examination but stays on in Paris for the summer in the hope of seeing Madame Arnoux. Arnoux takes him to a demi-mondaine fête at the Alhambra and he catches sight of Rosanette who, in the days of his affluence, will play a large part in his life. But he also goes to the party at Saint-Cloud to celebrate the name day of Marie Arnoux and there discovers the unhappiness that she is caused by her husband's infidelities. Frédéric finds himself more in love with her than ever.

He passes his examinations at the end of the summer and goes back to Nogent for the holidays, where his mother tells him that she has lost most of her fortune through bad investments and that he can no longer pursue his studies in Paris. He is obliged to enter an attorney's office. In Nogent, in boredom, he plays about with Roque's daughter Louise, a child of sixteen – her father we know is the rich man of the neighbourhood who has hopes of eventually having Frédéric as his son-in-law. Louise has a passion for the young man and Part One ends on their embrace, when he is about to leave again for Paris.[2]

> Elle ne répondit pas. Elle le regarda profondément, pendant long-temps. Frédéric avait peur de manquer la voiture; il croyait entendre un roulement tout au loin, et, pour en finir:
> – Catherine m'a prévenu que tu avais quelque chose . . .
> – Oui, c'est vrai! je voulais vous dire . . .
> – Eh bien quoi?
> – Je ne sais plus. J'ai oublié! Est-ce vrai que vous partez?
> – Oui, tout à l'heure.
> Elle répéta:
> – Ah! tout à l'heure? . . . tout à fait? . . . nous ne nous reverrons plus?
> Des sanglots l'étouffaient.
> – Adieu! adieu! embrasse-moi donc!
> Et elle le serra dans ses bras avec emportement.

Frédéric has decided to return to Paris, after two years of boredom at home, and after inheriting a large fortune from an uncle who has died intestate. In chapter one of Part Two, Frédéric, rich in his inheritance, departs. In the meantime Arnoux has fallen on evil days and has had to give up his paper. Frédéric has great difficulty in discovering his whereabouts. He eventually finds him and meets Rosanette again, and he is introduced to the life of the high *cocotterie*. This gives Flaubert the opportunity of describing Rosanette's ball, which will be described later. In chapter two Frédéric sets up in style in a private house. He meets the banker Dambreuse again who, now that he is rich, invites him to his house and tries to get him to invest money in his enterprises. He also meets Marie Arnoux again and feels his love stronger than ever. Chapter three shows the financial mess which Arnoux is in and Frédéric lends him the money he has promised to Deslauriers to found a paper. Deslauriers, always a traitor, calls on Madame Arnoux and tells her that Frédéric is in love with Rosanette. This chapter also gives the wonderful description of Frédéric taking Rosanette to the races, where he is seen with the cocotte by both Madame Arnoux and Madame Dambreuse. Rosanette makes certain that everyone should see with whom she has come. In chapter four the aristocratic student, Cisy, pretends to Frédéric that he has taken Rosanette away from him and makes disparaging remarks about Madame Arnoux. This leads to a duel with Frédéric which is described in Flaubert's most comic and grotesque style.

In chapter five, Frédéric, who has lost a great deal of money on the stock exchange and has no chance of being repaid his loan to Arnoux, begins to think more favourably of marriage with Louise Roque. His mother is now in favour of it, as there is a plan on foot to ennoble her son by taking over a title far back in her family. During his absence in Nogent, the treacherous Deslauriers tries to ingratiate himself with Madame Arnoux by telling her that Frédéric is engaged to Louise Roque.

In the meantime, in Nogent, Frédéric is giving Louise every hope that they would marry, when he receives letters from Paris – one from Dambreuse inviting him to dinner, the other from Rosanette wanting to borrow money. He is suddenly seized with nostalgia for the capital and the Boulevard and he leaves Nogent without having definitely decided anything with Louise.

In chapter six Frédéric, back in Paris, divides his time between Madame Arnoux and Rosanette. It is now 1847 and the political situation is becoming serious. Frédéric, more in love than ever with Marie Arnoux, manages to persuade her that Deslauriers was telling a false story. He succeeds in overcoming her resistance, so that finally he persuades her to make an assignation with him. He hires an apartment in the rue Tronchet for the purpose and prepares for her coming, with great luxury. He awaits her arrival all day, walking backwards and forwards to her house, but she does not come. He does not then know that this is on account of the serious illness of her little son, and believes that it is because she wants to disappoint him. It is 23 February 1848 and he wanders around the streets, hearing, but not noticing, the sound of firing in the distance. He encounters Rosanette and takes her back to the apartment he had prepared so lovingly for her rival. They become lovers and, as she sleeps, he weeps in the darkness. When she wakes and asks the reason for his tears, he answers that it is because he has had to wait so long a time to make her his.

Part One had ended with the embrace of Louise Roque and Frédéric; Part Two ends with his embrace of Rosanette.

Part Three runs from the February Revolution 1848 to the *coup d'état* of December 1851. Chapter one deals with the Revolution of February 1848, the sacking of the Tuileries and the Palais Royal, and gives a vivid picture of these historical events. Then comes the setting-up of the Second Republic; Frédéric thinks of entering public life and makes attempts at being elected, but, through the evil machinations of Sénécal, this ends in disaster and his political future lies in ruins. He returns to Rosanette and stays with her until the June Revolution, when he goes to Fontainebleau with her to escape from the events. He returns to Paris when he hears that Dussardier has been wounded.

In chapter two we see the old parties rearranging themselves under the Second Republic. All manage to settle down, especially after the June Revolution, when the government becomes conservative. Dambreuse, who, as Flaubert said, 'aurait payé pour se vendre', makes his peace with the régime. He was really of noble extraction, but when democracy was fashionable he dropped the apostrophe and became Dambreuse, pretending he really came of bourgeois extraction. He was above all a man of the Louis Philippe régime, but he managed, nevertheless, to make money out of the Second Republic – he probably would also have accepted the Second Empire if he had lived as long as that, and he might then have reverted to his noble origins.

Chapter two is important in describing the big party given by Madame Dambreuse to celebrate return to normality, and which balances Rosanette's ball earlier. Frédéric meets Marie Arnoux and he tries to talk to her to explain his conduct, but she treats him coldly. In chapter three he finally has a discussion with her and she tells him why she had missed her appointment with him. It looks as if everything is going to be at peace between them, when Rosanette appears to try to get some money from Arnoux. She treats Frédéric familiarly and shows what their relations have been, so that he feels that his chances with Madame Arnoux have again been wrecked. He wants to break with Rosanette, but she tells him that she is pregnant by him and he feels that he cannot abandon her. He is, however, completely out of love with her and blames her for the coldness between himself and Marie Arnoux. At this time Dambreuse's niece, really his illegitimate daughter, marries the ambitious Martinon. Madame Dambreuse is now alone in the house for most of the day. Frédéric, who has become less fastidious since he arrived in Paris, sees a great deal of her and eventually makes her his mistress. He is very proud of this high-class affair and is not loth that it should be generally known.

Chapter four brings us to early in 1851. Dambreuse falls very ill and soon dies, and his widow asks Frédéric to marry her. He accepts with alacrity, planning all that he will be able to do with his share of her immense fortune. It is then discovered that the banker, knowing of his wife's affair with Frédéric, has burnt the will in her favour and has left everything to his alleged illegitimate daughter. Pride prevents Frédéric from withdrawing from the marriage and Madame Dambreuse is very much touched by this, as she thinks his action is due to love of her, but he has never really loved her and has only been dazzled by her wealth and position, and anticipation of the glorious life he would be able to lead. While awaiting his marriage, he leads a despicable double life, spending the afternoon with Madame Dambreuse and the night with Rosanette, whom he finds more amusing than his fiancée. In the same chapter occur the birth and death of Rosanette's child.

Chapter five deals with the selling-up of Marie Arnoux's goods. Madame Dambreuse, who had always been jealous of her, found amongst her husband's papers proof of a debt of Arnoux to him. Urged on by the treacherous Deslauriers, who had never forgotten his failure with Marie Arnoux, she is persuaded to insist on repayment. Arnoux was unable to meet the debt and all his goods were ordered to be sold. Frédéric hears of this and tries to save him for the sake of his wife. He borrows a large sum of money from Madame Dambreuse, on the pretext of saving a friend from arrest. But it is too late – the Arnoux have left Paris. Frédéric thinks that it is Rosanette who has caused this disaster by trying to get payment from Arnoux for what he owed her, and also through jealousy of his wife. He finally separates from her. It is ironical that it is when she has done nothing that he punishes her.

Madame Arnoux's goods – all her most intimate possessions, many of them clothes that Frédéric remembers so well from having seen her wear them – are sold at a public auction. Madame Dambreuse insists on going to the auction and in spite of all Frédéric's entreaties bids for and secures a Renaissance casket which he particularly associates with Madame Arnoux. He accompanies her home and leaves her at her door, letting her know that everything is now over between them. He then countermands all the arrangements he has made for his marriage. By this time he has lost the largest part of his fortune through his extravagance – and generosity – and he longs for the peace of his home at Nogent. In the train on the way there he thinks again of Louise Roque, who had loved him simply in an innocent and uncomplicated way, and he thinks of paying court to her once more, also the memory of her dowry is not unwelcome to him. However, as he walks home through the town, he sees her, in wedding garb, coming out of the town hall on Deslaurier's arm, as his wife. He turns tail and takes the next train back to Paris. It is 2 December 1851, and the fighting for the *coup d'état* is already beginning. It is then that he witnesses the murder of the good and kind Dussardier by his friend the former revolutionary Sénécal, who has turned policeman:[3]

Entre les charges de cavalerie, des escouades de sergents de ville survenaient, pour faire refluer le monde dans les rues.

Mais, sur les marches de Tortoni, un homme, Dussardier, remarquable de loin à sa haute taille, restait sans plus bouger qu'une cariatide.

Un des agents qui marchait en tête, le tricorne sur les yeux, le menaça de son épée.

L'autre alors, s'avançant d'un pas, se mit à crier:

– Vive la République!

Il tomba sur le dos, les bras en croix.

Un hurlement d'horreur s'éleva de la foule. L'agent fit un cercle autour de lui avec son regard; et Frédéric, béant, reconnut Sénécal.

This ends the novel proper, but there are the two further chapters, six and seven, taking place sixteen years later, which are the Epilogue, and which will be discussed later.

L'Éducation Sentimentale is, however, not merely a love story, a tale of enduring love – although that runs right through it like a golden thread – but is, as well, the novel of human ambition – all the varieties of ambition of a number of different people. And it is, above all, the picture of an age, the well-defined period running from 1840 to the beginning of the Second Empire.

In *Madame Bovary* Flaubert had intended to paint for eternity, so that what he said would be as true in the future as it was in his own day. He took the greatest trouble to leave everything vague, to avoid local and temporary tittle-tattle; and he would not tie down his novel by contemporary problems. In *L'Éducation Sentimentale*, on the contrary, he wished to paint a very definite period in history, a fairly restricted period, all the details of which had to be correct. Writing to Barbès in October 1867, while he was composing the book, he said: 'Although my subject is one of analysis, I do touch on the events of the time.'[4] He did much more than that, and some of the episodes which he describes – such as the account of the Revolution of 1848 – are distinguished pieces of historical writing, which are essential for an understanding of the age.

The novel starts when the shadow of the Revolution of 1848 is beginning to be cast before it; it is the period of the running-down of the régime of Louis-Philippe, which, in 1830, had started out with so many high hopes and aspirations.

Flaubert, who grew to manhood during the period under review, and who had never liked or admired Louis-Philippe, wrote during the Revolution: 'There are many disconcerted faces that make me very happy to behold. I take a great delight in the sight of all these flattened ambitions.'[5]

The novel begins with the period of La Réforme, when there was an attempt at a campaign to improve the franchise, and the radicals wanted universal suffrage. At the time only those who had a certain income could vote. When a deputation went to Guizot to ask him to enlarge the franchise, he answered cynically: 'The remedy is in your own hands. Get rich!' There was a great deal of poverty at the time and also corruption, which made the rich richer and the poor poorer. Flaubert's novel is an account of the disillusionment with the reign, when all the aims of the Revolution of 1830 were failing.

Flaubert chose that period because, on the whole, it was the one that he knew best; the early part covers the years when he was a law student in Paris, when he was twenty, and he had also been in Paris for the February Revolution in 1848. We see the students of the time and attend their gatherings; we hear their discussions, understand their ideas and take part in their abortive revolts. We have glimpses of the lives of the poor, we sympathize with their problems and realize the need for change. All this is achieved with great sympathy and compassion, and with more absolute truth than in any novel by Balzac. Yet Flaubert, according to his theory of art, did not show bias towards any side.

Flaubert also gives us glimpses into the lives of the prosperous, into the lives of the rich bourgeoisie created by the régime of Louis Philippe, when they were allowed to make as much money as they liked, at the expense of everyone else, especially of the poor. People like the banker Dambreuse, who managed to make his peace with all the régimes, in particular the Orleanist. He would never have been in opposition to any form of government and would always have found valid reasons for accepting it.

All the milieus of the period are carefully built up from contemporary records and are correct politically and factually. However, it seems that the atmosphere of certain sections of society – such as the rich social life of the upper classes, or the life of the demi-mondaine class, of the kept woman – are in the mood of the Second Empire rather than that of the July Monarchy. This is not astonishing as that is the Parisian social life which Flaubert knew best; as it was when he lived there, part of every year, had his apartment there, and went about in society. Under Louis Philippe he was in Paris for only a little over a year, and even then only intermittently, and he lived mostly with students in the Latin Quarter, hardly going out at all except to his classes, to the law library and to cheap eating houses. After little more than a year, his nervous illness cut short his life in Paris and prevented him from continuing his studies. It was after the publication of *Madame Bovary*, in 1857, and especially after the great success of *Salammbô* in 1862, that he got to know Princesse Mathilde, the Emperor and Empress and many members of the aristocracy; he learned about the life of the big bourgeoisie under the Second

G. SAND

George Sand, the novelist. Flaubert kept this signed portrait of her in his bedroom.

Louis Bouilhet, poet and playwright. The closest friend of Flaubert's last ten years.

Empire but not before that, as he had no opportunity of knowing that kind of life when he was a poor student. His knowledge of the demi-monde also, which he shows in his description of the relations between Frédéric and the *grande cocotte* Rosanette, dates from this period – he could not have known it earlier. But when he was living in Paris in the eighteen-sixties, trying to get Bouilhet's plays produced and haunting the wings of various theatres, he met a variety of actresses and became intimate with them. That kind of life, which he described in *L'Éducation Sentimantale*, is very much more like that of the Second Empire than that of the July Monarchy. This was the hey-day of the demi-monde in Paris, of the cocotte, the kept woman, and there were many famous – or notorious – courtesans of the period – such women as Hortense Schneider, Appollonie Sabatier, Cora Pearl, Blanche d'Attigny, La Païva and Jane de Tourbey, with whom even the Emperor was implicated. Flaubert liked the company of such women and got to know them well. One can say that his picture of Rosanette and her life is the destruction of the Romantic myth of the courtesan.

All this social life – of high society and the demi-monde – as distinct from the political life, which is recorded accurately, with dates, is more typical of the light-hearted atmosphere of the last years of the Second Empire than of the waning years of the Louis-Philippe régime.

The chronology of events in the novel is, on the whole, carefully contrived when it is necessary for the truth of the narrative. And, even when there are some errors, these do not matter to the veracity of the book as one does not, as one reads, make a list of time of the events, month by month. For instance, one does not notice that a year – September 1843 to September 1844 – is dropped out. Then, at the beginning of Part Two, 1846 disappears altogether. Frédéric returns to Paris, with his fortune, in December 1845, and gives his house-warming party in January 1847, without anything being said about 1846. In the third chapter of Part Three, we pass in a few pages from August 1848 to May 1850. Then Rosanette announces to Frédéric, in January 1849, that she is pregnant, but she gives birth to the child only in February 1851 – a miraculous gestation of over two years. None of this, however, impinges on our consciousness, so cleverly is the narrative conducted.

There is, however, one discrepancy in dating which is noticeable, and thus worrying. In the first chapter of the Epilogue, when Marie Arnoux comes to see Frédéric in March 1867, she informs him that her husband is living in Brittany, with the family. Yet, in the second chapter, we are told that Frédéric and Deslauriers meet in the autumn of the same year, and, when Deslauriers asks him what has become of Madame Arnoux, Frédéric answers that she is living in Rome with her son, her husband having died the previous year. We cannot then help remembering that, in March that year, he was still alive and living with his children. This discrepancy in the time factor strikes the reader as a blemish. Otherwise, in essential historical events, the reader is confident that they happened as the author describes them.

The documentation which Flaubert carried out to obtain his knowledge of the age was fantastic. He read every newspaper of the time and consulted people who were implicated in the events. He visited factories in order to be correct in his details of manufacture – Arnoux, when his art shop and periodical failed, took up commercial art, manufacturing his own wares himself. Flaubert read every document concerning the Revolution of 1848, and indeed the most vivid parts of the book are the pictures of the Revolution and particularly the sack of the Tuileries Palace and the Palais Royal. He found out where the posts of the National Guard had been at the time. He also went so far as to find out whether, in 1848, one could go by train from Paris to Fontainebleau, as Frédéric escapes from the city there with Rosanette to avoid the fighting in the capital; in fact he discovered that the line had not yet been opened and he had to find another means of conveyance.

Most of these investigations were necessary for the truth of the narrative, but it is questionable whether all the details of technical research – such as those of the process of china manufacture in Arnoux's factory, or of the work done by Rosanette's parents in the poor life from which she escaped into prostitution – add anything to the novel. These minute and accurate details are, in a certain measure, *hors d'œuvre*, and are not really necessary to the artistic whole.

Most critics have considered *L'Éducation Sentimentale* as an autobiographical work. Du Camp said that he recognized everyone in it and all the events. But although a faint core of the characters may be found in real life, they are transposed and transmuted, and arranged according to a fictional pattern. It must not be forgotten that the book is a novel, and that the events are arranged according to a scheme which is more logical than real life. All the episodes except the initial love 'illumination' are invented. In the novel, after he has abandoned his studies in Paris through lack of success and lack of funds, the hero has gone back home to Nogent and settled in an attorney's office. Then he inherits a fortune from an uncle, returns to Paris to settle there, buying a house and spending his money lavishly, living a fashionable life, and vaguely considering going in for politics, or becoming a writer, or a painter. He keeps a woman but, at the same time, cherishes his vain passion for Marie Arnoux. He makes many attempts at becoming her lover, but fails through his timidity and weakness, and through her virtue. It is through frustration with her that he takes up with the demi-mondaine Rosanette; it is also through frustration that eventually, when she is a widow, he becomes engaged to be married to Madame Dambreuse, the wife of the financier.

All this is only in the novel and not in Flaubert's life.

It is true that there are some resemblances between the characters in the novel and people whom Flaubert had known. As he painted Rosanette, he undoubtedly thought of Apollonie Sabatier, 'la Présidente'. In the plan of the novel she is mentioned as 'la Présidente', though in the novel she is 'la Maréchale', and their personalities are very different.[6] Arnoux bears undoubted resemblances to Schlésinger.

Madame Dambreuse is certainly drawn from Madame Delessert, the fashionable hostess, who had been the mistress of Mérimée before becoming that of Du Camp, when he returned from the East, full of wordly ambition, in 1851. There are no obvious models for Sénécal or Dussardier in Flaubert's life.

Marie Arnoux is certainly intended for Élisa Schlésinger, but we know that more through the hero's life-long passion for her, from the way in which he falls in love with her, than from her character. In fact we know nothing deep about Madame Schlésinger at all, except that she was the wife of a shady businessman who was obliged to leave Paris in 1849, and Flaubert had none of the opportunity of getting to know her which Frédéric had with Marie Arnoux. He virtually ceased frequenting her when he fell ill and left Paris at the age of twenty-two. He did not write to her, but only to her husband as long as he was alive, and that was after publishing *L'Éducation Sentimentale*. We have therefore no way of knowing whether she bears any resemblance to Marie Arnoux, except in Flaubert's imagination.

Deslauriers, the treacherous Deslauriers, the close, life-long friend of Frédéric, bears some resemblance to Du Camp, who would certainly not have been pleased or flattered by the comparison. Yet there is something in Deslauriers' attitude to Frédéric which recalls Du Camp's to Flaubert. In the early days of their relationship, in their correspondence especially,[7] Du Camp had a romantic feeling towards his friend as Deslauriers had towards Frédéric:[8]

Puis, il songea à la personne même de Frédéric. Elle avait toujours exercé sur lui un charme presque féminin; et il arriva bientôt à l'admirer pour un succès dont il se reconnaissait incapable.

Deslauriers had also some of Du Camp's overriding ambition, but the difference was that the latter was very much more efficient and fulfilled all his ambitions whereas Deslauriers failed and was eventually a *raté*.

Du Camp certainly saw Frédéric as a faithful picture of Flaubert. He considered his friend weak and wavering, incapable of independent action, like the hero of *L'Éducation Sentimentale*, and as lacking in ambition – especially of the energy to achieve anything. This had been his opinion of Flaubert when they had been young together, and he did not alter it later with deeper knowledge of him. But he lost sight of what Flaubert was as an artist and what he was capable of enduring and achieving in the service of his art. He never deviated from that straight line towards his object, whereas Frédéric was an incurable amateur and dilettante, who did not know whether he wanted to be a politician, a painter or a novelist, and became none of them. Du Camp also did not see that Frédéric bore some resemblance to himself in his views on life.

The characters in the novel have only very small points of contact with the people whom Flaubert knew in real life – only as many as can happen with any novelist who must, after all, draw his material from somewhere.

The title of the novel is important as it is intended to deal with the total education of the various young men, the education of all their faculties and sentiments – not merely their proficiency in the passion of love. As Flaubert wrote to Mademoiselle Leroyer de Chantepie:[9] 'I want to write the moral history of the men of my generation, "sentimental" would be more correct. It is a book of love, of passion, as it can exist today, that is to say in a state of inactivity.' The book shows how they all deal with their lives, how they further their personal and selfish ambitions.

Although the events are important in the book, it is the depiction of the characters which makes the greatness of the novel, and there is a large gallery of wonderfully drawn portraits.

Flaubert, as a whole, had a low opinion of human nature – theoretically that is, for in real life all his geese were swans, and he was incapable of thinking ill of those whom he loved. But in the abstract he was incapable of thinking that anyone of intelligence could be admirable; and he could not see goodness anywhere except in very simple characters such as the idealistic and naïf Dussardier, the revolutionary in *L'Éducation Sentimentale*. Most of the characters in the novel are corrupt. But they are small-minded and mean rather than grandiosely evil. There are many more evil characters in Balzac than in Flaubert, who has never drawn anyone as black as Vautrin. Nearly all the characters are despicable, and Flaubert intended this; he said in the early plan for the novel that all were 'veules', even Madame Arnoux. That was however before he had seen Élisa Schlésinger again, and in the final version she is good and virtuous, and intended to be everything that was noble and beautiful; but she remains, on the whole, a shadowy figure, and Frédéric finds that she disappears from view when he tries to fix her in his mind. That is also the impression that the reader receives.

Most of the people in *L'Éducation Sentimentale* are self-seekers, with few ideas beyond their own selfish interests. We have seen how the banker Dambreuse was able to accommodate his beliefs to all parties and governments. It is true that there was a great deal of corruption towards the close of the July Monarchy. Nevertheless there were some people who were noble and selfless in their conduct, some who worked in a disinterested manner for the sake of learning, of art, or for the betterment of others; but Flaubert gives them no place in his novel, even though it is intended to be a complete picture of the age, of a whole generation. There are not even the long-suffering working-people, such as Catherine Leroux in *Madame Bovary*, who had toiled for half a century in the same farm, or Félicité in *Un Cœur Simple* from *Trois Contes*.

Frédéric is the main character in the novel, the sub-title of which is *Histoire d'un Jeune Homme*, and all the other characters revolve round him. He is charming and elegant and the author has conveyed this quality, while remaining critical of him. His character is carefully built up from his fresh youth, when he had not yet been spoilt by life, before he had become somewhat despicable. He is, however, weak and spineless rather than corrupt, like many of his contemporaries, but his susceptibilities are blunted in the end. Yet he possesses kindness of heart and good feelings, which are exemplified in his generosity to his poorer friends when he becomes rich. One of the saddest and grimmest scenes in the novel is the house-warming which he gives to the friends of his student days, and the way they mock at him and show no gratitude for the trouble he has taken to please them. They all come but behave atrociously: they criticize his entertainment; rough Sénécal strikes matches against the new wallpaper; Deslauriers is contemptuous of his library and declares that it is fit only for a little girl. Frédéric, he says, had bought most of the modern authors, but his friends say that 'Balzac est surfait, Byron démoli, Hugo n'entendait rien au théâtre' and so forth. They irritate Frédéric so much that he wants to throw them all out. Yet he has looked forward so much to entertaining them. As they go out they loudly criticize what he had given them, so that he can hear. Hussonnet says that the meal was badly chosen and too heavy; Sénécal declares that the whole house was futile; and the aristocrat Cisy opines that 'cela manquait de cachet'. Frédéric is left alone with the ruins of his party:[10]

> Il pensait à ses amis, et sentait entre eux et lui comme un grand fossé plein d'ombre qui les séparait. Il leur avait tendu la main cependant, et ils n'avaient pas répondu à la franchise de son cœur.

Frédéric's loyalty to his old friends is particularly seen in his attitude to his oldest school friend, Deslauriers, whom he never abandoned although he was often treated very badly by Deslauriers, and his kindness repaid with ingratitude; he even tries to blacken him with his friends, to obtain favours for himself; yet Frédéric never forgets him or neglects him and the novel ends on their meeting together.

Frédéric's kindness of heart is outraged at the hardness and cruelty of Madame Dambreuse after the death of her husband, when he has only just taken his last breath. In the room of death she has made a great show of grief, so that all are deceived; then she retires to her own room, where her lover joins her. He imagines that she must feel some grief at the death of the man with whom she has lived for so many years. When he sympathizes with her, saying that she must be sad, she answers cynically: 'Moi? Non pas du tout!'[11] Then she adds: 'Ah! Sainte Vierge! Quel débarras!' He cannot however help remarking: 'On était libre, pourtant.' Then she bursts out, in unguarded terms, against her dead husband:

Elle le dénigrait de plus en plus. Personne d'une fausseté aussi profonde, impitoyable d'ailleurs, dur comme du caillou, 'un mauvais homme, un mauvais homme!'
Il échappe des fautes, même aux plus sages. Madame Dambreuse venait d'en faire une, par ce débordement de haine. Frédéric, en face d'elle, dans une bergère, réfléchissait, scandalisé.

Frédéric's compassion is also seen in the ball given by *la Maréchale*, where we have the contrast between the extravagant luxury of the fare offered at the party, and the tubercular elderly courtesan spitting blood. He is the only person in the whole gathering who has noticed the episode, and, when he advises her to have treatment, she answers:[12] 'Bah! à quoi bon? autant ça qu'autre chose. La vie n'est pas si drôle!' Then he is suddenly seized with sadness, as he reflects on how much misery and heartache is hidden beneath the glittering exterior:

Alors il frissonna, pris d'une tristesse glaciale, comme s'il avait aperçu des mondes entiers de misère et de désespoir, un réchaud de charbon près d'un lit de sangle, et les cadavres de la Morgue en tablier de cuir, avec le robinet d'eau froide qui coule sur leurs cheveux.

Frédéric is a very representative Flaubert character and he suffers from what we nowadays know as Bovarysme – a man whose dreams can never be realized. The only difference between him and Emma Bovary is that, as he is an educated man, his dreams are of higher quality and are more sophisticated than hers. He, like Emma, can sit for hours and dream of escape with the object of his love:[13]

Quand il allait au Jardin des Plantes, la vue d'un palmier l'entraînait vers des pays lointains. Ils voyageaient ensemble, au dos des droma-daires, sous le tendelet des éléphants, dans la cabine d'un yacht parmi des archipels bleus, ou côte à côte sur deux mulets à clochettes, qui tré-buchent dans les herbes contre des colonnes brisées. Quelquefois, il s'arrêtait au Louvre devant de vieux tableaux; et son amour l'embrassant jusque dans les siècles disparus, il la substituait aux personnages des peintures. Coiffée d'un hennin, elle priait à deux genoux derrière un vitrage de plomb. Seigneuresse des Castilles ou des Flandres, elle se tenait assise, avec une fraise empesée et un corps de baleines à gros bouillons. Puis elle descendait quelque grand escalier de porphyre, au milieu des sénateurs, sous un dais de plumes d'autruche, dans une robe de brocart. D'autres fois, il la rêvait en pantalon de soie jaune, sur les coussins d'un harem; et tout ce qui était beau, le scintillement des étoiles, certains airs de musique, l'allure d'une phrase, un contour l'amenaient à sa pensée d'une façon brusque et insensible.

This is very like Emma's dream of elopement with Rodolphe.

Frédéric was a waverer who could never make up his mind about anything, nor come to any decision. We shall see this particularly in the final scene between him and Marie Arnoux. Flaubert does not seem to have thought this a great weakness, as he considered it also characteristic of Hamlet, who in his opinion was the greatest character of modern literature, and that it was his indecision which made him great. As he wrote to Louise Colet:[14]

It is, on the contrary, this perpetual state of flux in Hamlet, this vague atmosphere in which he lives, this lack of decision in will-power and lack of resolve in thought, which make it sublime . . . Ulysses is perhaps the strongest character in the whole of ancient literature and Hamlet in the modern.

Nevertheless Frédéric's lack of a decisive character, his in-ability to come to any conclusion drives him to behave very badly to all the women in his life and he has a satisfactory relation-ship with none of them. His behaviour is particularly despicable at the time of his engagement to Madame Dambreuse, when he spends the afternoon with her and the nights with Rosanette, while at the same time still thinking of Marie Arnoux. When Madame Dambreuse asks him how he spends his time, and why he does not come to see her more frequently, he answers that he has been ill. He takes a savage delight in telling the same lies to her as to Rosanette, and in sending to each a similar bouquet of flowers.

Frédéric is the chief person in the novel, but his life and fortunes are entwined with those of three women – Marie Arnoux, the prostitute Rosanette and the wife of the banker, Madame Dambreuse – of contrasting personalities, whose diversity is very well drawn.

We have seen how Frédéric first falls in love with Marie Arnoux and how she becomes a fixation in his life. We know very little about her and see her only through the hero's eyes. We see her clothes and the grace of her movements, but little else, and we do not know her tastes or her interests. We know that she is virtuous, that she does not approve of extra-marital affairs. In the first plan, as we have seen, Flaubert intended to make her more conventional and obvious. She was to be quite prepared to give herself to Frédéric, but his feelings were to cool off when she became more passionate, and vice versa. Then Flaubert thought that it would be a stronger situation if they did not become lovers. Pommier and Durry think that this is proof that, in real life, they had been lovers. The present author, however, does not believe this, as she does not think that Flaubert would have kept his love for her if this had been the case, since he normally wearied of what he had obtained. He was here discussing a situation in a novel and not in his own life. Pommier and Digeon, in an article entitled 'Du Nouveau sur Flaubert et son Œuvre', throw up their hands in horror at what they consider is an alteration in the truth of his narrative, because they insist on the autobiographical nature of the novel. (15) They call it 'rouerie artistique'. 'What?', they cry, 'this platonic love in which we see the most moving touch of the autobiography, the author only thought of after reflection and even through a calculation of artistic cunning!' This however does not prevent its being true, and the author could still have pondered whether this was the most artistic ending to a book which was a work of fiction and not an autobiography.

As Flaubert said, at first, in his plan, he wanted Marie Arnoux to be as cowardly and mean as Frédéric and Arnoux, but that was before he had seen Élisa Schlésinger after the lapse of fifteen years. When he saw her again, all his criticism fell away and she was for him once more *La Princesse Lointaine*. Marie Arnoux does eventually, against her will and ideals, fall in love with Frédéric, and, although she struggles against her passion, she does at last agree to an assignation with him, which the illness of her child prevents her from keeping. She thinks it is the hand of God that has intervened to prevent her from sinning. It is however somewhat strange that a woman as courteous as she did not send a word of explanation and apology to him when her son had recovered. It is true that there was the Revolution of February 1848 at the time, but she could have done so later in the following months. If this had happened then he would probably not have made Rosanette his mistress and would not have tied himself up in further lies and deceptions.

If she had turned up at the assignation, would Frédéric have made her his lover? It is hard to believe that he would ever have nerved himself to that pitch, that he could ever have taken such a resolution. The author, however, saves him from this dilemma, and the result is certainly more artistic and true. In the final scene between them we shall see the situation made concrete, but he has been taken by surprise and it all peters out.

Another important woman in Frédéric's life was Rosanette, the cocotte. Flaubert manages to convey her beauty and her charm, her good humour and her unscrupulousness, in the way she succeeds in playing off Arnoux, Frédéric and various other young men against one another, while holding her rich old protector, Oudry, in the background. Probably her attachment to Frédéric is greater than to the others, but this comes largely after she becomes pregnant by him. She would then like to be faithful to him and to marry him, but she is weak and pleasure-loving, and cannot resist the gift of money and other rich presents, so that faithfulness is not one of her virtues. Flaubert has cleverly shown the faults of her kind – her extravagance, her irresponsibility and her complete lack of care for the morrow:[16]

Celle de Rosanette l'amusait. On venait là le soir, en sortant du club ou du spectacle; on prenait une tasse de thé, on faisait une partie de loto; le dimanche, on jouait des charades; Rosanette, plus turbulente que les autres, se distinguait par des inventions drolatiques, comme de courir à quatre pattes ou de s'affubler d'un bonnet de coton . . . Elle fumait des chibouques, elle chantait des tyroliennes. L'après-midi, par désœuvrement, elle découpait des fleurs dans un morceau de toile perse, les collait elle-même sur ses carreaux, barbouillait de fard ses deux petits chiens, faisait brûler des pastilles, ou se tirait la bonne aventure. Incapable de résister à une envie, elle s'engouait d'un bibelot qu'elle avait vu, n'en dormait pas, courait l'acheter, le troquait contre un autre, et gâchait les étoffes, perdait ses bijoux, gaspillait l'argent, aurait vendu sa chemise pour une loge d'avant-scène. Souvent elle demandait à Frédéric l'explication d'un mot qu'elle avait lu, mais n'écoutait pas sa réponse, car elle sautait vite à une autre idée, en multipliant les questions. Après des spasmes de gaieté, c'étaient des colères enfantines . . . . Sans y prendre garde, elle s'habillait devant lui, tirait avec lenteur ses bas de soie, puis se lavait à grande eau le visage, en se renversant la taille comme une naïade qui frissonne; et le rire de ses dents blanches, les étincelles de ses yeux, sa beauté, sa gaieté éblouissaient Frédéric, et lui fouettaient les nerfs.

Then sometimes he calls on Madame Arnoux and finds her teaching her little boy to read; or the girl Marthe is practising her scales on the piano, with the mother at her sewing. Then it is his innocent pleasure to pick up her scissors when she drops them. There could not have been a greater contrast with Rosanette's boudoir.

Flaubert describes vividly Rosanette's loud-voiced vulgarity as in the scene at the races, when she is in a carriage with Frédéric, and Madame Arnoux, of whom she is jealous, passes by, and she shouts at her:[17]

– Donne-moi du champagne! dit Rosanette.
Et, levant le plus haut possible son verre rempli, elle s'écria:
– Ohé là-bas! les femmes honnêtes, l'épouse de mon protecteur, ohé!

Frédéric, knowing that he had been seen by Madame Arnoux, is full of embarrassment and hatred of Rosanette.

But perhaps the passage most revelatory of Rosanette's character is that in which Frédéric takes her to Fontainebleau to escape from the Revolution in Paris, and cannot help being disappointed at her ignorance and lack of knowledge of anything. When he tries to impress upon her the beauties of the palace, he is hurt by the triviality of her responses. They visit everything, the historic halls, the room where Napoleon had signed his abdication, the gallery where Monaldeschi was assassinated by order of Christine of Sweden, but all she can think of saying is: 'C'était par jalousie, prends garde à toi.'[18] Frédéric is much moved by these visions of the past, and tries to convey his emotion to her:

Frédéric fut pris par une concupiscence rétrospective et inexprimable. Afin de distraire son désir, il se mit à considérer tendrement Rosanette, en lui demandant si elle n'aurait pas voulu être cette femme.

– Quelle femme?
– Diane de Poitiers!
Il répéta:
– Diane de Poitiers, la maîtresse d'Henri II.
Elle fit un petit: 'Ah!' Ce fut tout.
Son mutisme prouvait clairement qu'elle ne savait rien, ne comprenait pas, si bien que par complaisance il lui dit:
– Tu t'ennuies peut-être?
– Non, non, au contraire!
Et, le menton levé, tout en promenant à l'entour un regard des plus vagues, Rosanette lâcha ce mot:
– Ça rappelle des souvenirs.

The only thing that seems to interest her is the pond with the carps, and she spends a quarter of an hour throwing pieces of bread into the water to see the fish bounding to catch them.

As we have seen, it is when Rosanette has not harmed him that Frédéric finally leaves her. He accuses her of having always hated Madame Arnoux and of wanting to ruin her:[19]

Ce que ça te fait? Mais tu te venges, voilà tout! C'est la suite de tes persécutions! Est-ce que tu ne l'as pas outragée jusqu'à venir chez elle! Toi, une fille de rien. La femme la plus sainte, la plus charmante et la meilleure! Pourquoi t'acharnes-tu à la ruiner?

Rosanette gives him her word of honour that she has done nothing, but he answers that her word of honour is valueless and he reminds her of her many infidelities to him:

– Cela t'étonne! Tu me croyais aveugle parce que je fermais les yeux. J'en ai assez aujourd'hui! On ne meurt pas pour les trahisons d'une femme de ton espèce. Quand elles deviennent trop monstrueuses, on s'en écarte; ce serait se dégrader que de les punir.

He tells her that he has never loved anyone but Marie Arnoux but, at this, Rosanette breaks out:

– Ça prouve ton bon goût! Une personne d'un âge mûr, le teint couleur de réglisse, la taille épaisse, des yeux grands comme des soupiraux de cave, et vides comme eux! Puisque ça te plaît, va la rejoindre.

Then Frédéric leaves her and she was never to see him again.

The third woman in Frédéric's life is Madame Dambreuse, the wife of the banker. She is very much a woman of the world, very much more sophisticated than Marie Arnoux. She is beautiful in a brittle way, very smart and at her best in society. She is very anxious to be a leader in the beau monde, and she knows what she wants. As Flaubert describes her:[20]

Il regardait cependant Madame Dambreuse, et il la trouvait charmante, malgré sa bouche un peu longue et ses narines trop ouvertes. Mais sa grâce était particulière. Les boucles de sa chevelure avaient comme une langueur passionnée, et son front couleur d'agate semblait contenir beaucoup de choses et dénotait un maître.

She was hard and temperamentally cold, but she fell in love with the handsome attractive young man who, through ambition, was only too happy to become her lover. However, he soon found her love too possessive, and he had to feign passion with her.[21]

Il reconnut alors ce qu'il s'était caché, la désillusion de ses sens. Il n'en feignait pas moins de grandes ardeurs; mais pour les ressentir, il lui fallait évoquer l'image de Rosanette ou de Madame Arnoux.

We have seen her cruelty after the death of her husband and her harshness to his illegitimate daughter. Although she obviously loves her young fiancé, she intends to be the master, and she is unwilling, to please him, to sacrifice a petty piece of vengeance against her rival, the purchase of a silver casket which has belonged to Marie Arnoux. He cannot bear to see it in anyone's hands but hers, and his fiancée's action is like an insulting slap in the face, so that he breaks off his engagement to her. Had they really become man and wife it is hard to believe that there was much happiness in store for them. So Frédéric himself breaks up two of his feminine relationships – the third was still to come.

Like Baudelaire, Flaubert was not very much interested in young girls and he knew none except his niece, about whom he was so much besotted that he could not see her clearly. So Louise Roque plays only a very small part in the novel. Yet, as she is drawn, there is something touching in her character, in her simple love for Frédéric, and in the way she goes from Nogent to Paris with her maid, during the Revolution, to find what has become of him. Eventually she abandons all hope of him when she hears that he is spending every night with Rosanette. Then she returns to Nogent, but it is not clear why she marries Deslauriers, who is unattractive and mediocre and who, it is quite clear in 1851, at the time of her wedding, will be a failure. She is very rich and could afford someone with more glamour and potentiality for success. She does not love him and does not remain with him for long.

In the early plan it was intended that the novel should be based on a triangle of characters, Monsieur and Madame Schlésinger and himself, the author. It was only later that many other important characters were added. Schlésinger became Arnoux, in the novel, without much difficulty and change. It is not in a conventional sense a triangle, as there is very little jealousy or ill will on Frédéric's part towards Arnoux. Arnoux is vulgar and self-indulgent, with an excessive love of wine, women and food. His infidelities are numerous and Frédéric is a witness of them and of the unhappiness that they cause his wife, yet he never dislikes him. There is something attractive and warm-hearted in him and even lovable. He has the saving grace of genuinely loving his wife and children and he feels remorse at the harm he is doing them, but he is too weak to alter. He cannot help harming them and eventually ruining them. When Frédéric first knew him, he was apparently the prosperous editor of a paper and the owner of an art shop. But his weaknesses make him a very bad businessman. He gradually loses all his money, which he largely squanders on his women, especially on Rosanette, for whose favours he is the rival of Frédéric. If any one person is responsible for ruining him – besides himself – it is she. After he loses his art shop, he sets up his own factory, manufacturing his ceramics, but that too fails and he is eventually reduced to selling religious objects before that business too goes bankrupt. He has, in the meantime, borrowed money right and left and, when he cannot repay it, his goods are sold and he has to flee Paris.

Flaubert has the gift of friendship and so too has Frédéric. Deslauriers is his first friend. They were at school together, where Deslauriers, who was by some years the elder, befriended him, attracted by his superior charm, which he himself lacks. He is intelligent and ambitious, very hard-working, and possessing the perseverance which Frédéric does not have. He does not however succeed, perhaps because he is physically unattractive, with no charm of personality. He is ambitious largely for money, but it is the power of money that he envies:[22]

Deslauriers ambitionnait la richesse, comme moyen de puissance sur les hommes. Il aurait voulu remuer beaucoup de monde, faire beaucoup de bruit, avec trois secrétaires sous ses ordres, et un grand dîner politique une fois par semaine.

His views are too violent, so that he could never have a following. At Frédéric's house-warming party he burst out against the social order:[23]

Je bois à la destruction complète de l'ordre actuel, c'est-à-dire de tout ce qu'on nomme Privilège, Monopole, Direction, Hiérarchie, Autorité, Etat! – et, d'une voix plus haute: – que je voudrais briser comme ceci, en lançant sur la table le beau verre à patte, qui se fracassa en mille morceaux.

These sentiments have been heard many a time before and since. Probably his treachery to his friends is also known. But Frédéric, who has great faithfulness in his make-up, feels tied to him for evermore by memories of childhood. The last person in the novel to whom he speaks is Deslauriers, being more intimate with him than with any of his other friends – indeed what other friends does he possess?

The other members of Frédéric's entourage appear shortly, from time to time, deftly sketched, in order to fill in one or other section of society. Cisy is the conventional and unintelligent member of the effete aristocracy. Martinon is the hard-working egoist, with no thought except for his own advancement, and he does nothing to jeopardize that. He seeks out the mighty of the land and marries the rich heiress of Dambreuse – he ends up as a senator. Hussonnet represents the journalists, the new form of journalism brought in by Émile de Girardin. Sénécal is the extreme revolutionary republican. He is a puritan who looks like an ecclesiastic, and he is opposed to all pleasure, all grace in life, which he thinks corrupt. He wants no kind of distinction, nothing that raises one man above the other, no honours:[24]

Tout ce qu'il jugeait lui être hostile, Sénécal s'acharnait dessus, avec des raisonnements de géomètre et une bonne foi d'inquisiteur. Les titres nobiliaires, les croix, les panaches, les livrées surtout, et même les réputations trop sonores le scandalisaient, ses études comme ses souffrances avivant chaque jour sa haine essentielle de toute distinction ou supériorité quelconque.

165

His idea of democracy is law and order under authority. When
Frédéric tells him that he is very hard for a democrat, when he
unfairly fines a worker, he answers:[25]

> La Démocratie n'est pas le dévergondage de l'individualisme. C'est
> e niveau commun sous la loi, la répartition du travail, l'ordre!
> – Vous oubliez l'humanité! dit Frédéric.

It is not surprising to discover later that he eventually becomes
a policeman, who kills the only true democrat and republican,
the only honest man in their group and one to whom, in any case,
he owes a great deal. We have seen that he kills Dussardier when,
during the *coup d'état* of 2 December 1851, he had cried 'Vive la
République'. Dussardier is happy enough to die then, as he thinks
that the Republic which was gained in 1848 has been ruined:[26]

> Est-ce que tout n'est pas fini, d'ailleurs? J'avais cru, quand la
> révolution est arrivée, qu'on serait heureux. Vous rappelez-vous
> comme c'était beau! comme on respirait bien! Mais nous voilà
> retombés pire que jamais.
> Et, fixant ses yeux à terre:
> – Maintenant, ils tuent notre République, comme ils ont tué l'autre,
> la romaine! ... D'abord on a abattu les arbres de la Liberté, puis
> restreint le droit de suffrage, fermé les Clubs, rétabli la censure, et
> livré l'enseignement aux prêtres en attendant l'Inquisition. Pourquoi
> pas? ...
> Il se prit le front à deux mains; puis écartant les bras comme dans
> une grande détresse:
> – Si on tâchait cependant! Si on était de bonne foi, on pourrait
> s'entendre! Mais non! Les ouvriers ne valent pas mieux que les
> bourgeois ... Il n'y a pas de moyen! pas de remède! Tout le monde est
> contre nous! ... J'en deviendrai fou si ça continue. J'ai envie de me
> faire tuer.

Perhaps he has some intuition that he will, in fact, be killed shortly
afterwards, and he certainly does nothing to save himself.

There is a sweet natural goodness in Dussardier which made
many people think him stupid and naïf. It is ironic to think that
once, when Sénécal is released from prison, Dussardier, who is a
very poor man, spends a large sum of money which he cannot
afford on a party to celebrate the occasion. Also he sacrifices the
whole of his life's savings in order to save Rosanette from being
sold up. Yet he is often horrified by the licence of the age and

says, to the mockery of his friends, that he would like to love one woman only for the whole of his life He gives all his time and energy to furthering the cause of the Republic and, eventually, dies for it. He is the one person who redeems the generally worthless characters in the novel.

In *Madame Bovary* Flaubert had been an incomparable painter of Rouen, which fills its pages. Now, in *L'Éducation Sentimentale*, he rivals Baudelaire in his depiction of Paris, and there are many scenes which could be part of the poet's *Spleen de Paris*. The Seine runs through the whole novel as a symbol, as it had done all through Flaubert's life. Most of the significant things which happen to Frédéric happen along the river, beginning with his picking up Marie Arnoux's shawl on the way from Paris to Nogent. The scenes along the river as they go by, with the little houses, the gardens of which run down to the river's edge, are very like what they are still today. But Paris itself particularly moved the author and he evoked it with great sensitivity and emotion:[27]

Les rues étaient désertes. Quelquefois une charrette lourde passait, en ébranlant les pavés. Les maisons se succédaient avec leurs façades grises, leurs fenêtres closes ... Un air humide l'enveloppa; il se reconnut au bord des quais.

Les réverbères brillaient en deux lignes droites, indéfiniment, et de longues flammes rouges vacillaient dans la profondeur de l'eau. Elle était de couleur ardoise, tandis que le ciel, plus clair, semblait soutenu par les grandes masses d'ombre qui se levaient de chaque côté du fleuve. Des édifices, que l'on n'apercevait pas, faisaient des réboublements d'obscurité. Un brouillard lumineux flottait au delà, sur les toits; tous les bruits se fondaient en un seul bourdonnement; un vent léger soufflait.

Il s'était arrêté au milieu du Pont Neuf, et tête nue, poitrine ouverte, il aspirait l'air. Cependant, il sentait monter du fond de lui-même quelque chose d'intarissable, un afflux de tendresse qui l'énervait, comme le mouvement des ondes sous ses yeux. A l'horloge d'une église, une heure sonna, lentement, pareille à une voix qui l'eût appelé.

There are, in *L'Éducation Sentimentale*, passages of descriptive writing which reveal what an incomparable prose artist Flaubert was – pictures like those of an impressionist painter. There are scenes in Fontainebleau, where Frédéric takes Rosanette during the Revolution of 1848, which resemble Sisley landscapes. Noth-

Flaubert the Master

ing like this had been achieved for Fontainebleau since Sénancour composed *Obermann* in 1804: [28]

> La lumière, à de certaines places éclairant à la lisière du bois, laissait les fonds dans l'ombre; ou bien, atténuée sur les premiers plans par une sorte de crépuscule, elle étalait dans les lointains des vapeurs violettes, une clarté blanche. Au milieu du jour, le soleil, tombant d'aplomb sur les larges verdures, les éclaboussait, suspendait des gouttes argentines à la pointe des branches, rayait le gazon de traînées d'émeraudes, jetait des taches d'or sur les couches de feuilles mortes; en se renversant la tête, on apercevait le ciel, entre les cimes des arbres. Quelques-uns, d'une altitude démesurée, avaient des airs de patriarches et d'empereurs, ou, se touchant par le bout, formaient avec leurs longs fûts comme des arcs de triomphe; d'autres, poussés dès le bas obliquement, semblaient des colonnes près de tomber.

There are many more such passages.

There is the unforgettable scene, with its marvellous effect of light, of the return from the races in the Champ de Mars, up the Avenue des Champs-Élysées: [29]

> Par moments, les files des voitures, trop pressées, s'arrêtaient toutes à la fois sur plusieurs lignes. Alors on restait les uns près des autres, et l'on s'examinait. Du bord des panneaux armoriés, des regards indifférents tombaient sur la foule; des yeux pleins d'envie brillaient au fond des fiacres; des sourires de dénigrement répondaient au ports de tête orgueilleux; des bouches grandes ouvertes exprimaient des admirations imbéciles; et, çà et là, quelque flâneur, au milieu de la voie, se rejetait en arrière d'un bond, pour éviter un cavalier qui galopait entre les voitures et parvenait à en sortir.
>
> Puis tout se remettait en mouvement; les cochers lâchaient les rênes, abaissaient leurs longs fouets; les chevaux animés, secouant leur gourmette, jetaient de l'écume autour d'eux; les croupes et les harnais humides fumaient, dans la vapeur d'eau que le soleil couchant traversait. Passant sous l'Arc de Triomphe, il allongeait, à hauteur d'homme, une lumière roussâtre, qui faisait étinceler les moyeux des roues, les poignées des portières, le bout des timons, les anneaux des sellettes, et, sur les deux côtés de la grande avenue, pareille à un fleuve où ondulaient des crinières, des vêtements, des têtes humaines, les arbres tout reluisants de pluie se dressaient, comme deux murailles, vertes. Le bleu du ciel, au-dessus, reparaissait à de certaines places, avait des douceurs de satin.

Flaubert always liked big scenes – the *pièces montées*. In *Madame Bovary* it had been the wedding breakfast and the agricultural show. In *L'Éducation Sentimentale* there is the same technique, and he usually has his scenes in pairs. There is the orgiastic and vulgar fancy-dress ball at the house of Rosanette contrasted with the sober and more boring party at the house of Madame Dambreuse. There is the lunch given by Frédéric to entertain his college friends contrasted with the one given by Cisy which was attended largely by the aristocracy. As was natural in the circumstances, and usual with Flaubert, food and drink play a very important part in the proceedings. There are few writers who enjoy the description of banquets more than he and there is not one of his novels which does not contain the description of some feast.

There are also, in *L'Éducation Sentimentale*, the description of the sack of the Palais Royal and the Tuileries Palace which Flaubert himself had seen during the February Revolution of 1848:[30]

Tout à coup *La Marseillaise* retentit. Hussonnet et Frédéric se penchèrent sur la rampe. C'était le peuple. Il se précipita dans l'escalier, en secouant à flots vertigineux des têtes nues, des casques, des bonnets rouges, des baïonnettes et des épaules, si impétueusement, que les gens disparaissaient dans cette masse grouillante qui montait toujours, comme un fleuve refoulé par une marée d'équinoxe, avec un long mugissement, sous une impulsion irrésistible. En haut, elle se répandit, et le chant tomba.

On n'entendait plus que les piétinements de tous les souliers, avec le clapotement des voix. La foule inoffensive se contentait de regarder. Mais de temps à autre, un coude trop à l'étroit enfonçait une vitre ; ou bien un vase, une statuette déroulait d'une console, par terre. Les boiseries pressées craquaient. Tous les visages étaient rouges ; la sueur en coulait à larges gouttes.

Then, in the official hall, the throne is insulted – working men, in filthy clothes, sit on it, demonstrate their power. Then they seize it and fling it out of the window, where it is carried away by the populace. A fiercer spirit breaks out:

Alors une joie frénétique éclata, comme si, à la place du trône, un avenir de bonheur illimité avait paru ; et le peuple, moins par vengeance que pour affirmer sa possession, brisa, lacéra les glaces et les rideaux, les lustres, les flambeaux, les tables, les chaises, les tabourets, tous les meubles, jusqu'à des albums de dessins, jusqu'à des corbeilles de tapisserie. Puisqu'on était victorieux, ne fallait-il pas s'amuser ! La canaille s'affubla ironiquement de dentelles et de cachemires. Des crépines d'or s'enroulèrent aux manches des blouses, des chapeaux à

plumes d'autruche ornaient la tête des forgerons, des rubans de la
Légion-d'Honneur firent des ceintures aux prostituées ... Et le délire
redoublait son tintamarre continu des porcelaines brisées et des
morceaux de cristal qui sonnaient, en rebondissant comme des lames
d'harmonica ...
Une curiosité obscène fit fouiller tous les cabinets, tous les recoins,
ouvrir tous les tiroirs. Des galériens enfoncèrent leurs bras dans la
couche des princesses, et se roulaient dessus par consolation de ne
pouvoir les violer.

These passages, amongst the most vivid in the novel, help to an
understanding of the atmosphere of the Revolution.

L'Éducation Sentimentale is a serious novel, but, nevertheless, it
gives Flaubert the opportunity of showing his gift for grotesque
comedy. There is the duel between Frédéric and Cisy.[31] At the
luncheon party given by the latter, the former thinks that his
friend has insulted Madame Arnoux and he flings a dish from the
table into his face, which breaks two bottles of wine and several
large plates before hitting him. Cisy, egged on by his friends,
challenges Frédéric to a duel. Neither of them knows anything
about fighting, neither has ever shot or fenced. There is all the
humour of finding seconds and arranging the conditions of the
contest, and meeting at dawn in the Bois de Boulogne. Both
heroes are terrified, but Frédéric manages to disguise his fear
under bravado while Cisy, when the duel is about to begin, faints
and falls to the ground. Then Arnoux arrives post-haste in a
carriage, thinking that Frédéric has been defending him, leaning
out of the door and shouting 'Stop! stop!' In the meantime Cisy
has recovered and it is discovered that he is bleeding from his
thumb, which he has scratched as he fell. He is bandaged and his
arm is put in a sling. Blood has flowed, so honour is safeguarded,
and the two enemies shake hands and go each his own way.

There is also the scene where Frédéric, after the Revolution of
February 1848, tries to enter politics and to become a candidate for
parliament. Flaubert must have enjoyed showing up the foolishness and inconsequence of all the speeches, with their clichés on
the abolishment of poverty and prostitution, of the Church and
privilege, of all law and order. There is the reciting of the
fashionable poem of the day, *La Casquette*:[32]

> Chapeau bas devant ma casquette,
> À genoux devant l'ouvrier.

Then comes the interruption of Frédéric's carefully prepared speech, by the patriot from Barcelona who speaks only Spanish. We have seen that the novel proper ends with the *coup d'état* of 2 December 1851. This marks the break-up of all the ties and hopes which had been cherished since the Revolution. Everything has now gone, in public and in private life. Frédéric has abandoned Rosanette, has broken off his engagement to Madame Dambreuse, and Marie Arnoux has left Paris for good. Everything gained by the Revolution of 1848 is finally buried on 2 December 1851. That ends the sentimental education of the young men of the story.

There is, however, the Epilogue of two chapters, taking place sixteen years later, in which Flaubert finishes off the events and brings his readers up to date. As in a classical play, he liked to round off his characters' lives and to show what they had become. The first of these chapters winds up the love story, which, as we have seen, is the centre and the core of the novel. It is the finest scene in the whole of Flaubert – one of the finest in French literature – and the reader feels that it must have had its counterpart in real life. It begins baldly, with a statement of the vain life which Frédéric has led, since we saw him last, returning defeated from Nogent, seeing his last hope of marriage destroyed by his friend Deslauriers; and then seeing another friend, Dussardier, murdered by Sénécal. Incidentally Proust greatly admired this opening:[33]

Il voyagea.

Il connut la mélancolie des paquebots, les froids réveils sous la tente, l'étourdissement des paysages et des ruines, l'amertume des sympathies interrompues.

Il revint.

Il fréquenta le monde, et il eut d'autres amours encore. Mais le souvenir continuel du premier les lui rendit insipides; et puis la véhémence du désir, la fleur même de la sensation était perdue. Ses ambitions d'esprit avaient également diminué. Des années passèrent; et il supportait le désœuvrement de son intelligence et l'inertie de son cœur.

Then one day in March 1867, towards evening, when he is alone in his study, a woman enters – it is Madame Arnoux. She comes on the pretext of returning to him a sum of money which he has lent her in the olden days, and she has enclosed it in a note case embroidered by herself with golden palm leaves.

After talking of many things in the past, she expressed a desire to go for a walk in the neighbourhood, and, like the two old characters in Verlaine's *Colloque Sentimental*, they evoke the past:

Dans le vieux parc solitaire et glacé
Deux formes ont tout à l'heure passé.

Leurs yeux sont morts et leurs lèvres sont molles,
Et l'on entend à peine leurs paroles.

Dans le vieux parc solitaire et glacé
Deux spectres ont évoqué le passé.

Marie Arnoux says:[34]

– Quelquefois, vos paroles me reviennent comme un écho lointain, comme le son d'une cloche apporté par le vent; et il me semble que vous êtes là, quand je lis des passages d'amour dans les livres.
– Tout ce qu'on y blâme d'exagéré, vous me l'avez fait ressentir, dit Frédéric. Je comprends Werther que ne dégoûtent pas les tartines de Charlotte.

Flaubert has here, and later, used ironically the clichés of Romantic literature, but the characters would have thought these things and they were no less sincere for being obvious. He acted in the same way in *Madame Bovary*, in the seduction scene at the Comices Agricoles when Rodolphe uttered the same kind of clichés, which were so subtly used as to be moving. Flaubert continues:[35]

Comme si la plénitude de l'âme ne débordait pas quelquefois par les métaphores les plus vides, puisque personne, jamais, ne peut donner l'exacte mesure de ses besoins, ni de ses conceptions, ni de ses douleurs, et que la parole humaine est un chaudron fêlé où nous battons des mélodies à faire danser les ours, quand on voudrait attendrir les étoiles.

When they get back to his house, she removes her hat and Frédéric sees, with a stab of pain, that she is now quite white – it was like a blow in his chest. To hide his disappointment and shock, he kneels down beside her, and, taking both her hands in his, he begins to murmur words of love.

– Votre personne, vos moindres mouvements me semblaient avoir dans le monde une importance extra-humaine. Mon cœur, comme de la poussière, se soulevait derrière vos pas. Vous me faisiez l'effet d'un clair de lune par une nuit d'été, quand tout est parfums, ombres douces, blancheurs, infini; et les délices de la chair et de l'âme étaient contenues, pour moi, dans votre nom que je répétais, en tâchant de le baiser sur mes lèvres. Je n'imaginais rien au delà. C'était Madame Arnoux telle que vous étiez, avec ses deux enfants, tendre, sérieuse, belle à éblouir, et si bonne! Cette image-là effaçait toutes les autres. Est-ce que j'y pensais seulement! Puisque j'avais toujours au fond de moi-même la musique de votre voix et la splendeur de vos yeux.

She accepts delightedly this tribute to the woman she once was but no longer is, and Frédéric, becoming drunk with his own eloquence, almost believes what he is saying.

Most readers consider that Frédéric no longer loves Marie Arnoux, but is only being courteous and kind. This sentence would lead to such an opinion and certainly this was Flaubert's intention in one of the first plans but, as has been frequently remarked, he changed his conception after he met Élisa Schlésinger again in 1865. It must, however, be remembered that Frédéric has never forgotten Marie Arnoux – as the beginning of the chapter proves – and she has made it impossible for him to love anyone else. Certainly now his passion rises – if only temporarily, but genuinely:

Il sentait sur son front la caresse de son haleine, à travers ses vêtements le contact indécis de tout son corps. Leurs mains se serrèrent; la pointe de sa bottine s'avançait un peu sous sa robe, et il lui dit presque défaillant:
– La vue de votre pied me trouble.
Un mouvement de pudeur la fit se lever. Puis, immobile, et avec l'intonation des somnabules:
– A mon âge! lui! Frédéric! . . . Aucune n'a jamais été aimée comme moi! Non, non! à quoi sert d'être jeune? Je m'en moque bien! je les méprise, toutes celles qui viennent ici.

He assured her that none ever came there on account of his love for her and he takes her in his arms:

Elle y restait, la taille en arrière, la bouche entr'ouverte, les yeux levés. Tout à coup elle le repoussa avec un air de désespoir; et comme il la suppliait de lui répondre, elle dit en baissant la tête:
– J'aurais voulu vous rendre heureux.

He feels a stronger passion than ever, 'une convoitise plus forte que jamais, furieuse, enragée'.

But then his mood changes and, as usual, irresolution seizes him. He does not know any more now then he does at any other time what it is he really wants – except that he does not wish to make a decision. He suspects that she has come to offer herself to him and he is now seized with perplexity. It is too late. He feels afraid, afraid of destroying his dream and his illusion. He could never have brought himself to have taken her. Also it would seem almost like incest at her age. Moreover he is afraid that he might grow tired of her later, and what a bother it might all be. And so, not to destroy his ideal, he turns away and lights a cigarette. Eleven o'clock strikes and she says that she will leave at quarter past. She sits while he walks about smoking, but they have nothing further to say to one another – the moment has passed. 'Il y a un moment, dans les séparations, où la personne aimée n'est déjà plus avec nous.' She knows that everything is now over and she accepts it. When it is almost half past, she rises, and taking her hat, she says:

– Adieu, mon ami, mon cher ami! Je ne vous reverrai jamais! C'était ma dernière démarche de femme. Mon âme ne vous quittera pas. Que toutes les bénédictions du ciel soient sur vous!
Et elle le baisa au front comme une mère.

Then she cuts a lock from her white hair, and, giving it to him, she leaves. With great intensity of emotion and economy of phrase, Flaubert makes us feel the dead weight of the vanished years, and the poignancy of the woman who has grown old:

Quand elle fut sortie, Frédéric ouvrit sa fenêtre. Madame Arnoux, sur le trottoir, fit signe d'avancer à un fiacre qui passait. Elle monta dedans. La voiture disparut.
Et ce fut tout.

This is how, for artistic reasons, Flaubert ends the affair. But, as we shall see, in real life, the dream which began so many years before on the beach at Trouville ended differently.

The dénouement of the love story is also not the end of the novel, and there is a second chapter in the Epilogue. Flaubert wanted to finish the book on a note of frustration, disillusionment and failure. When sending the book to a reviewer, he said that the sub-title *Histoire d'un Jeune Homme* is not correct: 'a bad title,' he said, ' the real title should be *Les Fruits Secs*.' It is an account of general failure. It is firstly the account of the failure of a régime, the decline and fall of the July Monarchy. It is also the chronicle of the failure of each of the characters in the book. All of them – like Emma Bovary – dream dreams beyond their powers of realization, although theirs is not an ending of high tragedy like hers, but sordid failure and the petering out of ambition. It shows the vanity of all dreams – that indeed was Flaubert's philosophy of life.

In *L'Éducation Sentimentale* everyone fails, even the most ambitious and unscrupulous place-hunters. At the end of *Madame Bovary*, the gross chemist Homais is left in command as the successful member of society, who reaches his full ambition when he is decorated with the cross of the Légion-d'Honneur. In *L'Éducation Sentimentale* no one succeeds, unless one makes the exception of Martinon, who becomes a senator; but he has counted for very little. In the final chapter, we are told what has happened to the characters since the end of the novel proper, since the *coup d'état* of December 1851. Sénécal has disappeared no one knows where, and he had, in any case, abandoned his early ideals and become a fascist. La Maréchale, Rosanette, had married her rich protector, become a widow, and grown stout; and there was nothing now left of the beautiful, gay young woman of sixteen years before. All their friends had failed in the same way. The ambitious Deslauriers, whose ruthlessness seemed to mark him out for success, through various failures of judgement and chance has eventually sunk down to be a small clerk in a provincial office.

And Frédéric, has he too failed? He is the hero of the book and, to reveal his philosophy of life, Flaubert needed a weak character who was bound to fail. It can certainly not be claimed that he has made a success with his life, in spite of all his advantages of fortune and gifts. He makes nothing of any of his talents, and he has become neither a great writer nor a great painter, nor has he become a public figure. He has squandered two-thirds of his fortune so that he can afford now to live only as a petty bourgeois. He has nothing to show for the sixteen years since the Second Empire was founded; he has done nothing in all this time, except travel a little, indulge in a few unsatisfactory love affairs and dream of what might have been in a more perfect love. His character is weak and ineffective, and he lacks the strength to succeed even in his love affair with Marie Arnoux – we have seen how this ended a few months before. Flaubert, analysing his character in one of his *Carnets,* says of him:[36]

Un défaut radical d'imagination, un goût excessif – trop de sensualité – pas de suite dans les idées – trop de rêveries, l'ont empêché d'être un artiste.

In the final chapter the two friends, Frédéric and Deslauriers, go over their past, trying to see the reasons for their failure, and also to find out what was the happiest time in their lives. They come to the conclusion that their best day was the one when they failed to go to the brothel. They had planned the visit carefully, to take place when the rest of the village was at Vespers; they had dressed themselves in their best clothes, had their hair curled – they were fifteen at the time – and each holding a bunch of flowers purloined from the garden of Frédéric's mother, they had gone to the house of ill-fame. But, when it came to the point and the women had smiled at them, Frédéric had thought they were laughing at him, and he fled leaving his friend behind. As Frédéric had the money, Deslauriers was forced to follow him. Now they vied with one another in adding comic details to the story.[37]

C'est là ce que nous avons eu de meilleur! dit Frédéric.
– Oui, peut-être bien? c'est là ce que nous avons eu de meilleur! dit Deslauriers.

This ending has been severely criticized as cynical and immoral, and frequently misunderstood. It has been thought that Flaubert was saying that their best moment had been when, as children, they had gone to the brothel. That was not however what Flaubert intended to say. On the contrary, he was saying that the best moment in their life had been when they had *not* carried out what they had planned. One of Flaubert's strongest beliefs was that happiness and fulfilment consist in anticipation and not in realization. The two youths had been frustrated in their attempt to reach sexual experience with the prostitutes, and so had not been disappointed or disillusioned. He believed that fulfilment cheapens aspiration. He himself was saved by his devotion to art, his worship of it, and this was the religion which, for him, made life worth living. Frédéric was lacking in such a faith.

However, in the last chapter, Frédéric is not completely open and frank with his friend. He does not mention his love for Marie Arnoux – he only answers casually when Deslauriers asks him what has become of her, saying that she is in Rome with her son and that her husband has died the previous year. He says nothing at all about her visit to him. His love for her has certainly been the greatest thing in his life; it has not reached complete fulfilment and so has not been spoilt by habitual disillusionment. He has kept her memory bright for sixteen years, never forgetting her, and why should he now no longer remember her? Like his creator he prefers memory to reality. He probably keeps her image in his shrine as Baudelaire has done that of his madonna:

> À la très-bonne, à la très-belle
> Qui fait ma joie et ma santé,
> À l'ange, à l'idole immortelle,
> Salut en l'immortalité!

Frédéric's feelings for his madonna could last him until the end, as Flaubert's were to do for Élisa Schlésinger.

Madame Bovary had been the sum of Flaubert's psychology. *L'Éducation Sentimentale* was the sum of his philosophy of life and this was what the public could not take. When the book came out, as we have seen, it was very unfavourably received. The truth is that the general public could not accept such a pessimistic, particularly drab view of life. As Flaubert said to the critic Céard:[38] 'The public only wants books which encourage its illusions, whereas *L'Éducation Sentimentale* . . .'

The general public was willing to accept catastrophe and noble tragedy; men crushed by fate or succeeding in defeating it even at great loss; but the characters in *L'Éducation Sentimentale* fail through their own weakness and inefficiency. Readers could not accept the general quality of greyness which pervaded the whole novel and its lack of purpose. It dealt with day-to-day events, which have little meaning and lead nowhere. It is intended to be banal and colourless, like real life. When he was composing *Madame Bovary* Flaubert had said that he would like to write a novel without any plot. One can say that he succeeded in this in *L'Éducation Sentimentale*.

The novel ends with the two heroes reviewing their life and considering it as ended, although they are only in their forties and could easily have twenty-five or thirty more years before them.

There is, however, no suggestion of how they might use them. They have no potentialities and will just drift aimlessly as they have done for sixteen years. Like most of the characters in the book, they are fundamentally frivolous and incurable amateurs who have no God. There is not one of them but prostitutes his art or his calling.

In Flaubert's own day, this disillusionment hurt and offended people even though their own ideals were materialistic. Flaubert saw the materialism but would not accept it; he was an idealist who could find no ideal but art great enough for his satisfaction. Henry James, writing in 1902, thought that the character of Frédéric was a mistake:[39] 'It was a mistake to propose to register in so mean a consciousness as that of such a hero, so large and so mixed a quantity of life as *L'Éducation Sentimentale* intends.' Today we, like Flaubert, have few illusions, and readers can now, without shock, accept the situation. We are used to heroes without ideals or purpose; our hero is the little man without any romantic glamour, leading a colourless and meaningless life. Frédéric Moreau is the ancestor of the anti-hero of the modern novel.

Part Two

The Third Republic

CHAPTER EIGHT

THE WAR AND THE COMMUNE

In the summer of 1870 Flaubert, in spite of his sadness, and even despair, on account of the death of so many friends in the past few months – Bouilhet, Sainte-Beuve, Duplan and finally Jules de Goncourt a few weeks previously – was working very hard. He was busy preparing the collection of Bouilhet's posthumous poems for publication, and his introduction to them: he was also trying to get an unpublished play of his friend, *Aïssé*, produced. He was, as well, working intermittently and in a desultory manner at his own *Tentation de Saint Antoine*. He was so busy, as he told Mademoiselle Leroyer de Chantepie, he had not the time nor the leisure yet to read a letter and a contribution which she had sent him, and he asked for leave to write to her later.[1] On the night of 14 to 15 July he took time off from his work to write to his niece, Caroline, when he experienced a temporary feeling of peace and almost happiness:[2]

I've rarely seen a night as beautiful as this one. The moon is shining through the tulip tree; the boats which pass cast shadows on the sleeping Seine, the trees are reflected in its waters, the sound of oars breaks the silence rhythmically; it is indescribable sweetness; it is, nevertheless, time to go to bed.

There is no word at all of the imminent war and he only sympathizes with her on the score of the terrible bourgeois she complains of living amongst.

Then, in the midst of this temporary respite and hard work, the Franco-Prussian war broke out on 15 July 1870, unexpected by him and by most people. It was fashionable then to despise

Prussia and to believe that Offenbach's *Grande Duchesse de Gérolstein* was a true picture of the country.

The first mention we have of the events in Flaubert's correspondence is in a letter to George Sand written the day after the declaration of war. He was disgusted at the enthusiasm for the conflict and, as yet, felt no patriotism. As he said to her:[3]

> I'm disgusted, distressed, at the stupidity of my fellow-countrymen. The incurable barbarity of humanity fills me with the blackest sadness. This enthusiasm which has, as motive, only one idea, gives me the longing to die so as not to see it. The good Frenchman wants to fight (1) because he thinks that he has been provoked by Prussia; (2) because the natural state of man is savagery; (3) because war contains an element of mysticism which carries away the masses. Have we returned to the great wars between races? I greatly fear it. The terrible butchery which is in prospect hasn't even a pretext. It is the longing to fight for the sake of fighting. I weep for the broken bridges, the blown-up tunnels, all that human achievement destroyed, in a word a radical negation.

He had not admired the Second Empire, but he thought that it should be defended to ensure law and order.[4]

He was, at first, cynically detached, but, before a week had gone by, he was beginning to feel anxiety and to be influenced by all those who talked of nothing but the war. The one person that he thought of incessantly was his niece, fearing that something might happen to her, even any unpleasantness. She was the person whom he loved most in the world. He did not yet realize the full significance of the war. Even at the beginning of August, he could still discuss it philosophically. As he said to George Sand:[5]

> Here is *natural man*. How can one then build up any theories? Praise, progress, enlightenment and the good sense of the masses, and the kindness of the French people. I assure you that here one would be lynched if one dared to mention peace. Whatever happens we are in regression for a long time.

However, as August advanced and events deteriorated, he began to grow anxious and involved, and he spent his time asking for news, trying to obtain any scrap that he could. Du Camp tells us that he believed every rumour that he heard, however far-fetched and improbable.[6] But one thing he would not believe in was the possibility of defeat, nor that the Germans would really reach

Paris and besiege it. He even believed an outlandish rumour that Bazaine had diverted the Moselle into a trench and had drowned twenty-five thousand Prussians there and many more elsewhere. [7]

In spite of his foolish optimism, things went from bad to worse and finally, on 1 September 1870, a hundred thousand French soldiers, under the leadership of their Emperor and Commander in Chief, were surrounded by the Prussians at Sedan and capitulated. They were carried off to Germany as prisoners. Flaubert wrote to Edmond de Goncourt that this was one of the worst defeats in French history but that he was confident that the country would rise again. [8]

With the complete *débâcle* at Sedan the war ceased being a mere dynastic struggle and became a national concern. The country as a whole would not accept defeat. It repudiated Napoleon with the Empire, and a Republic was declared on 4 September.

The news of the defeat at Sedan reached Paris on 3 September and Princesse Mathilde decided to leave the capital. She went first to Rouen and it was thought that she would spend some days with Flaubert, but she was advised to proceed immediately to Belgium, as feeling was high against the Bonapartes – she would not have consented to go to England. She spent the war months and the Commune in Brussels and returned to Paris only after peace was declared. It has never been decided whether all the cases of money, jewels and valuables with which she is alleged to have escaped really belonged to her – forty or fifty cases were mentioned. It is difficult in kingdoms to distinguish between what is private property and what belongs to the state. In any case, in revolutions, aristocrats have always escaped with as much loot as they could. Flaubert said goodbye to her in Rouen and then did not see her until after the war ended, in the middle of March 1871, when he spent four days in Brussels.

Now that the army was defeated Flaubert was seized with patriotism and with a longing to come to the help of his country, to save it from further defeat, and to prevent the occupation of Paris. He signed on as a male nurse at the Hôtel Dieu at Rouen, to occupy himself until he could leave to defend Paris, which he could not at the moment, as he was responsible for his mother. He had also enlisted in the National Guard as a lieutenant, and drilled his men by day and by night with great fierceness, threatening to run through the belly with his sword the first man who did not advance.[9] He shed no tears on the disappearance of the Empire, declaring that he had always been a republican, but he feared for the Republic. 'Whatever happens,' he wrote to George Sand,[10] 'the people now in power will be sacrificed, and the Republic will suffer the same fate. Please note that I'm defending it, the poor Republic, but I don't believe in it.'

In the meantime, in the midst of all these tragic events, Caroline, with her usual disregard for anyone's interests and comfort but her own, went off to London, with her maid, although there was no danger at Dieppe, where her country house was situated, nor yet at Rouen or at Croisset. She is alleged to have gone to her former governess Juliet Herbert, but we have seen that it may have been to a family called Farmer, friends of her grandmother. Her action left her old grandmother, who had brought her up since her birth, at Croisset, in imminent danger of invasion by the Germans, and preventing her uncle from going to the war, as he longed to do. But even in the midst of his anxieties and sorrows for France, like a Père Goriot Flaubert worried lest the food in England might not be nourishing enough for her, and that she might fall ill. He advised her to leave the bad climate of London and to take a flat in Brighton, where her maid could cook suitable meals for her. This was at a moment when the siege of Paris was in full swing and the people were starving.[11] He told her of the beauty spots that she should see in London and in the neighbourhood.

In the meantime, in England, with her natural regard for her own interests, and believing that the Prussians would win, she was learning German. Her uncle may have been ironic – though he would normally not have been capable of sarcasm with her when he wrote to her: 'I marvel at your energy in being able to learn German. But you're right to keep occupied; I am unable to do so. I listen incessantly for the sound of the drums.'[12]

After the defeat of the Imperial armies at Sedan, the war was continued by the new Republic. However, it pleased no one, neither those who regretted the Empire nor the advanced Republicans who thought it too reactionary, and there was great division of opinion. There were those who thought that the war was lost and that peace should be sought immediately at all costs; and there were those who thought that France should fight to the last man to defend the country.

Meanwhile the Prussians had been advancing on Paris and, by 20 September, they had completely cut off the capital from the rest of France. Then began the historic siege which was to last four months, although it was thought that the city could not possibly hold out for more than a few weeks. Flaubert was not in Paris during the siege, but its hardships and sufferings are known through the accounts of foreign correspondents and French writers. The population was reduced to eating rats and mice, cats and dogs, while the rich had cuts off the joints of the animals from the zoo – tigers and lions and the beloved pair of elephants, Castor and Pollux.

As is usual in France on these occasions – it happened also in 1940 – there were those who spoke of the defeat being a chastisement for the country, for its too easy living, for its *douceur de vivre*. This disgusted Flaubert, and he wrote to George Sand:[13] 'The ready-made phrases are not lacking. France will rise again! One must not despair! It is a wholesome chastisement! We were really too immoral, etc.!'

Flaubert considered that Paris should not capitulate and he declared that he would rather see it burnt to the ground, like Moscow, than yield and have the Prussians march into it.[14] He believed, as he said to Du Camp, that in a couple of weeks there would be a *levée en masse* and he got comfort from believing the wild rumour that a peasant, near Mantes, had strangled a Prussian with his own hands, and had torn him to pieces with his teeth.[15] He still hoped for victory by the armies of the Loire.

Up to this moment the Prussians had left the provinces in peace and Flaubert continued to live at Croisset with his old mother. But in October 1870 they advanced on Normandy and they were soon approaching Rouen. The armies commandeered food and stores and there was great hardship in the district. Flaubert describes the crowd, of close on three hundred poor people, converging on Croisset to beg for food at the door, and none were turned away. He thought then, with horror, of what would happen in the winter.[16] In the meantime the Prussians were approaching Croisset, one of the most comfortable houses in the neighbourhood. Flaubert was determined that he would leave the place the moment the first Prussian soldier crossed the threshold. He hid the manuscript and notes of *La Tentation de Saint Antoine* in a safe place in the grounds, and left with his mother and the old servant for Rouen, as yet free from Prussians. The Germans entered Croisset in the middle of December 1870, and Flaubert determined that he would return there only when the last of them had left. He resigned his commission in the National Guard, as discipline had completely disappeared and he could do nothing with the men.

His patriotism and love for his country had developed very much since the defeat of France and he suffered from the isolation of his country in Europe and the indifference of so many other countries to her fate. He wrote to Princesse Mathilde in exile:[17]

If the army of the Loire would march on Paris, then everything would not be lost, for the people of Paris will make a collective sortie, which will be terrible, I have no doubt. We have enough men and we shall soon have enough artillery, but what we lack are leaders, commanders. Oh! for a man! one single man! a good brain to save us! . . . The Prussians may spread indefinitely but, as long as Paris is not taken, France still lives.

Poor France, she who, for a century, has fought for America, for Greece, for Turkey, for Spain, for Italy, for Belgium, for everyone, and now everyone looks on coldly at her dying. How they hate us! And how they envy us, these savages! Do you know that they take pleasure in destroying works of art, luxurious objects, when they find them? Their dream is to destroy Paris, because Paris is beautiful.

I think constantly of the rue de Courcelles! And, on Sunday evening especially, I feel myself torn to pieces as if I were being cut in two.

It was true. England, which in the Crimean War had fought at her side was now against France. Her Queen, who fifteen years before had been charmed by the Emperor when she had visited Paris with her family, was now on Germany's side and wanted her to win. Her son-in-law, the Crown Prince, was leading the victorious armies in France.

Now that he had left Croisset, Flaubert begged his niece to return to her home in Dieppe, where everything was still safe, as her grandmother was pining away for lack of her. He said that he now deplored her plan of leaving France:[18]

We very rarely get letters from you, my poor Caro! Your last letter was that of the 15th. It seems to me that you could send us a letter by Dieppe c/o your husband as he tells us that he receives your letters regularly.

Your poor grandmother is getting worse and worse, morally speaking ... If the war continues much longer (which might easily happen) and if your absence continues, what will happen? Ah! what an unfortunate idea you had in going away! We would not (she and I) have suffered one quarter of what we have suffered, if you had remained with us.

But Caroline was deaf to all his entreaties. She returned to Dieppe only after the siege of Paris was well over, and the country had asked for an armistice, in the middle of February.

The siege of Paris was still continuing, but it was evident that it would soon have to be brought to an end as, by the New Year 1871, there was only sufficient food for a starvation diet for a couple of weeks.

The Prussians bombarded Paris in January 1871. On 22 January there was no food left, and civil war, and a rising of the populace, were imminent. The government then considered that an armistice must be sought. On 23 January Jules Favre led a deputation which called on Bismarck. The discussion continued for two days and Favre returned to Paris with the terms, but he went back to Bismarck on 25, 26, and 27 January. One of the difficulties was the question of the disarming of the National Guard, which Favre said would cause civil war. Eventually they were allowed to retain their arms, so that they could keep order, but this was the only concession. Favre returned to Paris in a state of collapse; he was a broken man and he fainted in the arms of his fifteen-year-old daughter.[19] At the stroke of midnight on 27 January the cannon ceased firing and the siege of Paris was over after one hundred and thirty days; the forts surrounding the town were then occupied by the Prussians.

The provinces were not consulted about the armistice nor informed immediately of it, and Gambetta received the telegram containing news of the capitulation only on 29 January. The Armistice was signed on 31 January and the blockade was raised on 1 February. The Armistice was, however, to take full effect only in March, after the Germans had triumphantly entered Paris. The Prussians took advantage of this to seize Dieppe and to levy an enormous tribute from the town, a million francs to be paid in three days, but this was finally reduced to four hundred thousand francs odd.[20]

After the signing of the Armistice the unpopular Gouverne-

ment de la Défense Nationale resigned to make way for the
National Assembly, to be elected at Bordeaux. Then, to the horror
and amazement of republican Paris, all the provinces, except for a
few of the larger towns, voted solidly for the extreme right
wing.

The peace terms were now being discussed at Versailles and, on
26 February, they were drawn up, but they were much more
severe than Thiers had anticipated: the cession of the provinces
of Alsace and Lorraine, and an indemnity of five milliards of
francs; but the occupation of Paris by the Prussian troops was the
final insult never to be forgiven or forgotten.

At first the people of Paris contemplated resistance, but it was
realized that this would do no good, as they had thrown away all
their trump cards, and it was finally decided to treat the invading
armies with silent contempt.

The march of the Prussian troops through Paris was to take
place on 1 March. At eight o'clock that morning a young lieutenant
and six troopers of the Fourteenth Prussian Hussars rode up to the
Étoile, jumped their horses over the chains and other obstructions
which Parisians had placed round the Arc de Triomphe, and
continued insouciantly through the sacred edifice.[21] This was the
beginning of the triumphal procession of the victors through the
capital of France. Thousands of Prussians marched through
Paris, completely boycotted by the inhabitants. As they rode
down the Avenue des Champs-Élysées a silent crowd glowered at
them. Not a shop or a café was open and no one spoke to them;
they were as isolated as if they had been lepers.

As soon as the last Prussian had withdrawn from the city, the
Parisians set to scrubbing the streets the enemy's feet had trodden
with disinfectant, cleansing the tainted pavement by the flames of
many bonfires. A huge beacon was kindled under the Arc de
Triomphe to purify the soil fouled by the invaders' tread. The
humiliation could finally be purged only in blood, but this
was not to happen until the following war. Now, in the Place de la
Concorde, the effigies of the towns of Alsace and Lorraine taken
by Germany, Metz and Strasbourg, were veiled in thick black
crêpe and remained so until November 1918, when the Germans
were defeated and the raped provinces returned to France.

Flaubert wrote to Princesse Mathilde after the Prussians had
tramped through Paris:[22]

Well! so it's all over! The shame is swallowed but not digested! I thought so much of you on Wednesday, and how I suffered! The whole day long I imagined that I saw the arms of the Prussians shining in the sunlight, down the Avenue des Champs-Élysées, and I heard, in imagination, their military bands, their odious bands, ringing out under the Arc de Triomphe. The man who sleeps in the Invalides must turn in his grave with rage.

The same gesture as was made in Paris on 1 March was also made in Rouen some days later, when Prince Frederick Charles came to review the troops and was received with silent contempt. It was Sunday, 12 March, and, from the previous Friday, all the houses had been hung with black flags. The Prussians tore them down, but they seemed to reappear as if by magic. All the shops had notices affixed to them saying 'closed on account of national mourning'.

Now that the war was over nothing could equal Flaubert's hatred and detestation of the Germans; he saw that he had never hated any people so much. He wrote to George Sand:[23]

I'll not try to tell you what I've suffered since the month of September. How did I not die of it? That is what astounds me. No one was as full of despair as I. Why? I've had bad moments in my life, I've suffered grievous losses; I've wept a great deal. I've swallowed down much agony. Well! all this accumulated suffering is nothing in comparison with this. I can't understand it! I can't console myself. I've no hope left. I didn't imagine that I was progressive, humanitarian, nevertheless! All the same I had illusions! What savagery! What retrogression! Bile chokes me! These officers who smash mirrors, in white gloves, who know Sanscrit and yet who fling themselves on Champagne; who rob you and send you their visiting cards; this war for money, these civilized savages, horrify me more than cannibals, and everyone will now imitate them.

But real peace was not yet to come, and a new form of disturbance and war was to start. The international war was replaced by civil war. The left-wing parties in Paris refused to accept the peace terms and determined to resist the recently elected government. On 28 March 1871, the Communards officially installed themselves in the Hôtel de Ville in Paris, and proclaimed the Commune, which was to last for two whole months and to end in what was called the 'Semaine Sanglante', when large sections of the city were burnt to the ground, including the Tuileries Palace and the Hôtel de Ville.

Flaubert remained with his niece in her villa near Dieppe for part of the Commune, but returned to Croisset at the beginning of April when all the Prussians had departed and the house was 'disinfected' of their presence.

He had never been politically minded, belonged to no party and was inexperienced and uninterested in political theories. He had not liked the Empire, had despised the new Republic and felt no affection for the Commune. He was no revolutionary, hated the manifestations of mass movements and disliked all forms of violence and the disruption of law and order. But he had loathed the German invasion so much that he had no hatred left for the Communards. The German invasion had been for him, as he said to George Sand,[24] 'one of these big upheavals of nature, the sort of cataclysm which occurs only once every six thousand years; while the insurrection of Paris, in my eyes, is a very clear event, almost simple'. After the German invasion he thought that nothing else could ever be a tragedy. He wrote to Madame Roger des Genettes:[25] 'Contrary to the general opinion, I can think of nothing worse than the German invasion. The complete destruction of Paris by the Commune would cause me less grief than the burning of a single village by these gentlemen.'

He considered that the worst aspect of the Commune was that it had displaced hatred, so to speak, and turned it from the Germans to the Communards. The bourgeois were even grateful that the Prussians were still occupying the country, and many used to say: 'Thank God the Prussians are still here.' As he wrote to George Sand:[26] 'The Prussians no longer exist. They are excused and admired. *Sensible* people want to become naturalized Germans. I assure you that it is enough to make you despair of the whole human race.' There was praise of the Germans in most quarters, and they were said to be more civilized than the Communards.

During the Commune the Civil War occurred, when Frenchmen fired on Frenchmen, and there was the second siege of Paris, by the regular forces, the Versaillais, from Versailles, where the government sat. They managed to enter the capital through a ruse on 21 May and then began the '*Semaine Sanglante*', when, in anger and despair, the Communards tried to burn all Paris. But the

Versaillais moved on inexorably and, on Whit Sunday 1871, they advanced to finish off the rebels holding out in their last stronghold in Père Lachaise Cemetery. They were surrounded on all sides, with their backs, literally, to the wall and their ammunition almost exhausted. Then one hundred and forty-seven Communards were lined up against the wall of the cemetery and shot.

Then followed the appalling reprisals from the Versaillais, though there were terrible atrocities on both sides. Most people had wanted the Versaillais to win and they had had a great fright during the Commune – especially during the *'Semaine Sanglante'* – and so the atrocities of the Communards were played up and those of the Versaillais, which were described as necessary to restore law and order, were minimized. But both sides were guilty of atrocities. On the side of the Commune there was the shooting of prisoners and hostages; there were the *pétroleuses*, with their bottles of petroleum which they threw into buildings to set them on fire. It was alleged that they poisoned the soldiers entering the town by offering them poisoned water to drink – this was certainly universally believed.[27] There was the senseless and particularly brutal murder of the Archbishop of Paris, Monseigneur Darboy, with other hostages, amongst them the confessor of the Empress, the seventy-five-year-old Father Deguerry. Prisoners had their ears torn off as they were marched away, and their faces were lacerated by the women in the crowds – it was like the torture of Mâtho in *Salammbô*, when he ran the gauntlet of death. But the atrocities were as bad – or even worse – on the side of the Versaillais, though perhaps less primitive. What made it so particularly vile was that most of it occurred when the conflict was over and the Communards could do no more. It was pure vengeance. After the capture of Montmartre, forty-nine Communards, including four women and three children, were made to kneel in front of a wall and were shot without a semblance of investigation.[28] There were the hundred and forty-seven Fédérés, mentioned earlier, shot at the 'Mur des Fédérés' in Père Lachaise Cemetery. There were shootings in most of the cemeteries of Paris and in the Luxembourg Gardens; nineteen hundred prisoners were shot in two days.[29] There were the same kind of denunciations as occurred in 1945, when Paris was relieved. The soldiers entered houses suspected of hiding Communards, dragged out everyone they found within and shot them on the spot without investigation. Undoubtedly the Communards lost more heavily than the Versaillais. In the *'Semaine Sanglante'* the Communards lost three thousand men and the Versaillais only one thousand. Historians now generally agree that during, the two months of the Commune, they lost twenty thousand killed.[30]

Flaubert has been severely criticized, especially by Sartre, for not having come out strongly in writing against the reprisals of the Versaillais when the Commune was over. He had not, however, been in Paris at the time. He heard of horrible atrocities on both sides, but he did not have a clear picture of what had happened. He thought that the Communards were madmen and he had no sympathy with their aims and ideals, but he felt no animosity against them. He was not, however, alone in remaining silent, and no writer raised his voice in protest. It is therefore strange that he should have been singled out for obloquy. All had suffered so much during the war, the Siege and the Commune, that they were weakened in every way, physically and morally. What they now wanted was a period of law and order in which to recover, and to get on with their own work. Those who were disinterested and public-spirited wished to reconstruct their country and to repair the disasters of the war.

Flaubert was however capable of moral courage and of coming out strongly for what he believed in. Victor Hugo had returned from Guernsey on the fall of the Empire and turned towards the left, as the revolutionary he liked to think that he was. He gave the impression that he supported and admired the Commune, and this disgusted many of his admirers, and especially Flaubert's friend Lapierre, the editor of *Le Nouvelliste de Rouen*, who published in his paper an article attacking him.[31] The offensive paragraph was the following:

A man whom France, for a time, had believed that she could count amongst her most powerful geniuses, and who had the talent to earn for himself many thousands of pounds of income, through his sonorous phrases and fantastic antitheses, a wretched poet; at times the supporter of the Monarchy, of Bonapartism, of Republicanism – you have guessed, Victor Hugo – has just given his opinion on the appalling tragedy which we are undergoing. This product of deep softening of the brain, or lunacy, is entitled *Paris et la France*.

Flaubert was outraged and he wrote immediately to Lapierre:[32]

It's to you *alone* that I'm writing, and so I'll be able, without any awkwardness, to unburden my heart to you.

Your paper seems to me to be on a slippery slope, and it is sliding down so swiftly that your issue of this morning scandalized me! The paragraph on Hugo goes beyond everything. 'France had believed that she could count amongst her most powerful geniuses.' This 'had believed' is sublime! It means 'Formerly we had no taste, but revolutions have enlightened us in the matter of art,' and finally he's only a *wretched poet,* 'who had the talent to earn an income' (are you now attacking money?) . . . 'with sonorous phrases and fantastic antitheses'. Try to imitate him, my good fellows! I find you all very comical! . . .

But Proudhon had already said 'It needs more genius to be a boatman on the Rhine than to compose *Les Orientales.*' And Augustine Brohan, during the winter of 1853, proved in *Le Figaro* that the same Hugo had never possessed any talent whatsoever. Don't imitate that clown and this strumpet! In the interest of public order, and the return of moral standards, the first duty is to speak about what one knows. Let us choose our arms. Don't let us put our enemies in the right; and, when you wish to attack the personality of a great poet, don't attack him as a poet; otherwise those who understand poetry will shun you.

There is too much literature here and I ask your pardon! But, as an old Romantic, I was, this morning, exasperated by your paper. The foolishness of old Hugo pains me too much as it is, without his being insulted in his genius. When our masters demean themselves, we must do like the sons of Noah, cover their shame! Let us at least keep our respect for what was great! Don't let us add to our ruins.

Goodbye, but I hope to see you soon. Bile chokes me and grief devours me.

This letter was written during the worst of the '*Semaine Sanglante*'.

Flaubert visited Paris early in June 1871 to work at various libraries on the research for his *Tentation de Saint Antoine.* The capital still presented a terrible sight, less than a fortnight after the end of the Commune. The Tuileries Palace and the Hôtel de Ville were gutted, mere shells, and would have to be pulled down. In the Place de la Concorde the tritons of the fountains were twisted into nightmarish shapes. Candelabras were torn from the ground and the effigy of Lille was decapitated. As Flaubert says in letters to various correspondents, the state of the city disgusted and impressed him less than the state of mind of the inhabitants:[33]

The smell of the corpses nauseates me less than the stink of egoism which breathes from all mouths. The view of the ruins is nothing in comparison with the utter imbecility of the Parisians. With few exceptions everyone seemed to me to be raving mad. Half the population longs to strangle the other half, which shares the same longing. That is clearly visible in the eyes of all who pass by.

During his time in Paris he went to visit Princesse Mathilde at Saint-Gratien. She had suddenly gone back there before the Germans had left.[34] Earlier she had planned to go to Italy and settle there.[35] However, she changed her mind, as she could not stay away from France. George Sand wrote to him to say how nice it was to have the Princess back again in France.[36] 'I received a kind little note from Princesse Mathilde. It is good and kind of her to come back to her friends at the risk of fresh disturbances.' Flaubert did not, however, share these sentiments, and he answered:[37]

You attribute your qualities to others, judging them *a priori* to be full of good feelings. This is a reference to one of your recent letters, where you consider the return of Princesse Mathilde to Saint-Gratien beautiful, kind and brave. I consider it all right, but for me, as I like her and her society is agreeable to me. As far as she is concerned, I consider that she should have stayed longer in exile. That would have been braver and of a prouder spirit. I wrote to her what I thought about the matter. Then, seeing that she was dying to get back to France, I said no more about it, and I was even of service to her, for it was one of my intimate friends who took all the necessary steps for this. She came back to France because she is a spoilt child who does not know how to resist her desires. Here is the whole psychology of the matter, and I made her a great concession (which she did not realize) by going out to see her at Saint-Gratien, in the midst of the Prussians. There were two officials at the door. Although I've no Emperor's blood in my veins, a blush rose to my brow as I passed in front of the sentry-boxes. Wasn't I prepared to do without my house while the Prussians were in it? I consider that she might have done the same. Keep this to yourself, naturally, and don't let's mention it again.

Especially galling to Flaubert was the fact that she owed her return to the good offices of the Emperor William I of Germany, who assured her that she need have no worry about Saint-Gratien. The Pavillon de Catinat would still be occupied by the Prussians, but the house would be vacated.[38]

Flaubert would not personally have accepted such a favour from the enemy. Writing to Ernest Feydeau, who was in Baden, he said:[39]

What sticks in my gullet is the invasion of the doctors, smashing mirrors with gun-shots, stealing clocks; this is new in history. I have such a deep grudge against these gentlemen, *that you'll never see me in the company of a German whoever he may be,* and I blame you for being now in their infamous country. Why? When are you coming home?

Flaubert kept to this resolve for the rest of his life. He never did speak to a German again, and never set foot in the country, though Maxime Du Camp continued to spend the autumn at Baden every year, and Turgenev, who had a house there, often invited him to stay.

The French poet, Jules Laforgue, who was Reader to the Empress Augusta from 1881 to 1886, describes Du Camp as coming to tea with the Empress, and being on the most friendly and intimate terms with her. Yet he was a born and bred Parisian, who had seen her husband ride triumphantly at the head of his victorious army, through the streets of his native city twelve years before. Flaubert would not have behaved thus however long he lived.

Princesse Mathilde settled down comfortably at Saint-Gratien but everything was not happy for her at first, as people were still suspicious of any Bonaparte, and she was thought by some to be plotting a return of the Empire. She answered indignantly:[40] 'Me, conspire! And especially to come here to conspire! Do they not know that I ask only for the preservation of my person and of Saint-Gratien; my *individual liberty*, as I wrote to M. Thiers?'

As soon as the Commune was over Flaubert settled down in his Parc Monceau apartment and especially at Croisset now that the Germans had vacated it. He set to work again on Bouilhet's *Dernières Chansons* and his introduction to the book; and took up again his efforts to have *Aïssé* published and produced. Also, when he had any time, he worked at his *Tentation de Saint Antoine,* after he was able to retrieve his text and notes.

CHAPTER NINE

THE GHOST OF THE
DEAD YEARS

It was after the Commune that Flaubert saw, for the first time for nearly ten years – and also for the last time – the great love of his life, Élisa Schlésinger. As was natural there was no communication between them during the war. As we know, it was a very unhappy time for her, as her daughter, now a German, was sympathetic to the Prussians and hoped that they would win. Her brother, on the other hand, was fighting on the French side. Élisa, although living in Germany, had remained very French, and her state, during the war, was not a happy one. Maurice Schlésinger had died in February 1871, before the war ended, and Flaubert heard the news only in April. He wrote to her in May, when she had not received the letter he had written to her the previous month:[1]

You didn't then receive a letter from me, a month ago, as soon as I heard of the death of Maurice? Now yours of yesterday gave me pleasure, my dear old friend, always dear, yes always! Forgive my selfishness. I had hoped, for a moment, that you would come back and live in France with your son (without thinking of your grandchildren) and I had hoped that the end of my life would be spent not far from you. As for going to see you in Germany, that is a country where I wouldn't willingly set foot. I've seen enough Germans during this past year to wish never to see another, and I don't accept that a Frenchman who respects himself should design to be for a moment with one of these gentlemen, however charming they may be. They've got our clocks, our silver, our lands, let them keep them, and let's not mention it any more. I wanted to write kind things to you, and here bitterness overflows! It is that I have suffered so terribly for ten months – suffered enough to go mad, and to kill myself! I have, nevertheless, gone back to work, and I try to get drunk on ink, as others get drunk on brandy, to forget public misfortune and my personal sadness.

Élisa came to Trouville, in the autumn of 1871, to settle business in connection with her inheritance there. She visited Croisset in November and stayed with Flaubert and his mother. What did they talk of on that occasion, and did they mention *L'Éducation Sentimentale*, which had appeared exactly two years before? We do not know. She was now free, and they could have spent the rest of their lives together as she was not happy in Baden, but she had commitments in Germany. There were her grandchildren there and her doctor, who understood her case, for her mental health was still precarious. She returned to Baden and Flaubert's mother died the following April. He felt unable himself to write to tell Élisa of his loss and he asked Du Camp to do it for him. He wrote to her again in May, when she thought he had forgotten her:[2]

How! You! You! You suspect your old friend? How can you imagine that he can have forgotten you, especially at a moment when his heart is so moved? If I did not write to you, it is because *I hadn't the strength to do so*. That is my excuse. I ought to have answered your first letter, it is true, but I was so tired!

Try to stay in Paris until 20 June; I expect to be there at that time, and we'll meet a bit.

The more my life advances, the sadder it becomes. I am about to enter into complete solitude. I make wishes for the happiness of your son, as if he were mine. I embrace you both – but you a little more, my ever beloved.

She came over to Paris in June 1872 for the marriage of her son. Flaubert attended the ceremony and wept tears of emotion. The young man had been born at the height of Flaubert's friendship with the Schlésingers, when he was a student in Paris. The wedding of her son is the last occasion when Flaubert saw Élisa, and she does not seem, this time, to have gone to Croisset. The last letter to her which has come down to us is the one of 5 October 1872. Were there other letters? Her great-grandson said that many were burnt, but this is very doubtful:[3]

My dear old friend. My old affection.

I cannot see your writing without being deeply moved. And so, this morning, I voraciously tore open the envelope of your letter. I thought that it was going to announce your visit. But, alas, no! That will be when? Next year? I'd like so much to receive you in my house and to have you sleep in my mother's bedroom!...

I spent the month of September in Paris. I'll go back there for a fortnight at the beginning of December, to have a bust made of my mother, and then I'll come back here for as long as possible. It is in solitude that I'm happiest! Paris is no longer Paris, all my friends are dead, and those that are left don't count much, or else are so changed that I don't recognize them any more. Here, at least, nothing irritates me, nothing afflicts me directly... They have given me a dog and I take walks with him, gazing at the effect of the sun on the leaves which are turning yellow, and, like an old man, I dream of the past, for I *am* an old man. The future has no dreams for me, but the olden days arise before me bathed in a golden haze. On this bright background, where dear ghosts hold out their arms towards me, the figure which stands out most brightly is yours!—Yes, yours! Oh! poor Trouville!

He said to several friends, amongst them Madame Roger des Genettes,[4] in letters on that same day that dear figures beckoned to him out of the past, but only to Élisa did he specify that it was chiefly hers.

Élisa Schlésinger went back to Baden in the autumn of 1872. She was permanently interned in the mental hospital in 1875 and eventually died there. It is said that she herself asked to be interned, and there was no one now in Germany to care for her or about what happened to her. Did Flaubert know of her final internment? It is impossible to imagine that he did not. He knew her son, and Maxime Du Camp spent the autumn every year in Baden. Did she know of Flaubert's death in 1880? Again it is unlikely that she did not. In 1881, the year after Flaubert's death, Du Camp suddenly encountered her, as he tells in his *Souvenirs Littéraires,* in a group of women coming out of the asylum for exercise.[5]

The woman who walked in front was very old, gloomy and centred in herself; her eyes were fixed on the ground, her arms motionless. She seemed to glide along by an internal movement, which pushed her forward, without moving her body. Her hair was white and in disarray, and escaped from under an old battered straw hat, from which hung a tattered flower. Her skin was brown, with livid patches under her eyelids. Her lips were flattened, her cheeks hollow and indicated the absence of teeth. A shaggy tuft of bristly hairs had probably been a beauty mark in her youth. The whole of her person was imbued with desolation.

This decrepit old woman, however, bowed to him as she passed, and then, suddenly, he recognized Élisa Schlésinger. If she was not too mad to recognize him, then she was not too mad to receive the news of Flaubert's death. She eventually died in the mental home at Baden in 1888, at the age of seventy-eight.

And so the end of Flaubert's great love, the Fantôme de Trouville, was more poignant and tragic than in *L'Éducation Sentimentale*, but it was nearer to his early draft, when he first heard of her mental illness and had planned then that the heroine of his novel should die mad in a mental hospital.

At the end Flaubert could say of Élisa Schlésinger, as Baudelaire had said of Apollonie in *Hymne*:

> Comment, amour incorruptible,
> T'exprimer avec vérité?
> Grain de musc qui gis invisible
> Au fond de mon éternité!

Flaubert's mother died on 6 April 1872. She had been in failing health since the war and several times he had thought that she was on the point of death. Her last letter to her granddaughter was written in a shaky hand, a few days before she died:[6]

My dear little girl, Gustave must have told you that I had a good trip, but what he could not tell you was all the gratitude that I felt for all your care of me. Farewell, my children, I embrace you from the depths of my heart. Your old mother Caroline Flaubert.

She died a week later. A few moments after she had taken her last breath, Flaubert wrote to the woman who had been as a mother to him, to George Sand:[7] 'My mother has just died. I embrace you.'

He was shattered by the blow and realized, as soon as she had gone, that she was the person in his life whom he had most dearly loved, and that nothing could ever take her place:[8] 'I've noticed during the past fortnight that my poor old mother was the being whom I most loved. It is as if they had torn out part of my entrails.'

He never really got over her death and, at the funeral of Leconte de Lisle's mother, he wept openly in the church and cried:

'Heavens above! Old women like that, we should not have to lose them.'[9]

Madame Flaubert left Croisset to Caroline, but with the proviso that her son was to live there for the rest of his life, as if he owned it.

During her lifetime she had looked after her son's financial affairs and had taken charge of the family fortune. Now this duty fell on Caroline – or she thought that it did. The inherent nastiness of her character, which had been kept in check by her grandmother's presence, began to appear, and she tried now to make her uncle economize. With her 'hôtel' in Paris, her villa near Dieppe, and her luxurious life, she grudged everything that he spent on himself, and she wrote harshly to him when he was still overcome by grief for his mother's death. He was so bitterly hurt that he could not refrain from showing his wound, though his remonstrances were very mild:[10]

Another disappointment! I must wait until Saturday to see and have my famous niece, and she doesn't tell me how long she will stay with me – nor anything about the Dantsick [*sic*] trip. I imagine that it won't take place at all.

As for your financial letter, what was the point of it? You're not wrong in imagining that it made me sad! There was no point in reminding me of my poverty. I think of it enough as it is!

Do you imagine that your remarks will change my character? Do you think that I can *investigate the expenses of my servants*? Suicide would be sweet beside such a prospect, there is nothing to do but groan and become resigned.

I still have my apartment in Paris for two and a half years more. After that I'll naturally give it up – and then that will be all. My life is abominably arid, without pleasure, without pastimes, without affection. But I shan't put asceticism to the point of worrying about my cook! There's enough sadness without that. Enough! Let's not mention it again. And so I'll see you on Saturday, my dearest Loulou. I embrace you very hard. Your old Nanny.

In spite of his unhappiness and worry, Flaubert finished *La Tentation de Saint Antoine* on 1 July 1872. He did not, however, wish to publish it then, as he was pledged to offer it to Michel Lévy, and he did not want to do so on account of the publisher's meanness in connection with the publication of Bouilhet's posthumous poems. He decided to put his manuscript away until his contract had run out, and then to publish it at the same time as his next book, which would be *Bouvard et Pécuchet*.

To take his mind off his troubles he went to Bagnères-de-Luchon with his niece for a holiday, which he did not enjoy, as he was not in the mood for a holiday and his mind was occupied with thinking of his modern novel, which was to be *Bouvard et Pécuchet*.

After his return to Croisset, Flaubert remained very solitary without his mother. He especially missed her at mealtimes, as he had never eaten alone. He had only the old servant Julie as company and he used to make her wear his mother's clothes to have the illusion that she was still with him. His niece came to see him as little as possible, and he was very lonely.

He now regretted not having followed the ordinary course of life – marrying and having children. Having, in his youth, been horrified at the thought of procreation, he now longed for children of his own, when he saw Maurice Sand's little girls. If Caroline had had children it would have been different, he would have loved them as his own, but she had been married for eight years and was still childless. He wrote to George Sand:[11]

What you tell me, in your last letter, of your dear little girls, moved me to the bottom of my heart. Why haven't I anything like that? I was born, nevertheless, with all kinds of affection. But one doesn't make one's destiny, one can only submit to it. I was cowardly in my youth, and was afraid of life. Everything has to be paid for!

She endeavoured to soften his loneliness, to take him out of himself; and she tried to persuade him to marry, but he had left it too late and was now over fifty. She wrote to him:[12]

And then why don't you marry? To be alone is hateful, is mortal, and cruel to those who love you. All your letters are dismal and tear my heart. Have you no woman whom you love or by whom you might be loved with pleasure? Take her with you. Is there no child anywhere of whom you might imagine yourself the father? Bring him up! Become his slave, and forget yourself in him.

He answered her:[13]

As for living with a woman, to marry as you advise me to do, that seems to me a fantastic prospect! I don't know why! But that is how it is! Try to understand the problem. Woman has never fitted into my life. Then I'm not rich enough, and then, and then! I'm too old ...

and too decent to inflict my personality permanently on someone else. There is in me an ecclesiastical residue that no one knows of. We can talk of all this verbally better than in letters.

He was however often full of affection and tenderness. He wrote once to his niece:[14]

This afternoon, as I was alone, I took a walk to the kitchen garden!!! It was a wonderful day. I remained contemplating nature, and I was seized with such violent tenderness for a little calf lying beside its mother on the dried leaves, lit up by the sun, that I kissed it on the brow, the said little calf!

Flaubert suffered another grief that autumn which affected him greatly – the not unexpected death of Théophile Gautier in October 1872. Gautier went far back into his literary life and was someone whom he had looked up to and revered. He received the news too late to be able to attend his funeral, and this grieved him, for he felt that the last of his literary friends in Paris had now gone.

It must not however be thought that Flaubert's life was wholly gloomy at this time. He continued to go to Paris and to receive his friends on Sundays for literary discussion, and he was more and more sought after by learned men of the day. He continued to see Princesse Mathilde at her new house in the rue de Berri in Paris, and at Saint-Gratien. Edmond de Goncourt, however, thought that the Princess's *salon* had lost a great deal of its brilliance and refinement since the war.[15] He wrote:

The Princess's *salon*, this *salon* of letters and art, this *salon* resounding with the fine speech of Sainte-Beuve, with the Rabelaisian eloquence of Gautier, the angry repartees of Flaubert, with the witticisms of my brother, this *salon* which, in the flatness of taste, resounded with noble ideas . . . this *salon* was dying out like fireworks in the rain.

And again: 'There is a decline in the quality of those who dine with the Princess; the invitations are now descending as low as to producers of vaudevilles.'

The Princess herself was now appearing in the light of an author, which she would probably not have dared to do in the days of Sainte-Beuve. She wrote an account of her dead griffon called Didi, under the title *Histoire d'un Chien*, which was printed and read one evening at Saint-Gratien. Goncourt called it 'la sensiblerie sans art d'une pensionnaire', but he did not take it on himself to criticize it, as he knew that that was not what she wanted. Flaubert, however, who believed that everyone was as sincere as he was, as a writer, felt it necessary to correct her style as she went along and did not advise publication. This drew from Goncourt the remark: 'Isn't he still young, the poor old fellow! She has such a childish pleasure in imagining her prose becoming printed matter, on beautiful paper, that it would indeed be foolish to wish to hinder publication'.

George Sand was trying to take him out of himself and she frequently invited him to visit her at Nohant, but all through 1872 he was unable to face society. However, in March 1873, he wrote to her that he was beginning to feel better and to emerge from the dark tunnel.[16] He even talked of going to two fancy-dress balls. In April he was, at last, persuaded to go to Nohant to share in natural family life, and he spent some days with her. In her memoirs she describes his excessive energy, and how he wore her out. It was like being assaulted by a battering-ram, she said, and she felt as if she had been trampled on.[17] At the parties there were wild dances, in the course of which each of the participants changed clothes several times. Flaubert ended up as a woman Andalusian dancer, and performed the fandango.

It was after the war that Flaubert formed the last great male friendship of his life, with Edmond Laporte. It is true that he had met him in 1865 through Duplan, but Flaubert did not take him fully to his heart until his more brilliant friends had died. He possessed a lace factory at Grand-Couronne a few miles down the river from Rouen, and Flaubert could see him frequently when he was at Croisset. He was not brilliant and he had not the literary knowledge and experience of Bouilhet, so that he could not give Flaubert any help or advice on artistic matters. He was, however, a man of great loyalty and faithfulness and there was nothing that he would not have done for Flaubert. He helped him with his research, and much of the work for *Bouvard et Pécuchet* was done by him.

During the war and the Commune, when he had leisure, Flaubert had been working on Bouilhet's poems for posthumous publication, and also trying to get his friend's play, *Aïssé*, produced. He was also trying to get the monument erected in honour of the poet in his home town of Rouen. Work for the latter dragged on for over ten years, with many recriminations, and it was erected only when Flaubert had been dead for two years in 1882.

As soon as the Commune was over, Flaubert started in earnest collecting money for the monument. His plan was to have something erected in the middle of the town, not a mere cross over the grave in the cemetery. He wanted it to be sited near the library, where Bouilhet had spent the last years of his life.

His first letter to the Municipality, with a view to obtaining a site, was dated 2 August 1871:[18]

Monsieur le Maire,
    At the time of the death of Louis Bouilhet, a subscription was opened to erect a monument to him. The Commission elected for that purpose, of which I am the Chairman, thought that a tomb was not the best way in which to honour the memory of our friend . . . Therefore, Monsieur le Maire, it proposes, to the town of Rouen, the construction of a little fountain, decorated with the bust of Bouilhet, in one of the streets or squares of Rouen. We can provide a sum of twelve thousand francs.
    It goes without saying, Sir, that the design of the monument will be submitted for your approval.
    I need not insist on the propriety of our idea, being convinced in advance that you will support it . . .
    We cannot make any plans or estimates without knowing the site that you will choose.

As he received no answer he wrote again in the following January, an immensely long letter.[19] The Conseil Municipal refused the offer by thirteen votes to eleven. Flaubert protested, and said that he was responsible to the subscribers who had entrusted their money to him. He complained of the grounds for the refusal: that Bouilhet was not a native of Rouen and that his literary merit was not sufficiently recognized – one can readily imagine what Flaubert's reaction to this last opinion was. He drew attention to the distinguished names of the subscribers, amongst them the Comédie-Française, various literary societies, Dumas and Turgenev. He pointed out Bouilhet's long association with Rouen – he had been at school there, had studied medicine there and had ended up as librarian – and that his literary value was recognized by every town in Europe, where his works were displayed in the windows of all the bookshops. 'If it had been a question of homage to one of the big tycoons of our department, whose

fortune is counted in dozens of millions, would you have refused?
I doubt it.'

The letter is written in Flaubert's most ironic and vituperative
style. 'Conservateurs qui ne conservez rien', 'Classes éclairées
éclairez-vous', 'À cause de ce mépris pour l'intelligence, vous
vous croyez pleins de bon sens, positifs, pratiques! Vous pratiques!
Allons donc! Vous ne savez tenir ni une plume ni un fusil.'

Not getting any answer or satisfaction from the municipality
he decided to publish his long letter. He sent it to *Le Temps*,
where it appeared on 24 January 1872. Then he had off-prints
made into a pamphlet, which he distributed to various public
men. This angered Rouen and probably was one of the reasons
why the negotiations for Bouilhet's fountain dragged on for ten
years. What is strange is that it should eventually have been
erected when Flaubert was no longer there, though the money
was there and it would have been a pity to waste it. The monument now stands against the wall of the Municipal Library and
does not deface it. The only drawback is that most people think
it is a bust of Flaubert.

Flaubert was also preparing Louis Bouilhet's posthumous
poems for publication, with his introduction. The volume
appeared in January 1872, although the preface was finished
before the war and is dated 20 June 1870. This is the only piece
of deliberate literary criticism which Flaubert ever produced, but
it must be admitted that many more acute observations appear in
his correspondence than in this preface. He could never have been
truly critical of Bouilhet and, moreover, his aim was to promote
interest in him. But even Flaubert could not arouse great enthusiasm for his poetry and, at times, there appears even his own
lack of deep appreciation. Flaubert, in any case, was not a great
reader of verse, for which he had no great liking. He gives a bald
and impersonal account of Bouilhet's life, but concentrates on the
man of letters, his high devotion to art, and his noble ideal of his
calling. He ends with a moving evocation of his personal loss:[20]

Puis, quand l'un sera mort – car la vie était trop belle – que l'autre
garde précieusement sa mémoire pour lui faire un rempart contre les
bassesses, un recours dans les défaillances, ou plutôt, comme un oratoire
domestique où il ira murmurer ses chagrins et détendre son cœur.
Que de fois, la nuit, jetant les yeux dans les ténèbres, derrière cette
lampe qui éclairait leurs deux fronts, il cherchera vaguement une ombre,

prêt à l'interroger: 'Est-ce ainsi? Que dois-je faire? Réponds-moi!'
Et si ce souvenir est l'éternel aliment de son désespoir, ce sera, du
moins, une compagnie dans sa solitude.

The collection was published by Michel Lévy. In the end, Flaubert paid all the expenses, as the publisher said that it did not sell,
but he had made no attempt to publicize it and the copies remained undistributed in the warehouse. It was this transaction
which caused the final break between Flaubert and Lévy, who had
published his two first books.

Flaubert finally managed to persuade the Théâtre de l'Odéon to
produce *Aïssé*. Its first night took place on 6 January 1872, but it
cannot be said to have been a success, as it had only, in all, twenty
performances. So bad was the organization that Flaubert had
to shift the scenery himself on the first night.[21]

At the same time he was working on two further plays, the
sketches for which he found amongst Bouilhet's papers, *Le Sexe
Faible* and *Le Cœur à Droite*. He eventually abandoned the second
as impossible to produce, but he did a good deal of work on *Le
Sexe Faible* and finished it in September 1872.

He tried to get it accepted by the Vaudeville Theatre and even
managed to obtain a theoretical promise from Carvalho, the
Director, in September 1873. It was, however, never produced, as
Carvalho wanted many alterations which Flaubert refused to
accept. Next it was turned down by the Théâtre Français and the
Théâtre de l'Odéon. Finally he was glad enough to have it accepted by the third-class Théâtre de Cluny, in September 1874.
Then he realized that the actors would not be capable of perform-
ing his play and he withdrew it.[22] He now abandoned all hope of
having it produced and put the manuscript away amongst his
papers. This was a wise move, as it is not a good play. The central
idea is that all men are weak and dominated by their women
folk, who eventually ruin them. The aim of all women is to lead
men on, to make them gross and degraded. The play is inspired
by many of Flaubert's own theoretical prejudices against women
and these were probably introduced by him during his revision
of the play.

In the meantime Flaubert was seized with a passion for the
stage, with the desire to produce a play entirely by himself, rather
than the working-up of someone else's sketches. This play was

Le Candidat, the only play written entirely by him (except his *Loys* XI, composed when he was sixteen, but never published or produced).

The first time we hear of the play is in a letter to George Sand on 20 July 1873, when he says that he has drawn up the plan of the play, which is twenty pages long. He mentions it also to Princesse Mathilde, in a letter the same day. He describes it more fully to Madame Roger des Genettes:[23]

If I ever write it and it is acted, I shall be torn to pieces by the populace, banished by the government, cursed by the clergy, etc. It will be complete, I assure you. This idea has occupied me for a month, and my plan fills thirty pages.

He showed the plan to Carvalho, who, he says, was delighted with it.[24] Carvalho was the Director of the Théâtre des Variétés, and he was, naturally, more excited at the thought of a play entirely by Flaubert than one hashed up from Bouilhet's notes.

Flaubert worked at it with his usual dramatic rapidity and had completed it on 26 November 1873. He then thought of plans for production. Carvalho was interested and, early in December, went down to Croisset to hear the play read:[25]

Carvalho arrived on Saturday at 4 o'clock. General embraces all round, according to the custom of theatre folk. At ten minutes to five began the reading of *Le Candidat*, which he interrupted only by praise … We dined at 8 o'clock and went to bed at 2 o'clock.

The result was that Carvalho accepted it for production. Flaubert was delighted and as he wanted his niece to share in his happiness he sent her a telegram to announce the news. It is touching and pathetic, his longing for her approbation:[26]

This afternoon, at 5 o'clock, I sent you a telegram to tell you that the reading of *Le Candidat* succeeded perfectly. It would be nice, if I could, before I go to bed, to receive an answer to my telegram. Shall I receive it?

On 11 December he went to Paris to present the play to the actors. They were well pleased with it. It was to be produced on 25 February 1874, but eventually it had its first performance on 11 March 1874.

Even before the first performance, doubt was expressed about the possible success of the play. The poet and critic Claudius

Popelin wrote to his father that he was going to the dress rehearsal.[27] 'It is not without anxiety that we see Flaubert embarking on the stage; he does not seem to us cut out for that. We are afraid of a failure which would cause him distress.' On 12 March he wrote again, after the first performance: 'I was yesterday at the first night of *Le Candidat* by my friend Flaubert. The day before I had seen the dress rehearsal which had not reassured me about the fate of the play, which I think doomed very soon to be withdrawn.'

The first night was a complete flop. There is a vivid but rather unkind account of the events in Goncourt's *Journal*:[28]

First one saw, on all faces, a pitying sadness; then the disappointment of the spectators, held back for a long time by respect for the person and talent of Flaubert, took its revenge in a kind of sneering whispering, in mockery of the pathos of the matter. No! those who do not frequent, as I do, this man of genius could not believe their ears. Amazement, hardly suppressed, increased every moment, faced with the lapses of taste, the lack of tact, the lack of imagination . . .

After the performance I went to greet Flaubert in the wings. I found him on the almost empty stage, in the company of one or two Normans. There was not a single actor on the stage. It was complete desertion, a flight from the author. In the staircases the actors were scuttling away. It was sad as well as fantastic, a regular rout. When he saw me Flaubert started as if waking up, and as if he wished to recover his official face, that of the strong man. 'Well! that's that,' he said, with wild, angry movements of his arms, and the contemptuous laugh of a man acting badly the part of 'don't care a damn!'

Goncourt added that everyone in the press was trying to soften the blow for Flaubert. He declared that if he personally had written such a play, he would have received nothing but abuse. Goncourt is however, ungenerous in this, as he always had a kinder, more flattering and fairer press than Flaubert.

Flaubert withdrew his play after the third performance, because he felt such sympathy for his actors, whom he admired greatly and whom he did not want to be made fun of, although he had advance bookings to the value of five thousand francs and he regretted the loss of the money. As he said to George Sand:[29] 'I don't want them to hiss my actors. On the second night, when I saw Delannoy going back to the wings with tears in his eyes, I felt like a criminal and I said to myself: "That's enough!" Three people moved me, Delannoy, Turgenev and my servant. Well! it's all over now!

I'm having my play printed and you'll receive a copy at the end of the week.'

The press was entirely hostile and no journalist said one kind word for the play. In fairness it must be admitted that it did not deserve to succeed. Flaubert did not proceed in the same way with his dramatic work as with his fiction. He wrote too quickly and did not submit to the necessary discipline, as he thought that he knew it all already and did not have the same ideal as for his novels. He once said to Goncourt:[30] 'The theatre is not an art, it's a secret.'

Flaubert managed, in his play, to offend everyone, all parties. The political situation in the seventies, in France, was very confused. There was republicanism, royalism – of two kinds, Bourbon and Orleanist – Bonapartism; there were conservatives, liberals and socialists. Flaubert was opposed to all of them and considered that there was nothing to choose between them. In his play he abused all sides and this destroyed all sympathy for the characters which they might have aroused. The play is also an attack against universal suffrage, which was one of the great 'superstitions' of the day. Flaubert thought that it increased egoism and stupidity. After the Commune he had said:[31]

The last god but one, which was universal suffrage, has just made a fool of its followers, by naming the 'assassins of Versailles'. What can one believe in? In nothing! That is the beginning of wisdom. It was time to get rid of 'principles', and to adopt science and investigation. The only reasonable thing (and I come back to that all the time) is a government of officials, always provided that these officials know something, indeed that they know many things. The people are eternal children, and they will always be (in the hierarchy of social elements) in the last row, because they are the large numbers, the masses, unlimited. It matters little if a great many peasants know how to read and no longer heed their parish priest; but it matters a great deal that many men, like Renan or Littré, should be able to live and be listened to. Our salvation now rests on a *legitimate aristocracy*, I mean by that a majority composed of something else than numbers. If they had been more enlightened, if there had been in Paris more people who knew any history, we would not have had to suffer from Gambetta, nor Prussia, nor the Commune.

It would have been difficult for Flaubert to write a satisfactory political play, as he had no political opinions or convictions.

Le Candidat is probably Flaubert's most pessimistic work, as it shows a general contempt for humanity without the traits of compassion which are to be found in all his novels.

The candidate himself is a possible character. Flaubert wished, in his case, to show how the desire to become a deputy can completely alter an ordinary father of a family. He is fairly well drawn and has some life, but neither he nor any of the other characters has any definite political opinions – not even selfish ones. The others are weakly drawn and the motives of their actions are not apparent; what is worse, one does not really know who is interested in whom, who loves whom, and what are their real feelings and opinions. The characters chop and change with the crudest self-interest, destroying continuity.

Flaubert, the great and supremely careful stylist, does not appear in this play and he made no attempt to suit the dialogue to the characters. This is particularly true of the conversation between the lovers, which is pure romanticism, and made the audience laugh. Flaubert was particularly hurt by this,[32] and he wrote to George Sand: 'They took, as a joke, poetic things. A poet says "The truth is that I belong to 1830, I learned to read in *Hernani* and I would have liked to have been Lara". Whereupon bursts of ironic laughter.'

What the audience chiefly objected to was the uniformly grey atmosphere which permeated the play – they would have preferred the lurid, if melodramatic, colouring of a Zola.

Amongst the criticism which Flaubert received, the most acute was that by George Sand. She loved him and greatly admired his work, but she did not think much of his play and this pained her very much.[33] She considered that he had not really observed his material, but had built on abstract ideas and prejudices. She thought that it was too realistic, too *true*, and had not sufficient illusion in it. In his fiction Flaubert understood that reality is not art, that art is not photography, and that there must be choice and even distortion, but he loses sight of that in his drama. She also thought it wrong that no character arouses any interest or sympathy, as this made it impossible to be moved by the play.

Le Candidat was produced once more by Antoine, at the Théâtre de l'Odéon on 20 April 1910, but it had only one performance. The columnist of *Comoedia* considered it a pity that more people should not have been given the chance to see the play, and he wrote favourably about it:[34]

Certainly *Le Candidat* deserved only mediocre praise at the time of its creation (and since, as it has grown old, it has not improved), but its author is amongst those to whom respect must remain due, even in the midst of their greatest aberrations. And then I say, and I am not afraid to repeat it, if Flaubert's comedy is a failure, it is far from being without qualities. The audience at the 'Odéon Saturdays' were aware of this and I had hoped that the audience tomorrow, Tuesday, could equally have verified it, but M. Antoine abandoned the plan of putting on *Le Candidat* once more.

Just before the production of *Le Candidat*, Flaubert at last agreed to the publication of *La Tentation de Saint Antoine*. He was now free from his contract with Michel Lévy and could offer his book to whomsoever he pleased. He had met a publisher called Georges Charpentier and had become friends with him and his family – he was even godfather to one of his children. He offered him *La Tentation de Saint Antoine* and he accepted it. Charpentier was to publish all his subsequent books as well.

La Tentation de Saint Antoine appeared on 1 April 1874. The first printing of two thousand copies was sold out in a week and it had to be reprinted. This is a great success for any age. Three other editions were sold out before Flaubert's death in 1880. The third edition was published in 1875; the fourth also in 1875; and the fifth in 1880. There were many others after that. The book was therefore one of the author's great successes financially.

He received a kind letter from Banville and one also from Hugo. A favourable article from Banville appeared but on the whole the press was unenthusiastic and did not really understand the work. There was, as usual, a vituperative article from the pen of Barbey d'Aurevilly, in *Le Constitutionnel* on 20 April 1874. He said that, for years before it appeared, *La Tentation de Saint Antoine* had been spoken of as a masterpiece, but that Flaubert, who did not write easily, needed much noise and turmoil whenever he gave birth, like the member of a savage tribe. Barbey d'Aurevilly declared that all the indigestible erudition required for *Salammbô* was also apparent here and was choking the author. He called the book a sad execution, the definitive extermination of Flaubert. He personally found no idea or plan in the work, and he ended by saying that the novelist was not a realist but a brutalist.

La Tentation de Saint Antoine was to have been translated into Russian and published in the Empire. Flaubert expected a good price for it, but the Tsar refused permission for it to appear on account of its alleged godlessness. The French version was also not allowed to be sold in Russia.

CHAPTER TEN

LA TENTATION DE
SAINT ANTOINE

The version of *La Tentation de Saint Antoine* which Flaubert finished in 1872 – the manuscript is dated 20 June 1872 – and which was published on 1 April 1874 is the third. The first was the one finished in 1849, under the posthumous influence of Alfred Le Poittevin, which he had read to his friends Maxime Du Camp and Louis Bouilhet and which they had advised him to throw into the fire and to forget all about. The second is the one on which he was working in 1856, after he had finished *Madame Bovary* and it was in the press. He would have published it then, if he had not feared that he might be taken to the courts again on the charge of offence against religion, and he went on to *Salammbô*. He had made certain changes in the first version, had shortened it and rendered it less romantic, but it was virtually the same work, merely revised and improved. The third version, published in 1874, was entirely rewritten, so that it became a totally new work. It has been reduced to a third of the size of the first version; it is also very much less romantic and emotional – much more intellectual and abstract. The three versions are preserved in the Bibliothèque Nationale in Paris – six volumes including several volumes of notes and plans.[1]

The initial inspiration of the whole work occurred when, at the age of twenty-three, in 1845, he saw the picture by Breughel depicting the temptations of Saint Anthony in the Balbi Museum in Genoa, and was shattered by it when the other pictures in the gallery left him cold. The final version is very much further from this original inspiration than the first or the second. There is also another more humble source. As a child he used to attend a mystery play depicting the life of Saint Anthony, which was performed every year in Rouen at the Foire Saint Romain. This too is nearer to the first version than to the final. In it the saint is shown at prayer in the desert, while his companion, the pig, sleeps peacefully at his side. Then Satan appears, followed by a retinue of little devils, and tempts him. He keeps on crying: 'Messieurs les démons, laissez-moi donc!' Flaubert used these words on the title page of the first two versions. But the demons will not leave him in peace, and they take away his beloved pig, while the hermit begs them to give it back to him. At this moment in the mystery play, the spectators usually joined Saint Anthony in his supplications. Then Satan appears again, vomiting flames, but finally God the Father sails in on his cloud of cotton-wool and sends the demons back to Hell, when they are about to demolish Anthony's hut. After which Anthony, who has been saved by God, kneels in worship of the Almighty.

The pig appears in the first and the second version but he has been dropped from the third. Flaubert continued to go to the puppet shows until adult life, and there is a story of a performance he attended with George Sand, Feydeau and Turgenev, after the book was published. The manager, catching sight of him in the tent, went to the front of the stage and announced loudly: 'Ladies and Gentlemen, the author of the play is present in the house, and he has paid us the honour of attending our performance.'[2] It is said that Flaubert was delighted by this.

The nineteenth century in French literature is the period of the great prose epics, relating the destiny of mankind, such epics as the *Ahasvérus* of Edgar Quinet. We can see their influence on many of Flaubert's boyhood works, such as *Smarh* and the first version of *La Tentation de Saint Antoine*. There is, however, a difference between Flaubert and the other writers of the prose epics. On the whole they described the ascent of man, in which they believed, and were inspired by fundamental optimism. Whereas Flaubert wished to denigrate man, to reveal his weakness and folly and show how, since the beginning of time, he had always been fallible, ignorant and blinded by his vanity, finding nothing to which to cling. The subject-matter which he chose for his final version gave him ample scope and opportunity for devastating criticism, free-thinking and scepticism. The other epic writers sought for some idealism and some belief which they could put in the place of Christianity. Flaubert, on the other hand, tried to show that there was no possibility of anything stable, that there was nothing satisfactory for man in any beliefs, which were all equally vain.

The work opens with a very beautiful and peaceful description of the Thébaïde, in great contrast with the turmoil in Anthony's heart. Flaubert is recalling the lovely Greek landscapes which had made such an impression on him during his journey to the East. This scene does not occur in the first two versions:[3]

C'est dans la Thébaïde, au haut d'une montagne, sur une plate-forme arrondie en demi-lune, et qu'enferment de grosses pierres.

La cabane de l'ermite occupe le fond. Elle est faite de boue et de roseaux, à toit plat, sans porte. On distingue dans l'intérieur une cruche avec un pain noir; au milieu, sur une stèle de bois, un gros livre; par terre çà et là des filaments de sparterie, deux ou trois nattes, une corbeille, un couteau.

A dix pas de la cabane, il y a une longue croix plantée dans le sol; et à l'autre bout de la plate-forme, un vieux palmier tordu se penche sur l'abîme, car la montagne est taillée à pic, et le Nil semble faire un lac au bas de la falaise.

La vue est bornée à droite et à gauche par l'enceinte des roches. Mais du côté du désert, comme des plages qui se succéderaient, d'immenses ondulations parallèles d'un blond cendré s'étirent les unes derrière les autres, en montant toujours; puis au delà des sables, tout au loin, la chaîne libyque forme un mur couleur de craie, estompé légèrement par des vapeurs violettes. En face, le soleil s'abaisse. Le ciel, dans le nord, est d'une teinte gris perle, tandis qu'au zénith des nuages de pourpre, disposés comme les flocons d'une crinière gigantesque, s'allongent sur la voûte bleue. Ces rais de flamme se rembrunissent, les parties d'azur prennent une pâleur nacrée; les buissons, les cailloux, la terre, tout paraît dur comme du bronze; et dans l'espace flotte une poudre d'or tellement menue qu'elle se confond avec la vibration de la lumière.

Anthony is outside his hut, on the top of a mountain; night is falling and he is worn out by a day spent in privations, fasting, prayer and hard toil. He is undernourished and weak, and so prepared to be the prey of all sorts of hallucinations. In the growing darkness, he feels his strength draining away, leaving him obsessed by many unworthy dreams, and he spends the night in horrible nightmares. Many commentators have seen in these visions the result of Flaubert's epileptic hallucinations. There is, however, nothing strange in them – or necessarily medical – and no need for this explanation. Anthony's physical condition would have made him liable to them. But Flaubert's hallucinatory experience made it easier for him to describe them. He said to Mademoiselle Leroyer de Chantepie that everything that was in Saint Theresa, Hoffmann and Edgar Poe was known to him, and that he understood hallucination thoroughly.[4]

At first Anthony regrets his childhood and his youth, especially his betrothed Ammonaria, whom he had once loved dearly. Then he weeps over all that he has sacrificed, over all that he might have achieved, if he had not become an ascetic and a hermit. He would have liked to have been a scholar or a philosopher; or else a soldier, or a collector of taxes in some port; or a rich merchant, with a wife and large family. From the darkness a voice whispers to him that this can still be remedied; and it offers him riches and women. Tables laden with food rise before him – these are the temptations of the vulgar appetites. Next he dreams that he is the confidant of an Emperor, rich and powerful. Afterwards he finds himself in a gorgeous palace at a feast given by Nebuchadnezzer. This gives Flaubert an opportunity he never misses of describing a banquet; and this one resembles that of the mercenaries in *Salammbô*.

All this is phantasmagoria, in his mind, but suddenly he comes to his senses and finds himself back in front of his hut. He scourges himself as a punishment for these visions, but then other visions rise up before him. The Queen of Sheba comes to visit him and offers herself to him. There is a moving scene describing her attempts at seducing him. In the earlier versions she is a somewhat vulgar and sensual temptress, but here she is beautiful and refined, one of the most delicate products of civilization.

Anthony makes the sign of the cross and is thus able to withstand temptation.

Next Satan appears, having taken on the shape of the hermit's former disciple Hilarion, who had greatly admired him. The Devil tempts him in his faith and makes him doubt all that he had previously believed in by many specious arguments. He points out to him all the obscurities, contradictions and inconsistencies, in both the Old and the New Testaments, and also in other religions besides Christianity. He discourses on all the religions of the world and makes them all sound ridiculous, and very like Christianity, in which Anthony had not yet doubted. All the religions of the world, since the beginning of time, pass before him, and none has been truer than any other. This was a favourite theme with nineteenth-century writers. We find it in Leconte de Lisle's work, especially in a poem entitled *La Paix des Dieux*, in which all the religions fade away and die. Man addresses all these Gods saying:[5]

> Vous en qui j'avais mis l'espérance féconde,
> Contre qui je luttais, fier de ma liberté,
> Si vous êtes tous morts, qu'ai-je à faire en ce monde,
> Moi, le premier croyant et le vieux révolté? –
>
> Et l'homme crut entendre alors dans tout son être
> Une voix qui disait, triste comme un sanglot:
> – Rien de tel, jamais plus, ne doit revivre ou naître;
> Les Temps balayeront tout cela flot sur flot.
>
> Rien ne te rendra plus la foi ni le blasphème,
> La haine, ni l'amour, et tu sais désormais,
> Éveillé brusquement en face de toi-même,
> Que ces spectres d'un jour c'est toi qui les créais.
>
> Mais va! Console-toi de ton œuvre insensée.
> Bientôt ce vieux mirage aura fui de tes yeux,
> Et tout disparaîtra, le monde et ta pensée,
> Dans l'immuable paix où sont rentrés les Dieux.

Then Hilarion shows Anthony all the heresies since the beginning of the world, each more monstrous than the other, and each proving only the infinite folly of man. Next come all the Gods, of all the religions, who have ever existed, some of them abominable and some grotesque, from the blood-stained Gods of primitive people to the poetic Gods of Greece. Eventually, as in Leconte de Lisle's poem, they all disappear into nothingness. At this point, in the published text, Anthony says: 'Tous sont passés!' but a voice says to him: 'Il reste moi!' This is Satan, who will now show him all the philosophies of the world and will tempt him with the gift of perfect knowledge.

However, in the original plan for the final version, a passage dealing with Christ – he had not had his place amongst the Gods – was to come at the end of the procession of the old Gods. It is to be found amongst the multitudinous notes for the work at the Bibliothèque Nationale. It must have meant a great deal to Flaubert as seven copies exist in the notes, as well as the fair copy.[6] It does not exist in any of the three versions of the work, but it was written only at the time of the third version, as it deals with Hilarion, who occurs only in the last version. It describes a vision of Christ in modern times. Louis Bertrand was shown the passage by Flaubert's niece, and he published it in his edition of the first version, though it is perfectly clear that it must belong to the third.

Bertrand says that Flaubert's niece told him that her uncle had omitted the passage out of deference for religion. This is very unlikely and would not have been at all in character. What is more probable is that he discarded it because it was not true to the fourth century and was thus an anachronism. It was a view of the founder of Christianity typical of the nineteenth century and found in many of the writers of the time – witness *Le Nazaréen* by Leconte de Lisle:[7]

> Quand le Nazaréen, en croix, les mains clouées,
> Sentit venir son heure et but le vin amer,
> Plein d'angoisse, il cria vers les sourdes nuées,
> Et la sueur de sang ruissela de sa chair.
>
> Mais dans le ciel muet de l'infâme colline
> Nul n'ayant entendu ce lamentable cri
> Comme un dernier sanglot soulevait sa poitrine,
> L'homme désespéré courba son front meurtri.
>
> Non! Une voix parlait dans ton rêve, ô Victime!
> La voix d'un monde entier, immense désaveu,
> Qui te disait: – Descends de ton gibet sublime.
> Pâle crucifié, tu n'étais pas un Dieu.
>
> Cadavre suspendu vingt siècles sur nos têtes,
> Dans ton sépulcre vide il faut enfin rentrer.
> Ta tristesse et ton sang assombrissent nos fêtes;
> L'humanité virile est lasse de pleurer. –
>
> Voilà ce que disait, à ton heure suprême,
> L'écho des temps futurs, de l'abîme sorti.

Flaubert's passage, which was never published by him, is as follows:[8]

Les rochers, la cabane, la croix et Hilarion même ont disparu. Antoine n'entend plus rien. Le silence, à mesure qu'il monte, lui paraît augmenter et les ténèbres sont tellement obscures qu'il s'étonne en ouvrant les bras de ne pas sentir leur résistance – et cependant elles l'étouffent comme du marbre noir qui serait moulé sur sa personne. Bientôt elles s'entrouvrent faisant comme deux murailles, et au fond dans un éloignement incalculable une ville apparaît.

Les fumées s'échappent des maisons, des langues de feu se tordent dans la brume. Des ponts en fer passent sur des fleuves d'immondices. Les voitures closes comme des cercueils embarrassent les longues rues toutes droites. Çà et là des femmes avancent leurs visages sous le reflet des tavernes, où brillent à l'intérieur de grands miroirs. Des hommes en costume sale et d'une maigreur ou d'une obésité grotesque s'entrecroisent comme s'ils étaient poursuivis, le menton bas, l'œil oblique, tous ayant l'air de cacher quelque chose.

Et voilà qu'au milieu d'eux Antoine aperçoit Jésus. Depuis le temps qu'il marche sa taille s'est courbée, sa chevelure a blanchi, et sa croix fait un[?] au milieu de son épaule. Elle est trop lourde. Il appelle. On ne vient pas. Il frappe aux portes, elles restent fermées. Il va toujours implorant un regard, un souvenir, on n'a pas le temps de l'entendre. Sa croix se perd dans les bruits. Il chancele [*sic*] et tombe sur les deux genoux. La rumeur de sa chute assemble les hommes de toutes les nations, depuis les Germains jusqu'à des nègres, et, dans le délire de leur vengeance, ils hurlent à son oreille : 'On a versé pour toi des déluges de sang humain, façonné des bâillons avec ta croix, caché toutes les hypocrisies dans ta robe, absous tous les crimes au nom de ta clémence. Moloch à toison d'argent, voilà trop longtemps qu'elle dure, ton agonie. Meurs enfin, ne ressuscite pas'.

Puis les autres, ceux qui l'aimaient, ayant encore sur leurs joues le sillon de leurs larmes lui disent: 'Avons-nous assez prié, pleuré, espéré? Maudit–sois tu pour notre longue attente, par notre cœur inassouvi!' Un monarque le frappe avec son sceptre, en l'accusant d'avoir exalté les faibles. Et le peuple le déchire avec les ongles, en lui reprochant d'avoir soutenu les rois.

Quelques-uns se prosternent par dérision. D'autres lui crachent au visage, sans colère, par habitude. Des marchands veulent le faire asseoir dans leurs boutiques. Les Pharisiens prétendent qu'il encombre la voie. Les docteurs ayant fouillé ses plaies prétendent qu'il n'y faut pas croire, et les philosophes ajoutent que ce n'était rien qu'un fantôme. On ne le regarde même plus, on ne le connaît pas. Il reste couché au milieu de la boue, et les rayons d'un soleil d'hiver frappent ses yeux mourants. La vie du monde continue autour de lui, les chars l'éclaboussent. Les prostituées le frôlent. L'idiot, en passant, lui jette son rire, le meurtrier son crime, l'ivrogne son vomissement, le poète sa chanson. La multitude le piétine, le broie, et, à la fin, quand il ne reste plus sur le pavé que son grand cœur tout rouge dont les battements, peu à peu, s'abaissent, ce n'est pas comme au Calvaire, un cri formidable qu'on entend, mais, à peine un soupir, une exhalaison.

On another page, there is the addition: 'Prouve que tu es Dieu, disent-ils. Appelle tes anges, défends-toi, allons, amuse-nous, fais des miracles. Tu n'es rien qu'un fantôme.'

After this vision Anthony cries: 'Horreur! je n'ai rien vu! N'est-ce pas, mon Dieu? Que resterait-il?'

If Christ did not exist as the son of God, as a divine being, what else could be left to him? Out of the darkness he hears a voice cry: 'Moi, dit quelqu'un.' 'Et Hilarion est devant lui, mais transfiguré, beau comme un archange, lumineux comme un soleil.' Then, on another page, 'la voix plus forte qu'un clairon. Il touche le ciel avec la tête.' Then the printed version continues and Anthony says: 'Qui donc es-tu?'.[9] And the vision answers: 'Mon royaume est de la dimension de l'univers, et mon désir n'a pas de bornes. Je vais toujours, affranchissant l'esprit, et pesant les mondes, sans haine, sans peur, sans pitié, sans amour et sans Dieu. On m'appelle la Science.' But Anthony answers: 'Tu dois être plutôt . . . le Diable.'

That is indeed who he is, Satan in the person of Hilarion. He shows his forked hoof to Anthony, then throws him on his horns and carries him away into the air.

Anthony is in despair because he has been shown that God does not really exist:[10]

Comment? mes oraisons, mes sanglots, les souffrances de ma chair, les transports de mon ardeur, tout cela se serait en allé vers un mensonge . . . dans l'espace . . . inutilement – comme un cri d'oiseau, comme un tourbillon de feuilles mortes!

Il pleure.

Oh! non! il y a par-dessus tout quelqu'un, une grande âme, un Seigneur, un père, que mon cœur adore et qui doit m'aimer.

Satan says that he will give him in exchange command of complete knowledge and, in chapter six, he shows him the wisdom of all the philosophies of antiquity, which he had learnt in his youth. However the Devil manages to show him the weakness of each, to make him doubt them all, and believe that nothing happens to man except in his own mind. Satan says to him:[11]

Mais les choses ne t'arrivent que par l'intermédiaire de ton esprit. Tel qu'un miroir concave il déforme les objets; – et tout moyen te manque pour en vérifier l'exactitude.

Jamais tu ne connaîtras l'univers dans sa pleine étendue; par conséquent tu ne peux te faire une idée de sa cause, avoir une notion juste de Dieu, ni même dire que l'Univers est infini – car il faudrait connaître l'Infini!

La Forme est peut-être une erreur de tes sens, la Substance une imagination de ta pensée.

Anthony has believed in knowledge and its power, and, with this disillusionment, he is seized with a sudden dislike of life and is tempted by suicide. Suicide would give him back power and make him the equal of God, for he would himself have made the choice between life and death, independently. He is however afraid of sinning, but Death points out to him all the philosophers who have killed themselves reasonably.[12] Death is no longer romantic as it was in the first *Tentation de Saint Antoine*; it is nothingness, 'le néant'. Anthony then comes to the conclusion that death is only an illusion which hides the continuity of life, but he asks:[13]

Mais la Substance étant unique, pourquoi les Formes sont-elles variées?

Il doit y avoir quelque part, des figures primordiales, dont les corps ne sont que les images. Si on pouvait les voir on connaîtrait le lien de la matière et de la pensée, en quoi l'Être consiste.

Then he is shown all the primeval figures, the fabulous beasts from all the folklores of the world. These creatures give ample scope to Flaubert for the expression of his gift for the description of the grotesque. Most of these creatures are frightful – half human beings, combinations of human beings and animals, of different animals, of vegetables and animals, every kind of natural aberration:[14]

Et toutes sortes de bêtes effroyables surgissent: le Tragelaphus, moitié cerf, moitié bœuf; le Myrmecoleo, lion par devant, fourmi par derrière, et dont les génitoires sont à rebours; le python Aksar, de soixante coudées, qui épouvanta Moïse; la grande belette Pastinaca, qui tue les arbres par son odeur; le Presteros, qui rend imbécile par son contact; le Mirag, lièvre cornu habitant les îles de la mer. Le léopard Phalmant crève son ventre à force de hurler; le Senad, ours à trois têtes, déchire ses petits avec la langue; le chien Cépus répand sur les rochers le lait bleu de ses mamelles ...

Ce sont des têtes d'alligators sur des pieds de chevreuil, des hiboux à queue de serpent, des pourceaux à mufle de tigre, des chèvres à croupe d'âne, ... des veaux à deux têtes dont l'une pleure et l'autre beugle, des foetus quadruples se tenant par le nombril et valsant comme des toupies, des ventres ailés qui voltigent comme des moucherons . . .

Les végétaux maintenant ne se distinguent plus des animaux. Des polypiers, qui ont l'air de sycomores, portent des bras sous leurs branches . . .

Puis les plantes se confondent avec les pierres. Des cailloux ressemblant à des cerveaux, des stalactites à des mamelles, des fleurs de fer à des tapisseries ornées de figures.

All these monstrous creatures exist in nature, which means that they must have been created, must have their place in creation. Everything then is possible and there is no such thing as beauty or ugliness; there need only be understanding. Anthony goes down further into life, to the very beginning, and he is no longer afraid:[15]

Et il n'a plus peur! Il se couche à plat ventre, s'appuie sur les deux coudes; et, retenant son haleine, il regarde.

Des insectes n'ayant plus d'estomac continuent à manger; des fougères desséchées se remettent à fleurir; des membres qui manquaient repoussent.

Enfin, il aperçoit de petites masses globuleuses, grosses comme des têtes d'épingles et garnies de cils tout autour. Une vibration les agite.

Then Anthony, in ecstasy, cries out:

O bonheur! bonheur! j'ai vu naître la vie, j'ai vu le mouvement commencer. Le sang de mes veines bat si fort qu'il va les rompre. J'ai envie de voler, de nager, d'aboyer, de beugler, de hurler. Je voudrais avoir des ailes, une carapace, une écorce, souffler de la fumée, porter une trompe, tordre mon corps, me diviser partout, être en tout, m'émaner avec les odeurs, me développer comme les plantes, couler comme l'eau, vibrer comme le son, briller comme la lumière, me blottir sur toutes les formes, pénétrer chaque atome, descendre jusqu'au fond de la matière – être la matière.

The original ending of *La Tentation de Saint Antoine*, written in June 1872, showed Anthony, after the above passage, gazing up at the orb of the rising sun and seeing a vision therein:[16] 'Les trois vertus théologales, la foi, l'espérance et la charité, s'y trouvent au milieu, debout, et leurs pieds portent trois rayons, trois glaives mystiques et qui s'abaissent presqu'au cœur de Saint A toine.'

La Tentation de Saint Antoine

This is a logical ending and it is reasonable that, after seeing the beginning of life, Anthony should see as the most important needs, Faith, Hope and Charity. However, the following year Flaubert crossed out this ending, and substituted the vision of Christ.[17] The final ending to *La Tentation de Saint Antoine* is the one published in 1874:[18]

Le jour enfin paraît; et comme les rideaux d'un tabernacle qu'on relève, des nuages d'or en s'enroulant à larges volutes découvrent le ciel.

Tout au milieu, et dans le disque même du soleil, rayonne la face de Jésus Christ.

Antoine fait le signe de la croix et se remet en prières.

It is hard to explain the need for this change, for the vision of Christ at the end. This is the only time he appears in the finished work and he has not been one of Anthony's preoccupations or interests. In fact, like so many of his contemporaries, Flaubert was inclined to put Christianity lower than what are called the pagan religions. Writing to George Sand he said:[19] 'My religious investigations have inspired in me such a disgust for theology and Christians, that I'm reading the philosophic works of Cicero with great delight. What a difference between that society and the one which succeeded it!'

The first two versions of *La Tentation de Saint Antoine* end with the sardonic laughter of Satan as he mocks the saint. But, in this final version, Anthony seems to have reached peace and serenity after having seen how life started and how everything hung together and made a unity. Would this have made him bow down before Christ? It certainly comes strangely after his satire and abuse against all religions, and their vanity. In real life Saint Anthony did, eventually, overcome temptation and return to the bosom of Christ. He had, however, never strayed so far from faith as Flaubert's Anthony, and his temptations were an attack against a man of profound beliefs who was only too human but not a disbeliever. The greatest temptation of Flaubert's Anthony was that of knowledge, and he did not withstand that but gained strength from it.

La Tentation de Saint Antoine is Flaubert's bitterest attack, up to that time, against mankind. In *Madame Bovary* he had portrayed the stupidity and folly of an individual, a silly woman, and the world and society were not implicated. In *L'Éducation Sentimentale* he had depicted the vanity and corruption of a whole society at a given period and the canvas is very much broader. In *La Tentation de Saint Antoine* it was the whole of mankind that he was indicting. According to Flaubert, from the very beginning man has shown himself vain and presumptuous, without coherence, without any hope of certainty or any stable belief. Yet he invented the myths, and, in his pride, thought that he had reached complete certainty; he was ready to massacre and to shed rivers of blood to support these unfounded creeds. Satan proves to Anthony that, at the end of all knowledge and learning, there is nothing, and that black is white and vice versa. Before he had met him, in the shape of Hilarion, Anthony had imagined that all that was needed to withstand temptation was strength of purpose. He did not reckon with the temptation of knowledge, which would undermine his faith and point out to him the impossibility of any belief or certainty.[20]

In the first two versions of *La Tentation de Saint Antoine* Flaubert had not been much concerned with the period in which the hermit had lived and he did not think of historical accuracy – as he had done when he had been writing *Salammbô*. Most of the details come from much later periods, especially from artistic sources of the twelfth and thirteenth centuries. In the final version, on the contrary, he wished as far as possible to be true to the historical period. There was a hermit and a saint called Anthony, who had lived in the fourth century. Something is known of his life and he was taken as the model of the typical hermit. He gave up all his property to follow Christ and to live in the desert. He suffered many temptations, which he finally surmounted, and he ended in adoration of Christ and in unity with Him. In spite of all his privations and suffering, he lived to the age of a hundred and five, and died about AD 355. Flaubert wished, this time, to give his saint the hallucinations, dreams and aspirations which would be of his time.

Jean Seznec has shown how, even in the final version of *La Tentation de Saint Antoine*, many of the hallucinations and visions of the saint come from very much later pictorial sources.[21] This is not, however, necessarily anachronistic for, if these artists were able to depict such beings, then so would Anthony, as these exotic creatures are not necessarily of any particular age, and a man of the fourth century would have been quite capable of imagining them. Flaubert even asked Maurice Sand to produce drawings for him of extraordinary animals which he invented.

Nevertheless many critics have considered that Flaubert made Anthony too learned for his time. Maxime Du Camp certainly thought so, and said that the hermit could not possibly have known all the heresies with which Hilarion tempts him.[22] Anatole France thought the same.[23] It must, however, be remembered that Anthony was a learned man, especially in theology and the history of the Church, so that it does not seem impossible that he should have known the religions of the world which had preceded Christianity. Coming as he did from the Near East, he would surely have known some of the oriental religions, and especially the Greek and Roman, though he might not have known all the pagan ones. He would, however, have been unlikely to have been able to conceive the beginning of matter and to wish, as he says, to 'descendre jusqu'au fond des choses'. That surely is a nineteenth-century conception. Taine thought that this idea was too scientific and modern for a fourth-century man, that it was too much like the zoology of Lamarck.[24] He also considered that Flaubert had shown an extraordinary knowledge of hallucinations, especially as they would strike an ascetic of the year 330, and of the effect they would have on a sick man.

There are some minor anachronisms which, in a work of this kind, are not of great significance. For instance Anthony is described as taking up a large tome of the life of the apostles, the pages of which flutter in the breeze. There would not have been paper at this time in Alexandria and, in any case, the real Anthony was unable to read.

Saint Anthony is assailed by many temptations, supernatural, spiritual and realistic, but, in this third version, the sensual ones are not really dangerous to him and he is able to conquer them. They come largely from the hallucinations in the mind of a man sick from privations, starvation and solitude. He realizes this and that these sensual gratifications do not really make up the good life, and they do not undermine his faith. The serious temptations are those of the intellect, the pitfall of the search for knowledge, as they seem noble and good. These, far more than physical and sensual pleasures, lead him away from God and his religion, eventually destroying his faith. The quest for certainty and knowledge makes him question everything. The Devil, in the shape of his close friend Hilarion, shows him – indeed proves to him – that what he had considered as the only true religion was, in reality, no more true than the others, and that many of the essential elements of Christianity were to be found in previous so-called pagan religions. He proves to him that it is no more sensible to believe in one than in the other. Anthony had always believed in the supremacy of Christ, but Hilarion shows him Apollonius of Tyana, who had been considered the rival of Christ and as great and supernatural as He. Apollonius had arisen at the time of the struggle between Christianity and paganism. There were many who followed him in preference to Christ, and many of his miracles were identical with those of Jesus, as, for instance, the raising of the dead girl. All this would naturally greatly worry Anthony. If he could believe Hilarion then what was there before him except despair? He would have lost everything, for he had sacrificed much to follow Christ. What was left to him if the Messiah was a fraud?

Flaubert gives Anthony a great many of his own doubts and beliefs, his own conceptions, but the two men were very dissimilar in character, and their positions were very different. Anthony, when attacked by temptations, especially those of the intellect, was a man of deep faith who had much to lose. Flaubert, at this time of his life, had no religious faith which could be undermined. He believed that all the harm in the world came from man's pride of intellect. He had held this conviction even as a boy when he composed *Mémoires d'un Fou* and *Smarh* – his certainty that man knew all the answers and that, eventually, he would master everything. Flaubert realized that, since the beginning of time, there had been the dogmatic holders of beliefs and creeds who each, in turn, had imagined that they possessed perfect truth and complete wisdom.

Flaubert wished to make Anthony reach the position in which he found himself, that of utter and complete scepticism, where he could come to no conclusion. 'Ne pas conclure,' he said about everything in life. So he gave Anthony, as final temptation, not worldly desire or pleasure, but the longing for ultimate truth. He inspired in his hero a disgust for all forms of religion, and disbelief in them. In spite of everything Flaubert himself was not without his religious feeling, but his religion was a belief in art, and he never doubted that. Hilarion does not tempt Anthony with doubt of art and disbelief in it, and one wonders how Flaubert would have extricated himself from this dilemma.

The real Anthony, in the fourth century, although suffering much from temptations, was able in the end to overcome them and bow down before God in prayer. That is why Flaubert had to end the work as he did, with the vision of Christ.

La Tentation de Saint Antoine is the one of all his books which Flaubert preferred. Was he right in this? How is it to be classified? Is it a novel or a play? He seems not to have wanted it to be a play, as, in the unpublished notes for the book, he says:[25] 'Enlever tout ce qui peut rappeler un théâtre, une scène, une rampe.' In its own day the work had interest chiefly on account of the widespread passion for the study of religions which the researches of Renan had encouraged and fostered. Today those still interested in an intellectual study of comparative religion will be fascinated by his material and his use of it. Those interested in classical philosophy will find much to engross them. There will be many to enjoy the use of the artistic sources.

But what is there today for the ordinary cultivated reader who has no specialized knowledge? There will be much that he will find boring and too long, and he will not be able to remember all the different pagan religions and heresies. He will particularly enjoy the passages of beautiful description, amongst the best which Flaubert has produced. There is the description of the Thébaïde, already quoted, and the description of the double port of Alexandria. There is the description of the Queen of Sheba:[26]

La Reine de Saba, se laissant glisser le long de son épaule, descend sur les tapis et s'avance vers Saint Antoine.

Sa robe en brocart d'or, divisée régulièrement par des falbalas de perles, de jais et de saphirs, lui serre la taille dans un corsage étroit, rehaussé d'applications de couleur, qui représentent les douze signes du Zodiaque. Elle a des patins très hauts, dont l'un est noir et semé d'étoiles d'argent, avec un croissant de lune, et l'autre, qui est blanc, est couvert de gouttelettes d'or avec un soleil au milieu.

Ses larges manches, garnies d'émeraudes et de plumes d'oiseau, laissent voir à nu son petit bras rond, orné au poignet d'un bracelet d'ébène, et ses mains chargées de bagues se terminent par des ongles si pointus que le bout de ses doigts ressemble presque à des aiguilles.

Une chaîne d'or plate, lui passant sous le menton, monte le long de ses joues, s'enroule en spirale autour de sa coiffure poudrée de poudre bleue, puis, redescendant, lui effleure les épaules et vient s'attacher sur sa poitrine à un scorpion de diamant, qui allonge la langue entre ses seins. Deux grandes perles blondes tirent ses oreilles. Le bord de ses paupières est peint en noir . . .

Elle secoue, tout en marchant, un parasol vert à manche d'ivoire, entouré de sonnettes vermeilles; et douze négrillons crépus portent la longue queue de sa robe, dont un singe tient l'extrémité qu'il soulève de temps à autre.

Or there is the picture of Venus Anadyomene:[27]

Elle a de grands cheveux blonds qui se déroulent sur ses épaules, les seins petits, la taille mince, les hanches évasées comme le galbe des lyres, les deux cuisses toutes rondes, des fossettes autour des genoux et les pieds délicats; non loin de sa bouche un papillon voltige. La splendeur de son corps fait autour d'elle un halo de nacre brillante; et tout le reste de l'Olympe est baigné dans une aube vermeille, qui gagne insensiblement les hauteurs du ciel bleu.

Flaubert was primarily a novelist, but it is difficult to see how *La Tentation de Saint Antoine* could be regarded as a regular novel. There are too many characters in it and they come and go, mostly as hallucinations in the mind of Anthony, without any real depth, and the reader is unable to identify himself with them. There are a few well-drawn characters, who appear for a short time, such as Apollonius of Tyana, and Simon and Helen. There is really only one character, who remains somewhat shadowy, so that we do not see him very well in his struggle with his various temptations. He is largely an intellectual abstraction, and the reader does not sympathize with him emotionally. He becomes most life-like when he is most like Flaubert – or rather when Flaubert incarnates himself in him. He has Flaubert's great *ennui*, his love of exotic climes, and his love of solitude, with the feeling of the soul trying to escape from its prison. These things, however, are less marked than in the first version, which is more autobiographical.

As we have seen, judging by the number of editions that it went through in the six years between its publication and Flaubert's death, *La Tentation de Saint Antoine* must have been read and have been a comparative financial success. Yet all the critics scorned it – more than they do today – except an erudite scholar like Taine, whose preoccupations it flattered.

CHAPTER ELEVEN

BANKRUPTCY

Flaubert did not seem to recover from his disappointment in *Le Candidat,* and it continued to prey on his mind. He remained in low spirits and depressed, so that his doctor insisted that he should have a rest and a change, and sent him to Switzerland. He went there at the beginning of July 1874. He seems to have been suffering from nervous prostration and high blood-pressure. He went to Kaltbad Rigi alone, as Laporte could only join him on the return journey. The trip was not a great success. Flaubert said that he did not care for Switzerland, a country without history, and he would have preferred the artistic beauties of the Vatican Museum to the beauties of nature. Writing to George Sand he said:[1]

As you know Switzerland, there is no point in my speaking of it, and you would despise me if I told you that I was dying of boredom there. I came through obedience because I was ordered to do so, to take the flush out of my face and to calm my nerves. I doubt if the remedy will have any effect; in any case it will have been deadly boring to me. I'm not *a man of nature* and I don't understand countries without any history. I would give all the glaciers for the museum at the Vatican. There one can dream. Anyway in about three weeks I'll be glued once more to my green table, in a humble abode where you seem no longer to want to come!

Moreover most of the guests at the hotel were Germans, and he had vowed never to speak to a German again. If such a life continued he would throw himself into the first glacier that he met, and the first week had seemed to him like three centuries. As he wrote to Princesse Mathilde:[2] 'I'm bored here to extinction. If such a life were to continue, I would throw myself over a precipice to shorten it. The prophecy of Popelin has been fulfilled; I smoke a lot. But that of Benedetti has failed – up to the present moment no Russian woman has offered me her heart.'

Nevertheless, in spite of his boredom, his trip seemed to have done him some good; he had taken some exercise; his face was less flushed and his breath less short.

He was working while he was in Switzerland, but not at *Bouvard et Pécuchet*, which he intended to write on his return; he was collecting the material for what was to become *La Légende de Saint Julien l'Hospitalier*. It is strange that this should have been so, but the story seems to have preoccupied him a great deal intermittently during his life, and he also worked at it after he had finished *Madame Bovary* in 1856.

Flaubert was back in Paris on 24 July 1874, and he continued very unsettled. He did not seem to be able to get down to his book, which he intended to begin on 1 August, but his mind was occupied with many other plans, especially a novel of the Second Empire entitled *Sous Napoléon III*.[3] He was to return to it again later, in thought, and it is a pity that he never wrote it. He did, in fact, begin *Bouvard et Pécuchet* in the first week in August, as on the sixth he sent his niece the first sentence of the book, telling her that it would be a long time before she would hear of it again, as he was floundering.[4] It is said that this first sentence was inspired by an event which occurred many years before, when Flaubert had sat, with Bouilhet, outside an old men's home in Rouen and had seen two such inmates appear. Flaubert had then said that he would like to write a novel about two such men.

At the end of the year, as we have already seen, he was again occupied with Bouilhet's play, *Le Sexe Faible,* but with no more success than previously.

Flaubert remained very lonely at Croisset and he could not grow accustomed to being without his mother, with whom he had lived for the whole of his life. Caroline does not seem to have gone to visit him as frequently as he would have wished; there were constant lamentations in his letters about her absence, and he implored her to come. But she was socially ambitious and was leading a gay and fashionable life in her house in Paris and her villa in Dieppe. There was an occasion when she proposed not to come and visit him for three months. He wrote to her on 28 August 1874:[5]

> How much *society you have*, my darling! And will this brilliant society, that stream of visits, really keep you at Neuville until the end of October? and from now until then, must the old man resign himself to do without your company at Croisset? No matter! when I get home, if you can't come, I'll go to see you myself, for I'm immeasurably lonely for you my poor child. I'm afraid that, as I grow older, I'll grow like your grandmother. I'm *going* that way. What is certain is that the Rigi did not do me much good, morally speaking. I think that these wonderful scenes have made me stupid.

He decided then to make a change and to leave his little apartment in the rue Murillo. He seemed to need a new living place after the publication of each of his books. He had moved from Croisset to the Boulevard du Temple in Paris when he had finished *Madame Bovary* and was awaiting its publication. Then, after the appearance of *L'Éducation Sentimentale*, in 1869, he had rented an apartment in the rue Murillo, to be nearer to Princesse Mathilde. Now that he had published *La Tentation de Saint Antoine*, he moved again, to Number 240 rue du Faubourg Saint Honoré, to the same block of flats where his niece now lived. This was to be his last move and it will be seen how disastrous it was. It was a bigger apartment than the rue Murillo and it had larger rooms. He was however in too low spirits, too discouraged to make any elaborate decoration and he merely altered the fittings he had had in the rue Murillo without buying anything new.[6]

This final move was the beginning of misfortune for Flaubert. He was never again to know any financial stability, never any peace. He moved in there on 10 May 1875, and before the end of the month disaster struck Caroline's husband, when he was threatened with bankruptcy and Flaubert sacrificed the whole of his fortune, all his security, and gave up his independence to save him.

There seem to have been difficulties in Commanville's financial affairs in 1871, but it was thought that this was the consequence of the war and the Commune. It seemed as if he then needed only an advance to extricate him from his temporary difficulties, but subsequent events might lead to the conclusion that matters were more serious, in 1871, than was thought – or admitted. From the evidence it looks as if Flaubert had tried to obtain a guarantee,

Flaubert the Master

a loan or an advance from Princesse Mathilde to help his nephew. It is only his excessive love for his niece that could have persuaded him to embark on such a course, for he would never have asked for anything for himself. His mother does not seem to have been informed about the matter, but she was in failing health at the time and was to die four months later. He wrote to his nephew on 27 December 1871:[7]

> Perhaps Rothschild will help us? Here is how the matter stands: The Princess wrote me a charming letter – and she is much distressed – in which she explains to me that she cannot help us.
>
> What I feared didn't happen, and we are greater friends than ever; and, before dinner, I had a very frank discussion with her.
>
> She first offered me to borrow on Saint-Gratien, which is not mortgaged. On my refusing she said:
>
> 'I'll go and see Rothschild. I'll find it for you.'
>
> 'But if he refuses?'
>
> 'We'll look elsewhere! You can count on me!'
>
> At this moment the guests arrived. After dinner we resumed the conversation, in a corner. In short I'm to go to her on Saturday morning, to find out the result of her efforts. Now that the ice is broken I can push her towards Royher, who was mentioned, or someone else.

The events are mentioned in *Gli Amici della Principessa Matilde*, a volume of letters edited by Marcello Spaziani.[8] There are letters here from Flaubert to the Princess which have not been published in the collected correspondence.

The Princess's lawyer does not seem to have been eager to carry out the requests and he seems to have been suspicious of Commanville. Indeed, if he had known as much about him as we now know, he would have been even less eager. He obviously thought that there was some plot between Flaubert and his nephew. Poor Flaubert, who understood nothing about business and who would, eventually, be responsible for the repayment of the loan.[9] After seeing the lawyer's letter he wrote to the Princess on 30 December 1871:[10]

> Princess, you never gave me greater proof of the frankness of your affection than in sending me your lawyer's letter (not very friendly towards me). I opened it only this evening when I arrived at my niece's house. M. Fraignaud has misunderstood the question, or rather the situation, and I believe that his zeal for you has led him somewhat astray. I beg you a thousand times to forgive me, but here is the exact

truth. Commanville had thought that your lawyer would come to him as a trusted agent, the accredited envoy of your Royal Highness, and that he need not use any cunning. On being asked when he needed the sum, Commanville answered 'At the end of the month'. But your lawyer was quite wrong when he imagined that his commercial existence could hang on this loan. Without in the slightest lacking in politeness or good behaviour, he treated him all the time as a man in a desperate condition, to whom one is giving charity. The expression is perhaps strong, but he was more than cold. There was no kind of plot between myself and my nephew. M. Fraignaud asked him what guarantees he intended to give your Highness. My nephew answered 'None', imagining that your Highness wished to avoid being known in the business, and a direct guarantee would cause this. Commanville added that his intention was to give me a mortgage on his property, so as to guarantee me against all eventualities. M. Fr. has therefore been wrong in writing to you 'Here is my opinion on the plot' . . . When M. Fr. mentioned the figure of 50,000 francs, he showed no astonishment since, a few days before, he had said that that sum would be sufficient. Asked about the period when he would repay the sum, he answered 'In April.' . . . Commanville said that he was certain to be able to pay back the money in April . . .

To sum up, Princess, my nephew wanted to give M. Fr. an honest and loyal explanation. He has always seen in the help which you proposed to give him, a matter of trust and honour and not a business transaction.

Need I add that I am ashamed to have given you so much trouble, and that I shall always remain, whatever may be your final decision, your very grateful and more than ever affectionate, Gustave Flaubert.

The Princess does not seem to have been allowed, by her lawyer, to accede to Flaubert's request. He wrote to her again in January 1872:[11]

Princess, I come, one last time, to importune you with this business, as boring for you as it is for me, which is saying a lot.

I did not understand your letter of yesterday evening.

(1) Rothschild asks for a fortnight to bring back your shares, and then, at the end of a fortnight, what will happen?

(2) Is M. Fr. sure to be able to lend the 50,000 francs on 1 February?

(3) If these two lenders are set aside, there remains the third plan which you mentioned.

You offered us your help with so much spontaneity and such warmheartedness that we had counted on it a little, and did not try elsewhere. We should therefore need to know if we can count on the

50,000 francs by 1 February. If we had that assurance we'd be free from anxiety, for my nephew has now sufficient to face all eventualities of this month.

I have another request to make, and that is to answer me as soon as possible, and categorically. Then I beg your forgiveness, while assuring you that I am, you know, always yours.

It is not clear what was finally decided or done, but Commanville seems to have been able to settle his affairs, as we hear no more about them in Flaubert's letters. Caroline continued her fashionable life in Paris and in Dieppe. Perhaps business looked up now that the war and the Commune were things of the past. We do not know what occurred in the years between 1871 and 1875, but what is certain is that Commanville did not keep his uncle informed of what was happening. Flaubert often wondered why he was never able to obtain money from his nephew, with whom he had left his capital, and he never had any statement of accounts.

For years Flaubert had left large sums of money with Commanville, who was to invest them and to pay him the interest at regular intervals; but, after 1874, he was finding it more and more difficult to get instalments from him, or answers to his letters. Also he was constantly receiving bills for things which he knew that he had given his nephew the money to settle. By the end of 1874 he was asking for elucidation of his affairs, but got no satisfaction. He had, however, no conception of the real state of his business. But, by May 1875, there was no possibility of hiding things from him any longer. In July matters had become desperate. Commanville could not settle with his creditors and there was no other issue but bankruptcy. Large sums of money were required immediately and there was even talk of selling Croisset. Flaubert was naturally appalled by this. The place did not belong to him, but had been left to Caroline, with the condition that he was to stay in it as long as he lived, though he would never have held her to that condition. He wrote to her:[12]

Well! I can't stand any more! I'm at the end of my tether! The pent-up tears are choking me, and I've opened the flood-gates. Then the thought of not having a roof of my own, a *home*, is unbearable to me. I gaze now at Croisset, with the eyes of a mother who looks at her tubercular child saying to herself: 'How much longer will he last?' I cannot get used to the possibility of a definitive separation.

However, he always thought of her first and of what it would all mean to her:

> But it isn't that which is worrying me most at the present moment. What rends my heart, my poor Caro, is your ruin! Your present and future ruin. To go down in the world is no joke. And all these grand expressions of resignation and of sacrifice do not console me at all, not at all!

He did not however hesitate. He sold his large farm at Deauville, which he had inherited from his mother and which was the main source of his income, and put all the money towards the fund to save his nephew from bankruptcy. He left himself almost destitute, but, as he said to Princesse Mathilde in September, he had received so good a price for the property that 'l'honneur sera sauf'. He wrote to her:[13]

> One must spare one's friends! I do not want to inflict on you the embarrassment of my gloomy self. I don't know how I didn't die of grief during the last four months. What I suffered cannot be imagined. Only since yesterday have matters been settled. *L'honneur sera sauf*.

It was only a short respite and the money was not sufficient to settle the whole of the deficit. Then the faithful Laporte, as usual, came to the rescue, and put the whole of his capital into the fund to save the nephew of his dearest friend from ruin. He also slept on New Year's Eve at Croisset so that on New Year's Day he should be the first to wish him better luck in the coming year and a change in his fortunes.

For the time being Commanville was saved, as Flaubert said to Turgenev,[14] but he did not know how he himself was to live, as he had nothing left. He told Edmond de Goncourt that his nephew owed him over a million francs.[15] He had, however, many friends who loved him dearly and would do anything for him. He wrote to George Sand to tell her of his misfortunes, that he was a finished man.[16] She could not bear anything to happen to him or for him to be unhappy. She offered to buy Croisset from him, and to allow him to live there during his lifetime. She imagined that it belonged to him and did not realize that any money she gave for the property would benefit only Caroline. He was, however, very much flattered that she should think of doing so much for him, and he told his niece of it with pride:[17]

Read what old Mother Sand writes about *it* [Croisset]. 'If it was not beyond my means, I would buy it, and you would spend your life in it. I have no money, but I'll try to place some capital. Answer me seriously, I beg you and, if I can do it, it will be done.'
Now! what do you say about that!

Flaubert now thought, for the first time in his life, of getting remunerated work. He asked his friend Bardoux if he could find him a librarianship, something like that of the Bibliothèque Mazarine. Bardoux had been a fellow-student of his at the law school and was now 'Sous Secrétaire d'État à la Justice'. They had remained friends through the years.[18]

Flaubert knew nothing about paid employment, never having done any in his life, and he was fifty-three – an old fifty-three. His niece also, with her usual lack of sympathy, was trying to urge him to find work. He said that he would write to Laporte on the subject, on whom he counted more and more:[19]

I shall follow your advice and ask his advice about a position. However the prospect disgusts me a lot! I, who was born so proud, to receive money from the public, to be ordered about, to have a master! Well! we'll see.
I kiss you tenderly. Your poor old uncle.

She was able to accept everything from him, without compunction, and now she was going to give up her own apartment and live with him in his. She was eventually even to crowd him out of this.

To take his mind off his worries, as he was unable to work at his novel *Bouvard et Pécuchet*, Flaubert decided to go on a visit to Concarneau, to his friend Georges Pouchet, the son of the man who had taught him natural science at school in Rouen, Félix-Archimède Pouchet. Flaubert went to Concarneau in the middle of September 1875 and intended to stay there until November.

He found it impossible to get on with *Bouvard et Pécuchet*. The immensity of the task was too much for him at this time, and he decided to abandon it until he grew stronger and calmer. He again thought of *Saint Julien l'Hospitalier*, which had preoccupied him for many years – as we have seen he had been working at it in Switzerland the previous year. He took out the material again – he must have brought it with him to Concarneau – and he decided to use it for a medieval romantic tale. He had written no short stories since his boyhood at school. He began work on its composition in September 1875,[20] and finished it very quickly – phenomenally quickly for him – for it was completed by February 1876, but it must be remembered that he had done work on it, even if only in research and documentation.

While in Concarneau, with his disgust for his present life, Flaubert was thinking about the vanished past. Concarneau was somewhat similar in atmosphere to the Trouville of his youth, and he was taking what Baudelaire would have called 'un bain de souvenirs'. When he got home, after he had finished *Saint Julien l'Hospitalier*, he felt that he would like to write a nostalgic work, something short and evocative. At the time he was worried about George Sand's health, and felt that he would like to write something to please her. She had frequently accused him of being deliberately depressing and pessimistic. She wrote him a long letter in December 1875:[21]

What shall we both do? You certainly are going to produce *desolation* and I *consolation*. I don't know what our destinies depend on. You watch the people pass, you criticize them, but you literally avoid passing an opinion on them, you are satisfied with merely painting them, hiding your personal opinion with great care, on principle. Nevertheless one sees it through your narrative, and you make the people who read you sadder. I would like to make them less unhappy. I cannot forget that my personal victory over despair has been through the effort of my will, and from a new way of understanding things which is the contrary of the one I formerly held.

I know that you blame the intervention of personal doctrine in literature. But are you right? Isn't it rather lack of conviction than an aesthetic principle? ... Art is not only painting. Real painting is moreover full of the soul of the man who pushes the brush. Art is not merely criticism or satire; criticism and satire only paint one facet of truth. I want to see man as he is. He is not good or evil, he is good and evil.

Flaubert answered her the same month:[22]

Your good letter of 18th, so tenderly maternal, made me think a great deal. I've re-read it about ten times, and I confess that I'm not sure that I understood it fully. In short, what do you want me to do? Make your teaching more precise!

I do everything I can to broaden my mind, and I work in the sincerity of my heart. The rest doesn't depend on me.

I do not produce *desolation* for the pleasure of it, believe me, but I cannot change my eyes. And as for my lack of convictions, alas, convictions smother me. I burst with suppressed anger and indignation. But, in the ideal I have of Art, I think that one must not show one's own, and that the artist must no more appear in his work than God in his. Man is nothing, the work of art everything. This discipline, which may come from a false point of view, is not easy to follow. And for me at least, it is a kind of permanent sacrifice that I make to good taste. It would be very pleasant for me to say what I think and to relieve Monsieur Gustave Flaubert, by phrases; but what is the importance of the said gentleman?

Then he thought of writing a gentle story to prove that he too could be tender and have feelings. *Un Cœur Simple* is the result of this desire. He wrote of it to Madame Roger des Genettes:[23]

Here am I back in the old house again, which I left last year three parts dead with discouragement. Matters are not very grand but they are at least bearable. I've put myself on my feet again and I want to write. I hope for a fairly long period of peace and one mustn't ask the Gods for more than that. So be it!... *L'histoire d'un Cœur Simple* is merely the account of a humble life, that of a poor country girl, religious and mystical, devoted without excess and soft as fresh bread. She loves, one after the other, a man, the children of her mistress, a nephew, an old man whom she looks after, then her parrot; when the parrot dies she has him stuffed, then, dying in her turn, she confuses the parrot with the Holy Ghost. This is not ironic as you might imagine, but, on the contrary, is very serious and very sad. I want to move people, to make sensitive souls weep, as I am one myself.

Unfortunately George Sand was never to see the tale. Flaubert began it in February 1876 and finished it on 17 August 1876, but she had died the previous June. When the whole collection was published in 1877, he wrote to her son, Maurice Sand:[24] 'I began *Un Cœur Simple* on her account alone; solely to please her. She died when I was in the middle of the work. Thus it is with all our dreams!'

Flaubert's close friendship with George Sand was sliding towards its close. From the end of 1875 she seemed in very poor condition, and she was always very careless about her health. She suffered from abdominal trouble but she does not seem to have consulted a doctor until May 1876, a month before she died. Her health continued to deteriorate, and she was always in great pain.

Her care seems to have been bungled, as she was treated for hernia when, in reality, she had abdominal cancer. Flaubert was growing very anxious on her behalf as we see from his letters to Maurice Sand's wife.[25] One of the longest letters George Sand wrote to him, eight printed pages, was on 12 January 1876, in which, in pain as she was, she discussed intimately the differences between them as writers. It is her profession of faith.[26] She ended:

> For the past three days I've been writing you this letter, and every day I'm on the point of throwing it into the fire, for it is long and diffuse, and probably useless. Very different temperaments on certain points come together with difficulty, and I fear that you will not understand me any better today than the last time. I send you, nevertheless, this scribbling, so that you should see that I'm almost as preoccupied with you as with myself . . .
> I embrace you for all of us.

The last letter she wrote to him was on 26 March 1876. Her last letter of all was to her doctor in Paris, the quack Henri Favre, who had diagnosed hernia.[27] It ended:

> I wonder where I am going and whether I may not expect a sudden departure one of these days. I would prefer to know it at once than to be taken by surprise. I am not one of those who grow emotional at suffering one of the great laws, or who revolt against the ends of universal life. I would, to get well, do everything that is prescribed to me, and, if I had a day of interval between my crises, I would go to Paris so that you could help me to lengthen my task; for I feel that I can still be useful to mine.

Two days later she took to her bed never to rise again and she died at 6 o'clock in the morning of 8 June 1876.

There were a great many people at her funeral, fifteen of them from Paris. Flaubert went in company with Prince Napoleon; Renan was also there. Flaubert wept floods of tears and he said that he felt that he was burying his mother for a second time. George Sand had not wished for any religious ceremony or any kind of service, for she remained a free-thinking deist until the end. However, her daughter Solange Clésinger, without authorization from anyone, went to the Bishop of Bourges and arranged for a Catholic funeral, while no one in the house defended the interests of the dead woman. Maurice Sand was so much overcome by grief that he did not have the strength to stand up to his sister.[28]

As Flaubert returned home after the funeral he heard of the death of Ernest Lemarié, one of his oldest, if not closest, friends. They had been to school together and it was he who had introduced Flaubert to Maxime Du Camp thirty-five years before, in Paris. He had also been saddened earlier in the year, on 8 March 1876, when he had heard of the death of Louise Colet. He had not seen her for more than twenty years and all his last meetings with her had been stormy and unpleasant. Nevertheless, on seeing the announcement of her death, he remembered the time, thirty years before, when he had been only twenty-five years old and was full of hope for the future. Now he was old and poor and felt that he might well be finished.

Some months later, on 3 March 1877, his brother-in-law, Émile Hamard, died. There could be no grief at this, for Hamard had sunk, over many years, into alcoholism and insanity. All his intrusions into the family had been disastrous and it had been necessary to have him restrained by law from interfering in his daughter's life. But at this death Flaubert remembered his sister's death thirty years before, his grief which had never grown less and which still burned in him. He recalled also Hamard's overwhelming sorrow.

Flaubert finished *Un Cœur Simple*, George Sand's story, on 17 August 1876. Then he decided that he would like to write about Saint John the Baptist, as the account of Herod and Herodias excited him. It was a strange plan, for hitherto there had been no indication that he was interested in that story or that period. Again he wrote quickly and he had finished the tale on 1 February 1877.

For some unknown reason Flaubert attended midnight mass on Christmas Eve at the local church. So strange did he himself consider the event that he mentioned it to every friend he wrote to at the time. To his niece he wrote on Christmas Day:[29] 'I too have had my diversions! I've been this evening to the mass at Saint Barbe, at the nuns', where I brought Noémie and Madame Chevalier. There you are! Isn't that beautifully romantic? And, to tell you the truth, I enjoyed it immensely.'

This action cannot be taken as a return to religion on account of unhappiness or grief, but it is certainly mysterious. Flaubert cannot have been in search of local colour for *Hérodias*, on which he was then working, as it has nothing to do with Christmas or any Christian ceremony. It might perhaps be that he was already planning the scene in *Bouvard et Pécuchet* where the two friends attend midnight mass and are very much affected by the experience, so that they turn to religion for a time.

Flaubert, in spite of his previous depression and poor health, started off 1877 in better physical condition and in a hopeful state of mind. He had a book almost ready for the press, and he had sold his first two tales to Russia with Turgenev's help.

Flaubert finished *Hérodias* on 1 February 1877. Then he went to Paris to negotiate publication. He was very much pleased with himself, for he had produced a whole book in little more than a year. He had the stories copied out and had the manuscript beautifully bound. He presented it to Edmond Laporte with the following inscription:[30]

En souvenir de l'été et de l'automne 1876. Vous m'avez vu écrire ces pages, mon bon cher vieux. Acceptez-les et qu'elles vous rappellent
Votre Géant,
Gustave Flaubert,
8 avril 1877.

Now that his work was finished Flaubert was leading a very busy social life in Paris and he felt that he could relax. He was seeing all his friends and dining with them. One new friendship which he valued greatly and which was to be one of the great consolations of his last years was that with Guy de Maupassant. Maupassant became Flaubert's disciple and never wrote anything without showing it to him. He was the nephew of the great friend of Flaubert's youth, Alfred Le Poittevin, the son of Laure Le Poittevin, the same age as he, who had been one of the company of actors in the billiard room at the Hôtel Dieu in Rouen, when they had been children. Guy de Maupassant had been born in 1850 while Flaubert was in the East, having left France the previous October. In spite of this some critics have tried to claim that he was his son. It is true that there was some mystery in the registration of his birth, but this was only so that it could appear that he was born in a château, and there is no proof whatsoever that Flaubert saw Laure de Maupassant, Guy's mother, for a very long time before his birth. Flaubert did not meet him until 1872, but sympathy arose immediately between the two men.

Maupassant adored the older writer and did everything he could to further his fame. He wrote a very favourable article on him which was signed Guy de Valmont and published in *La République des Lettres* in October 1876; he treated him as one of the great writers of the age.

Trois Contes appeared on 24 April 1877. It was a great and wide success – not a *succès de scandale* like *Madame Bovary*, nor a popular success like *Salammbô*, but a real success. In the three years between its publication and Flaubert's death in 1880, it went through five separate editions. If he could have written further books like this, his financial situation would have been permanently retrieved.

The book was a success with the intelligent critics as well as with the general public. On the whole the press was favourable, though there were, as usual, some carping reviewers, who did not see how Flaubert was developing, such as Brunetière in *La Revue des Deux Mondes* on 15 June 1877. The article which pleased Flaubert particularly was the one by Banville in *Le National* on 14 May 1877. He treated him not merely as a prose writer and a novelist, but as a poet:[31]

The illustrious author of *Salammbô* and of *La Tentation de Saint Antoine*, M. Gustave Flaubert, has just published a book simply entitled *Trois Contes*, but these tales are three masterpieces, absolute and perfect, created with the power of a poet, sure of his art, and of which one can only speak with the respectful admiration due to genius. I said a poet and this expression must be taken in its strictest meaning; for this great writer, of whom I am speaking here, has been able to conquer an essential and definitive form, where each sentence, each word has its *raison d'être*, necessary and inevitable, a language where it is no more possible to change anything than in an Ode of Horace or a Fable by La Fontaine. He possesses, to the highest degree, the intuition which reveals to us what no one has seen or heard, but, at the same time, he has studied everything and knows everything, having [joined to the original creator that he is, an impeccable craftsman]; and so he always finds the right word, and thus he can paint everything, even the most idealized eras and figures, without having recourse to a useless verb or a parasite adjective.

In June 1877 Flaubert returned to Croisset, which he had left nine months before, now full of hope and prepared to begin work again on *Bouvard et Pécuchet*, though he was not completely absorbed by it, as other plans came back into his fertile mind. He was particularly thinking of writing on *La Bataille des Thermopyles*, which was to recur to him, at intervals, through the rest of his life.

This period was a temporary lull in the storm of financial difficulties, when he felt, for the first time for a couple of years, that he might still recover. He had the joy of having created something without excessive expenditure of time. He had made some money on his book and the future did not seem to him quite so black.

CHAPTER TWELVE

TROIS CONTES

Trois Contes is the work which Flaubert composed more quickly than any other. He began writing in September 1875 and the tales were finished on 1 February 1877 – the book appeared in April that year – that is, one year and four months, which was very rapid for him when one thinks that each of his other books took him five years to write. The manuscript is kept in the Bibliothèque Nationale, with the notes and rough copies.[1]

SAINT JULIEN L'HOSPITALIER

The first story, *Saint Julien l'Hospitalier*, it is true had, for some reason, been occupying his mind for many years. It was the tale which he began with, in the autumn of 1875, when he could not work at his novel. As we have seen, he was already collecting material for it in 1856, after he had finished *Madame Bovary*, and, in 1874, in Switzerland. According to Maxime Du Camp, the idea of writing about Saint Julien l'Hospitalier came to Flaubert when he visited a church in Caudebec-en-Caux in 1846 with him, where there was a representation, in a stained-glass window, of the legend of Saint Julien.[2] Du Camp, however, is often inaccurate in his statements. A. M. Gomez proves that there is no stained-glass window in the church at Caudebec-en-Caux representing the life of Saint Julien, but only a statuette of the saint,[3] while A. Raitt points out[4] that the statue in the church is a mutilated one above the porch. He also remarks that there is however a stained-glass window representing the life of Saint Eustace, and Flaubert might have imagined that it was that of Saint Julien. Raitt also points out that Flaubert's interest in Saint Julien goes further back in his life than 1846. It has generally been over-looked that, as a schoolboy, he visited the church at Caudebec-en-Caux with a class from his school in 1835.[5] The boys were in the charge of E. H. Langlois, who had made a study of the stained-glass window in the Cathedral at Rouen depicting the life of Saint Julien. It is very likely that he drew the attention of the boys to the similarities between the story of Saint Eustace and that of Saint Julien, and that Flaubert remembered it later. Also, of course, he knew the window in the Cathedral at Rouen. Langlois taught him at school and was a friend of his family. It was natural, when he visited the church at Caudebec-en-Caux eleven years later with Du Camp, that he should recall the earlier visit. It can therefore be taken that his first interest in the saint came from his visit to Caudebec-en-Caux, when he was fourteen, and that his tale is a mixture of the story of Saint Eustace and Saint Julien. What is not known, as he does not mention it in his corres-pondence, is why he thought of the legend in 1856, when he had finished *Madame Bovary*.

When he had composed his tale Flaubert wished it to be believed that it had been inspired by the stained-glass window in the Cathedral in Rouen depicting the legend of Saint Julien, and he wished a reproduction of the illustration from Langlois' book to be used as a frontispiece to his tale.

The word 'inspiration' must be very loosely interpreted, as there is very little resemblance between the episodes as related by Flaubert and those depicted in the Cathedral window, and he could not have obtained his plot from it. It is impossible to find Flaubert's episodes in the window, and vice versa. There is, for instance, nothing in it about the saint's youth, or about the deer's prophecy – very important aspects of the story. On the other hand Flaubert did not take from the window the fact that the saint's wife accompanied him on his wanderings and later, with him, slept with the leper. It is probable that the sophisticated French nineteenth-century public could not have accepted that. As usual with Flaubert, very many sources have been suggested, most of them very learned.[6] A great many of them do not seem very likely, but what is probable is that the real sources are very few and very simple.

He obtained the idea and the background from Langlois' book, *Essai Historique et Descriptif sur la Peinture sur Verre*. There was also, most probably, Alfred Maury's *Essai sur les Légendes Pieuses du Moyen Âge*. Maury was a friend of his and it is certain that he knew his work and that he would have consulted him. Many critics claim that he owed something to a story from *Le Rhin* by Victor Hugo, 'La Légende du Beau Pécopin et de la Belle Aude'. This is somewhat far-fetched as the only resemblance between Hugo's and Flaubert's tales are that they are both medieval and of a legendary nature. Both Pécopin and Julien were devoted to the chase, but then so were most knights in the Middle Ages, particularly in literature. The psychology of the stories is however very different. There is no moral aspect in 'Le Beau Pécopin et la Belle Aude', and the fantastic element in it is more marked and more obvious, whereas in *Saint Julien l'Hospitalier* the moral problem is very important and the magical element can be interpreted rationally. The only real resemblance between the two tales is the description and the enumeration of the hunting dogs. Flaubert's passage could have been signed by Victor Hugo.

In the middle of the nineteenth century a great many medieval texts were republished. In 1839 there was *Le Livre du Roy Modus et de la Reine Ratio*, which deals with hunting and was republished and modernized by Elzéar Blaze. It was quoted in *La Chasse à Courre France* by J. la Vallée in 1839. The author of *Le Roy Modus et la Reine Ratio* was a Norman, H. de Ferrières, and it is certain that Flaubert borrowed from it.

To these texts could be added the *Acta Sanctorum*, the lives of the saints; and Jacobus de Voragine's *Golden Legend*. But these fade into insignificance in comparison with a modern and more popular source, *La Légende de Saint Julien le Pauvre d'après le Manuscrit de la Bibliothèque d'Alençon*, retold and modernized by Lecointre-Dumont and published in *Les Mémoires de la Société des Antiquaires de l'Ouest* in 1838. Flaubert would certainly have known it through his friend Alfred Maury, and it is probable that he obtained most of his plot from it. He could have dispensed with any other sources, so that he did not need the learned texts from the Bibliothèque Nationale in Paris.[8] He drew from it such important facts as Julian's prowess in hunting, his blood-lust and subsequent obsession with guilt.

Maury's *Essai sur les Légendes Pieuses du Moyen Âge*, which we have seen that Flaubert must have read, was published in 1843 and it included a footnote to Lecointre-Dumont's article; thus he

Madame Schlésinger in 1872, as she would have appeared when Flaubert last saw her.

Flaubert's mother in old age.

Flaubert's niece, Caroline.

Edmond Laporte. He became a close friend of Flaubert's after Bouilhet's death.

could have known of this vital text before he visited the church in Caudebec-en-Caux with Maxime Du Camp in 1846. It was, however, only in 1856, after he had finished *Madame Bovary*, that he undertook serious work on Saint Julien, though he postponed for twenty years the writing of it and might even not have composed it then if it had not been for the disaster in his financial affairs, which made it impossible for him to get on with *Bouvard et Pécuchet*.

Certainly Flaubert obtained from Lecointre-Dumont all that he needed to compose his tale. Largely from him he drew the psychological element absent from the usual accounts of the saint, and it is this aspect which interested him most. Flaubert builds up very carefully the blood-lust of the hero, since that is the most significant trait in his character, and the one which he had most difficulty in eradicating. We are shown this from Julien's earliest days, when, as a little boy, he kills a mouse in chapel and draws infinite pleasure and ecstasy from it. From that he graduates to larger animals. There is the pigeon whom he had first only winged and then strangles with his own hands, when he is only a child:[9]

Le pigeon, les ailes cassées, palpitait, suspendu dans les branches d'un troène.
La persistance de sa vie irrita l'enfant. Il se mit à l'étrangler; et les convulsions de l'oiseau faisaient battre son cœur, l'emplissaient d'une volupté sauvage et tumultueuse. Au dernier raidissement il se sentit défaillir.

The development and culmination of this vice is seen in the terrible slaughter at the hunt, when he leaves not one single animal standing. There is also the frustrated nightmare hunt when, after long abstinence, he yields to his passion for killing, but finds that he can kill nothing, and is left with the unsatisfied urge for slaughter. He arrives back in his castle at dawn, with the lust still strong in him. He discovers a man and a woman in his bed. In his passion he jumps to the conclusion that it is his wife with a lover, and he kills them both, thus releasing his pent-up feelings.

The tale begins with simple scenes as if from a fairy story, in primary colours like those of a stained-glass window or an illumination on a medieval manuscript. It is very different from the rich descriptions in *Salammbô*, or in the tale *Hérodias*. Flaubert has miraculously evoked the simplicity and naïvety of a medieval poem.

In a few simple words he manages to establish the uncomplicated characters of the parents of Julien. The father is described thus:[10]

> Toujours enveloppé d'une pelisse de renard, il se promenait dans sa maison, rendait la justice à ses vassaux, apaisait les querelles de ses voisins. Pendant l'hiver, il regardait les flocons de neige tomber, ou se faisait lire des histoires. Dès les premiers beaux jours, il s'en allait sur sa mule le long des petits chemins, au bord des blés qui verdoyaient, et causait avec les manants, auxquels il donnait des conseils. Après beaucoup d'aventures, il avait pris pour femme une demoiselle de haut lignage.

The mother is described in a similar manner:

> Elle était très blanche, un peu fière et sérieuse. Les cornes de son hennin frôlaient le linteau des portes; la queue de sa robe de drap traînait de trois pas derrière elle. Son domestique était réglé comme l'intérieur d'un monastère; chaque matin elle distribuait la besogne à ses servants, surveillait les confitures et les onguents, filait à la quenouille ou brodait des nappes d'autel. À force de prier Dieu, il lui vint un fils.

To celebrate the event there is an immense feast which lasts three days and three nights, lit up by torches and accompanied by the sound of harps. There are chickens as big as sheep and so many people come that they are obliged to drink out of helmets. Then one of the story's supernatural events occurs:[11]

> La nouvelle accouchée n'assista pas à ces fêtes. Elle se tenait dans son lit, tranquillement. Un soir elle se réveilla, et elle aperçut, sous un rayon de la lune, qui entrait par la fenêtre, comme une ombre mouvante. C'était un vieillard en froc de bure, avec un chapelet au côté, une besace sur l'épaule, toute l'apparence d'un ermite. Il s'approcha de son chevet et lui dit, sans desserrer les lèvres:
> – Réjouis-toi, ô mère! ton fils sera un saint!
> Elle allait crier, mais, glissant sur les rais de la lune, il s'éleva dans l'air doucement, puis disparut. Les chants du banquet éclatèrent plus fort. Elle entendit les voix des anges; et sa tête retomba sur l'oreiller, que dominait un os de martyr dans un cadre d'escarboucles.
> Le lendemain, tous les serviteurs interrogés déclarèrent qu'ils n'avaient pas vu d'ermite.

There is the possibility of a rational explanation, that the vision half seen in dim light might be due, in the mother, to the weakness, the haziness, of post-labour confusion of mind.

The father, as he sees his guests away from the gate, has a similar vision. A gypsy tells him that his son will be a great warrior, win much glory, and become a member of the family of an emperor. The lord looks to right and left, but sees nothing. The wind is beginning to drive away the mists of dawn. He attributes this vision to the fact of being tired and not having slept, but he might have thought that it was from having drunk too deeply from the wine at the feast.

These prophecies exactly suit those to whom they are addressed.

The father's influence is at first predominant and the boy's warlike qualities and his so-called manly characteristics are encouraged and fostered. He is trained in all the tasks connected with the chase – he trains dogs and falcons, learns how to lay snares, to distinguish the passage of deer and fox.

All this training eventually leads to the paroxysm and orgasm of killing which induces in him the overwhelming feeling of guilt:[12]

Redescendu dans la plaine, il suivit des saules qui bordaient une rivière. Des grues, volant très bas, de temps à autre passaient au-dessus de sa tête. Julien les assommait avec son fouet et il n'en manqua pas une.

Cependant l'air plus tiède avait fondu le givre, de larges vapeurs flottaient, et le soleil se montra. Il vit reluire tout au loin un lac figé, qui ressemblait à du plomb. Au milieu du lac, il y avait une bête que Julien ne connaissait pas, un castor à museau noir. Malgré la distance, une flèche l'abattit; et il fut chagrin de ne pouvoir emporter la peau.

Puis il s'avança dans une avenue de grands arbres, formant avec leurs cimes comme un arc de triomphe, à l'entrée d'une forêt. Un chevreuil bondit hors d'un fourré, un daim parut dans un carrefour, un blaireau sortit d'un trou, un paon sur le gazon déploya sa queue. et quand il les eut tout occis, d'autres chevreuils se présentèrent, d'autres daims, d'autres blaireaux, d'autres paons, et des merles, des geais ... Elles tournaient autour de lui, tremblantes, avec un regard plein de douceur et de supplication. Mais Julien ne se fatiguait pas de tuer, tour à tour bandant son arbalète, dégainant l'epée, pointant du coutelas, et ne pensait à rien, n'avait souvenir de quoi que ce fût.

He kills with the ease and facility one sometimes feels in a dream. Then an extraordinary sight makes him stop in his tracks:

Des cerfs emplissaient un vallon ayant la forme d'un cirque; et tassés, les uns près des autres, ils se réchauffaient avec leurs haleines que l'on voyait fumer dans le brouillard.

L'espoir d'un pareil carnage, pendant quelques minutes, le suffoqua de plaisir. Puis il descendit de cheval, retroussa ses manches, et se mit à tirer.

Au sifflement de la première flèche, tous les cerfs à la fois tournèrent la tête. Il se fit des enfonçures dans leur masse; des voix plaintives s'élevaient, et un grand mouvement agita le troupeau.

Le rebord du vallon était trop haut pour le franchir. Ils bondissaient dans l'enceinte, cherchant à s'échapper. Julien visait, tirait; et les flèches tombaient comme les rayons d'une pluie d'orage. Les cerfs rendus furieux se battirent, se cabraient, montaient les uns par-dessus les autres; et leurs corps avec leurs ramures emmêlées faisaient un large monticule, qui s'écroulait, en se déplaçant.

Enfin ils moururent, couchés sur le sable, la bave aux naseaux, les entrailles sorties, et l'ondulation de leurs ventres s'abaissant par degrés. Puis tout fut immobile.

La nuit allait venir; et derrière le bois, dans les intervalles des branches, le ciel était rouge comme une nappe de sang.

Julien s'adossa contre un arbre. Il contemplait d'un œil béant l'énormité du massacre, ne comprenant pas comment il avait pu le faire.

Then, on the other side of the valley, he catches sight of an enormous black stag, with his hind and all her little fawns, one hanging to her nipple. The stag is like a king with his long white beard and his sixteen branched antlers. Julian shoots at the fawns and kills them. The mother raises a cry that sounds to him almost human, and Julian shoots her down and lays her dead on the ground. The big stag then sees what was happening:[13]

Le grand cerf l'avait vu, fit un bond. Julien lui envoya sa dernière flèche. Elle l'atteignit au front, et y resta plantée.

Le grand cerf n'eut pas l'air de la sentir; en enjambant pardessus les morts, il avançait toujours, allait fondre sur lui, l'éventrer, et Julien reculait dans une épouvante indicible. Le prodigieux animal s'arrêta; et les yeux flamboyants, solennel comme un patriarche et comme un justicier, pendant qu'une cloche au loin tintait.

The bell sounds like a knell and the stag, like a prophet and a judge, repeats three times: "Maudit! maudit! maudit! Un jour, cœur féroce, tu assassineras ton père et ta mère." Il plia les genoux, ferma doucement ses paupières, et mourut.' Then Julien, overcome by grief and remorse, bends his head in his hands and weeps.

This prophecy is not merely dependent on blind fate, as prophecies are in most stories; the disaster will come not because it was foretold but on account of Julien's evil and cruel heart. When the time comes, he jumps to the conclusion, without stopping to think, that he has a right over the life of his wife, and he is not afraid to kill her, not thinking he is destroying his own dear parents. It is his own evil nature which brings about the tragedy and not the prophecy. This makes the action very much deeper and more significant for an understanding of his character. He is not a blind tool in the hands of fate.

Now, in his terror of being driven by his obsession to kill his parents, he decides to leave the country and go far away from them.

He wanders over the face of the world, experiencing many legendary adventures and fulfilling the prophecy made to his father by the gypsy, for he becomes a great warrior and eventually marries the beautiful daughter of an emperor.

He keeps away from hunting and no one can persuade him to take part in the pleasures of the chase, for he thinks, in this way, that he can exorcise the prophecy. But the longing for hunting is always with him, so that his wife encourages him, as she thinks that it will raise his spirits. Then one night, as he lies beside her in their bed, he hears the baying of a fox. The temptation becomes too great; he takes down his bow from the wall and goes out – he imagines that he sees wild animals passing beneath the windows of his room. His wife is astonished at this sudden resolution but he answers: 'C'est pour t'obéir!... Au lever du soleil je serai revenu'.

Then follows the second tremendous hunt, the phantom hunt. Flaubert liked such parallel scenes. There is the wedding breakfast in *Madame Bovary* contrasted with the dinner and ball at the Château de la Vaubyessart; the seduction scene of Emma by Rodolphe at the Comices Agricoles in contrast to that by Léon in the Cathedral at Rouen; and in *L'Éducation Sentimentale* the elegant dinner at the house of Madame Dambreuse, opposed to the more vulgar version at the house of the courtesan Rosanette. Now, in *Saint Julian l'Hospitalier*, there is the scene of real killing in contrast to the phantom hunt, the nightmare slaughter, when Julien is surrounded with animals and can kill none of them.

Les ombres des arbres s'étendaient sur la mousse. Quelquefois la lune faisait des taches blanches dans les clairières, et il hésitait à s'avancer, croyant apercevoir une flaque d'eau, ou bien la surface des mares tranquilles se confondait avec la couleur de l'herbe. C'était partout un grand silence; et il ne découvrait aucune des bêtes qui, peu de minutes auparavant, erraient à l'entour de son château.

Le bois s'épaissit, l'obscurité devint profonde. Des bouffées de vent chaud passaient pleines de vapeurs amollissantes. Il enfonçait dans des tas de feuilles mortes, et il s'appuya contre un chêne pour haleter un peu.

Then a wild boar shoots past him so rapidly that he does not have the time to bend his bow, and the animal disappears. Next he shoots an arrow at a wolf but misses him. He tries several times but always in vain:

Julien parcourut de cette manière une plaine interminable, puis des monticules de sable, et enfin il se trouva sur un plateau dominant un grand espace de pays. Des pierres étaient clairsemées entre des caveaux en ruine. On trébuchait sur des ossements des morts; de place en place, des croix vermoulues se penchaient d'un air lamentable. Mais des formes remuèrent dans l'ombre indécise des tombeaux; et il ensurgit des hyènes, tout effarées, pantelantes. En faisant claquer leurs ongles sur les dalles, elles vinrent à lui et le flairaient avec bâillement qui découvrait leurs gencives. Il dégaina son sabre. Elles partirent à la fois dans toutes les directions, et continuant leur galop boiteux et précipité, se perdirent au loin dans un flot de poussière.

It is so all through the night – the beasts mock him but he can touch none of them.

Alors son âme s'affaissa de honte. Un pouvoir supérieur détruisait sa force; et, pour s'en retourner chez lui, il rentra dans la forêt . . .

Il y avait dans son feuillage un choucas monstrueux, qui regardait Julien; et çà et là, parurent entre les branches quantité de larges étincelles, comme si le firmament eût fait pleuvoir dans le forêt toutes ses étoiles. C'étaient des yeux d'animaux, des chats sauvages, des écureuils, des hiboux, des perroquets, des singes.

Julien darda contre eux ses flèches; les flèches, avec leurs plumes, se posaient sur les feuilles comme des papillons blancs. Il leur jeta des pierres; les pierres, sans rien toucher, retombaient. Il se maudit, aurait voulu se battre, hurla des imprécations, étouffait de rage.

Et tous les animaux qu'il avait poursuivis se représentèrent, faisant autour de lui un cercle étroit. Les uns étaient assis sur leur croupe, les autres dressés de toute leur taille. Il restait au milieu, glacé de terreur, incapable du moindre mouvement. Par un effort suprême de sa volonté, il fit un pas; ceux qui perchaient sur les arbres ouvrirent leurs ailes; ceux qui foulaient le sol déplacèrent leurs membres; et tous l'accompagnaient.

Then he begins to run and they all run also, treating him with irony and disrespect. They stamp on his feet, they tickle him and pinch him. A bear knocks off his hat and a panther contemptuously spits out an arrow it holds in its mouth. All seem to be hatching some plot of revenge. He walks on, his arms outstretched, his eyes closed like a blind man, and he does not even have the strength to cry for mercy.

A cock crows and others answer. It is now daylight. He recognizes, beyond the orange trees, the roof of his castle.

This feeling of the animals surrounding him and crowding round him recalls a dream which Flaubert had had in the south of France in 1845, when he was on the way to Italy with his sister on her honeymoon. The circumstances are dissimilar but the atmosphere and emotion are the same:[14]

J'ai rêvé il y a environ trois semaines, que j'étais dans une grande forêt toute remplie de singes; ma mère se promenait avec moi. Plus nous avançions plus il en venait: il y en avait dans les branches, qui riaient et sautaient; il en venait beaucoup dans notre chemin, et de plus en plus grands, de plus en plus nombreux. Ils me regardaient tous, j'ai fini par avoir peur. Ils nous entouraient comme dans un cercle; un a voulu me caresser et m'a pris la main, je lui ai tiré un coup de fusil à l'épaule et je l'ai fait saigner; il a poussé des hurlements affreux. Ma mère m'a dit alors: 'Pourquoi le blesses-tu, ton ami? qu'est-ce qu'il t'a fait? ne vois-tu pas qu'il t'aime? comme il te ressemble?!' Et le singe me regardait. Cela m'a déchiré l'âme et je me suis réveillée ... me sentant de la même nature que les animaux et fraternisant avec eux d'une communion toute panthéistique et tendre.

Flaubert remembered this dream for thirty years and must have felt guilt all that time for the animals he had killed, guilt which he transferred to Julien. He was twenty-three when he had the dream and he wrote of it in 1845 in his *Notes de Voyages*.

When the cock crows and daylight begins to appear, Julien decides to give up the chase and to go home. Then suddenly he catches sight of three red partridges flying low over a field of grain. He unhooks his cloak and throws it over them as a net. When he has lifted it, he finds only one bird, dead for a long time, and rotten. This disappointment infuriates him more than any of the others. His thirst for slaughter seizes hold of him again and, as there are no animals, he wishes to kill human beings.

He jumps up the steps of the castle and bursts open the doors, but at the foot of the stairs the thought of his wife softens his heart. He gently enters the room where she normally sleeps, to kiss her in her dreams, but, as he bends over the pillow, he feels a beard against his cheek:[15]

Il se recula, croyant devenir fou; mais il revint près du lit, et ses doigts, en palpant, rencontrèrent des cheveux qui étaient très longs. Pour se convaincre de son erreur, il repassa lentement sa main sur l'oreiller. C'était bien une barbe, cette fois, et un homme! un homme couché avec sa femme!

Éclatant d'une colère démesurée, il bondit sur eux à coups de poignard; et il trépignait, écumait, avec des hurlements de bête fauve. Puis il s'arrêta. Les morts, percés au cœur, n'avaient pas même bougé.

Then he hears, coming nearer and growing louder, a cruel voice which he recognizes as the bellowing of the large black stag.

His wife then tells him that they are his parents who, after years of wandering, have at last discovered where he is and have found their way to his castle. She had fed them and had put them in his bed to await his return.

The dead are buried with great pomp and magnificence in the church of a neighbouring monastery. A monk with his cowl pulled down to hide his face follows the procession, but no one dares speak to him, for this is Julien, the parricide. He remains for the whole of the mass lying flat on the ground, his head in the dust, and his arms outstretched, as if he were crucified.

When the funeral is over he is seen departing towards the mountains. He turns his head several times and then disappears. They never see him again.

Julien becomes a wanderer on the face of the earth. He is often repulsed, often unhappy, and he throws himself into every danger, hoping to die. He is guilty of the sin of despair and is tempted by suicide. One day, leaning over a deep pool, he sees his reflection in the water and he thinks it is his father. He weeps and thinks no more of killing himself.

Finally he sets himself up as a river ferryman, and he lives in a hut made of mud, with, for sole furniture, a bed of dried leaves, a stool and a little table, and three clay goblets. There, year in and year out, he ferries men, goods and beasts across the river. Then, one night, there appears the celestial client, in the shape of the old leper:

Il était enveloppé d'une toile en lambeaux, la figure pareille à un masque de plâtre et les deux yeux plus rouges que des charbons. En approchant de lui sa lanterne, Julien s'aperçut qu'une lèpre hideuse le recouvrait; cependant il avait dans son attitude comme une majesté de roi.

Dès qu'il entra dans la barque, elle enfonça prodigieusement, écrasée par son poids; une secousse la remonta; et Julien se mit à ramer.

À chaque coup d'aviron, le ressac des flots la soulevait par l'avant. L'eau, plus noire que de l'encre, courait avec furie des deux côtés du bordage. Elle creusait des abîmes, elle faisait des montagnes, et la chaloupe sautait dessus, puis redescendait dans des profondeurs où elle tournoyait, ballottée par le vent.[16]

Only with great difficulty does Julien reach the other side and several times the boat is in danger of sinking, but he feels that he is bound on an important errand, by a secret order which he cannot disobey.

When they reach the hut, the leper demands food and drink, and then a place in his host's bed; and finally orders Julien to lie with him to warm him. He obeys and stretches out on him completely so that they lie mouth to mouth and breast to breast:[17]

Alors le Lépreux l'étreignit; et ses yeux tout à coup prirent une clarté d'étoiles; ses cheveux s'allongèrent comme les rais du soleil; le souffle de ses narines avait la douceur des roses; un nuage d'encens s'éleva du foyer; les flots chantaient. Cependant une abondance de délices, une joie surhumaine descendait comme une inondation dans l'âme de Julien pâmé; et celui dont les bras le serraient toujours grandissait, grandissait, touchant de sa tête et de ses pieds les deux murs de la cabane. Le toit s'envola, le firmament se déployait; – et Julien monta vers les espaces bleus, face à face avec Notre Seigneur Jésus, qui l'emportait dans le ciel.

After this follows a space in the text to show that the body of the story is over, and Flaubert ends the tale as if he had been telling it to an audience:

Et voilà l'histoire de Saint Julien l'Hospitalier, telle à peu près qu'on
la trouve, sur un vitrail d'église, dans mon pays.

Flaubert generally believed that character was a man's fate or
fatality, which eventually led to his doom, and from which he
could not escape. All he could, and should, do, was learn to
know himself and how to manage this character, to live with
himself, since he could not be changed. Julien is, however, an
exception to this, and he is the one character in Flaubert's work
who, in the end, redeems himself and improves himself. He
has sinned, but expiates his evil actions. He is the only one of
Flaubert's characters to have a sense of sin. He is able to repent
and to make amends for his past life, and become humble, sub-
missive and selfless. At the end, when he has become a ferryman,
there is nothing left of the glorious warrior who has conquered
the world; nor of the great hunter with his passion for killing;
nor of the brilliant son-in-law of an emperor. There is nothing
left but the poorest, the humblest and most penitent of Christians
whose only aim is to bring help to others.

Saint Julien l'Hospitalier is one of Flaubert's most perfect works
in construction and style – especially in its descriptive powers. It
is indeed a poem, as Banville declared. There is also the added
interest of the brilliant analysis of a psychological state, the gradual
development of the vice of blood-lust. This, however, if nothing
else, would have revealed that the story is a nineteenth-century
production, as it would not have occurred to a medieval artist or
writer.

The possibility and power of Saint Julien to redeem his past
and to become a saint is surely an optimistic conception not seen
elsewhere in Flaubert's writings.

UN CŒUR SIMPLE

Un Cœur Simple belongs to an unhappy period of Flaubert's life,
when he felt that everything was gone, when he had to sell up all
his property to pay his nephew's debts. He then dreamed, with
nostalgia, of the far-distant past. There is no evidence that he had,
before this, thought of writing anything similar. In 1876 he was
also worried about the state of health of George Sand, which
made him want to write something that would please her before

it was too late, to prove that he was not as hard as people thought – as she herself often imagined.

At the end of 1875, while he was composing *Saint Julien l'Hospitalier*, he was staying with his friend Georges Pouchet at Concarneau, which, in atmosphere, was very similar to the seaside resort associated with his early dreams, Trouville. Then, in contrast with the unpleasant present, he saw his early life in a golden haze and thought that everything then had been poetic and beautiful.

It was at this time also, in 1876, that Gertrude Collier, now Gertrude Tennant, came back into his life after nearly thirty years, and she had been associated with that happy life at Trouville. She came to see him in Paris, when he was writing *Un Cœur Simple*, probably early in 1876, as the first letter we have from him to her is dated 19 October 1876:[18]

How can I ever tell you the immense pleasure that your visit, your reappearance, gave me? It seemed to me that all the intervening years had disappeared and I was again embracing my youth. May God bless you for the kind thought.

The following year he wrote to her:[19] 'Do you know what I call you, in the depths of my being, when I think of you? (Which happens very often.) "My youth".' He wrote to her for Christmas 1876:[20] 'During all the long years when I lived without knowing what had become of you, not a day passed when I did not think of you.'

The last time that Flaubert had made a similar descent into his past had been in 1853, when he had revisited Trouville at the time of writing *Madame Bovary* and had wanted to review the scenes of his early life in order to cut himself off from them and start afresh. Then it had been a pleasurable excursion, a diversion. But, in 1875, he had wallowed in the past, trying to recapture its atmosphere rather than any particular events.

The work does not allow for Flaubert's usual habit of documentation, as the story is built on atmosphere and memories. Yet, even here, it can be seen that the habit dies hard and Flaubert did some research work, not all of it essential, on the diseases which might attack parrots, so that he could describe accurately and scientifically the death of Loulou. He studied the various forms which pneumonia takes, so that he could make no mistakes when he wrote of Félicité dying of that disease. He also obtained, from the Museum in Rouen, the loan of a stuffed parrot, so that he could describe its appearance at any hour of the day. But one cannot therefore talk of the sources of *Un Cœur Simple* in the way one talks of the sources of *Saint Julien l'Hospitalier* and *Hérodias*.

As the critics have been unable to find sources for the different episodes in the tale, they try to see all the characters as people whom Flaubert knew as a child. They have been mistaken and have exaggerated when they have tried to fasten particular episodes on to specific events in Flaubert's life. For instance they see the description of the children, Paul and Virginie, as counterparts of Flaubert and his young sister Caroline. But Virginie has certainly not the personality or intelligence of Caroline – nor her age. Paul is also very unlike what Flaubert was as a child, with his intellectual interests. He grows up to be a gambler without any intelligence or taste, and Virginie's death bears no resemblance to that of Caroline and does not cause her brother much grief. There is none of the close affection between Paul and Virginie that there had been between Flaubert and his sister.

Félicité may bear some infinitesimal resemblance to the old servant Julie who had brought up the Flaubert children. But their lives were very different. Julie must have been very much more intelligent, since she could tell Flaubert stories of the neighbourhood and be a companion to him after the death of his mother. Félicité could never have been that even if there had been someone with whom she could have behaved in a similar manner. She never receives any of the affection and consideration which are owed to her, whereas Julie was cherished by the whole family, treated like one of them, and loved and cared for to the end of her days, surviving all the children she had brought up. Félicité's real prototype is Catherine Leroux, in *Madame Bovary*, who spends half a century of devoted service in one farm, who is totally devoted, inarticulate, with no more intelligence than the beasts she tends, and who receives no better rewards for her life service than Félicité.

The critics also see in the arrival of Madame Aubain's daughter-in-law a reflection of the arrival of Louise Colet at Croisset in 1854. It is, however, difficult to see any connection between the two events, which have no resemblance to one another. Madame Aubain's daughter-in-law comes to prospect, to find out what kind of a home she is marrying into. But Louise Colet had come uninvited, and she certainly had not come to marry Flaubert. She was eventually evicted by him ignominiously.

As soon as he had finished *Saint Julien l'Hospitalier*, Flaubert thought of writing the story of the poor servant girl. It is not clear why he should have thought of writing it at that moment, except that he wanted to compose a tale which was entirely kind and consoling, though it need not have dealt with a very unintelligent servant. However, Flaubert was so constituted that he was unable to see kindness and goodness in a sophisticated and intelligent human being. That is why Félicité is so simple as to have no character at all, and no positive characteristics except her unreflective goodness.

At first the tale was to be called *Le Perroquet*, which means that the parrot episode was, from the very beginning, significant. There is the synopsis of a story with that title in the Flaubert papers at the Bibliothèque Municipale at Rouen[21] which is largely about the bird.

In February 1876, Flaubert started the story, which was still called *Le Perroquet*. It is virtually the same tale as *Un Cœur Simple*, except that Félicité does not play such an important part and very few of her adventures are related. The other elements – as for instance the Aubain family – do not occur in it either. In *Le Perroquet* Mademoiselle Félicité has a parrot given to her by a sailor nephew who has brought it back from his travels overseas. Her master dies, and the parrot also, which she then has stuffed and which becomes her most precious possession, her greatest confidant, to whom she tells everything. A procession is held in her home town for the feast of Corpus Christi, and she asks for permission to place her stuffed parrot on the altar of repose. The parish priest grants her request. The emotion of seeing him there is so overwhelming that it brings on a stroke, and she is taken away dangerously ill to the hospital. There she has mystical visions in which the parrot plays the part of the Holy Ghost. She confuses the sound of the chain of the incense-burner, in the procession, with the former sound of the parrot's chain. She is, however, afraid that thinking of the parrot in this way might be sinful, though her confessor assures her that this is not so. Soon afterwards she dies.

From this synopsis it will be seen how important a part the

parrot played in the original plan, at the expense of everything else. Félicité herself disappears almost entirely and there is no mention of all the things that happen to her in the finished story, which is very much more interesting than the short sketch. Also, as has already been stated, the Aubain family plays no part in it.

Un Cœur Simple is generally taken as a realistic tale, yet it is difficult to believe that so many disasters could happen to one human being. Everything turns out disastrously for Félicité. Her only love affair fails; the child of her mistress, on whom she had lavished her affection, as if she had been her own, dies; her nephew, to whom she had given all her love, dies of yellow fever in distant seas; then her parrot, her sole companion, dies too; her mistress, Madame Aubain, who has never been kind to her and has exploited her, but whom she nevertheless loves in her own dumb devoted way, dies also. After that she becomes deaf and blind and, finally, on her death-bed, she is left with a moth-eaten stuffed parrot to represent the Holy Ghost.

It must, however, be remembered that during the previous eight years or so Flaubert had lost everything which made life worth living. He had lost his dearest friends – Bouilhet in 1869, Sainte-Beuve the same year; Duplan and Jules de Goncourt in 1870; then, in 1872, the mother whom he had loved so dearly, and also Théophile Gautier; in 1876 he had lost his second mother, George Sand. And finally he had lost all his money in the ruin of his niece's husband. There did not seem to him to be anything left in his life.

Although Flaubert had intended *Un Cœur Simple* to be consoling, it turns out to be basically as pessimistic as his other work. Its message is that all we are left with at the end, in spite of all our goodness and effort, is a moth-eaten stuffed parrot to act as the Holy Ghost.

Saint Julien l'Hospitalier is written in the sophisticated, coloured style of a legend, even though with simplicity, and it is the most romantically written of all Flaubert's published works. But *Un Cœur Simple* has a colourless simplicity entirely suited to the subject, and everything is seen from the uncomplicated view of Félicité herself, so that there is nothing in it which could not have been seen or imagined by her. The method is reminiscent of the first volume of Joyce Carey's first trilogy, *Herself Surprised*, where the images are those which Sarah Monday, the servant, would have noticed. She has the same simplicity as Félicité and the same down-to-earth awareness of reality. The only events Félicité notices are those which touch her immediate entourage:[22]

> Puis des années s'écoulèrent, toutes pareilles et sans autre épisodes que le retour des grandes fêtes: Pâques, l'Assomption, la Toussaint. Des événements intérieurs faisaient une date, où l'on se reportait plus tard. Ainsi, en 1825, deux vitriers badigeonnèrent le vestibule; en 1827, une portion de toit, tombant dans la cour, faillit tuer un homme. L'été de 1828, ce fut à Madame d'offrir le pain bénit . . .
> Une nuit le conducteur de la malle-poste annonça dans Pont l'Évêque la Révolution de Juillet. Un sous-préfet nouveau, peu de jours après, fut nommé.

Félicité also thought that God must really have chosen a parrot for the Holy Ghost and not a dove, since doves cannot speak.[23] Taine considered this too sophisticated a thought for so simple a girl but, on the contrary, it is the kind of simple logic which she might have conceived.

The simplicity and unpretentiousness of the style in *Un Cœur Simple* does not exclude fine writing and poetic description. There is the quiet village asleep in the summer afternoon torpor:[24]

> Les jours qu'il faisait trop chaud, ils ne sortaient pas de leur chambre. L'éblouissante clarté du dehors plaquait des barres de lumière netre les lames des jalousies. Aucun bruit dans le village. En bas, sur le trottoir, personne. Ce silence épandu augmentait la tranquillité des choses. Au loin, les marteaux des calfats tamponnaient des carènes, et une brise lourde apportait la senteur de goudron.

There is also the return of the fishing boats at evening:

> Le principal divertissement était le retour des barques. Dès qu'elles avaient dépassé les balises, elles commençaient à louvoyer. Leurs voiles descendaient aux deux tiers des mâts; et la misaine gonflée comme un ballon, elles avançaient, glissaient dans le clapotement des vagues, jusqu'au milieu du port où l'ancre tout à coup tombait. Ensuite le bateau se plaçait contre le quai. Les matelots jetaient par-dessus le bordage des poissons palpitants; une file de charrettes les attendait, et des femmes en bonnet de coton s'élançaient pour prendre les corbeilles et embrasser leurs hommes.

It would not have been Flaubert if there had not been the description of a rich meal. Here it is the one offered to Madame

Aubain and her family, on the way to Trouville, by her farmer's wife.

Elle lui servit un déjeuner où il y avait un aloyau, des tripes, du boudin, une fricassée de poulet, du cidre mousseux, une tarte aux compotes et des prunes à l'eau de vie.

The tale ends with a typical Flaubert masterpiece, a piece of orchestration, like that of the Comices Agricoles in *Madame Bovary*, when Félicité is dying and the scene in the Corpus Christi procession in the street below blends with what is happening in the room of death above.[25] Félicité, lying in bed, only semi-conscious, imagines that she sees what is happening as if she were amongst the crowd. Her main concern is for Loulou. 'Is he all right?' she enquires anxiously.

Le clergé parut dans la cour. La Simonn grimpa sur une chaise pour atteindre l'œil de bœuf, et de cette manière dominait le reposoir.
Des guirlandes vertes pendaient sur l'autel, orné d'un falbala en point d'Angleterre. Il y avait au milieu un petit cadre enfermant des reliques, deux orangers dans les angles, et, tout le long, des flambeaux d'argent et des vases en porcelaine, d'où s'élançaient des tournesols, des lis, des pivoines, des digitales, des touffes d'hortensias. Ce monceau de couleurs éclatantes descendait obliquement, du premier étage jusqu'au tapis se prolongeant sur les pavés; et des choses rares tiraient les yeux. Un sucrier de vermeil avait une couronne de violettes, des pendeloques en pierres d'Alençon brillaient sur de la mousse, deux écrans chinois montraient leurs paysages. Loulou, caché sous des roses, ne laissait voir que son front bleu, pareil à une plaque de lapis.

Then the churchwardens, the choir and the children range themselves on three sides of the square. The priest slowly mounts the steps, and places on the lace cloth his large gold sun, which shines out brilliantly. There is a sudden deep silence, only broken by the incense-burners, sliding on their chains:

Une vapeur d'azur monta dans la chambre de Félicité. Elle avança les narines, en la humant avec une sensualité mystique, puis ferma les paupières. Ses lèvres souriaient. Les mouvements de son cœur se ralentirent un à un, plus vagues chaque fois, plus doux, comme une fontaine s'épuise, comme un écho disparaît; et, quand elle exhala son dernier souffle, elle crut voir, dans les cieux entr'ouverts, un perroquet gigantesque, planant au-dessus de sa tête.

We have in *Un Cœur Simple* the kind of characters we find elsewhere in Flaubert's work, with their crass selfishness and hardness. Madame Aubain does not realize all the devotion and affection which have been lavished on her by Félicité. When her little daughter is away at a boarding school, and no letter had been received from her for four days, she is most concerned on her behalf, but Félicité tells her, to encourage her, that she herself has received no word from her nephew Victor for six months, from his ship away in distant seas; she shrugs her shoulders and answers 'Ah! your nephew,' as if Félicité's anxiety were of a different and lower order. And, when it is heard that he has died of yellow fever, she shows her no kindness or sympathy. The only time that she shows human feeling is when she and the servant are sorting out dead Virginia's clothes:[26]

Ses robes étaient en ligne sous une planche où il y avait trois poupées, des cerceaux, un ménage, la cuvette qui lui servait. Elles retirèrent également les jupons, les bas, les mouchoirs, et les étendirent sur les deux couches, avant de les replier. Le soleil éclairait ces pauvres objets, en faisait voir les taches, et les plis formés par les mouvements du corps. L'air était chaud et bleu, un merle gazouillait, tout semblait vivre dans une douceur profonde. Elles retrouvèrent un petit chapeau de peluche, à longs poils, couleur marron; mais il était tout mangé de vermine. Félicité le réclama pour elle-même. Leurs yeux se fixèrent l'une sur l'autre, s'emplirent de larmes; enfin la maîtresse ouvrit ses bras, la servante s'y jeta; et elles s'étreignirent, satisfaisant leur douleur dans un baiser qui les égalisait.

C'était la première fois de leur vie, Mme Aubain n'étant pas d'une nature expansive. Félicité en fut reconnaissante comme d'un bienfait, et désormais la chérit avec un dévouement bestial et une vénération religieuse.

Félicité has a platinum-like goodness which nothing can corrode, and part of her goodness comes from the fact that she is unconscious of her qualities, as when she saves her mistress's children from a bull. Perhaps, if she had been more intelligent, she would have been less purely good, for she would have known it and it would thus have been alloyed.

Nevertheless, in spite of her simplicity, naïveté – even stupidity – she possesses positive characteristics, especially her power to give love and to serve. Her power of love in spite of loss and disappointment, still continues to demand a vessel to contain it, and she asks for nothing for herself. She loves little Virginia and also her nephew Victor as if they were her own children, and these are positive feelings. After the death of the little girl, when the mother's grief has grown less, when she has got used to it, it is Félicité who continues to tend her grave with great devotion. She can even feel love for her selfish and unsympathetic mistress. There is no struggle in her between evil and goodness, as she has no inclination towards sin, and so it is difficult to consider her virtuous or saintly. She has nothing to fight against and could be nothing else but good. She is a picture of utter purity and has none of the temptations of Saint Julien before his redemption.

But she possesses some commonsense and is capable of being astute in protecting her mistress's interests, so that even the hard-headed farmers, to whom she stands up, go away full of admiration for her business sense. She is also able, courteously, to get rid of some of Madame Aubain's guests who outstay their welcome. There is one of her uncles, who always arrives at meal times, with a filthy dog in tow who dirties all the carpets and furniture. His master generally drinks too much and then tells risqué stories. Félicité pushes him outside, always politely, saying: 'Vous en avez assez, M. de Gremanville! À une autre fois.' Then she closes the door behind him.[27]

Un Cœur Simple might have been sickly, with the undiluted goodness of the heroine, or else bitterly ironic. Félicité was, however, the kind of human being by whom Flaubert was always moved and whom he loved. There is no trace of irony in the story but only compassion for the life which fate has allotted to her and for the poor return she receives for so much devotion.

HÉRODIAS

The third story in the collection is yet another form of tale. It does not treat of contemporary life, as did *Un Cœur Simple*; nor of legendary times, as did *Saint Julien l'Hospitalier*, which could dispense with realistic or historical facts. *Hérodias* deals with the beginning of Christianity. It is a piece of historical writing, with verifiable facts which cannot be invented or inflated through imagination. Flaubert, as we shall see, took a great deal of trouble concerning these facts, and was very anxious to be faithful to history.

The first two stories took, as their subject matter, almost th entire life of the main character. But *Hérodias*, like a Frenc classical play, strictly observes the unity of time, and the whole action takes place in twenty-four hours, from dawn one day to dawn the following day. The passage of time, as in many scenes in *Madame Bovary*, is shown by the position of the sun. The fact that the action takes place in twenty-four hours means that great conciseness was needed and this concision has often been criticized. But, by a clever use of flash-back, Flaubert manages to convey – as in a classical play – a very much longer space of time.

Hérodias has been very much more commented on than either of the other stories. This is not due to preference or admiration but to the fact that more objective and learned criticism was possible. The critics have said that the story was concise to the point of obscurity, but they often lose sight of the fact that it and its events are more obscure to the modern public than they were to the people of Flaubert's day, with their widespread interest in and knowledge of the study of comparative religion. There was, at the time, great interest in the dawn of Christianity on account of Renan's writings, the beautifully and poetically written *Vie de Jésus*, *Vie des Apôtres* and *Histoire du Peuple d'Israël*. His books were read by a very large public when dry and learned treatises would not have evoked any interest. Through Renan's writings the public was able to see the people of these lands as real people, human beings like themselves. In the nineteenth century there would not have been the abysmal ignorance of biblical history which exists in our modern times.

The sources of *Hérodias* are not obscure. The most important consists of two short passages from the Gospels of Saint Mark and Saint Matthew. Flaubert also read Renan's *Vie de Jésus* and *Vie des Apôtres*; and he studied Flavius Josephus, who wrote in Greek *La Guerre des Juifs* and *Antiquités Juives*, translated by l'Abbé Glaive and published in 1846, in French, which is probably the version that Flaubert read. He was a Jew, born in Jerusalem, thirty-seven years after Christ, who died in Rome under the Emperor Trajan. Flaubert found in his work much historical material. When he wanted documentation for the Roman side of the background, he applied to Suetonius. He filled in the picturesque scene from his imagination and from his memory of his visit to Palestine in 1850.

There is no evidence to prove when Flaubert first thought of writing *Hérodias*, except the time when he began it, as there is no mention of it before that. But the story does not seem to go far back into his life. The first mention we have of the tale is in a letter to Madame Roger des Genettes, when he was finishing *Un Cœur Simple*, in April 1876:[28]

Do you know what I would like to write after this? The story of Saint John the Baptist. The nastiness of Herod towards Herodias excites me. It is still only in the state of a vague dream, but I would very much like to go deeply into the idea. If I begin it, it will give me three stories which would be enough to allow me to publish in the autumn a quite amusing volume.

There is no evidence that he was reading anything for the story before that. However he had always been interested in religion, not just one religion, but religion in general, all religions.[29] We know how much he admired the writings of Renan.

As we have seen in *Salammbô* he was also very much interested in clashes between the different races, and the conflicts amongst the sects of Jews in this period, when the teaching of what was to be Christianity was beginning to spread in the Holy Land, are clearly recognizable. He said, about his future tale, 'the question of races overshadows everything else.'[30]

The story is, however, not merely a study of the races and their clashes, for it would not have been a work by Flaubert if it had not included, in addition, psychological analysis. However, in the short space of time at his disposal – only twenty-four hours – he could not go in for the analysis in depth which he had practised in *Madame Bovary* and in *L'Éducation Sentimentale*. He therefore took his characters at a moment of crisis – as in a classical play – and, in his depiction of the different races, he chose certain outstanding types and features to symbolize them. For instance, Vitellius and his son Aulis are symbolic of the sophistication and corruption of the Roman Empire, and Aulis represents its grossness – he spends his time eating, and then vomiting in order to be able to eat again.

The two characters to whom Flaubert gave most attention were the Tetrarch Herod and his wife Herodias. Herod's meanness and cowardice towards her fascinated him. Flaubert shows these characteristics in most men – in Rodolphe in *Madame Bovary*, in

Arnoux and Frédéric in *L'Éducation Sentimentale*, and so on.

Herod was an official who stood between the Romans and the Jews, and he had to be careful not to offend the overlords or go counter to their wishes. As the story opens he is seen against the background of political unrest. He is worried about the state of the country and he longs for the arrival of the Romans to make sure that law and order will be observed, but, at the same time, he is worried about what they might do. He is also at odds with Herodias and anxious about her vilification by John the Baptist and what influence it may have on his career. He is beginning to grow tired of his relationship with her, but he is weak in her presence; and he is now to be completely overcome by his sensual passion for Salome.

Flaubert saw Herodias as a kind of mixture of Cleopatra and Madame de Maintenon. She is, however, far less assured and certain of herself than either of them. She is always anxious lest she should lose the love of Herod, and especially her power over him. She knows that she is growing old, that he is ruled by his senses, and that her influence is waning. She realizes that she is unpopular with the people in general, and that many consider that she is living in sin with him, for she has left her first husband, his brother Philip Herod, to follow him. She knows also that John the Baptist preaches against her and calls her an adulterous whore. She wants to use her influence with the Tetrarch to have him destroyed. He has cried out against her before the assembled people:[31]

Ah, c'est toi, Jézabel!

Tu as pris son cœur avec le craquement de ta chaussure. Tu hennissais comme une cavale. Tu as dressé ta couche sur les monts, pour accomplir tes sacrifices!

Le Seigneur arrachera tes pendants d'oreilles, tes robes de pourpre, tes voiles de lin, les anneaux de tes bras, les bagues de tes pieds, et les petits croissants d'or qui tremblent sur ton front, tes miroirs d'argent, tes éventails en plumes d'autruche, les patins de nacre qui haussent ta taille, l'orgueil de tes diamants, les senteurs de tes cheveux, la peinture de tes ongles, tous les artifices de ta mollesse; et les cailloux manqueront pour lapider l'adultère.

She knows that Herod is moved by and afraid of John the Baptist, and she is in constant fear that he might, one day, listen to the prophet and repudiate her, and she knows that he would not hesitate to sacrifice her to his ambitions if it was necessary. She is willing to go to all lengths to retain her hold over him, prepared even to sacrifice her daughter by her first marriage, whom she has brought to Palestine in order to tempt him, as she knows how weak he is when he is governed by his passions.

Salome has, in her physical make-up, much of Salammbô. Her appearance at Herod's birthday feast is very like that of Salammbô at the banquet of the mercenaries, and Herod is as thunderstruck at her vision as Mâtho had been at that of the Carthaginian princess:[32]

> Mais il arriva du fond de la salle un bourdonnement de surprise et d'admiration. Une jeune fille venait d'entrer.
>
> Sous un voile bleuâtre lui cachant la poitrine et la tête, on distinguait les arcs de ses yeux, les calcédoines de ses oreilles, la blancheur de sa peau. Un carré de soie gorge-pigeon, en couvrant les épaules, tenait aux reins par une ceinture d'orfèvrerie. Ses caleçons noirs étaient semés de mandragores, et d'une manière indolente elle faisait claquer de petites pantoufles en duvet de colibri.
>
> Sur le haut de l'estrade, elle retira son voile. C'était Hérodias, comme autrefois dans sa jeunesse. Puis elle se mit à danser.

In Flaubert's tale, Salome is a very young girl and she has much less personality than the biblical character. She is completely under the thumb of her mother – rather in the way that Salammbô was under the influence of the priest of Tanit.

Salome has her wonderful looks and her talent for dancing, which she uses to captivate Herod, at her mother's behest, scarcely knowing what she is doing. Her dance, minutely described here, is supposed to have been modelled on a bas-relief in the Cathedral at Rouen. This relief is, however, static and shows only one movement. Flaubert is far more likely to have been thinking of the dance which he had seen the courtesan Kuschiuk Hânem perform in Egypt more than twenty-five years before, the 'Danse de l'abeille', and which he had recorded in his correspondence and in *Notes de Voyage*.[33] This was to be the most important scene in the tale and Flaubert was most anxious about it. He wanted it to have the same impact on his readers as it had on Herod – as it had had on him when he was a young man:[34]

> Ses pieds passaient l'un devant l'autre, au rythme de la flûte et d'une paire de crotales. Ses bras arrondis appelaient quelqu'un, qui

s'enfuyait toujours. Elle le poursuivait, plus légère qu'un papillon, comme une Psyché curieuse, comme une âme vagabonde, et semblait prête à s'envoler.

Les sons funèbres de la gingras remplacèrent les crotales. L'accablement avait suivi l'espoir. Ses attitudes exprimaient des soupirs, et toute sa personne une telle langueur qu'on ne savait pas si elle pleurait un dieu, ou se mourait dans sa caresse. Les paupières entre-closes, elle se tordait la taille, balançait son ventre avec des ondulations de houle, faisait trembler ses deux seins, et son visage demeurait immobile et ses pieds n'arrêtaient pas . . .

Puis ce fut l'emportement de l'amour qui veut être assouvi. Elle dansa comme les prêtresses des Indes, comme les Nubiennes des cataractes, comme les bacchantes de Lydie. Elle se renversait de tous les côtés, pareille à une fleur que la tempête agite. Les brillants de ses oreilles sautaient, l'étoffe de son dos chatoyait; de ses bras, de ses pieds, de ses vêtements jaillissaient d'invisibles étincelles qui enflammaient les hommes . . . Sans fléchir ses genoux en écartant les jambes, elle se courba si bien que son menton frôlait le plancher . . . . Ensuite elle tourna autour de la table d'Antipas, frénétiquement, comme le rhombe des sorcières.

Herod is moved by the dance beyond reason and sense; he is out of his mind and is ready to promise her anything. He says that anything she asks for she can have, even to half of his kingdom. But Salome is only a little girl who does not understand what it is all about and she runs back to her mother to find out what she should demand. She is told to ask for the head of John the Baptist on a platter. She is so young and foolish that, by the time she has got back to the Tetrarch's table, she has forgotten the name of the victim.

Elle y monta, reparut; et, en zézayant un peu, prononça ces mots, d'un air enfantin:
– Je veux que tu me donnes, dans un plat, la tête . . . . Elle avait oublié le nom, mais reprit en souriant:
– La tête de Iaokanann!

Herod visibly crumples up. In spite of his wife, he does not wish for the prophet's death and he is afraid of him. But the whole hall has heard the promise he has made, and there are many men among them who wish for the destruction of John. All have their eyes now on him and he is forced to order the decapitation of the prisoner.

However, John's prestige is so great that the official executioner, Mannaeï, although during his forty years of office he has despatched many hundreds of victims, returns from the cells trembling, with his teeth chattering, saying that he could not kill him, as an angel, with a flaming sword, had been standing outside the door, although no one else had seen him.

Then the rage of Herodias, in her frustration, bursts out, and Herod also cannot contain himself at having been disobeyed.[35]

La fureur d'Hérodias dégorgea en un torrent d'injures populacières et sanglantes. Elle se cassa les ongles au grillage de la tribune, et les deux lions sculptés semblaient mordre ses épaules et rugir comme elle.

Antipas l'imita, les prêtres, les soldats, les Pharisiens, tous réclamant une vengeance, et les autres, indignés qu'on retardât leur plaisir.

Mannaeï is sent out again, and, after what seems an interminable time, the head of John appears at the open door, held aloft by the executioner. He places it on a platter and offers it to Salome. Finally, after being taken round all the tables of the notables, it reaches the platform and the Tetrarch's high-table, and is placed before him. He looks at it and the tears run down his cheeks as he fully realizes what he has done. He went against his own wishes and instincts when he acquiesced to Salome's desire.

The guests leave one by one, realizing that Herod would like to be alone on such an occasion. The torches are extinguished and there is only Antipas alone in the darkening hall, his head bowed into his hands, gazing at the severed head:[36]

La lame aiguë de l'instrument, glissant du haut en bas, avait entamé la mâchoire. Une convulsion tirait les coins de la bouche. Du sang, caillé dōéjà, parsemait la barbe. Les paupières closes étaient blêmes comme des coquilles.

Herod must eventually have left the hall, though we are not told this, for finally the scene is bare and there is only the severed head in the midst of the débris of the feast, as an object of no importance to anyone.

Then, as the sun gradually rises, two messengers arrive with good news of Christ and impart them to Phanuel, a member of the Essenian followers of John the Baptist, who has been a witness of the events of the evening. He points to the terrible object lying on the table, but they say: 'Take comfort, he has gone to the kingdom of the dead to announce the coming of Christ.'

The three men take up the head and set out for Galilee. They do not carry away the whole body, as in the Bible account, but only the head, the noblest part of the prophet, and it becomes symbolical of Christianity, for as they proceed on their way it becomes heavier and heavier, so that they have to carry it alternately.

It is interesting here to compare with *Hérodias* Oscar Wilde's *Salome,* which he claimed had been inspired by Flaubert, though the works are of very different quality. Wilde entitles his play *Salome*, and he gives her more importance and maturity than Flaubert does. It is she herself who desires the head of John the Baptist. When she is offered it on a charger, it is laid on the ground beside her. She kisses the dead head's eyes and lips, and then executes a sensual dance round the platter. Herodias plays a small part in the play and Herod is a decadent neurotic, resembling one of the poets of the yellow nineties in England. It is impossible to imagine him as a real leader, as Flaubert describes him, or as anyone to be entrusted with responsibilities.

Flaubert was very much concerned lest *Hérodias* should resemble *Salammbô* too closely and, in fact, there are strong points of likeness between the two works. The opening scene in *Hérodias*, with the sun rising over the citadel of Machaerous and the Dead Sea, is very like that in *Salammbô* where the sun appears over sleeping Carthage. When composing both scenes he was thinking of the Palestinian countryside which he had seen in his youth on his visit to the East:[37]

Un matin, avant le jour, le Tétrarque Hérode Antipas vint s'y accouder, et regarde.

Les montagnes immédiatement sous lui commençaient à découvrir leurs crêtes, pendant que leur masse, jusqu'au fond des abîmes, était encore dans l'ombre. Un brouillard flottait, il se déchira, et les contours de la mer morte apparurent. L'aube, qui se levait derrière Machaerous, épandait une rougeur. Elle illumina bientôt les sables de la grève, les collines, le désert, et, plus loin, tous les monts de la Judée, inclinant leurs surfaces raboteuses et grises. Engaddi, au milieu, traçait une barre noire; Hébron, dans l'enfoncement, s'arrondissait en dôme; Esquol avait des grenadiers, Sorek des vignes, Karmel des champs de sésame; et la tour Antonia, de son cube monstrueux, dominait Jérusalem. Le Tétrarque en détourna la vue pour contempler, à droite, les palmiers de Jéricho; et il songea aux autres villes de sa Galilée: Capharnaüm, Endor, Nazareth, Tibérias où peut-être il ne reviendrait plus. Cependant le Jourdain coulait sur la plaine aride.

Toute blanche, elle éblouissait comme une nappe de neige. Le lac, maintenant, semblait en lapis-lazuli; et à sa pointe méridionale, du côté de l'Yemen, Antipas reconnut ce qu'il craignait l'apercevoir. Des tentes brunes étaient dispersées; des hommes avec des lances circulaient entre les chevaux, et des feux s'éteignant brillaient comme des étincelles à ras du sol.

Even if this passage recalls *Salammbô*, it is a beautiful piece of description in its own right and reveals Flaubert's great talent as a nature artist.

There is also the feast for the celebration of Herod's birthday, which resembles in certain respects the banquet of the mercenaries in *Salammbô*. In that novel Hamilcar visits his treasures in the cellars of his palace, and particularly his beloved elephants. The Tetrarch visits his horses, his most treasured possessions, and he is afraid that Vitellius, as Roman overlord, might deprive him of them. This is a wonderful picture of physical animal perfection:[38]

Des chevaux blancs étaient là, une centaine peut-être, et qui mangeaient de l'orge sur une planche au niveau de leur bouche. Ils avaient tous la crinière peinte en bleu, les sabots dans des mitaines de sparterie, et les poils d'entre les oreilles bouffant sur le frontal, comme une perruque. Avec leur queue très longue, ils se battaient mollement les jarrets. Le Proconsul en resta muet d'admiration.

C'étaient de merveilleuses bêtes, souples comme des serpents, légères comme des oiseaux. Elles partaient avec la flèche du cavalier, renversaient les hommes en les mordant au ventre, se tiraient de l'embarras des rochers, sautaient par-dessus les abîmes, et pendant tout un jour continuaient dans les plaines leur galop frénétique; un mot les arrêtait. Dès que Iaçim entra elles vinrent à lui, comme des moutons quand paraît le berger; et, avançant leur encolure, elles le regardaient inquiètes avec leurs yeux d'enfant. Par habitude, il lança du fond de sa gorge un cri rauque qui les mit en gaieté; et elles se cabraient affamées d'espace, demandant à courir.

Antipas, de peur que Vitellius ne les enlevât, les avait emprisonnées dans cet endroit, spécial pour les animaux, en cas de siège.

Hérodias is probably the least popular and admired of Flaubert's three tales, and this has generally been attributed to the fact of its concision and erudition. Yet, in achievement, it is not inferior to the other two. The style is as beautiful and the psychology more subtle and deep. Also the evocation of history is extremely well done as well as being accurate. Taine, who knew the difficulty of such a work, considered it the masterpiece of the collection. He thought it a miracle that the author had been able to include so much in so short a space. He realized that Renan had needed many volumes to reach the same conclusions:[39]

In my opinion the masterpiece is *Hérodias*. *Julien* is very true, but it is the world imagined by the Middle Ages, and not the real Middle Ages themselves; that is what you wanted, since you wished to produce the effect of a stained-glass window; that effect is there; the pursuit of Julien by the animals, the leper, all the pure ideal of the year 1200. But *Hérodias* is Judaea thirty years after Jesus Christ, real Judaea and much more difficult to render, because it is a question of another race, of another civilization, of another climate. Yes! you were right to say to me that nowadays history and fiction cannot be distinguished one from the other – yes! but on condition that they are written as you write them. These eighty pages have taught me more about the origins and background of Christianity than the work of Renan; nevertheless you know how much I admire *Les Apôtres*, his *Saint Paul*, his *Antéchrist*. But all the customs, the feelings, the scenery can only be conveyed by your method and your clear-sightedness. By art and style, you have got round the great difficulties, shown up the horrors and the indecencies; one can see Vitellius and Salome, and there are no coarse words, no crude words; nothing is left out; the two main aspects of Salome are there. There are even the shrieks of John.

Trois Contes is a collection of short stories. The question has often been discussed whether there is any unity between the three tales, any connecting link or thread. Or are they merely grouped by chance, because their author thought that they would make an attractive book? In his correspondence Flaubert does not mention any connecting link. Some critics have professed to see a unity but have not produced any good grounds for their opinion.

The printed order is somewhat mysterious. It is not the chronological order of composition, as *Saint Julien l'Hospitalier* was the first to be written. It is not the chronological order of the period in which the stories take place – it begins with the modern period, then follows the Middle Ages, and finally there is the beginning of Christianity.

All the stories tell of a state of holiness, and perhaps Flaubert wanted to show in his arrangement an ascending order of saint-hood, and the power of sacrifice of three different types of character. Félicité has perfect innocence and goodness, but she is

273

completely unreflective; there is no conflict in her and she could not be anything but good. Her sainthood might then not be considered of the highest.

Julien, through most of his life, was far from good and he gave way to temptation. He sinned very greatly and, although he was able to repent and to redeem his wickedness, there is some admixture in his sainthood, although there was choice left to him.

John the Baptist shows prophetic faith in contact with worldly ambition and self-protection. He willingly accepted his sacrifice, knowing what he was doing and knowing that there was no possibility of worldly salvation for him. There was no evil or ignorance in him and so his sainthood is of the highest quality of the three.

It is also possible to believe that Flaubert intended to give his readers, in *Trois Contes*, an anthology of his various styles of writing. Ever since his earliest days there had been the three forms of inspiration in his writings, exemplified by the different kinds of books that he composed. There is the realistic modern, as shown in *Madame Bovary*; the historical, as exemplified in *Salammbô*; the legendary, as shown in *La Tentation de Saint Antoine*. In *Trois Contes* he plaited all the strands into one single tress; he gathered together, in one single bouquet, all the flowers of his art. His style, art and method could be studied in this one book alone.

CHAPTER THIRTEEN

THE FINAL YEARS

The year 1877 opened for Flaubert, on the whole, hopefully. There seemed to be a temporary lull in his financial disasters, now that all his money had gone to save his nephew. He also had great hopes for *Trois Contes*, which he had nearly finished and of which he had already sold two tales. He was now beginning to be appreciated by the rising generation of writers, and a group of them invited him, Zola and Edmond de Goncourt to a banquet held at the Restaurant Trapp, near the Gare Saint Lazare. This banquet is generally taken as the foundation of the Naturalist Movement and most of the young hosts were followers of Zola – Huysmans, Maupassant, Paul Alexis, Octave Mirbeau and others.[1] The menu consisted of 'Potage purée Bovary; Truite saumonée à la Fille Élisa; Poularde truffée à la Saint Antoine; Artichaut au cœur simple; Parfait naturaliste; Vins de Coupeau; Liqueurs de l'assommoir.'

Later in the year *Trois Contes* was even recommended in the catalogue of a Catholic bookseller.[2] How different now was his reputation!

He was also beginning to be known abroad. What gave him particular pleasure was an article by George Saintsbury in the *Fortnightly Review*,[3] the most intelligent criticism which was published on him during his lifetime. Saintsbury realized his importance in the development of the novel. But what pleased Flaubert most of all was the preference of the critic for the *Tentation de Saint Antoine* over his other works. He thought it the highest expression of dream literature. Saintsbury also agreed with Flaubert's general views on literature, and advised the practice of his theories. He praised Flaubert for not using literature as a vehicle for personal feelings and experiences. He was also now being sought out by publishers and editors of reviews for contributions. Juliette Adam approached him to give her something for the review which she founded in 1879, *La Nouvelle Revue*, in opposition to *La Revue des Deux Mondes*. She was a very remarkable woman who died at the age of one hundred, in 1936, and she had been one of the leading journalists in the early years of the Third Republic. She was a Republican who never forgave the Germans as long as she lived. At first she was a supporter of Gambetta but cooled towards him when he abandoned the policy of 'La Revanche'. She had one of the most influential and brilliant political *salons* of the time, but attracted also literary men and artists. She got to know Flaubert in 1878 and she was one of the people who was most active in trying to obtain for him, in 1879, the librarianship of the Bibliothèque Mazarine. He promised her the book on which he was working at the time, *Bouvard et Pécuchet*, if she did not press him too hard as to time. It appeared posthumously in her review, from 15 December 1880 to 1 March 1881. However, liberal-minded as she was alleged to be, Flaubert's novel was more brutally mutilated than even *Madame Bovary* had been by *La Revue de Paris* in 1856. She cut out the scene in the cellar between Pécuchet and the servant girl Mélie, from whom he contracted venereal disease (chapter seven); also the supremely comic scene, describing the copulation of the peacock and the peahen and the discomfiture of Madame Bordin (chapter ten), as well as, in the same chapter, the discussion between Bouvard and Pécuchet on how to preserve the virtue of young Victor. There are other similar excisions.

One can imagine what Flaubert's attitude would have been to such treatment, especially coming from a literary friend.

The lull in financial disaster was, however, only short-lived and, in 1878, Ernest Commanville was in as great difficulties as ever. He was continuing his wild speculations, hoping to recoup himself thereby and using for that the money which Flaubert and Laporte had raised to save him from bankruptcy. As usual his uncle could never obtain from him any information about what was happening, and when eventually he did get some, it was worse than the previous time. He was constantly being presented with unpaid bills which he thought had been settled a long time ago; he found his name guaranteeing matters about which he knew nothing. He himself had been given no money for over two years, contrary to the 1875 arrangement, and when he had paid his last instalment on the Bouilhet monument he had absolutely nothing left. He had often to borrow money from the servants and found difficulty in getting Commanville to reimburse them. His niece, who gave up few of her own luxuries, was always complaining of his extravagance – especially of the amount of wood that he burned in an effort to heat damp and cold Croisset and of the occasional cigar that he still smoked. She said to Edmond de Goncourt: 'He's a strange man, my uncle, he does not know how to stand up to adversity.(4) If he had heard of this, it would have struck his sense of irony, as he reflected that his adversity was entirely due to her and her husband. He was, however, so infatuated by her that he regretted his poverty more for her sake than for his own.

As usual the faithful Laporte came forward to help his friend's nephew and mortgaged what was left of his private possessions – except the house in which he lived – but his factory had just gone bankrupt and he could not do very much this time. He touchingly said to Flaubert that now that he was in the same boat as his friend it made them more alike.

Laporte's small amount of money was not sufficient, this time, to float Ernest Commanville. His condition was becoming desperate and it looked as if the sawmill, his only remaining asset, which he had been trying to save from the wreck, would have to be sold. In desperation Flaubert thought of applying to his friends for aid for his nephew. He sought the help of Edgar Raoul-Duval, a lawyer and member of parliament, and a man of means, a close friend of his. And especially of Madame Pelouze, a rich widow who owned the Château de Chenonceaux, which she had very well renovated. She was very fond of Flaubert and he often stayed with her in her château and, in the midst of his present poverty, enjoyed its luxury. She was a well-read woman and he enjoyed discussing literature with her. He used to say that collections of Ronsard's poetry were brought to the dinner table. He once read her some cantos from Bouilhet's *Melaenis*, and this brought back to him the happy past.

It is easy to imagine what it cost a man of Flaubert's pride and independence to go, cap in hand, to his friends for financial help – he would, indeed, have done it only for his niece. There was a later occasion, when he might have applied for something for himself, but he could not do it. 'If I could write more comfortably from my bed,' he wrote to Turgenev,[5] 'I would explain to you how I cannot approach Madame Pelouze directly myself. Get someone else to speak to her, well and good! But to ask her for something for myself, no!' But he could make requests for his nephew – or rather for his niece. His own request would have concerned the librarianship at the Mazarine.

Madame Pelouze does not seem to have been eager to come to Commanville's aid as his treatment of his uncle was well known. Flaubert was afraid that he might have lost her friendship on account of this step.[6] It is said that she was asked to advance on loan fifty thousand francs, but it is not known whether she granted this and it does not seem likely. Bart, however, declares that she provided the money in cash, but he does not quote any proof and there is nothing in the published correspondence about it.[7]

The year 1879 was the worst in Flaubert's life. It began with the removal of all the Commanvilles' furniture into his apartment, as they had given up their home in Paris and the villa at Dieppe.[8] He was, however, anxious to keep something of his own there. 'As for the furniture,' he wrote to Caroline,[9] 'I wish, I even insist (if I can express myself thus) to retain, in my study, my leather furniture. I am indifferent to the rest.' He thought, however, that it would be impossible for the three of them to live in so small a lodging and he contemplated going there only when they were away.[10]

Next, on 25 January, he fell on some ice and broke his fibula. It does not seem to have been a very grave accident, but there was a bad sprain as well as the fracture. He was a very heavy man, which made it difficult for him to get about, and he was in great pain. The faithful Laporte, as usual, rallied round and came out to Croisset to act as a hospital nurse to his friend, and he spent nights on a sofa in his room to be available at any moment. Indeed Flaubert called him his 'Sister of Charity'. Once, when the river was so swollen that the ferry boat could not cross, he removed his trousers and waded across.[11]

The financial difficulties did not cease and there came a moment when the sale of the sawmill had to be accepted, even if it did not sell at its true worth. Flaubert hoped that, as the chief creditor,

Maxime Du Camp, another close friend of Flaubert's last years.

Guy de Maupassant, Flaubert's disciple and friend during his last ten years.

Portrait of Flaubert
in his great-coat, by
Paul Baudouin.

Flaubert's last letter.

he would now receive some money, but he had no guarantee and received nothing. Again he did not understand what was happening and came to the conclusion that, as usual, he had been told nothing or given wrong information, and that the charges on the estate were more extensive than he had been told. He had always understood that the sawmill was worth six hundred thousand francs – this was when he was asked to advance the money – but now he was informed that it was not worth more than two hundred thousand. It sold, in fact, at a slightly higher price than was expected, and Flaubert was very anxious that friends – especially Laporte and Raoul-Duval – should be repaid what they had lent, whatever happened to the family. He wrote to Caroline:[12] 'I think constantly of this. Shall we be able to repay our *friends*? What do you think? This idea pursues me everywhere, as if I'd committed a crime. Oh! curses on commerce! What shame!' And again: 'We must do everything to avoid despoiling our friends. We should be, you and I, scoundrels, if they lost a penny. We *should* not have done that. As far as I'm concerned, remorse tears me to pieces.'[13]

His wishes were, however, not followed.

In the midst of his complete destitution, he thought of asking his brother for help, knowing that he would not refuse him. It would humiliate him to beg, but less so than to receive the money from strangers. His brother received him very cordially and affectionately, and offered the allowance before he was asked. They were happy to see one another and spent the whole day together. But Flaubert never received the allowance. Although Achille was perfectly lucid that day, he was already a very sick man, suffering from softening of the brain, senile decay, from which he was to die a few years later, and he did not remember what he had promised. He already looked as if he were ninety years old.[14] It was a pity that the allowance did not materialize, as he was a very rich man and would not have missed it.

Flaubert's state of destitution did not remain hidden from the general public and the press got hold of it. An article was published in *Le Figaro* on 17 February 1879, telling of his lamentable state of affairs and saying that something must be done to remedy it. He was furious, as he had always hidden his life from the general public, considering that it was no concern of theirs.

Even before the article in *Le Figaro*, friends knowing his disastrous financial state were considering trying to obtain paid work for him – amongst them Princesse Mathilde, Madame Brainne and Edmond de Goncourt. Taine had even suggested that he should become a candidate for membership of the French Academy, but he would not consider that as he thought it an empty honour.[15] It would, however, have permitted him to sell his books, but his difficulty was to write a sufficient number to sell. In a moment of discouragement he had let himself go to show his unhappiness to the Princess and she had come forward immediately with her offer of help. He answered her:[16]

Your letter of a week ago, my dear Princess, moved me to tears (you know that, like Goncourt, I'm an old sentimental fool). Yes! I was moved to the depths of my heart by the sensitivity of your attention.

Keep your goodwill towards me, but, for the moment there's no hurry. I gave in to a mood of discouragement, in writing to you.

I am unhappy because I see those who are near and dear to me suffer, and I am upset in my work; but my soul is free and my conscience is clean, and my body strong and that is the main thing. We shall discuss all this towards the end of January, when I shall be in Paris.

He also wrote to Edmond de Goncourt:[17] 'What do you mean by this sentence: "I've been busy on your behalf . . . but with decent discretion?" The Princess, on the other hand, sends me allusions to a post, to a position worthy of me. I'm very grateful to her, in advance, but it is as useless as these exhortations to apply for the French Academy.'

He wrote more explicitly still to Madame Brainne:[18]

As for a post, an employment, my dear friend, never! never! never! I refused one offered to me by my friend Bardoux. It is like the Cross of Officier de la Légion-d'Honneur which he was also offering me.

Putting things at their lowest one can live in an inn on fifteen hundred francs a year. That is what I'd do rather than accept one penny from the budget.

Do you know this aphorism, which is mine? 'Honours dishonour; titles degrade and employment stupefies.' And moreover am I capable of filling a post, of whatever kind? The very next day I'd be thrown out, for impertinence or insubordination. Misfortune does not make me more tractable, on the contrary! I am, more than ever, intransigently idealistic, and resolved to die rather than make the slightest concession.

At this time employment for him was only a vague plan, but there arose later a definite project which was seriously considered.

The librarian at the Bibliothèque Mazarine, Sylvestre de Sacy, was known to be dying, and it was only a question of time and not a very long time. Flaubert's friends thought of the possibility of this post for him. After some discussion, he was attracted by the idea, as he felt that it would not disgrace him – there had been literary predecessors, amongst them Sainte-Beuve. The thought of the nice house, with a view on the river, appealed to him and the good salary. The post was in the gift of the Ministry of Instruction, and the Minister, Agénor Bardoux, was a friend of Flaubert and favourable to him. Unfortunately the government fell at the end of January and Bardoux was succeeded by Ferry, who was not interested in him.

Flaubert's friends mismanaged the affair. They thought that their only task was to persuade Flaubert to accept nomination. Turgenev went down to Croisset to talk to him, and he put the post in a very favourable light so that Flaubert became eager for election. He promised him too much – he was on his way to Russia and he proceeded too hurriedly. He counted too much on Gambetta, thinking that Juliette Adam would persuade him, and he bearded him at a public reception. He however refused all persuasion and Ferry did nothing. Flaubert also had the humiliation to read, in *Le Figaro* of 15 February, an account of Turgenev's interview with Gambetta.

It was objected, in several quarters, that Flaubert had no qualifications for the appointment, which was indeed true. But what was more fatal to him was that there was another candidate, Baudry, the son-in-law of Sénard – he who had defended Flaubert at his trial in 1857 – who had helped the government in the recent elections and gratitude was felt towards him.

Baudry was finally elected on 17 February 1879.

Zola wrote Flaubert a very kind letter which reveals the warmth of his heart:[19]

I wanted to write to you, my dear friend, to tell you that we were all of us clumsy in your affair. I beg you to take the matter philosophically, as an observer, as an analyst. Our greatest clumsiness was in having done things too hurriedly, to go and remind Gambetta of his promise, at a moment when, for the past week, he was overwhelmed with demands of all sorts. Madame Charpentier was in bed

and we had to use Turgenev who, the next day, was leaving for
Russia, and who was obliged to hurry matters too much. The occasion
was a bad one and all sorts of unfortunate circumstances arose . . .

In short my opinion is that a woman was necessary for you to carry
off the matter quickly. You had nothing to do with all this, you've left
nothing of yourself in it, and, tomorrow, if you agree, everything can
be repaired.

He then went on to talk of the article in *Le Figaro*, saying that no
one minds what a paper says, and he begged him not to take it all
too seriously. He ended:

Do not be too sad, I beg you again. On the contrary, be proud. You
are the best of all of us. We do not wish you to be unhappy.

As for your life, somewhat disturbed at the moment, it will all settle
itself, be assured of that. Get well quickly, and you will see that everything will be all right.

I embrace you.

Émile Zola.

Flaubert remained very much humiliated at having allowed
himself to be put in the position of begging for a favour. His
friends, however, still continued to work on his behalf. They
planned to obtain for him a state pension, which they disguised
under the title of a supernumerary librarianship at the Mazarine,
without any duties attached to it. Flaubert considered it as a charity
and refused it. It would have been more simple to have said to
him that it was an honour, a civil list pension. His friends, however, did not rest, but it took them nearly six months to persuade
him finally to accept the pension.

In order to raise his spirits, after all the misfortunes he had
suffered since the beginning of the year – his broken leg, his
financial disasters, and his disappointment over the librarianship
of the Bibliothèque Mazarine – some of his close friends organized
a feast for him to celebrate Saint Polycarp, whom he had adopted
as his patron saint on account of the pessimism of his sayings,
especially 'Lord! in what a century have you caused me to be
born!' It was Lapierre, the editor of the *Nouvelliste de Rouen*, who
had invented the celebration, and it was held at his house on
24 April 1879. Flaubert was still very lame, so his servant was
invited to look after him. His old friend, the actress Suzanne
Lagier, was also invited, to please him. The guests were all in

fancy-dress and the dishes were called after the main works of the author. There was a wonderful Savoy cake in the centre of the table, inscribed in sugar, 'Long live Saint Polycarp!'[20] At dessert Madame Pasca read a poem especially written for the occasion by a Monsieur Boisse, a councillor at the Law Courts, of which three verses are quoted here:

> Monsieur Flaubert, en ce beau jour de fête,
> Retrempez-vous dans le sein d'vos amis;
> Pour que d'leurs vœux, elle soit l'interprète
> Ils ont fait v'nir une artist' de Paris.
>
> Monsieur Flaubert, votre patron se nomme
> Saint Polycarpe, un savant bien distingué,
> On dit partout que c'était un brave homme
> Mais il paraît qu'il n'était pas très gai.
>
> Il s'écriait, ce pauvre Polycarpe,
> En ce bas mond' tout va de mal en pis;
> Et cependant il pince de la harpe,
> Tout, comme un autre, au sein du Paradis.

The following day Flaubert described the feast in a letter to his niece, and how his plate and glass were crowned with a wreath of flowers.[21]

It was finally Guy de Maupassant who persuaded Flaubert to accept the pension. He was now working at the Ministère de l'Instruction Publique and was concerned with literary pensions and prizes. He made his friend see that there was no disgrace in accepting a literary pension from the state, that it was an honour, that there were hundreds of writers receiving pensions and that many of them were comparatively rich:[22]

I've just been speaking with M. Charmes and we are of the same opinion. *Everybody, everybody,* considers the offer of a pension, by the Ministry to a man of letters, as a proof of esteem. All the princes in the past have given them to their great men; why should our government not do the same thing, and what is changed, that a thing considered up to now as an *honour* should be for you painful and humiliating?

He wrote to an unknown correspondent in June:[23]

It's done and I've given in! My intractable pride had held out until now. But alas! I'm at the point of being in danger of dying of hunger – or almost. And so I accept the post in question, three thousand francs per annum, with the promise of being used for nothing whatsoever, for you understand that, if I was forced to live in Paris, I'd be poorer even than before.

He went to Paris in June to discuss the matter with the Minister of Education, Jules Ferry, and told him of his consent. However he heard finally and officially only in October that he was to receive an annual pension of three thousand francs, to be backdated to 1 July – the first month after he had consented to accept it. The Minister's letter was, he said 'ultra aimable'.[24]

This visit was saddened for him, in his friendship with Princesse Mathilde, by the news which they do not seem to have heard until the end of the month, that the Prince Imperial had been killed on 1 June in the Zulu War. Flaubert knew how grieved she would be, for the young prince represented for her the future of Bonapartism in France, and she remained above everything else a Bonaparte. Her brother's two sons were nothing to her beside the Emperor's heir. After she came back from the funeral in England, Flaubert wrote to her:[25]

What an abominable week you have just spent, my dear good Princess. What a journey and what sights! Last Saturday I did nothing but think of you. This morning the papers inform me that you have come back to Paris. Send me a word how you are . . .
The best part of my year will be in the month of September, when I shall go to see you at Saint-Gratien.
Until then, Princess, I am as always, as I kiss your hands,
your faithful and old devotee.

Flaubert was tired and depressed all the time that he was in Paris and he did not feel up to going about much, but he spent a great deal of time at the Bibliothèque Nationale amassing material for his *Bouvard et Pécuchet*. He saw Jane de Tourbey again – now Comtesse de Loynes – and he said that the only happy day he had spent in the whole of the year was the morning he had had lunch with her in the Parc des Princes. They had always kept in touch. She had written to him sympathetically when his mother had died and when he had lost his money, and he had written to her to commiserate with her when her husband had left her, in 1876.

She was very kind to him and must have felt true affection for him, though there was little physical attraction left in the old man, stout, lame, bald and red-faced, with only a couple of teeth left in his head. He wrote to her after he had returned to Croisset to thank her for the day they had spent together:[26]

How long it is since I've heard news of you, my dear beauty, my true friend. And first, how is your *humour*? For health only comes afterwards. Are you still in the Bois de Boulogne? Where did you spend your summer? This evening the rain is falling; the fine days are over. Mine have disappeared this long time! Do you know that the only *piece of good luck* that fate has granted me this year, well frankly it was the morning when I had lunch with you at the Parc des Princes, in the month of June, this summer. What beautiful eyes! How pretty you were! so that, for two hours, I loved you madly, as if I'd been eighteen. Besides I love you always, adorable creature that you are.

I searched on your behalf (according to your orders) for a house in this neighbourhood but, up to now, it has been impossible to find anything worthy of your grace.

When shall we meet again? I'm going again to spend the whole of this winter at Croisset, to finish my eternal book. But perhaps, from the month of April, I'll stay the whole year in Paris, without leaving. Then we'll make up for lost time. We'll see one another shan't we? So long as there aren't too many bourgeois in your house, too many men ... I kiss you most tenderly on both your hands.

Your faithful old friend.

It was at this time that Caroline Commanville developed ambitions to become a painter, whether to bolster up her pride, which had been undermined by the changed conditions of her life, or else to try to retrieve her financial state, is not known. But she embarked on the plan with the ruthlessness which she showed in her other dealings with her uncle, and she used him shamelessly for her own interests, making him write in her support to his important friends – Popelin, Edmond de Goncourt, Princesse Mathilde and so forth. For the purpose of acceptance by the Salon of 1879, she painted a portrait of Doctor Cloquet, one of the most eminent medical men of the day. He had been a close friend of her grandfather Doctor Flaubert, and had gone on the trip to Corsica with young Gustave when he had passed his *baccalauréat* in 1840. He was to live to the age of ninety-three. By dint of great effort and influence, the portrait was eventually accepted and hung at the Salon of 1879.

Flaubert went back to Paris in September. This was his last visit to the capital, the last time that he saw his friends there, and the last time that he stayed with Princesse Mathilde at Saint-Gratien. Primoli describes the visit in his diary, and relates how Flaubert declared what had been his showpiece, before the war and after *Salammbô* had appeared, a monologue describing Mathô.[27] 'Nothing could give an idea,' he wrote, 'to someone who had not heard him, of Flaubert reading, reciting, intoning his works. It is Lemaître acting a boulevard play. The words fall from his lips with the noise of a cascade, which flows through his whole body. He seemed to become the barbarian Mathô, whose adventures he was relating.'

However, the peace and freedom from most pressing anxiety, obtained from the prospect of the pension, was short-lived and, by the time he got back to Croisset, in September 1879, Commanville was again in serious financial difficulties. He never told Flaubert what was happening and he still continued his wild speculations. As a result of this his uncle lost his last valuable asset, his friendship with Laporte, which was, with his love for his niece, the most precious thing in his life, his last close male friendship.

When Commanville's affairs deteriorated in September 1879, Caroline insisted on her uncle writing to Laporte to obtain a further guarantee from him, to ask him to pledge his last remaining asset, the house in which he lived. Laporte had sacrificed a great deal for his friend – he did not begrudge this for him – but he did not see why he should sacrifice anything further for the nephew in whom, rightly, he had no confidence, as he knew well that this further capital would go the way of the rest of his money and also of Flaubert's. He also knew that his friend was now comparatively safe from complete destitution, with his pension and the money he might earn from his books. He knew however that he was completely under the domination of his niece and her husband, and he wrote this time very firmly to Commanville to say that he could not accede to his request. Commanville took care not to answer himself, but got his uncle to write, knowing that Laporte would refuse him nothing. Flaubert wrote on 28 September 1879:[28]

A letter from you, which Commanville has just shown me, astonishes me. It seems to me that you do not understand the matter. Faucon could ask you for the immediate repayment of fourteen thousand francs before the end of the year. He agrees to put it off for a year and for this small service he asks us for twenty-five thousand francs . . . These twenty-five thousand francs . . . we shall have to find if you don't consent to renew your pledge. I don't understand what is stopping you. But whatever you decide, my dear friend, nothing will be changed between us two. However, before you decide, I *beg you* to think over the matter seriously.

Laporte answered immediately on receipt of this letter on 30 September 1879:[29]

This is what I feared, my dear Giant. You are brought into a discussion from which you should have been excluded. I cannot accept you as judge in a matter, where your nephew, on the one hand, and a friend on the other, are of different opinions. If we state our grievances and our reasons, what will happen? You will be obliged to put one or other in the wrong and your affectionate relations with that one could be affected. Let me discuss the affair with Commanville alone. If a few temporary annoyances result from that, you will, at least, not have had to take sides for or against anyone. Be assured, my dear Giant, that I shall always love you with my whole heart.

Laporte managed to refuse Commanville this further guarantee and Flaubert understood perfectly well that his friend, who was in such financial difficulties himself, should be unwilling to make further advances. His niece and nephew, however, made him feel that Laporte had acted treacherously towards him, and they insisted, for their honour, on his making a complete break with him. Caroline even told him that Laporte had guaranteed the earlier loans out of personal vanity, to gain intimacy with Flaubert.

Flaubert suffered a great deal from this interruption in his friendship, the only close friendship still remaining to him, and he did not at all understand what had happened, except that his dear niece imagined that she had been insulted and humiliated. He wrote to her in October:[30]

I've received a letter from Laporte . . . His tone is friendly as in the past. As he has not been seeing me, he'll come this week I'm sure. This wait is agony to me . . . What am I to say to him? I'm perplexed and in despair. When shall I have peace? . . . This affair with Laporte fills me with such bitterness and wrecks my life to such an extent that I haven't the strength to rejoice over a lucky event which has happened to me.

This was the formal announcement from Jules Ferry of the award of his pension. In December, he wrote to her again:[31] 'I continue to think very often of my ex-friend Laporte. That's a matter I've not been able to stomach easily.'

At the New Year, Laporte, who was broken-hearted at the loss of his friendship with Flaubert, attempted a reconciliation, and there is a touching letter from him, copied out by Flaubert, to send to his niece:[32]

My dear old friend. Whatever may be the feelings which others may have inspired in you towards me, I do not wish my New Year to come again without your receiving a mark of my affection and all my best wishes. Accept them without fear; it is perhaps the best of all your friends who is sending them. I embrace you.

He even added wishes for the niece, who was responsible for the mischief: 'I send to Madame your niece the homage of my deep respect.' Laporte did not receive an answer and Caroline did not mention his letter to her uncle, so that he asked her again what she thought of it:[33] 'You say nothing about Laporte's letter, of which I sent you a copy.'

The break between Flaubert and Laporte became complete and they never wrote to one another again nor ever met again.

Early in 1880, when Commanville's affairs seemed somewhat better – and Flaubert's also, for it was then that the negotiations to produce an opera from *Salammbô* seemed most advanced, when there was the possibility of the publication of *Le Château des Cœurs*, and a new edition of *L'Éducation Sentimentale* – Laporte wrote to Commanville to ask for some repayment of his loans. He seems to have sent to both Flaubert and Commanville a bailiff's summons. Flaubert was bitterly hurt and insulted, though he had no reason to be as, by his own wishes, he was no longer a friend of Laporte's. He said to his niece:[34] 'The chivalrous summons of Laporte has deeply upset me, as if someone had spat in my face.' It is not known how the matter was finally settled, as it is not mentioned any more in the correspondence.

Laporte, who had genuinely loved Flaubert, and had shown it in every possible way, never really got over the break with him. Lucien Descaves, who met him in 1906, a quarter of a century after the events in question, said that he was still inconsolable and deplored the ungrateful and underhand dealings which had led to the break between them.[35]

Flaubert's growing friendship with Guy de Maupassant was some consolation to him for the loss of intimacy with Laporte. As has been seen, Maupassant was the son of his childhood friend, Laure le Poittevin, the sister of Alfred. He became his disciple and it is probably due to Flaubert that he became a great stylist. As we have seen, it is Maupassant who finally persuaded him to accept the state pension in 1879. Flaubert, on his side, was responsible for saving his young disciple from a lawsuit for obscenity in 1880. Maupassant was summonsed on account of a poem, *Au bord de l'eau*, alleged to be obscene. It had appeared as long ago as 1876 under the name of Guy de Valmont, in *La République des Lettres*. It was now republished under his real name in *La Revue Moderne et Naturaliste*. The action was, however, stopped on account of a letter which Flaubert published in *Le Gaulois* on 21 February 1880, and which poured scorn on the summons.

Flaubert and Maupassant shared a common delight in obscenity and pornography, but whereas Flaubert kept it out of his published works and confined it to his correspondence, Maupassant published his abroad. Goncourt gives an account of a little playlet by him, which was performed privately every year after 1875, and which disgusted even Suzanne Lagier, free as she was normally in her speech, so much that she left before the end. The play, *Feuille de Rose*, was acted in a studio in the rue de Fleurus by Maupassant and a few of his friends. Goncourt has described the first performance:[36]

C'est lugubre ces jeunes hommes travestis en femmes, avec la peinture sur leurs maillots d'un large sexe entrebaillé; et je ne sais quelle répulsion vous vient involontairement pour ces comédiens s'attouchant et faisant entre eux le simulacre de la gymnastique d'amour. L'ouverture de la pièce c'est un jeune séminariste qui lave des capotes. Il y a au milieu une danse d'almées sous l'érection d'un phallus monumental et la pièce se termine par une branlade presque nature.

The next day Flaubert talked enthusiastically about the play and said that it was 'très frais'.

The play would leave our modern permissive performances far behind.

Maupassant's first important story, *Boule de Suif*, was published in *Les Soirées de Médan* in February 1880 and Flaubert hailed it for the masterpiece that it was. Maupassant's affection and admiration were very sweet to him at the end of his life. When he died it was Maupassant who washed him and laid him out ready for burial.

The work on which Flaubert was labouring during the last years of his life was *Bouvard et Pécuchet*, and he had been carrying out an immense amount of research for it since 1874, after the publication of *La Tentation de Saint Antoine*, with only the gap while he was composing *Trois Contes*. His researches were encyclopedic and dealt with almost every branch of knowledge – agriculture, geology, archaeology, medicine, education, philosophy, religion, physical culture and many other subjects – and he had read many hundreds of books in the process. His friends were beginning to be anxious lest his sources were becoming too learned and he too much divorced from life. Taine was very much worried about the harm that this might do his reputation. He wrote to Turgenev to express his fear and begged him to use all his influence with Flaubert to persuade him to change his plan. Taine knew that he had a great regard for the Russian novelist, and valued his opinion:[37]

The object of this letter is our friend Flaubert, and I beg you to destroy it when you've read it. You'll see that the matter is delicate. It is a question of his novel about the two retired employees who practise the sciences. He read it to me, or I've read nearly the whole of it at his house. I promised not to speak of it to anyone but you, who have also read it. When I'd finished, he asked me for my opinion. I put him off and asked for time to think it over, and I'm consulting you. My opinion is that the book, even if carried out as well as possible, could not be good; the comic element which he thinks he has included will miscarry like a rocket which has misfired. The two heroes being limited, stupid like Henri Monnier's characters, their misadventures, disappointments are necessarily flat; one expects them and they interest no one. It is like two snails trying to climb to the top of Mont Blanc, the first time they fall one smiles, but the tenth time is unbearable. Such a subject could only furnish, at most, a short story of a hundred pages ... Whatever may be the talent employed in carrying it out, I foresee a failure with the public, even worse than *L'Éducation Sentimentale* ... Think it over and tell me whether I'm right. You are a master in the matter of fiction, the first, in my opinion, of all our contemporaries. You must be able to judge and to predict better than I. If Flaubert had written none of his book, I would speak to him immediately and frankly. But he has been working on it for two or three years, and, even supposing my opinion had any weight with him, he would suffer very much at the thought of so much effort and work wasted. On the other hand, he counts on spending another three years on it; would it not then be cruel, if he is wrong, to allow him to throw so much time into the same abyss? I've always been sincere with him. I like him and admire him very much. He is a big-hearted man, loyal and estimable. I would like to behave to him as a good and loyal old friend, but I don't know what to do. He would bear me no grudge for my frankness, but I'm afraid of discouraging him without advantage. On the other hand, it pains me to see him get lost in an impasse ... Once again tell me what I should do. If my impression is false, so much the better, a thousand times the better. But, if you think it right, what are we to say to our friend?

Flaubert was not solely occupied with preparing *Bouvard et Pécuchet*, but he toyed with many other plans. In spite of his worries, his imagination was very fertile. There were many books which he thought of writing, particularly the story of the Battle of Thermopylae, which went back very far into his life. He even considered returning to Greece, with Georges Pouchet, in order to obtain details for the background. There was the plan of writing a novel taking in several generations of a Rouen family which Goncourt mentions. But the work which is most regretted is one dealing with the Second Empire, which seems to have greatly occupied his mind, and which he thought of in many forms. It is given the title *Le Préfet*, or *Un Ménage Parisien sous Napoléon III*. It is discussed in *Carnet* 20, which M. J. Durry has fully studied in her *Flaubert et ses Projets Inédits*.[38] It would probably have been a kind of continuation of *L'Éducation Sentimentale*, doing for the Second Empire what that novel had done for the earlier period.

There was also a story told by Charles Lapierre which Flaubert had thought promising and which he said that he would turn into a novel.[39] Lapierre was dining one evening at Croisset and told many strange stories, amongst them one about a most curious woman, Mademoiselle de P. She came from the Norman nobility and her life was made up of scandalous adventures. Thanks to protection in high places, she was appointed as reader to the Empress

Eugénie, in the last years of the Empire, but she got herself dismissed from Court as the result of an open liaison with a smart, gay young officer in the Imperial Guard. After that she became, in 1869, one of the most sought-after of the queens of the Parisian demi-monde. All the high dignitaries of the Empire, foreign diplomats, lords of finance, writers and artists used eagerly to frequent her boudoir. She was, it was said, beautiful enough to damn a saint. Like all her rivals in elegance and luxury, she disappeared during the war, but she was found afterwards in the circle of Thiers. Then her star waned and she sank into the lowest harlotry; she was able, however, to rise again, no one knows how, and became the mistress of a cavalry officer, eventually dying the legal wife of an admiral.

When Flaubert heard the story, he jumped up in excitement and delight, crying: 'Do you know Lapierre, you've just given me the subject of a novel, the counterpart of my Bovary, a Bovary of high society, what an attractive figure!' And he went to put down the story which he had just heard and to annotate it. He never wrote the novel and it is sad that the notes were never found. It is a pity that he did not write about the Second Empire, which he knew so well – the Court, the bourgeoisie and the demi-monde.

One of the most remarkable features of Flaubert's last years was the number of women friends who were prepared to comfort him, love him and care for him. Plain and grotesque-looking, with many unpleasant physical characteristics, he had the power of awakening affection in members of the opposite sex. It is unlikely that there was anything physical in their relationship – except perhaps with Madame Brainne, though even there no evidence exists of such intimacy – but he knew how to talk to them, about themselves and what interested them, and he was never bored with them. Also he appreciated their letters and never failed to answer, creating a special intimacy in their correspondence.

He was still keeping up his confidential correspondence with Madame Roger des Genettes, telling her all the intimate details of his everyday life, and advising her on hers. As we have seen, she had taken the place in his life of George Sand after her death and that of his mother. He did not see her now as much as he would have wished, for her health was fragile since her paralytic stroke, and she lived quietly in the country, coming rarely to Paris or to Rouen.

There were also Madame Pelouze, the owner of the Château de Chenonceaux, and Princesse Mathilde; and we have seen that the beautiful Comtesse de Loynes still treated him with warm affection.

Then there were those whom he called his three angels, Madame Lapierre, her sister Madame Brainne and Madame Pasquier (on the stage, Madame Pasca). Madame Lapierre was the wife of the editor of the *Nouvelliste de Rouen* and it was in her house at Rouen that the celebrations for the feast of Saint Polycarp took place. Madame Pasca became a singer after the death of her husband, who was a rich industrialist, and she had some notable successes on the stage in Paris, in Dumas' play *Les Idées de Madame Aubray* and in some operettas by Meilhac and Halévy.

Madame Lapierre wrote to Flaubert once:[40] 'I have the intention, next week, of spending a day at Rouen to go and embrace you. I embrace my dear Flau whom I love so much. I thank him for his affection and his concern for his friends, and for everything affectionate which comes from him.' She and her sister often went out to Croisset to see him, and a card to him informed him: 'Friend Flaubert is warned that his beautiful friends propose to go and ask him for lunch next Friday. They send a thousand marks of affection.' Madame Pasca, who did not live in Rouen, never went without going out to Croisset to see Flaubert. All three 'angels' realized how much kindness and softness there existed in the gruff old bear, and he was grateful to them for their affection.

Léonie Brainne, however, was the closest to him of the three and he was most intimate to her in his correspondence. His letters to her have come to light only since the war, and it is easy, from them, to see why so many should have imagined that they were lovers. He wrote to her once:[41]

What can I say to you? that you wrote me a darling letter. I've re-read it three times, as if I was a youth. Why am I that no longer, why am I that no longer? Why did I meet you too late? My heart remains intact, but my feelings are sharpened on the one hand and dulled on the other, like an old knife which has been too often sharpened, which has notches and breaks easily. It seems to me that I am not worthy of all that you give me, and the comparison which I make between the two of us humiliates me. 'To have a little place in my life,' you say. No! it isn't little and it is everything which touches me, penetrates me. That is why I am constantly in a state of agitation. I have gleaned on your lips, my dear beauty, something which will remain in the depths of my heart whatever may happen. How easy it would be for me to write endearments to you, to make phrases to you! But I spare your good taste. You might think that they weren't true.

But this is not the letter of a conquering lover. He liked to write to her in an intimate and flirtatious manner, with risky allusions, which he knew that she would understand and which would not commit him:[42]

When are you coming back? When shall I see you? When shall I be allowed to kiss you? At the moment I'm dreaming of your shoulders, of your legs in their red stockings, of your gentle mischievous eyes, and I long to devour you, that is the truth. I'd love to be the bath-tub which surrounds you! Such is my character (and *sometimes* my temperament). 'So much the worse for the ladies.' Much love from your old affectionate.

And again:[43] 'I kiss all the parts of your lovely person which you surrender to my not respectful friendship. For you are not yet worthy of respect, my dear beauty! – but always enviable, and desired.'

There are many more such allusions interspersed in his letters.

But Madame Brainne was a very good friend to him and, at the moment of his financial disasters, she came forward, like George Sand, with the offer of financial help. 'I am moved to tears,' he wrote to her,[44] 'by your offer of help, my dearest friend. Perhaps I shall take advantage of it but, for the moment, I only need to thank you.' She wrote to him once:[45]

I didn't go to embrace you this afternoon, for fear of stumbling into a large masculine company. Tell me when I shall have the chance of finding you at home and expressing to you the immensity of my love. How are you? Whatever you may think about it, my concern for you is very great, and I love you with infinite tenderness. Your dedicatory inscription is a glorification for my vanity and a satisfaction for my heart, which belongs to you this long time. I embrace you as much as I can, but not as much as you deserve.

Your best and most faithful, Léonie.

One of the great joys of Flaubert's last year resulted from his having got in touch again with Gertrude Collier, now Gertrude

Tennant. As we have seen, she came into his life again in 1876, when he was thinking about the past and when he was composing *Un Cœur Simple*. He had not seen her for nearly thirty years, since she left Paris in 1847.

In the early days it was the gentler younger sister who seemed to attract him most, and it was even thought that he might marry her. Gertrude seemed to him and to his sister hard and authoritarian, but, nevertheless, he may have cherished for her deeper feelings than he knew at the time, or would admit; and perhaps, at bottom, he preferred her sharpness to the sweetness of the younger sister. As she left he gave her his precious copy of Montaigne's *Essays*, inscribed 'Souvenir d'une inaltérable affection'. When he was in London in 1851, he met Henrietta again and a correspondence ensued between them for a time. He did not meet Gertrude and, when he spoke of her to Henrietta, she asked him not to mention her to her sister – there was obviously no love lost between them. He sent Gertrude a copy of *Madame Bovary*, when it was published in 1857, inscribed in the same way as the Montaigne *Essays*. She did not care for it and expressed surprise that he could ever have written such a book. They do not seem to have corresponded until 1876, and it is not known what prompted her then to break the long silence and to come to France. She probably wanted to visit Paris after the war for the sake of her children, now grown-up, and Flaubert was the only person left in the country whom she still knew. Perhaps she had treasured affection for him for all these years, and now that she was growing old would like to see him again. Certainly what she wrote after his death to his niece would support this belief. He was now fifty-four and she fifty-seven and one wonders whether she was shocked by his appearance. She had last seen him thirty years before, when he was still like an athletic young Greek god – as she described him. Now he was stout and bald, with long scanty locks, a red face, with only a couple of teeth left in his head, and his saliva blackened from his mercury treatment.

He wrote to her affectionately and with delight at the thought of seeing her again:[46]

My dear Gertrude, I am lonely for you. That is all that I can say to you. The kind gesture which urged you to try to see me after so many years must be followed up. It would be cruel now to start your forgetfulness again. And first write to me to tell me what is happening to you and your beautiful children. Then, this winter, you must come back to Paris to spend the whole season there. Dolly needs it for her scientific studies, and Evelyn for her singing ... Yes, dear Gertrude, life is so short that one must spend it as far as possible with those whom one loves. Would you like Caroline to look for an apartment for you to rent, in January? Do that! do! pray!

Then he tells her that, with her, he is embracing his youth. He wrote to her for Christmas:[47]

On this day the English celebrate! and I imagine you as much as I can, at home and surrounded by your beautiful children, with the Thames at your feet. As for me, I'm completely alone. My niece and her husband have been in Paris for the past six weeks. I shan't go to join them until the beginning of February, to get on more quickly with my work, so as to be able to publish my little book of tales in the spring ... If you are glad that I'm lonely for you, be so completely, dear Gertrude! ... Blessed be the inspiration which urged you to come and find me! But I shan't let you go any more. We must write and see one another, musn't we? The great age we have both reached permits us to cease being modest. It is true that three-quarters of the people that I know are stupid. I imagine that noble England is the same as witty France in this respect. And so one must only be with those who please one, that is to say with those whom one loves ... Ah! Trouville! the best part of my youth was spent there. Since we were there together on the beach, many waves have flowed over it. But no storm, dear Gertrude, has wiped out these memories. The perspective of the past: does it embellish everything? Was it really so beautiful and so good? What a lovely corner of the world and humanity it was, with you, your sisters, mine. Oh! abyss, abyss! If you were an old bachelor like me, you would understand it better. But no! I feel that you understand me.

At this moment of the year one wishes one another all sorts of things. What can I wish you? It seems to me that you have everything. I regret not being a believer so that I could pray heaven for your happiness.

He told her about his *Trois Contes* and was very much hurt when she expressed surprise that, after his other works, he should have written a tale entitled *Un Cœur Simple*.[48] 'A question: Why do you seem so astonished that I could have written a story entitled *Un Cœur Simple*? Your amazement intrigues me. Do you then doubt my faculty for affection? You certainly haven't got that right.'

They do not seem to have met as often as he would have wished. Did she find that too many things separated them after thirty years? Some remarks of his might lead to this conclusion:[49]

Why do you say that so many things separate us? For me there is only one and that is space! As for the rest, I pass through it all and I am attached to you in every meaning of the expression! How I long to see you! How many things I would have to say to you, alone with you, at the fireside. Do you know what I call you in the bottom of my being, when I think of you (which happens very often)? I call you my youth. Blessings on you and on all those you love, and, from the bottom of my heart, I am yours.

She sent him a picture of her daughter which greatly moved him, as it reminded him of what she had been at the same age.[50] What he really wanted was to persuade her to come and visit him at Croisset, which she had never seen, as it had not yet been bought when he knew her earlier. It was his real background and it was where he had written all his books. 'You've never come to Croisset,' he said to her.[51] 'You must get to know my real home. My lair.'

They do not seem to have met for a year, and no letters have reached us. As we have seen, however, 1879 was a very unhappy year for him. In October that year she seems to have broken the long silence and asked him whether he would be in Paris. He told her then that he could not move until the spring of the following year, as he wished to finish the first volume of his *Bouvard et Pécuchet*. He was also prevented from moving by his poverty, as he had not the money to stay in Paris. Anyway his niece was occupying his apartment.

The last letter from Flaubert to Gertrude Tennant is dated 13 January 1880, when he wrote to send her his sympathy for the loss of her daughter Evelyn in marriage:[52]

Don't be sad, my dear Gertrude. Remember that you have others who need you, and who will always need you. Your letter touched me to the heart, my dear old friend. How I would love to see you often, and for a long time, alone the two of us. We've got so many things to say to one another, haven't we?

I wish Evelyn all the happiness which her character and her extraordinary beauty deserve. A poet as a husband! A bourgeoise wouldn't have done that, and I love you all the more if that could be possible. To be a poet, young and rich, and to marry the woman one loves! There could be nothing better than that! and I envy your son-in-law, as I look back on my own life, so arid and so solitary.

He died four months later, so that meeting in Paris in the spring, which they had planned and to which they had looked forward for over a year, never took place.

Flaubert was often lonely during his last years, in spite of his hard work at his book, and he regretted not having children round him. He agreed, at the end, that he had taken a wrong turning in his life. Zola said that Flaubert admitted to him that he was sorry that he had not married and had children.[53] He once asked Heredia to take him to a children's party, which greatly moved him.[54] He wrote to his friend Gustave Toudouze:[55] 'I envy you since you are happy. Take care of your happiness. Love your wife and give your little boy big warm kisses. You are on the right and true path, don't leave it.' His niece relates a story how, in the last year of his life, she visited a friend with him, whose newly born baby was in a cradle in the room with them. On the way back he kept on repeating, 'A little creature like that in a home, there's nothing better than that in the whole world.'[56]

He lived a great deal in the past and, like Félicité in *Un Cœur Simple,* he was a fetichist for things of former days. He asked his niece about the whereabouts of the old hat which his mother had worn gardening, about her shawl and the little paper fan she had used in Italy, when she had come to meet him on his return from the East, so that he could gaze at them continuously. Like Charles in *Madame Bovary*, he liked Julie, the servant, to wear her mistress's dress and come and sit with him in the evening after dinner. Then he gazed at the old checked dress, dreaming of the departed, until tears rose to his throat and choked him. This was seven years after his mother had died.

In February 1880 Maxime Du Camp wrote to Flaubert to tell him that he had just been elected a member of the Académie Française. It was what he had always wanted and Flaubert was pleased for his sake, though he did not want it himself. Some people have thought that he was envious and jealous of Du Camp but this was certainly no longer true. He was, perhaps, envious when Du Camp was made an Officier de la Légion-d'Honneur in 1852 for his contribution to learning after his trip to the East. But, by 1880, Flaubert genuinely did not hanker for honours. As we know he had refused to allow his name to be put forward for election to the Académie when Hugo had offered to support him. He had also refused to be nominated for promotion in the Légion d'Honneur.

The year 1880 opened more hopefully for Flaubert. There seemed a chance of his nephew being able to start again in business with a new sawmill, and he went to Russia to prospect and to obtain wood. Flaubert was overjoyed and he wrote to his niece to express his delight and his hope that all their troubles were now over.[57] He also thought that it was time now that he should regain possession of his apartment and one can sense in his remarks the suppressed irritation of the past years:

And now let's talk a little about *our*, or rather *my* apartment. Well! here Madame are my wishes. I ask to be liberated from my enemy, *the piano*, and from another enemy which strikes me on the forehead: *the stupid hanging lamp* in the dining-room. It is very inconvenient if one has anything to do at the table. And as, this summer, I'll need that table for my copyist, take away that machine and put back my simple lamp which I had in Boulevard du Temple. Free me also of all the rest – it would be simpler! the sewing machine, the plaster casts, your bookcase with the glass front, your chest. I was so much inconvenienced by all this, the last time I was there, that my clothes had to remain on the chairs. Finally store this excessive furniture at Bedel's until your next move. But make arrangements so that I shall be in my own home and so that I shall have elbow-room. Since this apartment is no longer to be of use to you, empty it. And please note that I shall need it in May and June, and that I shall be back there in September.

I'm planning to turn your bedroom into a boudoir. The divan that I shall put there can be used by you or Ernest this summer, if need be (it clutters up the dining-room and is in danger of breaking the windows). Naturally don't remove the curtains or the carpets. I can *endure* the big linen-cupboard in my bedroom, on account of its contents which are difficult to remove. The wall-brackets, as well as the crystal chandelier, and the Venetian glass in my study don't worry me.

As for your bedroom, my future boudoir, I know that it would be convenient for you to put the piano there. If you don't know where to accommodate it, that is an added reason for removing your royal bed from that room, which won't be of any use to you this summer, then I would submit to the piano without too much grumbling. But I beg of you, my dearest, clear the place for me.

He wrote again the following day:[58]

I don't want to displease my dearest, nor myself either. So here is what must be done: Keep your bedroom as it is, *but* clear away the piano (that's agreed), also the hanging lamp in the dining-room, the sewing-machine, the chest and the divan, or at least the chest. You could put the divan in the anteroom. Also arrange for the passage to be clear. In a word only keep what is absolutely useful for sleeping and dressing; take the bust back into your room (or leave it on top of the bookcase).

It is sad to think that Flaubert never went back to his apartment in Paris, for two months later he was dead.

He was now in a happier frame of mind, and he planned a celebration for Easter Sunday, 28 March, paid for out of some money he had hidden away for the purpose. He invited Daudet, Zola, Maupassant, Goncourt and his publisher Charpentier. It was to be an all-male affair and the guests were to spend the night at Croisset. Goncourt has given an account of the festivities.[59] He was much more favourably impressed by the beauty of the property than he had been when he visited it in 1863 and had been shocked that there had been silver, not gold plate, on the table. He said now that the hospitality was very good and the meal excellent, with the cream sauce going with the turbot like a dream. They drank many different kinds of good wines and Flaubert was in great form, telling many gross stories, as he liked to do in an all-male gathering, and there was much laughter. Next day they talked all the morning, then, after luncheon, separated, and Flaubert promised that he would meet them in Paris in May.

However the grandest celebration that year was the one for the feast-day of Saint Polycarp, on 27 April, only ten days before he died. He himself has given an account of it in a letter to his niece the following day.[60] The party was planned and given, as usual, by Monsieur and Madame Lapierre. Flaubert received thirty letters from different parts of the world and various telegrams. The Archbishop of Rouen, some Italian cardinals, various corporations of the town, as well as a religious object shop sent kind messages. He was given various presents, amongst them a pair of silk socks, a scarf, a picture of Saint Polycarp and an alleged tooth of the saint. Box after box of rare flowers came from Nice, and all the dishes were called after his books. He was very much touched by all the trouble that was taken for his pleasure.

It was a good thing that he had this banquet as one of the last memories of his life.

Flaubert had hoped to complete the first volume of *Bouvard et Pécuchet* before he went to Paris at the beginning of May 1880, but he could not get it finished in time and he decided not to postpone his visit any longer, as he had told so many friends that he was coming and had made so many engagements. He decided to leave the one remaining chapter unfinished and to complete it on his return. He then wrote his last letters to his friends announcing his arrival. The last letters in the *Correspondance Générale* are dated 3 May 1880, one to Guy de Maupassant and one to Théodore de Banville. There is however one further letter, written to Claudius Popelin on 6 May, two days before he died:[61]

My dear friend. Now I don't count on you any more [that is, to visit him at Croisset] as I'm beginning my packing, and you'll see me either Sunday evening or Monday morning. *But* I hope that, this summer, I'll have a fairly long visit from you. I embrace you, your old Gustave Flaubert.

On this Popelin has pencilled a note to the effect that this was Flaubert's last letter. Then, on Saturday 8 May 1880, the day before he was to leave for Paris, he died.

Lapierre was the first to hear of the death and informed the press and all the friends. The Commanvilles and Maupassant arrived the same evening, and it was the latter who prepared him for burial and watched over him for three nights. Nobody but the housekeeper and the doctor saw him as he was dying, and what Caroline was later to relate was invented. Edmond Laporte was not informed and he heard the news only the following day from the announcement in the press. He went out immediately to Croisset and asked to be allowed to see his dear old friend one last time but, through Caroline's orders, he was refused admission; she thus kept up her animosity towards him even beyond death.[62] There is some confusion over the circumstances surrounding his death. According to his housekeeper's account he had got up, had had a very hot bath and then had been overtaken by some weakness. She could not get hold of his usual doctor but fetched a Doctor Tourneux, who seems to have been the first person to see Flaubert dead – indeed dying. René

Dumesnil, himself a trained doctor, later discussed the matter with Tourneux.[63] The latter said to him that none of the symptoms, at the time of death, had been epileptic, but were more like those of apoplexy. There do not seem any valid reasons for doubting his testimony. There is the suggestion that death might have been due to the syphilis, from which he had been suffering for many years.[64] It is impossible from such a distance to diagnose accurately the true causes of his death, but it matters very little now whether it was epilepsy, apoplexy or syphilis. There is, however, one suggestion which is important, as it would affect our view of the man, and that is that he committed suicide. A certain Doctor Ledoux claimed that he had strangled himself in his bath.[65] The evidence is not at all convincing and it is not shown how it could have happened. Ledoux said that there was a police report – a *procès-verbal* – and that seals were affixed on the door of the study where Flaubert had died. This would not tally with the suggestion that he had strangled himself in his bath, for he would not have transported himself, dead or dying, from the bathroom to the study. There is nothing very suspicious in a police report, as he had died suddenly. Ledoux tried to obtain a copy of the report, but found that none were preserved after ten years.

It does not seem possible or likely that Doctor Tourneux should have lied and his testimony is clear. He was not Flaubert's regular doctor, nor a friend, and there was no reason why he should hide the fact of suicide. The suggestion of suicide seems very fanciful. It is difficult to see how, physically, he could have achieved it. He had, apparently, just come from his bath, which had probably been very hot, and he was waiting for his breakfast. It seems that the hot bath might have brought on an apoplectic stroke in someone with high blood pressure, as Flaubert seemed to have had. All his plans were ready for him to go to Paris the following day, and he had made many assignations with friends. He wanted to finish the book on which he had been working for so many years – certainly the first volume, of which only one chapter was left to complete and for which the notes were prepared. He had been postponing his visit to Paris in order to finish it, but, in the end, he felt that he could not postpone his visit any longer, but would complete the remaining chapter on his return. He would surely not have killed himself before that was done. He had a puritanical sense of duty towards his art, and would not have given up a piece of work unless forced to do so. He would not have killed himself through despair, for he obtained a fierce kind of ecstasy from viewing the worst, gaining strength from its awareness. As he wrote to Ernest Feydeau: 'People like us must have the religion of despair. One must be equal to one's destiny, that is to say impassible like it. By dint of saying "That is so! that is so!" and of gazing down into the black pit at one's feet, one reaches calm.'[66]

Flaubert, out of deference to his niece's religious beliefs and principles, left no conditions and did not insist on a lay funeral. The funeral took place on Tuesday, 11 May, and three hundred people came to it, mostly writers from Paris, amongst them Daudet, Zola, Goncourt, Coppée, Banville and Maupassant. Maxime Du Camp, Flaubert's oldest remaining friend, did not attend, pleading illness, but it may have been because he did not care for Caroline – as none of the friends did. She even accused him to her uncle of having been rude to her, a couple of months before he died.[67] Du Camp was not in any hurry to write, and did so only on 17 May:[68]

You understood, didn't you, my dear Caroline, that I must have been ill not to go to Croisset, and not to have written to you immediately. I've just suffered from an attack of nephritis, which made me incapable of doing anything, except to suffer from this death.

Then he went on to talk of Flaubert, the companion of the whole of his life, whom he had loved so much. He added that he had not even been able to send her a telegram to tell her that his heart was with her. It must be admitted that his excuses are somewhat thin. Goncourt has given a long and full account of the sordid events of the funeral and its aftermath in his *Journal*.[69]

The procession wound its way from the house where Flaubert had spent the largest part of his life and had written all his books, to the little parish church at Canteleu. After a short funeral service it went to the cemetery at Rouen, passing beside Bouilhet's grave, and arrived at the family plot. Then there happened what had occurred at his sister Caroline's funeral thirty-four years before. The grave had been dug too short and the grave-diggers had the greatest difficulty in fitting in the coffin. It could neither be pushed in nor pulled out, the funeral party had to leave the cemetery before the grave was filled in, and there were cries of 'Enough, enough! wait until afterwards.'(70)

A picket of the Garde Nationale fired a volley over the grave – the traditional honour paid to members of the order of the Légion-d'Honneur. Flaubert had asked that there should be no speeches and only Lapierre spoke a few brief words.

Goncourt has described all the journalists, with pieces of paper in the hollow of their hands, taking notes of the people who were present; they were also talking loudly of the meal they were going to have afterwards in Rouen, and even of the local brothels they were going to sample.

'Oh! the sad and heart-rending funeral Flaubert had!' wrote Goncourt.

He described how the son-in-law had ruined Flaubert, that he was not only a dishonest man but, commercially speaking, a swindler. He pocketed a twenty-franc piece which his uncle had given him to pay the locksmith. He could not make out whether the niece – whom he called 'les petits boyaux de Flaubert' – was evil in her own right or only the unconscious instrument in the hands of her scoundrel of a husband, who exercised over her the power which scoundrels have over honest women.

Before the funeral Commanville spoke all the time of the money which could be made from the works of the dead man, suggesting that his love letters should be sold and even giving the impression that he was capable of blackmailing the surviving ladies. This went on until the Monday and when Maupassant and Pouchet put Flaubert in his coffin the body was already beginning to decompose.

On the evening of the funeral Commanville cut himself seven slices of ham at dinner and then took Maupassant into the garden, to the summer-house, and kept him there a prisoner, with hypocritical expressions of affection for the dead man, while he discussed literary possibilities for over an hour.

In the meantime Caroline Commanville took Heredia aside on another seat and complained that Maxime Du Camp had not even sent her a telegram, and that Zola and Daudet had not liked Flaubert. This, in point of fact, was not true. Then she told Heredia that he was a gentleman and that she needed the devotion, in these sad circumstances, of a man of the world who would defend her from the members of her own family. She was indeed accused of being very cruel to her cousin, Achille Flaubert's daughter, Juliette. Then she burst into tears with such tender abandon, and brought her head so near to Heredia's breast that he said that, if he had made a movement, she would have thrown herself into his arms. Then she took off her glove and let her hand hang at the back of the seat, so near to his mouth that she seemed to be asking for a kiss. Goncourt did not know whether this was sudden true love in a woman overcome by grief, or whether it was play-acting to advance her husband's frauds. And Goncourt added: 'Ah! my poor Flaubert, here round your corpse are human documents with which you could have made a provincial novel.'

Caroline was not slow in realizing all that her uncle had left. She sold the house for one hundred and eighty thousand francs. She said, to defend her action:[71] 'We have sold Croisset, my husband was never well there, and the property was a heavy charge on us. A good price was offered to us for it.' Then she added: 'In a few days I had to leave all my memories of childhood behind me, and those even dearer to me, connected with my beloved uncle, and this seemed to me like a second death.' When her uncle was alive she went little enough to Croisset to see him.

The house was pulled down and an ugly factory erected in its place. The only thing left of Croisset was the little summer-house by the Seine, which became a small Flaubert museum.

Caroline exploited Flaubert's fame and literary remains for half a century until her death in 1931, and became very rich in the process. However, although she did bowdlerize the letters, she is responsible for publishing most of the correspondence. Her house at Antibes, Villa Tanit, became, in her lifetime, a centre for Flaubert studies and she was glad of the fame which her dead uncle brought her. Unfortunately, after her death, much material was, through her wishes, scattered in various libraries, and much was sold and disappeared.

When Ernest Commanville died in 1890, she married Franklin Grout, the brother of a friend of hers, Frankline, who had married Auguste Sabatier, a Professor at the Faculty of Protestant Theology in Paris. Franklin Grout was a psychiatrist, the son of a Rouen doctor, who eventually joined Doctor Blanche at his mental nursing-home in Paris, and looked after Maupassant when he died there.

Jacques Émile-Blanche, the son of Franklin Grout's partner, tells us in *La Pêche aux Souvenirs* that Caroline shamelessly exploited her uncle after his death, that she had become even more snobbish and pushing, and she now had the money to support her pretensions.[72]

Maurice Barrès was told, when he visited Croisset, that Madame Franklin Grout never came there, not even for the celebrations, but had herself represented by a young woman.[73]

From beyond the grave Flaubert would have been pleased at the worldly success and prosperity of his beloved niece, and glad too that it was he who had been able to provide for her so lavishly and luxuriously.

CHAPTER FOURTEEN

BOUVARD ET PÉCUCHET

The book on which Flaubert was working during the last years of his life – and before that as well – was *Bouvard et Pécuchet*. As we have seen it was published posthumously by Juliette Adam, in her *Nouvelle Revue*, in 1880 and 1881. The manuscript and notes are preserved in the Bibliothèque Municipale at Rouen.[1] As we have seen, his niece tells us that the initial idea came when Flaubert and Bouilhet were sitting outside an old men's home in Rouen and saw a couple of inmates coming out, and Flaubert thought that he would like to write about such men.[2] It is also clear that he must have read a story entitled *Les Deux Greffiers* by B. Maurice, published in 1859, in a paper called *L'Audience*, on which Bouilhet and various other friends worked. It is true that it had already appeared on 14 April 1841 in *La Gazette des Tribunaux* and, in May the same year, in *Le Journal des Journaux*.[3] He is, however, more likely to have read it in *L'Audience*, when he was only nineteen and beginning to study law, than in the other papers.

The two clerks, who are close friends, withdraw when they reach their retirement, to the country with their families, and decide to spend their life pleasantly in rural pursuits, such as fishing. They find that, eventually, they grow bored and they return to their former work and dictate to one another. The story is short and simple and there is no more to it than that.

After Flaubert's death Madame Ernest Daudet discovered *Les Deux Greffiers* and Flaubert was accused of plagiarism. It is very likely that he did in fact read the tale but the resemblances between it and his novel are very slight. In *Les Deux Greffiers* it is solely weariness of excessive leisure which drives the friends back to routine work; but the implications in *Bouvard et Pécuchet* are vastly different. After Bouvard receives his legacy he and his friend Pécuchet retire to the country. After trying many and various occupations for which they are utterly unsuited and unprepared, after losing most of their money, and recognizing their incompetence, they return to their earlier occupation of copying. The essence of *Les Deux Greffiers* is that it is merely boredom that drives the clerks back to their former work, whereas the interest in *Bouvard et Pécuchet* lies in all their attempts at self-education and culture, and their failure in everything that they undertake.

Like *La Tentation de Saint Antoine*, *Bouvard et Pécuchet* is a work that goes far back into Flaubert's life. Critics tend to exaggerate when they see the origins of the novel in the essay which he wrote, at the age of fifteen, about the genus clerk entitled *Le Commis*, on the model of the fashionable physiologies of the time, where the clerk is studied as a species of animal. The only resemblance between the two works is that *le commis* is a clerk and Bouvard and Pécuchet are copyists – a kind of clerk.

Flaubert probably did not think about *Bouvard et Pécuchet* until after he had published *Salammbô* in 1863, when there exists the first plan of the novel.[4] This is the earliest extant plan and he must have been seriously thinking of the book then, but he allowed himself to be diverted into writing *L'Éducation Sentimentale*, probably, as we have seen, because he heard at that time that Élisa Schlésinger had been interned in a mental home, and this brought back to his memory his relationship with her with renewed poignancy. He then worked on that book for six years and shelved *Bouvard et Pécuchet* until after the war and the Commune, that is until after the publication of *La Tentation de Saint Antoine* in April 1874, and the failure of his dramatic venture, *Le Candidat*, at the end of March the same year. Then he began serious work on *Bouvard et Pécuchet*, and was occupied with it for the six years until his death, except for the short interruption of little more than a year between 1875 and 1877 while he was composing *Trois Contes*.

What are we to call the book? Flaubert himself called it a novel and we should follow suit. When he was beginning writing in 1874, he said to Madame Roger des Genettes that his 'novel' was to be called *Les Deux Copistes*.[5] And, when the book was almost finished in December 1879 – the first part at all events – he wrote to Gertrude Tennant that the first volume of his 'infernal novel' would be finished the following year; he does, however, admit that it will be a very peculiar novel, in which love will play no part whatsoever, and that those who read it to find out whether the Baroness will marry the Viscount will be disappointed.[6]

At first Flaubert intended to call the novel *Les Deux Cloportes*, the two woodlice, which reveals his contempt for his two main characters. However he gradually grew fond of them and made them more interesting, and eventually he said that they were not fools. In one of the plans he says: 'Ce ne sont pas précisément deux imbéciles, ils ont beaucoup de sentiment et d'embryons d'idées qu'ils ont du mal à exprimer.'[7] At the beginning, as he had first painted them, they would not have been able to understand and to discuss the learned books – religious and philosophical – which they were able to do later. They would also have been incapable of the judgement necessary to make a selection of the foolish things which they found in the books they studied. At first they did not possess a developed critical sense, but afterwards they were able to judge what they read and were capable of compiling, not just copying, *Le Dictionnaire des Idées Reçues*.

Even in the earliest conception of the novel, the texts which the two men were to copy were to play an important part. In the 1863 plan, when the novel was called *Les Deux Cloportes*, it was to be in three parts, in one volume, and the third part was to be entirely made up of foolish quotations which the two friends copied. One of the texts in Part Three was to be *Le Dictionnaire des Idées Reçues*.[8] Much later, this third part became so important that it needed a whole volume to itself, not just part of a volume. However, this volume was dropped in plans later than the 1863 one. But when, in 1877, he took up the book again, after the interlude of *Trois Contes*, the separate section made up entirely of foolish quotations had again become important to him, and is discussed in all the plans of the novel during the last three years of his life, though we do not know excatly what it would have been. It was now to be a whole volume.

The amount of research which Flaubert carried out in order to write *Bouvard et Pécuchet* was colossal. Writing to Madame Roger des Genettes in January 1880, he said:[9]

Do you know the number of volumes I had to absorb for my two men? More than fifteen hundred. My bundle of notes is eight inches high.

There are eight volumes of notes preserved in the Bibliothèque Municipale at Rouen, in the 'Dossier Bouvard et Pécuchet'.[10] However, all these documents do not refer to *Bouvard et Pécuchet*, and they have not been fully sorted or classified. There are many which were not intended for it. Amongst them is *Les Mémoires de Madame Ludovica*, which as we have seen was used for *Madame Bovary*. There are very many cuttings from the press, especially for 1848, which served for *L'Éducation Sentimentale*; and there are many notes which were also intended for that novel, as, for instance, the material on ceramics. We have also seen that the first sketch for *Un Cœur Simple*, entitled *Le Perroquet*, is amongst the documents.

There are all the rough copies of the novel – 'les brouillons' – in three volumes.[11] That is as far as the novel went when its author died, that is chapters one to nine and most of chapter ten. There is also the fair copy of the same chapters ready for publication.[12] There is the manuscript of *Le Dictionnaire des Idées Reçues*, and of the plans, following the 1863 plan, before the second volume was conceived.[13]

Although the documents contain the notes which Flaubert took when he was describing the disastrous experiments which the two friends undertook – gardening, horticulture, chemistry, geology and so forth – nevertheless the largest bulk of the documents were intended for Volume Two, which was, in his last plan, to consist entirely of quotations from the foolish things said by scholars and thinkers. This was what the two men were to copy when they abandoned their independent work. It is the material collected by Flaubert's friends, Duplan and Laporte. It is true that Duplan died in 1870, before the book was begun, but we have seen that, even in the 1863 plan, the copying of quotations was to be an important part of the third section of the novel and was to take up the whole of one book. For instance *L'Album de la Marquise*, in Duplan's hand, must have been made before the war, refer to the earliest plan and be intended to be part of the 'Sottisier'.[14] However, after the 1863 plan, there are others amongst the papers at Rouen. They are not dated but they must have been made after 1863 and before 1877, when Flaubert took up the book again, after having dropped it to write *Trois Contes*. There are several versions of what is really one plan (gg10), differing only in details. In this plan there are ten chapters, as we have them in the printed version; but it gives also two further chapters, eleven and twelve, which would have finished off the novel in one coherent volume. Chapter eleven was to discuss what the two men were copying when, in chapter ten, they returned to their former occupation. Chapter twelve was to be a kind of conclusion, showing what had happened to the characters in the novel, and tidying up all the loose ends. This plan seems, to one reader at least, a more satisfactory one than that finally adopted; one chapter for what the two men were copying seems sufficient in the balance of the novel, and a whole volume seems excessive. As he accumulated the material, Flaubert found that it could not all be fitted into one chapter and he thought of the separate volume. This is, in a way, a kind of return to the first plan of 1863, when he had conceived that one third of the novel, one whole part, should be devoted to the quotations. The first mention we have of the second volume is in a letter to Caroline, of December 1877, when he took up the novel again.[15] It is clear that henceforth, in the final writing of the book, the second volume is firmly entrenched in the plan, and that it meant a great deal to him.

When Flaubert died in 1880 he had almost finished Volume One, the ten chapters of which it now consists. Chapter ten was not quite completed, but he left full and thorough notes of how this was to be done. This is the novel as it has reached us in published form. Flaubert would have finished that chapter when he got back to Croisset from Paris in 1880. He had, however, written nothing of Volume Two, and there are no plans or scenarios amongst his notes, but only the raw material which the two men were to copy. He said, on several occasions, that he would only need six months to write it and that it was almost finished. This would mean that it would have to be a very different kind of book from Volume One, as there are no plans, no divisions into chapters, no description of characters, no action. It is very hard to see how this volume could be part of the same novel. It is, however, also clear that in the latter stages of the composition this second volume was a very important part of the conception –

though it is hard to see why – and he even believed that the first volume would be incomprehensible without it.[16] He had taken almost six years on Volume One and yet contemplated writing Volume Two in six months, though he said that it would consist mostly of quotations. This would have made a monstrous volume made up of raw material and not really a book at all – certainly not a novel.

Alberto Cento has produced a critical edition of Volume One, and this is the most complete edition yet.[17] He is planning to bring out the second volume, but this can certainly not be done in the same way, as there are no notes to explain what Flaubert intended. All that he will be able to do is to publish the vast amount of material which Flaubert had collected, in categories and under various headings. This has already been partially done in the notes at Rouen. This is all that Geneviève Bollème has done in her *Le Second Volume de Bouvard et Pécuchet*. It is hard to believe that this is what Flaubert would eventually have agreed to for his second volume, and that he would have been satisfied with something as monstrous as a mere compilation. It must be remembered that he was a novelist and a psychologist, and he could surely not have been satisfied with a novel having no analysis of the characters, and not taking them into account. After all the men were to compile the *Dictionnaire des Idées Reçues*, and it should be shown how they could do this. In the plan gg10, he had taken into account the character of the collectors of material, and shows how they change as they work:[18]

Ils copient tous les m.s. et papiers imprimés qu'ils trouvent, cornets de tabac etc. Journaux, lettres perdues, affiches . . . Ils en ont beaucoup car aux environs se trouve une fabrique de papier en faillite, et ils obtiennent des masses de vieux papiers. Mais bientôt ils trouvent le besoin d'un classement. Morceaux de style médical, agricole etc. Ils font des tableaux, des parallèles antithétiques comme 'crimes de Paris, crimes du peuple' etc. Mais souvent ils sont embarrassés pour ranger le fait à sa place, et ils ont des cas de conscience. La difficulté augmente à mesure qu'ils avancent dans leur travail, ils continuent cependant. Ils font le Dictionnaire des Idées Reçues et le catalogue des idées chic. Annoter au lieu de copier.

However the final idea of Volume Two was very much more complicated than chapter eleven of the scenario – they were now reading many sophisticated and learned works, not just copying odd pieces of paper.

Then, in the plan gg10, there is chapter twelve, the conclusion:

Un jour ils trouvent par hasard un brouillon d'une *lettre écrite par le médecin*. Le préfet lui ayant demandé si Bouvard et Pécuchet n'étaient pas des fous dangereux. La lettre est une espèce de rapport confidentiel expliquant que leur manie est douce et que ce sont deux imbéciles inoffensifs. Elle résume et doit rappeler au lecteur tout le livre. 'Qu'allons-nous en faire? La copier parbleu. Oui copions.' Ils copient. Finir par la vue des deux bonshommes penchés sur leur pupitre et copiant.

The two men had here learnt humility, had learnt to know themselves, and were satisfied to be merely copyists.

This is the ending of the book, in its first conception before Volume Two had become so important and pretentious even, and was more in keeping with their characters as we have grown to know them.

Alberto Cento, Geneviève Bollème, and D. L. Demorest all assume that chapters eleven and twelve of the plan gg10 were to be part of an introduction to Volume Two, though they do not show how this can be.[19] They have not considered that they could be part of a plan which had been discarded. In fact they do not seem to consider that there could have been a change of plan in 1877, when Flaubert took up the book again after writing *Trois Contes*, and gave more importance to the quotations – we have seen that the second volume was not mentioned until 1877. That is in fact what the present author believes. If chapters eleven and twelve of plan gg10 were to be part of Volume Two then there would be some repetition in the notes for the end of chapter ten, which was to be the ending of Volume One, as Flaubert left them when he planned to go to Paris in May 1880. There is no evidence anywhere that chapters eleven and twelve were to be used in Volume Two, or that the volume was to consist of anything else but quotations. The fictional elements would not have fitted in with the lists of citations.

At first, in the 1863 plan – indeed in gg10 as well – the copying was quite simple and not selective, and was only intended to give practice in the art of calligraphy; the two friends were to copy everything that came into their hands, at random. Then they found L'*Album de la Marquise* and copied that and recognized its humour.[20] There was, of course, no Marquise, but Flaubert chose to put in her autograph album many idiotic quotations from well-known writers who were supposed to be her friends. As, for instance, from Barbey d'Aurevilly: 'J'ai bu à longs traits dans la coupe d'opale de ses épaules la cruelle ivresse des bonheurs non partagés.' And from Alexandre Dumas: 'Blanche colombe brisée jusque dans l'âme, elle cachait son front sous son aile pour pleurer.' This text, as has been said before, was in the hand of Duplan and must go back to the eighteen-sixties. There was also, at the same time, *Le Dictionnaire des Idées Reçues*, which he tells Bouilhet in 1850, when he was at Damascus, was completely finished and that he wanted to publish it with a long explanatory preface.[21] This would have been then a separate book, published under his own name. There was also, in the 1863 plan, the *Catalogue des Idées Chic*. All these were still in the plan gg10, ten years later. Then he resorts to the subterfuge of pretending to have found the entire volume of quotations, of the various texts.[22] 'Avant la copie, après l'introduction, mettre en italiques, ou en note, qu'on a retrouvé par hazard [*sic*] leur copie, l'Éditeur en donne afin de grossir le présent volume.' The novelist has then found, for chapter eleven, all that the two friends had copied. All this is before 1877.

In the final plan, or conception – for we have no plan – when the friends begin copying again, they go to the books and authors in whom they had formerly believed, which had deceived them and in which they now find only absurdities, inanities and stupidities. This is when they compile Volume Two.

It is here that the enormous bulk of the notes which are preserved in the Bibliothèque Municipale in Rouen were to be used. There would, however, have been far too many of them and the weight of stupidities, far from adding strength to the argument, would have ended in weakness and boredom. It is inconceivable that Flaubert could have used all of them, even if sorted into different categories. The point is soon appreciated that many of the greatest minds, at times, wrote nonsense.[23] Flaubert cites the following, which are chosen from amongst hundreds. Bernardin de St Pierre: 'Le melon a été divisé en tranches par la nature afin d'être mangé en famille; la citrouille, étant plus grosse, peut être mangée avec les voisins.' Fénelon: 'L'eau est faite "pour soutenir ces prodigieux édifices flottants que l'on appelle des vaisseaux".' Raspail: 'Une garde-malade, si peu lettrée qu'elle soit, est souvent un grand médecin.' Chateaubriand: 'Sans religion on peut avoir de l'esprit mais il est difficile d'avoir du génie.' Sainte-Beuve, in *Port-Royal*: 'Une longue incubation de piété mûrissante.' While the Bishop of Metz pronounced in 1846: 'Les inondations de la Loire sont dues aux excès de la Presse et à l'inobservation du Dimanche'. And Lamartine described the sun setting behind the towers of Notre Dame Cathedral in Paris, when that is in the east.[24]

When Flaubert began thinking of composing *Bouvard et Pécuchet*, he declared to Madame Roger des Genettes, to Ernest Feydeau and to Madame Brainne that he was undertaking the book solely for the purpose of pouring scorn on his contemporaries, to empty his bile on them.[25] This statement cannot really refer to Volume One as it was planned and as it has come down to us. The misfortunes of Bouvard and Pécuchet, in most of their undertakings, are not due to the deficiencies of the scientific knowledge of the day, but to their own, because they embark on experiments for which they are not equipped or educated. They are too ignorant to be aware of their lack of preparation and they never learn to learn. It is not the lack of knowledge of the day which Flaubert is attacking in the first volume, but lack of method and training. When the book was nearly finished, he wrote to Gertrude Tennant that the sub-title should have been 'du défaut de méthode dans les sciences'.[26] One cannot say that the whole world deserves to be drowned in vomit and bile because two extremely foolish elderly men embark on experiments for which they are unsuited. Where Flaubert does pour out his anger and his scorn is on the other members of the community, whom he shows as selfish, self-interested and gross. Bouvard and Pécuchet start out by being simple and naïve, but always kind – indeed the only kind members of the village – and they are never vile. Eventually they become more human through their self-education, more evolved as human beings, and they can even be the spokesmen for their author.

Flaubert does make the two friends symbolical of the ignorance of average people. They have the same amateurishness which he deplored in other characters – in Frédéric and Pellerin in *L'Éducation Sentimentale*, for instance. They never take long enough to go into anything thoroughly, to master anything. When they do not understand something, they conclude that it is not worth knowing. That is why they chop and change so frequently and can keep their mind and attention on nothing. Consequently, 'N'ayant pu la comprendre [medicine] ils n'y croyaient pas.'[27] Flaubert was here symbolizing one of the great weaknesses of humanity in general and of his own country in particular. It is not love of learning which he intended to satirize, nor learning itself. But he wished to give a warning to those who embarked on subjects without being prepared for them, who had not learnt to learn.

The main idea of Volume Two, which the quotations were intended to prove, is that mankind in general is despicable, conceited, arrogant and self-important. Even many of the best writers, who should have learnt wisdom, imagine that they know everything. Even those with the highest reputation are as faulty as the rest. Most of them talk in clichés, use rough and ready formulas without thinking them out, in order to make statements and to adopt the ideas which they imagine everyone should hold. In a way only Bouvard and Pécuchet are exempt because, although they are simple and limited in intelligence, they are innocent and honest, and they see through the falsities. The question which Flaubert asks, in the persons of the two men, is why there are so many things which we would like to know, and which remain beyond our grasp. That was Flaubert's own question, and it is the tragedy of all mankind. Bouvard says:[28] 'La science est faite suivant les données fournies par un coin de l'étendue. Peut-être ne connaît-elle pas tout le reste qu'on ignore, qui est beaucoup plus grand et qu'on ne peut découvrir.' The conclusion is that man must learn humility, and that all the mischief comes from our terrible ignorance.[29] 'The harm comes from our gigantic ignorance. What should have been investigated was believed without discussion. Instead of examining things one only affirms them.'

The philosophy of the book is that all our efforts here below will be in vain, on account of our vanity, our self-sufficiency, and our conceit. Like Bouvard and Pécuchet most of us are deceived by everything and we do not realize our incapacity for understanding, but think, in our overweening vanity, that we know everything. The conclusion is that we must not believe in the absolute power of science and knowledge.

(*Bouvard et Pécuchet*, the first volume, as far as it goes, has been published, ending with the notes for the completion of chapter ten, and it makes a perfectly reasonable novel if we take no account of Volume Two, but substitute for it chapters eleven and twelve, from the earlier plan gg10. As has been said previously, this seems, to this author at least, more satisfactory than the novel planned in two volumes. Flaubert talked of the book as a novel and Volume One can be considered as such, but Volume Two would only have spoilt this plan – in any case the most significant part could be included in chapter eleven.)

The novel begins beautifully with the well-balanced sentence we have mentioned already: 'Comme il faisait une chaleur de 33 degrés, le boulevard Bourdon se trouvait absolument désert.' The author makes us realize, with great economy of phrase, the simple naïveté of the two men, their lack of intellectual subtlety, the interest and excitement which each feels when he discovers that the other has written his name in his hat, which he places on the seat beside him. It seems miraculous to each of them that the other should have had the same idea, and they think that there must be some hidden affinity and bond between them. It is friendship at first sight, a kind of *coup de foudre*. They talk together and discover that they are both copyists, and that their characters are complementary. Bouvard is stout, florid, fullblooded, a widower with a liking for good living and coarse stories. Pécuchet, on the contrary, is philosophic, thin, prudish and a virgin, although he is forty-seven.

They soon spend all their time together and discover that their education has been defective, but they try to improve it by going together to lectures, to museums and picture galleries. The way that they educate themselves, and the touching belief that they have in learning and what is found in books, is moving. They go for country walks together and develop a liking for rural life which makes them grow disgusted with their town life. They are very simple, unsophisticated and platitudinous and their sentiments come straight out of *Le Dictionnaire des Idées Reçues*. Flaubert does not mean us to be completely contemptuous of them nor to make a mock of them. From contact with one another they develop and grow deeper. He says in the plan gg10: 'Par le seul fait de leur contact, ils se développent et désirent acquérir des idées.' They were not exactly fools but had ideas and feelings which they had great difficulty in expressing, through lack of experience. With growth and development they became discontented with their life and their profession, although before they knew one another they were calm and content with their lot. So Flaubert intended them to grow and be improved by their studies and their friendship.

Then Bouvard inherits a fortune from the man he had always imagined was his uncle but was in reality his illegitimate father. He has no idea but that he will share his inheritance with his friend. This contrasts with the similar event in *L'Éducation Sentimentale*, where Frédéric inherits from an uncle and his friend Deslauriers assumes, to Frédéric's irritation, that he will go shares with him in it.

Bouvard and Pécuchet, now that they are rich, decide that they will settle in the country, as they are tired of city life, and that they will become real countrymen, living off their own lands. They decide to buy a property and farm it themselves. With his usual thoroughness, Flaubert did not merely dump them haphazard anywhere, but, with Laporte, wandered round Normandy to find the most suitable place to lodge them. They chose the little village of Chavignolles.

At first they bask in happiness in the rural atmosphere of their property; but then they have the plan of working their lands themselves and they take up various forms of agronomy. They buy books to study the subjects, but do not understand what they are reading, as they are ill-prepared for the task; they try all sorts of conflicting methods, which together could not possibly succeed. A simple, uneducated peasant can grow vegetables and fruit, can prune trees, but Bouvard and Pécuchet follow the printed word so slavishly that they fail in everything. One cannot attribute their failures to the weakness of science and learning, since they embark on experiments for which they are totally unprepared and unsuited. When they fail in one subject they jump to the next, imagining they will be more successful there, and do not wait to master the previous subject. The greatest genius in the world could not have mastered in a lifetime all that they tried to do in a few months. One knows, each time, that they will fail in what they embark on, and this becomes tedious and monotonous. How could they imagine that, in a few weeks, after having read some texts, they could practise medicine and attempt cures? One is inclined to agree with Taine, when he said[30] that the two friends were like two snails trying to climb to the top of Mont Blanc, the first time that they fell one smile, but the tenth time was unbearable.

In his preparation for this part of his book Flaubert went in for immense research to discover what the two friends might have read, and also what mistakes an ignorant man of the middle of the nineteenth century might make. All this the reader finds very time-consuming, and would like to be spared some of it. The point could have been made with very much less expenditure of effort, on the part of both the author and the reader.

Bouvard and Pécuchet fail in their experiments because they have not learnt to know themselves nor their capacities. They suffer, as do most of Flaubert's characters, from Bovarysme, that is to say that they see themselves other than they are and undertake things for which they have no talent or possibility of success. This made them incurable amateurs. They have, however, regret for their ignorance, like *Le Bourgeois Gentilhomme*, and wish to remedy it. They are willing to spend all their money on improving themselves. They are very different from, and vastly superior to, Homais in *Madame Bovary*, who only wants to make a parade of erudition and learning – not caring whether they are true or false – in order to enhance his prestige or advance his own interests. Homais succeeds through self-interest and because he does not care for truth, but Bouvard and Pécuchet fail, often through their best qualities. Although most of their failures are their own fault, there are some which are gratuitous and for which they cannot be blamed – except through lack of personal supervision. One of these episodes is the farcical dinner which they give in order to show off their house and garden to the neighbourhood. The dinner fails largely through the inefficiency of the servants. It is reminiscent of the house-warming party given by Frédéric Moreau to his friends when he comes into his inheritance. Bouvard and Pécuchet's guests behave with the same ill manners as those of Frédéric, criticizing the food that they are given and making fun of the layout of the garden, which, it must be admitted, is most peculiar. When the guests have departed, the friends express the same sad disillusionment which Frédéric feels after his party and, 'dégoûtés du monde, ils résolurent de ne plus voir personne, de vivre exclusivement chez eux pour eux seuls.'[31]

After the more learned subjects they take up literature and are enthusiastic for the historical novel, especially for Scott. Then they carry out some research and discover his historical inaccuracy and this turns them against him. When they get on to dramatic works, and read them in parts, Bouvard's performance, modelled on the style of Lemaître, reminds one of Flaubert's showpiece, his recitation in the part of Mathô from *Salammbô*. When they discuss theories of beauty they show how much they have developed since the early days of their studies, as they now served judgement and maturity. Flaubert found himself growing more interested in them and more sympathetic. He said, in plan gg10: 'Ils peuvent, après une étude, formuler leur opinion (la mienne) par des considérations sous forme d'axiomes.'[32] In the early days, when he called them the woodlice, he would not have identified himself with them. Now they were raising themselves up and becoming more subtle. In the early days of their education, they would have been incapable of grasping the abstract subjects which they eventually studied; they would have been unable to argue intelligently on religion with the parish priest, as they are now able to do. In their early experiments they fail through ignorance, but, when they study philosophy and religion, Flaubert shows the impossibility of reaching any certain conclusion, since each thinker believes that he has the monopoly of truth. Bouvard and Pécuchet are right here to express doubt in everything – Flaubert's doubt.

In the beginning, in the village, the inhabitants merely have contempt for the two friends, on account of their ignorance and failures; they treat them with ironic amusement, and cheat them whenever possible. Now that they have raised themselves up, have improved themselves, thinking themselves superior and showing it, they arouse hostility and are pursued with venom and ill will. Bouvard and Pécuchet have to pay for this superiority through suffering. As the author declares: 'Une faculté pitoyable se développa dans leur esprit, celle de voir la bêtise et de ne plus la tolérer.'[33]

Shortly afterwards they find a dead dog in a field and think a great deal about death and about the vanity of their life, with their unfulfilled ambitions and unsatisfied desires. They consider suicide to end it all:[34]

Ils examinèrent la question du suicide. Où est le mal de rejeter un fardeau qui vous écrase? et de commettre une action ne nuisant à personne? Si elle offensait Dieu, aurions-nous ce pouvoir? Ce n'est point une lâcheté, bien qu'on dise, et l'insolence est belle de bafouer, même à son détriment, ce que les hommes estiment le plus.

They think of the manner of their death and decide on hanging. But, in the end, it is a quarrel which decides everything, a question of a cup, belonging to Bouvard, broken by Pécuchet. In a fury at his friend's recriminations, the latter runs up to the attic, taking the candle with him. Bouvard, alone and groping his way in the dark, follows him upstairs and finds him with a rope in his hand. 'Wait for me, wait for me!' Bouvard cries, for, in death, they must not be divided, and he climbs on to the other chair. Then suddenly they remember that they have not made their wills, and they climb down, weeping copiously with disappointment. They lean out of the sky-light to recover, and, in the white landscape, under its coverlet of snow, they see processions of little lights, on a level with the ground, all going the same way towards the church, for it is Christmas Eve and people are going to attend midnight mass. Bouvard and Pécuchet are moved by curiosity and go out to follow them into the church:

Le serpent ronflait, l'encens fumait. Des verres suspendus dans la longueur de la nef, dessinaient trois couronnes de feux multicolores, et, au bout de la perspective, des deux côtés du tabernacle, des cierges géants dressaient des flammes rouges. Par-dessus les têtes de la foule et les capelines des femmes, au delà des chantres, on distinguait le prêtre, dans sa chasuble d'or; à sa voix aiguë répondaient les voix fortes des hommes emplissant le jubé, et la voûte de bois tremblait sur ses arceaux de pierre. Des images, représentant le chemin de la croix, décoraient les murs. Au milieu du chœur, devant l'autel, un agneau était couché, les pattes sous le ventre, les oreilles toutes droites.

La tiède température leur procura un singulier bien-être, et leurs pensées, orageuses tout à l'heure, se faisaient douces, comme des vagues qui s'apaisent.

Ils écoutèrent l'Évangile et le Credo, observaient les mouvements du prêtre. Cependant les vieux, les jeunes, les pauvresses en guenilles, les fermières en haut bonnet, les robustes gars à blonds favoris, tous priaient, absorbés dans la même joie profonde, et voyaient sur la paille d'une étable rayonner comme un soleil le corps de l'Enfant-Dieu. Cette foi des autres touchait Bouvard en dépit de sa raison, et Pécuchet malgré la dureté de son cœur.

Il y eut un silence; tous les dos se courbèrent, et, au tintement d'une clochette, le petit agneau bêla.

L'hostie fut montrée par le prêtre, au bout de ses deux bras, le plus haut possible. Alors éclata un chant d'allégresse qui conviait le monde aux pieds du Roi des Anges. Bouvard et Pécuchet, involontairement, s'y mêlèrent, et ils sentaient comme une aurore se lever dans leur âme.

As we have seen, it was probably for this description that Flaubert went to midnight mass on Christmas Eve 1876, which he mentioned to so many of his friends, as it must have moved him deeply.

Bouvard and Pécuchet now feel that it is not mere chance which has turned them away from death at that particular moment. They both remember their early faith and their emotions at religious ceremonies. They now read the Gospels:

L'Évangile dilata leur âme, les éblouit comme un soleil. Ils apercevaient Jésus, debout sur la montagne, un bras levé, la foule en dessous l'écoutant; ou bien au bord du lac, parmi les Apôtres qui tirent des filets; puis, sur l'ânesse, dans la clameur des *alleluia*, la chevelure éventée par les palmes frémissantes; enfin au haut de la croix, inclinant sa tête, d'où tombe éternellement une rosée sur le monde. Ce qui les gagna, ce qui les délectait, c'est la tendresse pour les humbles, la défense des pauvres, l'exaltation des opprimés. Et, dans ce livre où le ciel se déploie, rien de théologal au milieu de tant de préceptes; pas un dogme, nulle exigence que la pureté du cœur.(35)

They then start studying religious history and practices. Pécuchet even goes in for physical mortification and self-flagellation. They go on pilgrimages to religious places, but the selling of pious objects at the church porches shocks them, as it has so many pilgrims at Lourdes. Now that they show interest in religion and practise it, they are received at the local *château* and are flattered by this attention. Their minds, however, have been made independent by their studies, and they can no longer accept all the religious mandates, but discuss them with the parish priest, bringing forward rational and free-thinking arguments and investigating the truth of religious texts. They are soon dropped by the *bien-pensants*, who are horrified when Pécuchet declares that he thinks as much of Buddhism as of Christianity, because it had already recognized the vanity and nothingness of things here below; because its practices were austere, its flock larger than the Christian, and because it believed in reincarnation.

Their incursion into religion fails like all the rest and they are evicted from the château, which they leave without saying farewell.

Their last experiment is in education. They adopt a boy and a girl, Victor et Victorine, the children of a jail-bird then in prison, who were being taken away to a reformatory. Their kind hearts are touched, so that they wish to give them a better life, in which they can develop freely and naturally. Then they think of bringing them up and educating them. The two men must have been over seventy at the time – too old for bachelors to embark on such a task without any experience of children.

We do not know exactly how long the development of Bouvard and Pécuchet has taken, but there are a few dates which act as signposts and we realize that the novel must have covered a period of between twenty and thirty years. The novel begins in 1837 and it is in 1839 that Bouvard receives his legacy; and one of the last dates is that of the Italian war, which took place in 1860. We have some account of the Revolution of 1848, and the beginning of the Second Empire. They cannot have known the Franco-Prussian war, as that would have made too great a difference in their lives. The Revolution of 1848 and the *coup d'état* of 1851 might have passed almost unnoticed in a country village but not foreign invasion. They are forty-seven when the novel starts and so, at the end, they must be over seventy. But dates do not matter, as the village does not alter in essentials during the period.

Their scheme for the education of the children is their last important venture. It is similar to their early experiments – they read and study all sorts of contradictory texts, without choice or discernment, or any continuity. This last exploit leads to their undoing. With the usual foolish self-confidence of their earlier experiments, they form theories of education, obtaining their material from learned works, and still keep their touching belief in the printed word, in what is in books. They chop and change as their methods fail.

They cannot, however, be held entirely responsible for this failure, as they have very unpromising material. The boy is a cruel sadist who boils their pet cat in a pot, and becomes a thief like his father. The little girl is corrupt sexually, in spite of her youth, and sleeps with the travelling journeyman who comes to the house to work. As he is finishing the chapter on education, Flaubert comes to the pessimistic conclusion that it can do nothing. 'I want to prove,' he wrote to Maupassant,[36] 'that any education, of whatever kind it might be, doesn't mean much, and that human nature means everything, or nearly everything.'

The authorities hear of the exploits of the children and decide that Bouvard and Pécuchet are incapable of looking after the young and that they must be removed from them. But, in the meantime, the educators have decided that there is nothing to be done with them, and they abandon their plan of training them, making up their mind to find places for them as servants. 'Il y a des natures,' said Pécuchet, 'dénuées de sens moral, et l'éducation n'y peut rien.'[37]

They soon grow bored with their inactivity and, with their usual optimism, they do not lose hope, but decide that what has failed with children might well succeed with adults. They plan to give a lecture in the Hôtel de la Croix d'Or. Chapter ten stops at this point when, dressed in their best clothes, left over from better days, they set out for the hotel. Flaubert has, however, left full notes of how the chapter which was to be the last of Volume One, was to be finished. Bouvard and Pécuchet were each to give an address. Pécuchet's was to be pedantic, preaching governmental economy and that all taxes were to be reduced. Bouvard's speech was to be colloquial and familiar; he was to speak against the celibacy of the clergy, the futility of adultery, and to preach the emancipation of woman; he also demanded a brothel in Chavignolles.

The meeting eventually breaks up in disorder, and Bouvard and Pécuchet return home very tired and retire immediately to bed, little dreaming of the turmoil they have aroused.

Next day they discuss their speeches over their luncheon, and plan future pronouncements. Pécuchet, being very pessimistic, sees everything very black. He cannot believe in anything good in the future, and prophesies that the world will be taken over by America, with men enslaved to machines, and finally the planet will end through the disappearance of heat.

Bouvard, on the contrary, is optimistic, and sees Europe regenerated by Asia, with nothing but progress for mankind. There would be all sorts of wonderful inventions, aerial and submarine travel and interplanetary excursions. Paris would become a regular paradise, artificially heated by reflection of sunlight, and illuminated by walls painted with phosphorus. Evil would vanish from the world through the disappearance of want.

As they are discussing all these matters the police and the mayor arrive and all sorts of accusations are launched against the pair, on the score of their speeches and the behaviour of the children; and one of them is accused of being the father of Mélie's unborn child – she has been their servant but now works at the inn.

Bouvard is picked upon as the father as he is considered the richer of the two, and he is advised to pay her an allowance. There is talk of putting them both in prison as dangerous criminals, but the doctor arrives on the scene, and declares that it is not in prison that they should be confined but in a lunatic asylum, as they are mad. He says that he will write to the Préfet on the matter. The children are taken away from them as they are considered unfit to look after them, but that is the least of their preoccupations.

Everything has now failed them; they have squandered their life and their fortune and have nothing left. They suddenly think that the good time of their life had been before they had cherished all these ambitions, when they had done what suited them, what they were intended for, the simple task of copying. Like Don Quixote, whom they resemble, they repent of their past and their illusions and abandon them. They had believed in science and knowledge, in the same way as Don Quixote had believed in romance. He had mistaken windmills for giants, while they, in their archaeological days, had believed that an old ship-wrecked vessel, buried in the sand, was a prehistoric fossil. Each, on his own, decides that he wants to return to copying, though he hides his decision from his friend, only smiling as he thinks of it. Finally, not being able to keep it a secret any longer, they confess to each other that they want to copy, as they had done formerly. They have a double desk made, where they can sit opposite one another, and they buy all the utensils that they need for their work, and begin copying.

This is how the first volume was to end; the second would consist of what they are copying. This is all that was intended to go into Volume One and there is no indication that the chapters eleven and twelve of the gg10 plan were to be fitted in anywhere, as Alberto Cento and Geneviève Bollème said that they were to be. (This plan has already been mentioned, and how the two further chapters which followed chapter ten, were to finish the novel in one volume, taking no account of Volume Two.) Chapter eleven is entitled *Leur Copie* and it relates how the friends copy everything that they can find, amongst them old notes bought by weight from a bankrupt paper manufactory. It goes on to say that they soon feel the need to put some order in their copying and they recopy what they have already written. They put together various examples of different styles of prose; group together various kinds of crimes and various aspects of nature. They compile *Le Dictionnaire des Idées Reçues* and *Le Catalogue des Idées Chic*. They put annotations at the foot of each page.

Chapter eleven also deals with the fate of some of the inhabitants of Chavignolles: Marescot has left the village for Le Havre, and eventually becomes a notary in Paris. Mélie marries Beljambe the innkeeper, and, after his death, weds Gorju and lords it over the inn.

Chapter twelve is entitled *Conclusion* and tells how, amongst the old papers, Bouvard and Pécuchet find the draft of the letter from the doctor to the Préfet, which was mentioned at the end of chapter ten, in which he explains that the two men are not dangerous but only two harmless fools. Flaubert adds that here a summary is made of all that they have done, which is to be, for the reader, the criticism of the whole book.

When they find this letter Bouvard and Pécuchet ask themselves what they are to do with it. They decide that there can be no two opinions on the matter and that it must be copied like the rest. The novel is to end by a picture of the two men bent over their desk and copying. 'Finir par la vue des deux bonshommes penchés sur leur pupitre, et copiant.' 'Joie finale, ils ont trouvé le bonheur.'

Critics have been somewhat contemptuous of the characters in *Bouvard et Pécuchet*, and have considered them the merest types, barely differentiated, and mechanically treated. That is, for instance, the opinion of Brombert.[38] Not everyone, however, will agree with this verdict. Some believe that Flaubert exemplifies here the talent he had shown in *Madame Bovary* and in *L'Éducation Sentimentale* in the depiction of a great variety of characters, who make up the social scene and background. There are many different well-drawn characters in a variety of milieux. There is the Comte de Faverges, of the bien-pensant château society, a society which could be still found today in country districts in France. The Count is able, like the banker Dambreuse in *L'Éducation Sentimentale*, to fit in with any régime. He says to the parish priest:[39] 'Il faut rétablir l'obéissance. L'autorité se meurt si on la discute! Le droit divin il n'y a que ça! – Parfaitement, Monsieur le Comte!' This was a few days before the *coup d'état* of 2 December 1851.

There was also the notary Marescot and his silly wife:[40]

On les introduisit dans une salle à manger, que décoraient des pla
de vieille faïence, une horloge de Boule occupait le panneau le plu
étroit. Sur la table d'acajou, sans nappe, il y avait deux serviettes, une
théière, des bols. Madame Marescot traversa l'appartement dans un
peignoir de cachemire bleu. C'était une Parisienne qui s'ennuyait à la
campagne. Puis le notaire entra, une toque à la main, un journal de
l'autre; et tout de suite, d'un air aimable, il apposa son cachet, bien que
leur protégé fût un homme dangereux.

There is the parish priest, Father Jeufroy, who is very much
better and more fully drawn than Bournisien in *Madame Bovary*,
as he knows his subject better, his arguments are better mar-
shalled and he is less of a caricature. These are all minor characters,
but they are deftly drawn and have verisimilitude. The realism
with which the various milieux are painted show Flaubert's talent
for description, as, for instance, the dinner which the Count
offers to the important people of the district:[41]

Il jugea bon d'offrir un déjeuner aux notables du pays.
Le vestibule où trois domestiques les attendaient pour prendre leurs
paletots, le billard et les deux salons en enfilade, les plantes dans des
vases de la Chine, les bronzes sur les cheminées, les baguettes d'or aux
lambris, les rideaux épais, les larges fauteuils, ce luxe immédiatement
les frappa comme une politesse qu'on leur faisait; et, en entrant dans
la salle à manger, au spectacle de la table couverte de viandes sur des
plats d'argent, avec la rangée des verres devant chaque assiette, les
hors-d'œuvre çà et là, et un saumon au milieu, tous les visages s'épan-
ouirent.

We have noted Flaubert's great liking for feasts and this one
does not disappoint:[42] 'Et pendant que les plats se succédaient,
poule au jus, écrevisses, champignons, légume en salade, rôtis
d'alouettes, bien des sujets furent traités.' We are, however,
somewhat surprised that someone of the social experience of the
Count should serve Madeira and Sauterne right through the meal.
Flaubert's disgust with the people of his time, his psychological
pessimism, are seen in his portrayal of the inhabitants of Chavignolles, and in the contempt they arouse in him. In this he certainly
vomited his bile against the human race. There is no one here
who has any decent feelings, altruism or disinterestedness; there
are not even the good humble characters of his other works,
such as Catherine Leroux in *Madame Bovary* and Félicité in *Un
Cœur Simple*. The only people in the neighbourhood who have

any decent feelings and generosity are the two friends; they stand out head and shoulders above the rest, and, throughout the novel, we grow to love them. We laugh at them at first and their pretentious failures but eventually we grow to appreciate their disinterested love of learning and knowledge. They are the only people in the village moved by kindness and compassion. They are outraged at the sight of one of the villagers ill-treating an animal.[43]

Le vieux cheval, effrayé par les paons, cassa sous une ruade une des cordes, s'y empêtra les jambes, et, galopant dans les trois cours, traînait la lessive après lui.

Aux cris furieux de Madame Bordin, Marianne accourut. Le père Gouy injuriait son cheval: 'Bougre de rosse! carcan! voleur!' lui donnait des coups de pied dans le ventre, des coups sur les oreilles avec le manche d'un fouet.

Bouvard fut indigné de voir battre un animal.

Le paysan lui répondit: – J'en ai le droit: il m'appartient!

Ce n'était pas une raison.

Et Pécuchet, survenant, ajouta que les animaux avaient aussi leurs droits, car ils ont une âme, comme nous, si toutefois la nôtre existe.

They are also moved to pity at the cruel treatment meted out to the two children Victor and Victorine. They treat them with affection and kindness, the first kindness they had ever met, and it is not wholly their fault that the experiment fails so lamentably.

Flaubert believed that the evil and second-rate people are always triumphant in the end. Mélie, Marescot and Gorju come out of the events successfully and Bouvard and Pécuchet alone fail, largely because they have no sense of reality.

Bouvard and Pécuchet are the main characters in the novel, in fact the only ones fully drawn. They are generally thought of together, yet they are very different and they complement one another. Bouvard is an extrovert, sensual, cheerful, *bon vivant*, more of a man of the world than his friend, and he knows how to talk to women. Pécuchet is slightly built, an introvert, more reflective than his companion, and probably more intelligent. He has no understanding of women and, as we have seen, he is still a virgin although middle-aged. Bouvard hankers after social life and enjoys their short period of worldly success at the château. Whereas Pécuchet likes solitude and retirement and does not ask for anything more than the company of his friend. Like Flaubert, both men are unattractive physically but are, nevertheless, able to arouse affection. They have the simple naïve vanity of the uneducated, which has in it some touching quality. When they are in the process of educating the children, they see themselves as being successful and famous and having their own institute of education:[44]

> Un rêve magnifique les occupa; s'ils menaient à bien l'éducation de leurs élèves, ils fonderaient plus tard un établissement ayant pour but de redresser l'intelligence, dompter les caractères, ennoblir le cœur. Déjà ils parlaient de souscriptions et de la bâtisse.
>
> Leur triomphe chez Ganot les avait rendus célèbres, et des gens les venaient consulter, afin qu'on leur dise leur chance de fortune.

The strongest characteristic, however, in the two companions was their gift of friendship. In this they resembled Flaubert himself, who possessed many close friends who loved him dearly, whom he loved and whom he served devotedly. Friendship was probably the richest thing in his life and the friendship between Bouvard and Pécuchet reminds one of that between Flaubert and Bouilhet. They loved one another with disinterestedness and unselfishness; even with all their disasters, which each could have blamed on the other, they never thought of doing so, or of parting when everything went wrong, but stuck together to the end, contemplating ending their days together. Bouvard had sacrificed the whole of his inheritance to their relationship. They had an ennobling and enriching effect on one another, in their pursuit of learning and wisdom. As Flaubert said in the plan: 'Ils n'ont pas perdu leur temps, car leur cœur s'est attendri et leur esprit agrandi.'[45] At the end, as they bend over their double desk, they are very different from the pair of simple bourgeois who had sat on the seat on the Boulevard Bourdon, on that hot summer afternoon when each had been struck with amazement to discover that his companion had also had the idea of putting his name in his hat. Their creator, who, at the beginning, had mocked at them and had called them woodlice, ended fully on the side of the grotesque friends, for they shared his love of learning and scholarship, though they did not know how to use it.

There are not in *Bouvard et Pécuchet* the numerous beautiful landscapes which embellish *Madame Bovary* and *L'Éducation Sentimentale*. There are, however, some which reveal Flaubert's

powers as a descriptive artist. We have seen the moving picture of
the two friends when they attend midnight mass, after their
abortive attempt at suicide. There is also the evening which
they spend in their garden, after a succulent meal, when they
decide that all forms of diet are a farce.[46]

> Puis, comme autrefois, ils allèrent prendre le gloria sur le vigneau.
> La moisson venait de finir, et des meules, au milieu des champs,
> dressaient leurs masses noires sur la couleur de la nuit bleuâtre et douce.
> Les fermes étaient tranquilles. On n'entendait même plus les grillons.
> Toute la campagne dormait. Ils digéraient en humant la brise, qui
> rafraîchissait leurs pommettes.
> Le ciel, très haut, était couvert d'étoiles, les unes brillant par
> groupes, d'autres à la file, ou bien seules à des intervalles éloignés.
> Une zone de poussière lumineuse, allant du septentrion au midi, se
> bifurquait au-dessus de leur tête. Il y avait entre ces clartés de grands
> espaces vides, et le firmament semblait une mer d'azur, avec des
> archipels et des îlots.

That was one of the happier moments of their existence, but there
was the sad time when they tried to recapture their early serenity:[47]

> Et ils se rappelèrent le temps où ils étaient heureux . . .
> Ils voulurent faire, comme autrefois, une promenade dans les
> champs, allèrent très loin, se perdirent. De petits nuages mouton-
> naient dans le ciel, le vent balançait les clochettes des avoines, le long
> d'un pré un ruisseau murmurait, quand tout à coup une odeur infecte
> les arrêta, et ils virent sur des cailloux, entre des ronces, la charogne
> d'un chien.

The contrast between the peace of nature and the decay of the
carrion is well drawn. Anthony Thorlby calls it a resounding
cliché.[48] The passage is very like *Une Charogne* by Baudelaire,
published more than twenty years before, and which Flaubert
must have known, as the poet sent him his 1861 edition of *Les
Fleurs du Mal*. It was this vision which gave Bouvard and Pécuchet
the idea of suicide:

> Les quatre membres étaient desséchés. Le rictus de la gueule découv-
> rait sous des babines bleuâtres des crocs d'ivoire; à la place du ventre,
> c'était un amas de couleur terreuse, et qui semblait palpiter tant
> grouillait dessus la vermine. Elle s'agitait frappée par le soleil, sous le
> bourdonnement des mouches, dans cette intolérable odeur, odeur
> féroce et comme dévorante.

Cependant Bouvard plissait le front et des larmes mouillèrent ses yeux.

Pécuchet dit stoïquement: – Nous serons un jour comme ça!

L'idée de la mort les avait saisis, ils en causèrent en revenant.

The great difference between Baudelaire and Flaubert is that the spiritual element which makes the beauty of the poem is absent from the prose passage. Flaubert's description is colder and more clinical, more realistic and less poetical, less emotional than Baudelaire's description of a dead dog:[49]

Rappelez-vous l'objet que nous vîmes, mon âme,
Ce beau matin d'été si doux;
Au détour d'un sentier une charogne infâme
Sur un lit semé de cailloux,

Les jambes en l'air, comme une femme lubrique,
Brûlante et suant les poisons,
Ouvrant d'une façon nonchalante et cynique
Son ventre plein d'exhalaisons.

Le soleil rayonnait sur cette pourriture,
Comme afin de la cuire à point,
Et de rendre au centuple à la grande Nature
Tout ce qu'ensemble elle avait joint; ...

– Et pourtant vous serez semblable à cette ordure,
A cette horrible infection,
Étoile de mes yeux, soleil de ma nature,
Vous, mon ange et ma passion!

Oui! telle vous serez, ô la reine des grâces,
Après les derniers sacrements,
Quand vous irez, sous l'herbe et les floraisons grasses,
Moisir parmi les ossements.

Alors, ô ma beauté! dites à la vermine
Qui vous mangera de baisers,
Que j'ai gardé la forme et l'essence divine
De mes amours décomposés!

It must not be forgotten that *Bouvard et Pécuchet* is intended to be a comic novel, though perhaps it is a bitter comedy. The novel abounds in comic scenes which make the reader laugh aloud, and long for cinema treatment, with actors of the comic calibre of a

Charlie Chaplin. There is the scene of the move from Paris to
Chavignolles, when the pantechnicon, with Pécuchet on board,
breaks down, smashing some of the contents, and is further
delayed on account of the drunkenness of the driver. In the meantime Bouvard, who has taken the wrong coach, after too good a
luncheon, suddenly finds himself at Rouen.

There is the comic scene of the suicide, already mentioned,
where Bouvard calls to his friend to wait for him to die, and they
remember then that they have not made their wills. There is also
an amusing scene when the two friends are studying medicine,
with a dummy figure, and they put on white coats in order to be
more professional.

There is humour in the scene where they try to raise the
temperature of the bath water by muscular movement, but
succeed only in catching cold; and in the fact of the two elderly –
indeed old – men embarking on gymnastic exercises intended for
the training of young military men. There is the very funny
scene where Pécuchet argues religion with Father Jeufroy, in a
rainstorm and sharing the same umbrella – the priest's:[50]

Des gouttes d'eau tombèrent. Le curé déploya son parapluie; et
Pécuchet, quand il fut dessous, osa prétendre que les catholiques
avaient fait plus de martyrs chez les juifs, les musulmans, les protestants
et les libres penseurs que tous les Romains autrefois . . .

La pluie augmentait, et ses rayons dardaient si fort, qu'ils rebondis-
saient du sol, comme de petites fusées blanches. Pécuchet et M.
Jeufroy marchaient avec lenteur, serrés l'un contre l'autre, et le curé
disait:

– Après des supplices abominables, on les jetait dans des chaudières!
– L'Inquisition employait de même la torture, et elle vous brûlait
très bien.
– On exposait les dames illustres dans les lupanars! . . .
Le vent chassait, balayait la pluie dans l'air. Elle claquait sur les
feuilles, ruisselait au bord du chemin, et le ciel couleur de boue se
confondait avec les champs dénudés, la moisson étant finie. Pas un
toit. Au loin seulement, la cabane d'un berger.
Le maigre paletot de Pécuchet n'avait plus un fil de sec. L'eau coulait
le long de son échine, entrait dans ses bottes, dans ses oreilles, dans
ses yeux, malgré la visière de la casquette; le curé, en relevant d'un bras
la queue de sa soutane, se découvrait les jambes, et les pointes de son
tricorne crachaient l'eau sur ses épaules comme des gargouilles de
cathédrale.

Il fallut s'arrêter, et tournant le dos à la tempête, ils restèrent face à face, ventre contre ventre, en tenant à quatre mains le parapluie qui oscillait.

M. Jeufroy n'avait pas interrompu la défense des catholiques.

There is also the supremely humorous scene where Bouvard makes love to Madame Bordin, under the cover of drying sheets laid out on the clothes lines, while two peacocks copulate nearby.[51]

Bouvard s'assit par terre à côté de Madame Bordin...

La grande lumière éclairait son profil; un de ses bandeaux noirs descendait trop bas, et les petits frisons de sa nuque se collaient à sa peau ambrée, moite de sueur. Chaque fois qu'elle respirait, ses deux seins montaient. Le parfum du gazon se mêlait à la bonne odeur de sa chair solide, et Bouvard eut un revif de tempérament qui le combla de joie...

Les draps, autour d'eux, les enfermaient comme les rideaux d'un lit.

Il se pencha sur le coude, lui frôlant les genoux de sa figure.

– Pourquoi? Hein? pourquoi?

Et, comme elle se taisait et qu'il était dans un état où les serments ne coûtent rien, il tâcha de se justifier, s'accusa de folie d'orgueil:

– Pardon! ce sera comme autrefois! voulez-vous?

Et il avait pris sa main, qu'elle laissait dans la sienne.

Un coup de vent brusque fit se relever les draps, et ils virent deux paons, un mâle et une femelle. La femelle se tenait immobile, les jarrets pliés, la croupe en l'air. Le mâle se promenait autour d'elle, arrondissait sa queue en éventail, se rengorgeait, gloussait, puis sauta dessus en rabattant ses plumes, qui la couvrirent comme un berceau, et les deux grands oiseaux tremblèrent d'un seul frémissement.

Bouvard le sentit dans la paume de Mme Bordin. Elle se dégagea bien vite. Il y avait devant eux, béant et comme pétrifié, le jeune Victor qui regardait.

Flaubert, as he told his friend and publisher Charpentier, had procured a pair of peacocks, in order to study them in the act.[52] At this moment Gouy's old horse breaks loose and gallops round the yard, becoming entangled in the washing and the line, which snap, dragging the clean linen in the mud. It is now that, as we have seen earlier, Gouy ill-treats the horse to the anger of Bouvard. Pécuchet, arriving at that moment on the scene, adds his say, and declares that it was wrong to beat an animal, as he had a soul like ours – if indeed we had one.

– Vous êtes un impie! s'écria Mme Bordin.

Trois choses l'exaspéraient: la lessive à recommencer, ses croyances qu'on outrageait et la crainte d'avoir été entrevue tout à l'heure dans une pose suspecte.

– Je vous croyais plus forte, dit Bouvard.

Elle répliqua magistralement:

– Je n'aime pas les polissons.

Et Gouy s'en prit à eux d'avoir abîmé son cheval, dont les naseaux saignaient.

Brombert says:[53] 'Yet this strange enterprise, which is precisely an encyclopedic inventory of failure, diagnosing, among other things, the very breakdown of Culture, is prophetic not only of subsequent developments in Western society, but also of the kind of literature ultimately represented by the arid and clownish bitterness of a Samuel Beckett.'

It is hard to see what exactly he means by this. It is true that Beckett's work is bitter and reaches the extremest form of pessimism. It is true that *Bouvard et Pécuchet*, as we have it, is a novel of failure, and the heroes fail in everything which they undertake – in practical science, in philosophy, in religion, in education and in love – but a great deal of this failure is due to their own inefficiency and ignorance, and not through a failure of the subjects themselves – an inefficiency and ignorance which they share with the bulk of mankind. Flaubert had no faith in men in general, but he does not seem ever to have lost faith in real learning; or indeed in the good life, in culture, if only men could improve themselves and become different. Bouvard and Pécuchet are very different from Beckett's characters and Flaubert did conceive of their abandoning their human arrogance and becoming humble. He also conceived of their reaching total happiness and fulfilment. As they bend over their copying, they reach 'joie finale, ils ont trouvé le bonheur'. This is nearer to Pascal's state of mind, after his night of ecstasy, when he reached 'renonciation totale et douce', than it is to the mood of Beckett's heroes. How many people here below can claim to have 'trouvé le bonheur'?

It is true that this is in the plan gg10, chapter twelve, and might not have been the mood of Volume Two. Perhaps there they would have found no joy in their copying, and have only felt contempt and disgust for mankind, which had thought itself so intelligent and so fine.

It is possible to feel that one need not be sorry that Volume Two of *Bouvard et Pécuchet* was never written, but one reader, at least, regrets that the novel was not completed from plan gg10 in the twelve chapters.

CONCLUSION

When a list of the eight or ten greatest novels of the world is made, two, or at least one, of Flaubert's novels will figure on it – either *Madame Bovary* or *L'Éducation Sentimentale*, or both. If a list of the five or six greatest novelists of the world is made, again Flaubert's name will be represented on it. Is this only lip-service, a critical attitude of mind which does not involve the emotions or the spirit? Few will admit having been swept off their feet and radically altered by him as many were by Keats, by Baudelaire, by Rimbaud, by Eliot or by Beckett. Many feel greater love for other novelists, according to their taste – for Balzac, for Stendhal, for Tolstoi, for Dostoevsky, for Proust and so forth. In the near-century since his death Flaubert's work has aroused admiration rather than deep love. Was this because, as George Sand used to say, he kept himself too much out of communion with his readers and did not show them his deeper self? But Flaubert thought that the author, in his work, should be like God in the universe, felt everywhere and visible nowhere.[1] Few of us however have made a close and intimate friend of God. He used to say that the author should hide his life, that he should be like the hero from Leconte de Lisle's poem *Les Montreurs* from his collection *Poèmes Barbares*:

> Dans mon orgueil muet, dans ma tombe sans gloire,
> Dussé-je m'engloutir pour l'éternité noire,
> Je ne te vendrai pas mon ivresse et mon mal,
>
> Je ne livrai pas ma vie à tes huées,
> Je ne danserai pas sur ton tréteau banal
> Avec tes histrions et tes prostituées.

Flaubert was like one of those beautiful shells, hidden in the impenetrable depths of the Pacific Ocean, with the most wonderful colours in the universe, which no one can see, not even themselves, who grow and die, with their beauty totally unseen, until some foreign hand ravishes them from the deep. There is nothing but darkness where they come from, and they can only be seen by God.

Yet those who know Flaubert's writings well and have grown fond of them find that their interest in them grows deeper with time, and they never re-read one of his great works without finding something new each time, and something valuable.

We have seen, in *The Making of the Master*, how *Madame Bovary* remained, on the whole, Flaubert's most popular work with the general public, except perhaps in his own day, when the favourite was probably *Salammbô*. Flaubert himself was always annoyed when people praised *Madame Bovary*, for he considered *L'Éducation Sentimentale* vastly superior, and the indifference of the public to it was a great grief to him. Today critics are inclined to agree with him in his verdict, and to see in it the deepest and most perfect of novels.

Yet Henry James, in 1883, in *French Poets and Novelists*, said of *L'Éducation Sentimentale*:[2] 'The book is a *dead* one . . . like masticating ashes and sawdust . . . elaborately and massively dreary.' He talks about there being no more interest in it than in a heap of gravel. 'That imagination, invention, taste and science should concentrate themselves in human entertainment, upon such a result, strikes us as the most unfathomable of anomalies.' He said again in *Notes on Novelists* in 1902:[3] 'Thus it is that, as the work of a "grand écrivain" with beautiful passages and a general emptiness, with a kind of leak in its stored sadness, moreover, by which its moral dignity escapes – thus it is that Flaubert's ill-starred novel is a curiosity for a literary museum.'

James, although he admired Flaubert, thought him ultimately a failure, but nevertheless more important than if he had been a success. He says, in *The House of Fiction*:[4] 'He is, none the less, more interesting as a failure, however qualified, than as a success however explained.'

Flaubert stretches right across the nineteenth century, from 1820 to 1880, and he thus co-existed with the great movements in the novel, at a time when it was becoming the most important of the literary forms, taking the place in prestige of drama – realism and naturalism – and, although he owed something to all of them he was bound by none, so that he did not depend on temporary fashion or taste. He never became the leader of a movement with disciples. There is not a school of Flaubert. He was therefore able to become a classic of the nineteenth century, dealing with eternal values and, like the great writers of the seventeenth century, make a bid for immortality. His work has not aged during the past century and the chances are that it will not do so later.

It is due to Flaubert that the novel has become one of the great art forms of European literature, with the highest ideals. Henry James, who knew Flaubert and his writings, said so in *The Art of Fiction*, as did Walter Pater in his *Essay on Style*.

Flaubert may not have had the immediate contemporary influence of a Zola, whose abstract theories were more easy to assimilate and imitate – they were also more likely eventually to be proved wrong as they were categorical and rigid. Flaubert, on the contrary, refused to form any opinion on anything, as he thought man incapable of any certainty, and so 'il ne faut pas conclure'.

Proust, who did not greatly admire Flaubert, except perhaps in the narrow sense as a stylist – or perhaps only did not care very much for his work – nevertheless owed him a great deal, without realizing how much. From Flaubert he obtained the art of expressing his characters indirectly, through a *monologue intérieur*. This method of characterization is one of Flaubert's greatest contributions to the art of fiction and, as we have seen in *Madame Bovary*, it is very different from the direct method of characterization practised by Balzac and Stendhal.

Flaubert, like Proust, also saw time as destroying and memory as preserving and, although he did not build a theory on it, he used the preserving qualities of involuntary memory, and this is done through images, which are his method for preserving the past.

Most of the critics through the ages, when they have studied Flaubert, have concentrated on pure stylistic considerations, on verbal considerations, and have often not gone beyond that. This aspect is undoubtedly valid and his books are as strictly composed as plays. He knew exactly how long each section was to be before he started writing. Purely verbal style also meant a great deal to him and he submitted his writings to the ordeal of 'le gueuloir', that is to say that passages were bellowed out, in the open air for preference, to test the melody and harmony of the sentences. He once said to Goncourt, when he had almost finished *Salammbô*, 'I've only half a dozen or so of sentences to write, mais j'ai toutes mes chutes de phrase' – that is to say his cadences.[5]

He did not believe, as did most of his contemporaries, in an author developing his own particular style, which was hall-marked by his genius, and which he then used in everything that he wrote. Maupassant quotes him as saying:[6] 'He did not think of styles as a series of particular moulds, each of which belonged to one writer, and into which he poured all his thoughts.' On the contrary, with his ideal of keeping himself out of the picture, he considered that each work needed the style that suited it, and that this must be found. Maupassant again quotes him as saying:[7] 'Whatever may be the thing that one wants to express, there is only one word to express it, only one verb to animate it, only one adjective to qualify it. One must look for them until one finds them, that word, that adjective, that verb, and never be satisfied with the approximation.' We have seen this theory fully exem-plified in the style of *Trois Contes*.

Although Flaubert did not write verse, he was in reality a lyric artist who thought in the form of poetry, though it is un-certain whether he really appreciated it. He knew Baudelaire's work in his middle period, and they shared many literary and artistic theories. Baudelaire presented him with both editions of his *Fleurs du Mal*, and Flaubert thanked him for them, expressing admiration for the book, but, in his letters, there is no proof that he admired the best poems which it contained, such as *Le Voyage* or *Le Cygne*, but concentrated on the more obvious, such as *Une Charogne, La Géante, Le Chat* and so forth. He never doubted the greatness of Hugo and continued to admire him all his life. Amongst his poetry his greatest admiration went to *La Légende des Siècles*, which appeared when he was composing *Salammbô*. He does not seem to have noticed *Les Contemplations*, which came out when he was publishing *Madame Bovary*. That collection would probably have seemed to him too personal, and a confession.

It is strange that he should have continued to admire Hugo to the end as there was so much in him which was contrary to his deepest beliefs and ideals. Hugo was actively engaged in more causes than almost any other poet in the century, and Flaubert refused to express any political or social ideas, or to take any part in the movements of his time.

Where Flaubert is most like Baudelaire is in his depiction of the modern city, and he is a wonderful poet of Rouen and of Paris – especially of the latter; many of his scenes are like Baudelaire's in his *Spleen de Paris*. They were both composing them at the same time, in the last years of the Second Empire. Flaubert described Paris in the summer, when the students have gone home for the vacation:[8]

Il remontait, au hasard, le quartier latin, si tumultueux d'habitude, mais désert à cette époque, car les étudiants étaient partis dans leurs familles. Les grands murs des collèges, comme allongés par le silence, avaient un aspect plus morne encore; on entendait toutes sortes de bruits paisibles, des battements d'ailes dans les cages, le ronflement d'un tour, le marteau d'un savetier; et les marchands d'habits, au milieu des rues, interrogeaient de l'œil chaque fenêtre, inutilement. Au fond des cafés solitaires, la dame du comptoir bâillait entre ses carafons remplis; les journaux demeuraient en ordre sur la table des cabinets de lecture; dans l'atelier des repasseuses, des linges frissonnaient sous les bouffées du vent tiède. De temps à autre, il s'arrêtait à l'étalage d'un bouquiniste; un omnibus, qui descendait en frôlant le trottoir, le faisait se retourner; et parvenu devant le Luxembourg, il n'allait pas plus loin.

There are many more, too many to quote.

In his novels Flaubert liked big scenes standing out from the story and not merely continuing the narrative. This liking for great separate scenes probably came from his early passion for the stage. There are the many battle scenes in *Salammbô*, the banquet, the scene in the tent, the death of Mathô. In *L'Éducation Sentimentale* there are the scenes of the Revolution, the sack of the Palais Royal, the scene between Madame Arnoux and Frédéric. There are many big scenes in two of the *Trois Contes* – in *Saint Julien L'Hospitalier* and *Hérodias*; there are in *Bouvard et Pécuchet* the many comic dramatic scenes.

F. M. Wetherill, in his book *Flaubert et la Création Littéraire*, says on several occasions that Flaubert had no imagination, but it is hard to see how such an opinion on a writer whose images were as rich and as various as Flaubert's could be defended. He had great power of evoking a scene which he had beheld, of reaching its essence in images, and he had the faculty of imagining himself into the lives of the characters he was depicting.

One of the great characteristics and ornaments of his style was the image, and its richness can be seen in D. L. Demorest's book *L'Expression Figurée et Symbolique dans L'Œuvre de Gustave Flaubert*. In fact his mother thought that his love of images had dried up his heart. But he said to George Sand, late in his life, in 1872:[9] 'No, literature is not what I like best in the world. I did not explain myself properly (in my last letter), I was only speaking in the abstract, nothing more. I'm not such a pedantic fool as to prefer phrases to human beings. The longer I live the more acute my sensibility becomes.'

On the contrary Flaubert was one of the great psychologists in nineteenth-century fiction, and he achieved his knowledge of human beings through observation of all the various people whom he met and not through abstract theories, like so many of his contemporaries who, like Zola, created their characters through imperfectly known and undigested so-called scientific research. He saw each man as a unique example, an individual, himself alone, and not merely the product of his glands, his heredity, his physical make-up, but someone alone in his own right, possessing himself alone. He believed that a man's character was his fate about which he could do very little. He could get to know himself so as to cure his Bovarysme, that is being other than he is, and prevent his character from destroying him. Bouvard and Pécuchet reach self-knowledge in the end and learn humility, being willing finally to be what they are suited to being, mere copyists. Only one person, in the whole of Flaubert's work, manages to conquer his character, to alter it and to redeem himself, and that is Saint Julien.

Flaubert was a very great psychologist and we have seen, through his novels, a great number and variety of characters, very acutely drawn, so that, even in an intellectual work like *Bouvard et Pécuchet*, and especially in *L'Éducation Sentimentale*, there is an immense gallery of portraits, which make up the warp and woof of the social scene. This makes one regret that he never got down to writing the novels he planned to compose dealing with the social life of the Second Empire.

In his characterization he wished for moderation and there are none of the people larger than life who are to be found in

Balzac and Dickens. 'Pas de monstres, pas de héros,' he used to say. In spite of his low view of human nature he drew no characters as evil as the worst in Balzac.

On the whole he elected to depict unattractive characters, few, if any, of whom one would choose to have as friends. Marie Arnoux is an exception and he manages to convey her charm though, as a person, she remains shadowy, and one knows her less profoundly than the other characters.

In his last novel he took as his heroes two physically very unattractive figures, grotesque even, whom he managed, at the end, nevertheless to make sympathetic. They are the ancestors of the many unattractive heroes of modern fiction – Gully Jimson in Joyce Cary's novel *The Horse's Mouth*, Bloom in *Ulysses* by James Joyce, Samuel Beckett's heroes in all his novels and plays. They are the beginning of the anti-hero of modern fiction.

Brombert quotes Sartre as declaring that Flaubert hated the working class:[10] 'Il mange de l'ouvrier.' But this is not true. It is correct that he despised every class of society; nevertheless his kindest portraits are those of working-class people, and he does not treat them with irony or contempt – witness Dussardier in *L'Éducation Sentimentale*, Catherine Leroux in *Madame Bovary*, Félicité in *Un Cœur Simple* and many others.

In his psychology Flaubert was not concerned with the problem of good and evil, and did not depict the clash between good and bad impulses in his characters, what Baudelaire called, in *Les Fleurs du Mal, Spleen et Idéal*. His characters are not worried with the problem of sin, except Marie Arnoux, who does recognize that such a problem exists and is the only character he has depicted with a sense of guilt. She feels responsibility towards her husband and her children, and struggles against her personal desires. She then believes that the illness of her little boy has come as a retribution for having been prepared to yield sinfully to Frédéric. The others have no clash in their personalities; they are ambitious self-seekers who think only of themselves; and they fail because they have no love and no guilt, no passion or sense of direction. The clearest example of this is Frédéric, who thinks only of gratifying his own desires, can keep to nothing, address himself to nothing, has no real passion for anything, does not know what he wants and makes nothing of his life.

Generally speaking little has been known, or investigated, about

Flaubert himself as a human being. The material exists in great wealth, but it has not been fully studied, and so a false picture has been normally painted of him. Because most critics have judged him by his published writings, he has had the reputation of being a pessimist and a cynic who disliked the whole human race. In practice he loved most of his fellow-men, and his friends could do no wrong. Theoretically his philosophy was sad and he mostly wrote his letters when he was depressed and low in spirits, and he expressed then a longing for death, saying that he would welcome a stroke which would carry him off. Yet he is described by others as the gayest of companions, who was sought out by his friends, who played the fool – an actor *manqué*, who wore out his friends by his excessive energy, as George Sand discovered when he visited her at Nohant. All this he kept up to within a few days of his death. He had, in spite of everything, a love of life and its ordinary pleasures – friends, food and drink. He was never a wet-blanket at a party and was welcomed by everyone. He was not like Baudelaire who, towards the end of his life, was often left alone in a café on account of the bitterness of his attitude to life. Flaubert loved society, even the frivolous Court society and, in this, he was unlike Bouilhet, who preferred solitude. He got on well, even in the smartest gatherings, although he needed solitude for his work. He never, however, got used to eating alone and liked company at his meals.

He was the best of friends and greatly put himself out for those who were his intimates. He spent hours of time he could ill afford, working on their writings, to improve them, trying to obtain contracts for them. There was all his labour on Bouilhet's posthumous work; and a certain Madame Régnier asked him to take charge of her novel, at the moment when he was finishing *L'Éducation Sentimentale*. 'I should be very happy, Monsieur,' she wrote to him,[11] 'if you would be kind enough to take charge of the fate of the novel in question.' He did all that he could for her.

During the war his chief anxiety was for his friends, lest they should suffer hardships. He was particularly concerned about Ernest Feydeau, who was partially paralysed and did not have a great deal of money. He wrote to his old friend Doctor Cloquet:[12]

My dear good friend, I am appealing to your charity to do me a service. My poor friend Feydeau, now lives in the same town as you, rue Neuve-Chaussée No. 7. He has taken refuge there with his wife and two children. His paralysis is increasing and for lack of communication with Paris he is in the greatest distress. I would be *personally* grateful to you if you would go to see him (as if from yourself, by chance) and to help him with your advice and from your purse, which I imagine better filled than mine.

After the war, as his condition had still further deteriorated, he tried to obtain a state pension for him. Writing to Raoul-Duval, he said:[13] 'My dear friend, I BEG you to take into consideration the enclosed note – and to try to obtain some money for poor Feydeau who is in a state worthy of pity. Paralysed, with two children! – and a lot of unpaid bills. Thank you in anticipation, yours ever.' Flaubert enclosed a note on behalf of Feydeau, and stated his physical and financial state. Eighteen months later Feydeau died.

When money was borrowed, from his friends, to save his nephew from bankruptcy, he was most anxious that they should be repaid first, whatever happened to himself. He was sad when his poverty prevented him from giving money to the widow of his servant Narcisse. He wrote to Caroline:[14] 'For several years now I've not even been able to answer the widow of Narcisse, and this silence on my part has lain heavy on my heart, like a bad deed.' We know of his extreme goodness to his niece, to his mother and to his servants. He was simple and kind and, in many ways, childlike, which was what his friends found especially attractive in him. 'He had a kind heart,' wrote Zola,[15] 'full of childlike qualities and innocence, a warm heart, which burst out in indignation at any wound. That was his potent charm, which made all of us love him like a father.' And Madame Daudet said:[16] 'My husband never called him anything but "kind Flaubert". Kind he was and compassionate, and faithful in friendship, high above all the meanness of the profession.' Anatole France said of him:[17] 'He had a prodigious capacity for enthusiasm and sympathy. That is why he was always furious. He used to battle on the slightest pretext, always having some offence to avenge. He was very like Don Quixote, whom he admired so much . . . They were two good brave hearts. Both carried on a dream of life, with heroic pride, which it was easier to make fun of than to equal. I had scarcely been five minutes with Flaubert, than the little drawing-room, hung with oriental rugs, was dripping with the blood of twenty thousand slaughtered bourgeois!' Flaubert himself said to Goncourt:[18] 'It is indignation alone which sustains me. When I am no longer indignant, I shall fall down flat!'

His friends loved him because they knew that they could trust him and his constant goodwill towards them. Du Camp said that he was very easy to cheat; since he could not tell a lie himself, he could not conceive of anyone wanting to deceive him.[19] He never behaved shabbily to a friend, except once to the faithful Laporte, and that was not wholly his fault. Nevertheless he should have known his friend better and not have believed his niece, especially after all he had done for him.

There was universal sorrow when he died, and Maupassant wrote to Caroline:[20]

Dear Madame, your letter did me good as I am in a very sad moral state. The more the death of poor Flaubert fades into the distance, the more his memory haunts me, the more my heart aches and the lonelier my mind becomes. His image is ceaselessly before me, and I see him standing before me, in his great brown dressing-gown, which grew more voluminous when he lifted his arms as he spoke. All his gestures come back to my mind, all the intonations of his voice pursue me, and the phrases he used to say, are in my ear still, just as he pronounced them . . . These blows bruise our mind and leave in it continual suffering, which remains in all our thoughts.

My poor mother, over there, has been greatly hit by it, and it seems that she remained alone, shut in her bedroom, for two whole days, weeping. For her it is her last friend who dies, it is henceforth a life without echo of all these good memories of her youth; it means never to be able to recite with anyone that litany 'Do you remember?' At this moment I feel, in an acute form, the uselessness of living, the sterility of all effort, the monotony of events and things and that moral isolation in which we all live and which I felt less when I could speak with him, for he possessed, as no one else, that feeling of philosophers which opens on everything new horizons, which keeps your mind on the heights from whence one contemplates the whole of humanity, from whence one understands 'the eternal misery of things'.

Here, Madame, are sad matters, but sad things are better when one's heart grieves than matters of indifference.

What his friends especially missed, after he was gone, was his gaiety and sense of fun in social gatherings. Even in his most unhappy periods this never flagged. This may seem strange to those who judge him as pessimistic and sad, from his correspondence. Often, after being sunk in despair, he would suddenly change, put on a woman's dress, dance a Spanish dance and become the regular actor he would have liked to have been. His love of pornography was part of this *joie de vivre*, and appreciation of the grotesque humour of life. To him it was the highest comedy if he could find pompous men in high places involved in such situations. This struck his sense of irony and caused him acute pleasure. It filled him with delight when he heard that his enemy, the Public Prosecutor, Pinard, who had taken such a high moral tone at his trial of *Madame Bovary* in 1857, was discovered, twenty years later, to be the author of a collection of lewd verses.[21] 'Pinard my enemy,' wrote Flaubert to his niece, 'the author of obscene verses found in the *Prie Dieu* of Madame Gros . . . What a joke! what a joke!' He was also delighted at the story of the men found in the act of homosexuality in a urinal in the Champs-Élysées in Paris, one of whom was Eugène Lebègue, Comte de Germiny, son of a former Governor of the Banque de France who, when he was arrested, struck one of the policemen. 'This is one of those anecdotes,' wrote Flaubert,[22] 'which bring consolation and help to make life bearable!'

Yet Goncourt said that Flaubert was only a 'faux cochon', trying to be the equal of his friends, who were true 'cochons'.[23] This may well have been true.

It is often declared, and believed, that Flaubert had led a sedentary and uneventful life, and that nothing had happened to him. Henry James wrote:[24] 'The fewest possible things appear to have even succeeded in happening to him.' Such a statement could only have been made through ignorance. He was not a globe-trotter as Gautier had been, but he did a good deal of travelling at a time when this was not easy. As a young man, he went on a journey on foot, with Du Camp, through the primitive province of Brittany. He had the journey of two years in the East, enduring great hardships and dangers, in disturbed country, mostly on horseback through the desert. Later he went to Carthage and the neighbouring country in North Africa. He travelled extensively in France, when the railway service was not yet developed. In his private life, he had a trial for obscenity; he was bankrupted by his own niece. He was involved in the Revolution of 1848, nearly killed in the *coup d'état* of 1851, and he was a member of the National Guard, and a male nurse, during the Franco-Prussian war in 1870, and his home was occupied by the invader.

It is perhaps strange that, with his compassion and kindness, Flaubert should have had an obsession with sadism. This was not in his personal character, nor in his dealing with people. No acts of cruelty or unkindness, no examples of even mental cruelty, have ever been attributed to him. Yet there was a streak of sadism in his literature, his talent and his imagination, which is to be found in most of his early writings, in his works of boyhood. There is no doubt that he enjoyed describing horrors, and dwelling on them. Later he read the Marquis de Sade with great interest and excitement, and Goncourt expressed surprise that he should try to find meaning in this 'madman'.[25] He describes the kind of objects which Flaubert kept as mementoes[26] – the autograph confession of a pederast, who killed his lover through jealousy, and was eventually guillotined, after confessing all the details of his passion and crime; and the letter of a whore describing all the sordid and cruel tricks of her trade.

In his fiction there are also examples of his interest in horrors, often it seems for their own sake. These can be found in *La Tentation de Saint Antoine*, in *Saint Julien l'Hospitalier* and especially in *Salammbô*, which has so many sadistic scenes that it horrified some nineteenth-century readers, even Sainte-Beuve. There are the terrible battle scenes, the elephant charges, the torture of the prisoners; the description of the diseases of Hannon; the crucifixion of the lions, the death of the mercenaries in the Défilé de la Hache; and finally the torture and terrible death of Mathô. Only someone obsessed with sadism could have painted such pictures. Yet, in his private dealings, he was the kindest of men. Once, when he had said something about Bouilhet which was repeated to him and which had hurt him, he had been much upset by the occurrence:[27]

Yesterday evening I saw 'Monseigneur' (we dined together at Magny's) and I *excused myself to him*, for the poor fellow was much distressed at the way I had treated him. 'Monseigneur' is so kind . . . It seems that either you or your grandmother recounted the scene to the Achilles, for Madame Achille repeated it to Bouilhet himself. In short I felt remorse, and I begged his forgiveness, for you know that I don't like to hurt those whom I love.

Another marked feature of Flaubert's personality was his passion for erudition and learning, for their own sake and not for the use that he might make of them. If he had not been a great creative writer, he might well have become a distinguished scholar. He had scientific blood on both sides. His father was a famous surgeon and his mother the daughter of a doctor. We know the amount of research work which he carried out in connection with all his books. One cannot feel that all this work was essential – especially in the case of *Bouvard et Pécuchet*, which it even overweights. A great deal of it seems a waste of a good life, and he might have written other books in the time taken for collecting the material to prove the inanity of the human race.

He had a horror of the stupidity of mankind, with its conceit and its ill-considered theories which it took for profound and immutable truths; he felt this stupidity as a material thing that could hit him physically. He once wrote:[28]

> I feel, against the stupidity of my time, floods of hatred which choke me. Shit rises to my mouth as in the case of a strangled hernia. But I want to keep it, fix it and harden it; I want to concoct a paste which I shall cover the nineteenth century, as one paints, with cow dung, Indian pagodas.

So great was his contempt for his age that he did not wish to please it in his writings, and the consequence was that he managed to please posterity. He never sought success, nor tried to repeat something which had already been a success. He genuinely did not desire to receive honours from his contemporaries – certainly not after the war, when his disgust had developed to greater depths. There are no mention of them in his letters, and he positively did not want them. He refused to allow his name to be put forward for promotion in the Légion-d'Honneur, nor to be nominated as a candidate for election to the French Academy, when Hugo's support would probably have ensured his success. Perhaps he might have accepted them if they had come earlier, for he did accept the cross of Chevalier de la Légion-d'Honneur from Princesse Mathilde, but she was a personal friend and it was like the gift of a trinket from her hands. By the time he could legitimately hope for honours, he had come to despise all those in power, and to have such contempt for them that he did not want to be singled out by them for praise. He believed that nothing could be hoped from man in general, as he was incurable. This was the lesson which the second volume of *Bouvard et*

Pécuchet would have established, if he had finished it, and whic[h]
called his intellectual testament. Man is weak and fallible [and]
arrogantly over-confident in his powers and potentialit[ies].
Flaubert could have echoed Isabelle in *Measure for Measure* by
Shakespeare:

> but man, proud man!
> Dressed in a little brief authority –
> Most ignorant of what he's most assured.

He imagines that, with his knowledge, he can master the universe.
From Spencer Flaubert borrowed the theory that scientific knowledge, however great, does not give him the key of creation. We
are learning that today to our great cost. The nineteenth century
was the beginning of the period of infinite belief in the powers of
science to explain everything, and eventually conquer everything.
Flaubert intended to show up the weaknesses of that knowledge,
even in the most intelligent and advanced of human minds, and
show that it can never be anything but imperfect. That, in Flaubert's opinion, was man's tragedy, for, if knowledge is unreliable,
where can one look for certainty? He then reached the formula
'ne pas conclure', that is, not to make up one's mind about anything. This led him to the consciousness of failure, and all his
books depict failure in some form, so that it became almost an
obsession with him, and, looking at his own life, he saw failure
everywhere. There was the failure of his health; the break-up
of his family through death; there was the final failure of his great
love, his failure in passion; there was the failure with the public
of what he considered his great book; the failure of his one
dramatic venture; the failure of his fortune; his failure to finish
Bouvard et Pécuchet. There was failure of romantic love in *Madame
Bovary*, failure of a whole generation in *L'Éducation Sentimentale*,
of religion in *La Tentation de Saint Antoine*, and of knowledge in
Bouvard et Pécuchet.

In his longing for absolute certainty, Flaubert himself would
have welcomed religious faith, and he needed it. Although a
sceptic, he was not a materialist. He was a man of deep religious
feelings and needs, if not of any beliefs. He lost his faith when
very young – the whole of the home atmosphere was against it –
but not his thirst for religion nor his aspirations for the infinite.
Mauriac wrote[29] that Flaubert kept his heart to the end, which

could always be touched, and that he behaved as if humanity, in its search for light, always knocked at the wrong door. A few weeks before he died, Flaubert wrote to his niece:[30] 'I'm torn between faith and philosophy.'

He did not, however, consider that faith gave man the right to importune God, to try to influence him in his own affairs. One should not go, as a suppliant, cap in hand, asking for favours. He wrote to Feydeau:[31] 'Let's have the modesty of wounded animals, who withdraw into a corner and remain silent. The world is full of people who bellow against Providence. One must, if only on the score of good manners, avoid behaving like them.' To George Sand he wrote:[32] 'To accuse Providence is a mania so widespread that one should abstain from it, if only through good manners.' In the last difficult year of his life, he said:[33] 'Providence doesn't exactly bury me under roses, but I don't accuse her, being convinced of the necessity of things.' He himself gained strength and human dignity from trying to look straight at what was crushing him, and trying to understand it. He was the 'roseau pensant' of Pascal's *Pensées*, the most feeble thing in creation, but which understands what is destroying it. He himself was invigorated from gazing into the abyss at his feet, and saying to himself:[34] 'It is so, it must be so, it cannot be otherwise'; and this brought him exaltation.

By what then did he live, this theoretic extreme pessimist? By a kind of priesthood and sainthood in art, which demanded the same sacrifice as religion would have done. Art brought him the same joy, mingled with pain, that religious experience might. He declared:[35] 'I love my art with a frenzied and perverse passion, as the ascetic loves the hair-shirt which scratches his belly.' Zola once said that Flaubert had entered literature as formerly one entered a religious order, to experience all its joys and to die in it. And Mauriac said that he had substituted Art for God and, in so doing, had become guilty of idolatry.

Anatole France wrote to him:[36] 'I consider you, whatever may happen to you, as the happiest of men, for you have written what you wanted to write.'

Although he felt the need for religious feeling and would have welcomed faith, Flaubert did not feel the need for political involvement, and felt no urge to sublimate his desire for faith in politics and a wish to work for the betterment of the world. As far as society was concerned, all he asked was to be allowed to observe it, but not to improve it, as he had no zeal in that direction. He remained to the end anti-clerical and, on the whole, anti-Christian – one of his reasons for disliking Socialism was that he considered it a new form of Christianity. He also thought that it was completely materialistic, had no mysticism and inevitably led to authoritarianism, and he shows this in the career of Sénécal in *L'Éducation Sentimentale*. He did not believe in egalitarianism, he said, but in justice for everyone and, at the end of his life, after the war, he favoured a government by an élite, though it is hard to imagine that he would have found anyone worthy of that party. He was ignorant and innocent politically, because he was not interested in such questions. He despised all parties, could have belonged to none of them and he could not become interested in social progress. Yet he did his duty by his family and his friends, giving them devoted service; and he carried out his civic duties during the war. What he asked for from society was peace around him and this was largely due to the exigencies of his life as an artist. That was why, in 1870, although he had never liked the Second Empire, he thought at first that it should be supported as long as it had a chance of surviving, but he did not regret its passing. His strongest feeling was in being anti-bourgeois, but he never made it quite clear what he meant by bourgeois, and one suspects that it was everything he disliked. Yet there was much, in his own life, which was by any standards bourgeois. He married his niece in the most bourgeois manner possible and said that he would prefer her to marry a rich Philistine than a poor artist. It is true that, on personal grounds, he was unsure of the man, and his instinct was sounder than his opinions. He married her thus, in an effort to ensure her future prosperity, and it was this bourgeois marriage which eventually ruined him financially. This would have struck his grim sense of irony, if he had been capable of irony with regard to his niece.

Flaubert remained, all his life, faithful to the ideal of perfect eternal love, disinterested love, and he had a nostalgia for it. However he never really found it, not even in imagination, and he has not painted a single satisfactory love relationship in all his writings. Even the great love of his life with Élisa Schlésinger, depicted in the relationship between Frédéric Moreau and Marie Arnoux in *L'Éducation Sentimentale*, peters out into nothingness on account of the lack of decision and the feebleness of the hero. Would Flaubert himself have been capable of a satisfactory love affair with any of the many women who loved him? It does not seem at all likely. For most of his life, until within eight years of his death, he lived with his widowed mother, very much under her thumb. There were also his homosexual tendencies to inhibit him. After her death, George Sand tried to persuade him to marry, to fill the loneliness of his home life. Although he regretted then not having married when he was younger, he thought that it was by now too late. Could he then have married one of the women who were devoted to him? Élisa Schlésinger was his 'Princesse Lointaine', locked into his walled-up chamber, and there could have been no marriage between them, for he would always have been inhibited before her by his adoration, and she was too old for him. Louise Colet tried to marry him but that failed and, at that time, Flaubert had no need of marriage. Amélie Bosquet was too coarse-grained, and she would probably have offended him in his daily life. In any case he had ceased seeing her when his need was greatest, after his mother died. Jane de Tourbey had, by then, become Comtesse de Loynes and was very rich, but one cannot see her giving up her title, social position and ambitions, and living in his *garçonnière*, with all the paraphernalia of his notes and documentation. Madame Roger des Genettes was near to his age, being only three years older, and she came from the same social professional background as he. She could have made a civilized home for him, but he generally treated her as a mother figure, and she might have driven him distracted with her conventional religious practices. Also, in her latter years, she was an invalid through paralysis. Moreover she could not have given him the children for whom, in his latter years, he craved. A year before he died, he wrote to Frankline Sabatier:[37] 'You are wrong in thinking that the details concerning your child do not interest me. I adore children and I was born to be an excellent papa, but fate and literature decided otherwise. It is one of the sad facts of my old age not to have a little creature to love and to caress. Embrace yours for me.'

If his niece could have given him great-nephews and great-nieces, it might have filled the loneliness of his last years. He was probably right when he thought that he was not suitable to be a husband, and one cannot imagine a normal woman of his age fitting into his ascetic writer's life. What he wanted most with his women friends was to write affectionate letters to them, and to dream of them. When George Sand wanted him to marry, after the death of his mother, she was probably thinking of someone much younger and simpler than his correspondents. A simple woman who would not have made great demands on him for companionship, someone like Louis Bouilhet had in Léonie Leparfait, someone on whose bosom he could die. Who would not be jealous of the women in his life, as Louise Colet had been; who would not be hurt by the letters he received from other women, for that was one of the great pleasures of his life. She would have looked after his material life as his mother had done, and perhaps given him the child for which he longed. But this was not to be.

His niece lived with him for thirty-five years, and outlived him by half a century, yet she never said an interesting or an acute thing about him. She was dry and arid and did not really appreciate him. She did not read his books and knew nothing about them, but only made money from them after he had died. Those to whom he went for appreciation and understanding in his work were George Sand and Madame Roger des Genettes; and his close men friends.

The truth is that Flaubert probably never had a full relationship with any woman, except with Louise Colet, when he was young, and that ended in disaster. There is no proof that he had any sexual relationship with the many women in his life, though some think there is doubt about Madame Brainne and Juliet Herbert – Mademoiselle Leroyer de Chantepie he never even met. Perhaps normal sexuality meant nothing to him ultimately, and the only physical relationships he appreciated were homosexuality and prostitution. He kept, to the end, a romantic feeling for prostitution and brothels. There are many passages in his letters – most of them excised on publication – where he speaks of the physical orgies he enjoyed on his visits to Paris, but one cannot be sure whether he was speaking the truth or whether, as Goncourt claimed, he was only trying to appear as a 'cochon' to keep his end up with his friends. One cannot imagine such situations in connection with Edma Roger des Genettes and the correct, even prim, Amélie Bosquet.

In spite of all his women friends, and his affectionate correspondence with them, the really deep relationships in his life were with men. In his youth, in Alfred Le Poittevin, he had a hero with all the glamour of an older man, who was an idealist and marked him for life. In Maxime Du Camp he had the sophisticated man about town, who showed him things he would not have known otherwise. Although their friendship, later, wore thin, it never disappeared and they remained, to the end, what they had been as boys, 'Solus ad Solum'. Du Camp has always had a poor press, but he was a better friend to Flaubert than critics allow. He helped him to the best of his ability, and would have done more if he had been allowed to, but he was too much of his own time to understand him fully and this need not be attributed to jealousy. He was ambitious and he wanted to succeed in the worldly sense – he did, in fact, get all the honours to which he aspired – but he wanted his friends also to be successful. He was not an acute literary critic, and he genuinely thought that Flaubert was mistaken in many of his enterprises – but then so did others amongst his contemporaries. He has always been accused of treachery because he wrote, in his *Souvenirs Littéraires*, that Flaubert had suffered from epilepsy, but this was probably because he wanted to keep dark a more serious disease – indeed one considered shameful – syphilis, of which he knew since it had been contracted while he was with Flaubert in the East.

Louis Bouilhet was of the same literary family as Flaubert, who had the same ideals and ambitions, and it was generally believed that Flaubert would not have become the pure artist that he did without his help and advice. He was the closest and most intimate friend of his life, in every way.

Turgenev was the literary adviser and confidant of the last years, but they did not meet frequently enough to be close in everyday life.

Duplan and Laporte were of the 'faithful dog' variety of friends, who could not be of help to him in literature, but collected documentary material for him. All the close friends, except Laporte, he lost through death, but, as we have seen, Laporte was reft from him through the rapaciousness and selfishness of his beloved niece.

Flaubert was responsible for giving dignity and prestige to the novel, and for raising it to the heights of one of the noblest forms of literature, and this affected not only France but the rest of

Europe as well. When there were attempts in England to improve the standard of fiction, it was to Flaubert that the authors turned. Flaubert was the first novelist to believe that perfection was an essential attribute of fiction. Before him novelists had written well, if they happened to write well – as Mérimée did – but this was merely considered as a personal idiosyncrasy, and no one thought it adverse criticism to declare that Balzac's style was clumsy and his planning confused. On the whole, poetry and drama were considered nobler forms of literature than fiction. Flaubert established the novel as their equal.

Now that the novel is established as one of the great literary forms, is Flaubert's work finished and can he be discarded as an anachronism? Or is there any further interest in him for the modern reader: any spiritual or intellectual sustenance? He is not the kind of author who suddenly seizes hold of a reader, ravishing him from this world, with visions of another and a finer world – as Baudelaire and Rimbaud do. He would not have tried, with Baudelaire, to 'plonger au fond de l'inconnu pour trouver du nouveau', as he would not have believed in the possibility of the 'nouveau' having any value. Yet he had, temperamentally and spiritually, nostalgia for the mountain heights, and was an idealist who found it hard to endure the conditions of life, though he tried to bear them with pride and dignity, and without complaining.

He is not an author for wild popularity or enthusiasm, but the educated and sophisticated reader, who is not carried away by 'trends', finds acute pleasure in a work of art, perfect in form, with a harmonious and melodious style, and with deep understanding of human nature, shown in many characters, in diverse layers of life, not hindered by time and fashion, but eternally true and universal. This he will find particularly in his greatest work *L'Éducation Sentimentale*.

But Flaubert is not merely the author of impassible and abstract novels whom one need not bother to know as he has kept himself out of his writings. Since the thirteen volumes of his correspondence have been published – four since the last war – he appears, as a man, as one of his greatest creations. His correspondence, one of the most interesting in French literature, may well seem to the future to be his greatest work. It fills in his life the position that Gide's *Journal* occupies in his. Gide said that

Flaubert's letters had been, for many years, his Bible, his bedside book, and he had then only known the early and very incomplete editions. There is, in the *Correspondance*, the variety of the *Journal*, with more spontaneity and more naturalness, with more genuine sincerity. It is a valuable treasure-chest of discussion of an enormous number of literary and moral topics, over half a century, as he began writing letters as a small boy, discussed with emotion, humanity and wisdom, and Flaubert is a wonderful companion on this journey through a life, and a marvellous showman of the accumulated richness.

Thus the *Correspondance* may, in the future, become Flaubert's most popular and widely read book, the one in which he has most fully distilled his personality and his wisdom.

BIBLIOGRAPHY

A

The fullest edition of Flaubert's works, up to date, is the one published by Conard, in twenty-nine volumes, and it is the one used throughout this book, except where otherwise stated. It is not completely satisfactory, especially in the matter of the *Correspondance*. A useful edition, for those who want only the novels published by Flaubert himself, is that of the Éditions de la Pléiade, in two volumes by Gallimard. Only the books useful for Flaubert's life and works, after the publication of *Madame Bovary*, are given here; the others were listed in the bibliography of the first volume, *The Making of the Master*.

B

ALBALAT, A. *Gustave Flaubert et ses Amis.* 1927.

ALBALAT, A. *Souvenirs de la Vie Littéraire.* 1924.

AURIANT, *Les Secrets de la Comtesse de Castiglione.* 1935.

BART, B. *Flaubert.* 1967.

BENEDETTO, L. F. *Le Origini di Salammbô.* 1920.

BERTRAND, G. E. *Les Jours de Flaubert.* 1947.

BERTRAND, L. *Gustave Flaubert, avec des Fragments Inédits.* 1912.

BOLLÈME, G. *La Leçon de Flaubert.* 1964.

BOLLÈME, G. *Le Second Volume de Bouvard et Pécuchet.* 1966.

BONWIT, M. *Gustave Flaubert et le Principe d'Impassibilité.* 1950.

BROMBERT, V. *The Novels of Flaubert.* 1966.

CARLUT, C. *La Correspondance de Flaubert.* 1968.

CASSAGNE, A. *La Théorie de l'Art pour l'Art en France chez les Derniers Romantiques et les Premiers Réalistes.* 1906.

CASTEX, P. *Flaubert, L'Éducation Sentimentale.* No date.

CENTO, A. *Flaubert, Bouvard et Pécuchet. Étude Critique, précédée des Scénarios Inédits.* 1964.

COETLAND, P. *The Sentimental Adventure.* 1967.

COLLING, A. *Gustave Flaubert.* 1947.

DEMOREST, D. L. *L'Expression Figurée et Symbolique dans l'Oeuvre de Gustave Flaubert.* 1931.

DEMOREST, D. L. *À travers les Plans, Messages et Dossiers de Bouvard et Pécuchet.* 1931.

DEMOREST, D. L. and DUMESNIL, R. *Bibliographie de Gustave Flaubert.* 1947.

DESCHARMES, R. and DUMESNIL, R. *Autour de Flaubert.* 1912.

DIGEON, C. *Le Dernier Visage de Flaubert.* 1946.

DU CAMP, M. *Souvenirs Littéraires.* 1883.

DUMESNIL, R. *En Marge de Flaubert.* 1928.

DUMESNIL, R. *Gustave Flaubert, l'Homme et l'Oeuvre.* 1967 edition.

DUMESNIL, R. *L'Éducation Sentimentale.* 1935.

DUMESNIL, R. and DEMOREST, D. *Bibliographie de Gustave Flaubert.* 1937.

DUPUY, A. *En Marge de Salammbô. Le Voyage de Flaubert en Algérie-Tunisie, avril-juin* 1858. 1954.

DURRY, M. J. *Flaubert et ses Projets Inédits.* 1950.

FAGUET, E. *Flaubert.* 1899.

FAY, P. B. *Sources and Structure of Flaubert's Salammbô.* 1914.

FERRIÈRE, E. L. *L'Esthétique de Flaubert.* 1913.

FINOT, A. *Maxime du Camp.* 1949.

FISCHER, E. *Études sur Flaubert Inédit.* 1908.

FLAUBERT, G. *Lettres Inédites à Raoul-Duval.* 1950.

FLAUBERT, G. *Lettres Inédites (Publiées par Auriant).* 1948.

FLAUBERT, G. *Lettres inédites à la Princesse Mathilde.* 1927.

FLETCHER, W. J. *A Critical Commentary on Flaubert's Trois Contes.* 1968.

FREJLICH, H. *Flaubert d'après sa Correspondance.* 1933.

GAULTIER, J. DE *Le Bovarysme.* 1892.

GAULTIER, J. DE *Le Génie de Flaubert.* 1913.

GÉRARD-GAILLY, É. *Flaubert et les Fantômes de Trouville.* 1930.

GÉRARD-GAILLY, É. *Les Véhémences de Louise Colet.* 1934.

GÉRARD-GAILLY, É. *Le Grand Amour de Flaubert.* 1944.

GIRAUD, R. *The Unheroic Hero.* 1957.

GUILLEMIN, H. *Flaubert devant la Vie et devant Dieu.* 1939.

HAMILTON, A. *Sources of the Religious Element of Flaubert's Salammbô.* 1917.

HOLDEN, W. H. (editor) *Second Empire Medley.* 1952.

JAMES, H. *French Poets and Novelists.* 1884.

JAMES, H. *The House of Fiction* (edited by Leon Edel). 1957.

JAMES, H. *Notes on Novelists.* 1914.

LETELLIER, L. *Louis Bouilhet.* 1919.

LEVIN, H. *The Gates of Horn.* 1963.

LOMBARD, A. *Flaubert et Saint Antoine.* 1934.

LUBBOCK, P. *The Craft of Fiction.* 1921.
LUKACS, G. *The Historical Novel* (translated by Hannah and Stanley Mitchell). 1962.
KENNEY, H. *The Stoic Comedians.* 1962.
MARTINO, P. *Le Roman Réaliste sous le Second Empire.* 1913.
MAUPASSANT, G. DE *Études sur Gustave Flaubert,* in *Oeuvres Posthumes II.* 1917.
MAURIAC, F. *Trois Grands Hommes devant Dieu.* 1931.
MAYNIAL, W. *Flaubert.* 1945.
MAYNIAL, W. *Flaubert et son Milieu.* 1927.
NADEAU, M. *Gustave Flaubert Écrivain.* 1969.
PROUST, M. *Chroniques.* 1927.
RICHARD, J. *Stendhal et Flaubert Littérature et Sensation.* 1954.
RICHARDSON, J. *Princesse Mathilde.* 1969.
SAND, G. *Correspondance* (Calmann Lévy). 1892.
SARTRE, J.-P. *Situations II.* 1950.
SEILLÈRE, BARON E. *Le Romantisme des Réalistes. Gustave Flaubert, etc.* 1914.
SEZNEC, J. J. *Nouvelles Études sur la Tentation de Saint Antoine.* 1949.
SPAZIANI, M. *Gli Amici della Principessa Mathilde.* 1960.
SPENCER, P. H. *Flaubert.* 1952.
SUFFEL, J. *Gustave Flaubert.* 1958.
THIBAUDET, A. *Gustave Flaubert.* 1935 edition.
THORLBY, A. *Gustave Flaubert and the Art of Realism.* 1956.
TILLETT, M. *On Reading Flaubert.* 1961.
TROUBAT, J. *Souvenirs du Dernier Secrétaire de Sainte-Beuve.* 1890.
TURNELL, M. *The Novel in France.* 1950.
VALÉRY, P. *La Tentation de Saint Antoine,* in *Variété V.* 1944.
WETHERILL, P. M. *Flaubert et la Création Littéraire.* 1966.
WILSON, E. *The Triple Thinkers.* 1938.
ZOLA, É. *Les Romanciers Naturalistes.* 1881.

C

Below are listed some articles dealing with Flaubert's writings which have appeared in papers and reviews. Only those which throw some special light on the novelist are given, and those not used by their authors in subsequent works.

The Fortnightly Review, 1 April 1878. Saintsbury, G. 'Flaubert'.
Mercure de France, 1 May 1952. Pommier, J., and Digeon, C. 'Du Nouveau sur Flaubert et son Oeuvre'.
French Studies, October 1965. Raitt, A. 'The Composition of Flaubert's Saint Julien l'Hospitalier'.
Preuves, February 1965. Sarraute, N. 'Flaubert le Précurseur'.

Bibliography

Revue de Littérature Comparée, 1936. Bar, M. 'Don Quichotte et le Roman Réaliste en France'.

Revue des Deux Mondes, 15 July 1910. Bertrand, L. 'Les Carnets de Flaubert'.

Revue d'Histoire Littéraire de la France, 1919. Giraud, J. 'La Genèse d'un Chef d'Oeuvre'.

Jan.-March 1953. Bauchard. 'Sur les Traces de Flaubert et de Madame Schlésinger'.

NOTES

B.N.=Bibliothèque Nationale; B.H.V.P.=Bibliothèque Historique de la Ville de Paris; LOV=the Spoehlberch de Lovenjoul Collection at Chantilly.

INTRODUCTION

1 LOV AIV., letter to George Sand, 18 October 1871.
2 Auriant: *Les Secrets de la Comtesse de Castiglione*, p. 85.
3 LOV AV, letter to Duplan, 27 March 1867.
4 LOV AV, letter to Duplan, July 1868.
5 (a) LOV AV fol. 366, 20 October 1857: Râlant, beuglant, pâle, épouvanté, la merde au cul, la bave aux lèvres, et la gueule cassée, il décharge, dans son agonie, sous le clitoris rubicond de Dorothée furieuse.
   (b) LOV AV, 17 March 1864: La Princesse continue à me blaguer sur Dorothée. C'est m'honorer infiniment trop. Ton géant d'ailleurs *raté* quelquefois maintenant. Il est vrai que les récents affronts avaient une raison extrinsèque. La Dame schlinguait atrocement. Pour me prouver ma virilité, je suis retourné à une ancienne et alors, oh! alors!

Part One: The Second Empire

CHAPTER ONE: AFTER MADAME BOVARY

1 *Taine: sa Vie et sa correspondance* (Hachette 1904), Vol. II, p. 234.
2 *Vide* Starkie: *Flaubert: The Making of the Master*, p. 245 *et seq.*
3 Letellier: *Bouilhet*, p. 253.
4 *Correspondance*, Vol. IV, pp. 161–2, letter to Madame Pradier, February 1857.
5 LOV CI, letter from Bouilhet, some time in 1857.
6 *Correspondance*, Vol. IV, p. 175, letter to Feydeau, April 1857.

7 *Ibid.*, pp. 177, 179 and 186, letters to Duplan, May 1857.

8 *Ibid.*, p. 208, letter to Duplan, 22 July 1857.

9 *Ibid.*, p. 217, letter to Bouilhet, 22 August 1857.

10 *Ibid.*, p. 226, letter to Duplan, end of September 1857.

11 *Ibid.*, p. 226, letter to Duplan, end of September or beginning of October 1857.

12 *Ibid.*, p. 229, letter to Charles Edmond, 21 October 1857.

13 LOV CI, letter from Bouilhet, September 1857.

14 *Vide* Starkie: *The Making of the Master*, p. 243.

15 *Correspondance*, Vol. IV, p. 410, letter to Duplan, 1 January 1861.

16 *Ibid.*, p. 246, letter to Mlle Leroyer de Chantepie, 23 January 1858.

17 *Ibid.*, p. 251, letter to Mlle Leroyer de Chantepie, 6 April 1858.

18 *Vide* Starkie: *The Making of the Master*, p. 63.

19 *Correspondance*, Vol. IV, p. 256, letter to Louis Bouilhet, about April 1858.

20 *Vide* Starkie: *Petrus Borel, the Lycanthrope*.

21 Aimé Dupuy: *En Marge de Salammbô*, p. 25.

22 B.H.V.P., *Carnet No. 10*, p. 50.

23 *Ibid.*, p. 24.

24 *Correspondance*, Vol. IV, p. 266, letter to Feydeau, 20 June 1858.

25 *Notes de Voyages*, Vol. II, p. 347.

26 LOV CI, letter from Bouilhet, 28 August 1860.

27 *Ibid.*, letter from Bouilhet, March 1861.

28 *Ibid.*, letter from Bouilhet, 1 September 1861.

29 B.H.V.P., *Carnet No. 2*, p. 5, headed 'Notes Générales', October 1859.

30 *Correspondance*, Vol. IV, p. 286, letter to Feydeau, 19 December 1858.

31 *Ibid.*, p. 390, letter to Maxime Du Camp, 15 August 1860.

32 *Ibid.*, p. 206, letter to Baudelaire, 22 July 1857.

33 *Ibid.*, p. 407, letter to Baudelaire, 22 October 1860.

34 *Ibid.*, p. 124, letter from Baudelaire, 26 June 1860.

35 Goncourt: *Journal*, Vol. I, 6 May 1861.

36 *Correspondance*, Vol. IV, p. 427, letter to the Goncourts, early May 1861.

37 Goncourt: *Journal*, Vol. I, 6 May 1861.

38 LOV BII, letter from Du Camp, 11 July 1862.

39 *Correspondance*, Vol. IV, p. 446, letter to Mme Sandeau, 1 September 1861.

40 *Ibid.*, Vol. V, p. 16, letter to Mlle Leroyer de Chantepie, 24 April 1862.

41 *Ibid.*, p. 24, letter to Duplan, 10 June 1862.

42 *Ibid.*, pp. 25–6, letter to Duplan, 12 June 1862.

43 *Ibid.*, p. 39, letter to A. Baudry, 23 August 1862.

44 *Ibid.*, p. 34, letter to Mme Roger des Genettes, July 1862.
45 *Correspondance*, Supp. Vol. I, p. 316, note 2.
46 *Correspondance*, Vol. V, p. 94, letter to General Bougenel, June 1863.
47 LOV BII, letter from Du Camp, 10 December 1864.
48 Descharmes and Dumesnil: *Autour de Flaubert*, Vol. I, p. 164.
49 *Salammbô*, p. 504; letter from Berlioz, 4 November 1862.
50 Descharmes and Dumesnil: *op. cit.*, pp. 187–99.
51 *Ibid.*, pp. 188–92.
52 *Correspondance*, Vol. VI, p. 391, letter to Caroline, 23 June 1872.
53 *Ibid.*, Vol. VIII, p. 270, letter to Caroline, 12 June 1879.
54 *Ibid.*, p. 273, letter to Caroline, 15 June 1879.
55 A. Jullien: *Ernest Reyer*, pp. 64–6.
56 Descharmes and Dumesnil: *op. cit.*, p. 199.
57 *Ibid.*, p. 40.
58 Dumesnil: *En Marge de Flaubert*, pp. 117–18.
59 *Correspondance*, Vol. V, pp. 89–90, letter to Duplan, beginning of April 1863.

CHAPTER TWO: BLUE STOCKINGS AND COURTESANS

1 *Correspondance*, Vol. IV, p. 303, letter to Feydeau, January 1859.
2 *Ibid.*, Vol. III, letter to Louise Colet, 1 September 1852.
3 *Vide* Starkie: *The Making of the Master*, pp. 63–6.
4 B.N. N.A.F. 23, 825.
5 *Vide* Starkie: *op. cit.*, pp. 267–8, for his letter.
6 *Correspondance*, Vol. IV, p. 169, letter to Mlle Leroyer de Chantepie, 30 March 1857.
7 *Ibid.*, p. 168, letter to Mlle Leroyer de Chantepie, 30 March 1857.
8 Letter from Mlle Leroyer de Chantepie B.N. N.A.F. 23,825, 23 March 1857.
9 *Ibid.*, 14 September 1859.
10 *Correspondance*, Vol. V, p. 95, letter to Mlle Leroyer de Chantepie, 22 June 1863.
11 *Ibid.*, p. 157 letter to Mlle Leroyer de Chantepie, 6 October 1864.
12 Letter from Mlle Leroyer de Chantepie, B.N. N.A.F. 23,825, 28 July 1868.
13 *Ibid.*, 15 August 1868.
14 *Correspondance*, Vol. V, p. 386, letter to Mlle Leroyer de Chantepie, 15 July 1868.
15 Letter from Mlle Leroyer de Chantepie, B.N. N.A.F. 23,825, 28 July 1868.
16 *Correspondance*, Vol. V, pp. 394–6, letter to Mlle Leroyer de Chantepie, August 1868.
17 Letter from Mlle Leroyer de Chantepie, 2 September 1868.

Notes

18 *Correspondance*, Vol. VII, pp. 304 et. seq., letter to Mlle Leroyer de Chantepie, 17 June 1876.
19 *Ibid.*, Vol. IV, p. 234, letter to Mlle Leroyer de Chantepie, 4 November 1857.
20 LOV BI.
21 *Correspondance*, Vol. IV, p. 350, note.
22 *Bulletin des Amis de Flaubert*, 27 December 1965; A. Dubosc: *Amélie Bosquet*.
23 *Correspondance*, Vol. IV, p. 350, letter to Amélie Bosquet, November 1859.
24 B.N. N.A.F. 23,828, unpublished portion of letter to Amélie Bosquet, 24 August 1861.
25 *Ibid.*, April or May 1863.
26 *Ibid.*, August, 1863.
27 LOV BI., letter from Amélie Bosquet, August 1866.
28 LOV BI., letter from Amélie Bosquet, 17 July 1866.
29 *Correspondance*, Vol. V, p. 259, letter to Amélie Bosquet, December 1866.
30 LOV BI, letter from Amélie Bosquet, 14 December 1866.
31 *Ibid.*
32 *Correspondance*, Vol. V, p. 320, letter to Amélie Bosquet, September 1867.
33 *Ibid.*, p. 325, letter to Amélie Bosquet, September 1867.
34 B.N. N.A.F. 23,824.
35 LOV BI, letter from Amélie Bosquet, 10 December 1869.
36 *Correspondance*, Vol. II, p. 399, letter to Louise Colet, 15 April 1852.
37 *Ibid.*, Vol. III, p. 69, letter to Louise Colet, 17 December 1852.
38 *Ibid.*, p. 116, letter to Louise Colet, 9 March 1853.
39 *Ibid.*, Vol. IV, p. 34, letter to Louise Colet, 23 March 1854.
40 Madame Roger des Genettes: *Quelques Lettres*, p. 104, 14 April 1888.
41 *Correspondance*, Vol. IV, p. 360, letter to Mme Roger des Genettes 1859–60.
42 *Ibid.*, p. 362, letter to Mme Roger des Genettes, 1859–60.
43 *Ibid.*, p. 364.
44 *Ibid.*, Vol. V, p. 159, letter to Mme Roger des Genettes, October 1864.
45 *Ibid.*, Vol. VI, p. 402, letter to Mme Roger des Genettes, 18 August 1872.
46 Mme Roger des Genettes: *op. cit.*, pp. 108–9.
47 *L'Œuvre*, 20 November 1931; Deffoux: *Le Pupitre de Flaubert*.
48 Mme Roger des Genettes: *op. cit.*, letter 30 August 1890.
49 *Ibid.*, letter 27 November 1890.
50 Goncourt: *Journal*, Monaco edition, Vol. V, p. 85, 6 April 1862.

51 *Bulletin des Amis de Flaubert*, No. 13, 1958.
52 *Correspondance*, Vol. IV, p. 275, letter to Feydeau, 24 August 1858.
53 *Ibid.*, Supp. Vol. I, p. 254, letter to Mme Sabatier, March 1860.
54 The fullest account of her career is given in Auriant: *Les Secrets de la Comtesse de Castiglione*.
55 Auriant: *op. cit.*, p. 77.
56 *Ibid.*, p. 72.
57 Holden (editor): *Second Empire Medley*, p. 55.
58 Auriant: *op. cit.*, p. 88.
59 Goncourt: *Journal*, Vol. III, p. 167, 20 January 1869.
60 Suffel: *Gustave Flaubert*.
61 Auriant: *op. cit.*, p. 77.
62 *Ibid.*
63 Suffel: *op. cit.*, p. 63.
64 Auriant: *op. cit.*, p. 66.
65 *Le Figaro Littéraire*, 11 July 1953; J. Bertaut: *Une Égérie de la Troisième République*.
66 LOV CI fol. 408.
67 *Correspondance*, Supp. Vol. I, p. 239, letter to Jane de Tourbey, 15 May 1858.
68 Auriant: *op. cit.*, pp. 84–5 note.
69 LOV AV fol. 113, letter to Bouilhet, 10 May 1855.
70 Spencer: *Flaubert*, p. 63, note 4.
71 *Correspondance*, Vol. VI, p. 153, note, letter to Caroline, 22 September 1870.
72 Bart: *Flaubert*, p. 771, note 22.
73 *Correspondance*, Supp. Vol. III, p. 48, letter to Mme Brainne, 7 September 1872.
74 *Ibid.*, Vol. VI, p. 412, letter to Caroline, 8 September 1872.
75 *Ibid.*, Supp. Vol. III, p. 143, letter to Laporte, 19 September 1874.

CHAPTER THREE: SALAMMBÔ

1 B.N. N.A.F. 23, 656–62.
2 *Ibid.*, 23, 659–62.
3 *Ibid.*, 23, 656.
4 Seznec: *Nouvelles Études sur La Tentation de Saint Antoine*, p. 9.
5 *Correspondance*, Vol. V, p. 27, letter to Chevalier, 24 June.
6 *Oeuvres de Jeunesse*, Vol. II, pp. 4–5.
7 *Mémoires*, Vol. V, p. 96.
8 *Correspondance*, Vol. V, p. 56, letter to Sainte-Beuve, 23–24 December 1862.
9 Faguet: *Flaubert*, p. 46.
10 Ferrière: *L'Esthétique de Flaubert*, p. 272.

11 B.N. N.A.F. 23,662, fol. 148.
12 Fay: *The Chronological Structure of Salammbô*, p. 12.
13 Michelet: *Histoire Romaine*, 1833 edition, p. 249.
14 *Salammbô*, p. 4.
15 *Ibid.*, p. 19.
16 *Ibid.*, p. 24.
17 *Ibid.*, pp. 104–6.
18 *Ibid.*, p. 129.
19 *Ibid.*, p. 246.
20 *Ibid.*, p. 248.
21 *Ibid.*, p. 265.
22 *Ibid.*, p. 270.
23 B.N. N.A.F. 23,662, fol. 220.
24 *Salammbô*, p. 273.
25 *Ibid.*, pp. 349–50.
26 *Ibid.*, p. 379.
27 *Ibid.*, p. 370.
28 *Ibid.*, p. 386.
29 *Ibid.*, p. 385.
30 *Ibid.*, p. 388.
31 *Ibid.*, pp. 400–401.
32 Michelet: *op. cit.*, p. 286.
33 *Salammbô*, p. 403.
34 *Ibid.*, pp. 412–13.
35 *Ibid.*, pp. 413–14.
36 B.N. N.A.F. 23,662, fol. 220.
37 *Salammbô*, p. 265.
38 B.N. N.A.F. 23,662, fol. 219 verso.
39 *Ibid.*, fol. 219.
40 *Salammbô*, p. 227.
41 *Ibid.*, p. 376.
42 *Ibid.*, p. 376.
43 *Ibid.*, p. 21.
44 Gérard-Gailly: *Les Véhémences de Louise Colet*, pp. 191–3.
45 *Revue d'Histoire Littéraire de la France*, July–September 1964.
46 *Ibid.*
47 *Correspondance*, Vol. V, p. 86, letter to Froehner, 21 January 1863.
48 James: *French Poets and Novelists*, p. 210.
49 Bart: *Flaubert*, p. 431.

CHAPTER FOUR: PRINCESSE MATHILDE AND GEORGE SAND

1 Viel-Castel: *Mémoires*, Vol. VI, p. 209.
2 *Correspondance*, Vol. V., p. 75, letter to Gautier, 19 January 1863.

3 LOV BII, fol. 329, letter from Goncourt, 1863.
4 Spaziani: *Gli Amici della Principessa Matilde*, p. 99.
5 *Correspondance*, Vol. VI, p. 83, letter to Caroline, 14 October 1869.
6 *Ibid.*, Vol. V, p. 279, letter to Princesse Mathilde, some time in 1867.
7 *Ibid.*, Vol. VI, p. 17, letter to Princesse Mathilde, some time in 1869.
8 Goncourt: *Journal*, Monaco edition, Vol. V, p. 148, 16 August 1862.
9 Primoli: *Preface to Flaubert: Lettres Inédites à la Princesse Mathilde*, p. iv
10 The famous actor of the Romantic period.
11 *La Presse*, 31 October 1866.
12 Goncourt: *Journal*, Vol. III, p. 81, 28 October 1866.
13 *Ibid.*, p. 228, 7 August 1868.
14 Primoli: *op. cit.*, pp. vii–xi
15 Communicated by J. Richardson, from the Primoli papers. The *Correspondance* incorrectly states (Supp. Vol. II, p. 15, note 4) that Flaubert wrote it on either Princesse Mathilde's or Princesse Julie's autograph book, though Flaubert states himself that he had written it on Princesse Primoli's autograph book. *Correspondance*, Vol. V, p. 167, letter February 1865.
16 *Correspondance*, Vol. V, p. 398, letter to Princesse Mathilde, 15 August 1868.
17 *Ibid.*, p. 329, letter to Princesse Mathilde, some time in 1867.
18 *Ibid.*, p. 233, letter to Princesse Mathilde, 1866.
19 *Ibid.*, Vol. VI, pp. 21–3, letter to Caroline, 23 May 1869.
20 *Ibid.*, p. 94, letter to Princesse Mathilde, November 1869.
21 Duruy's letter communicated by J. Richardson, from Primoli Collection.
22 *Correspondance*, Vol. V, p. 223, letter to Princesse Mathilde, 16 August 1866.
23 *Ibid.*, p. 229, letter to Princesse Mathilde, August 1866.
24 *Ibid.*, Vol. VI, p. 100, letter to Princesse Mathilde, 31 December 1869.
25 *Ibid.*, Vol. V, p. 74, letter to George Sand, January 1863.
26 George Sand: *Correspondance*, Vol. IV, p. 338 (Calmann Lévy edition).
27 Suffel: *Gustave Flaubert*, p. 71.
28 Richardson: *Princess Mathilde*, p. 107.
29 Sand: *Correspondance*, Vol. V, p. 167, letter to Flaubert, 15 January 1867.
30 *Ibid.*, letter to Flaubert, pp. 99–101.
31 Goncourt: *Journal*, Monaco edition, Vol. VI, p. 146.
32 Maurois: *Lélia*, translated by G. Hopkins, p. 426.

33 Sand: *Correspondance*, Vol. V, p. 126, letter to Flaubert, 10 August 1866.

34 *Ibid.*, p. 131, letter to Flaubert, 12 August 1866.

35 *Correspondance*, Supp. II, p. 68, letter to George Sand, 1 September 1866.

36 Sand: *Correspondance*, Vol. VI, p. 249, letter to Flaubert, 25 October 1872.

37 Maurois: *op. cit.*, p. 246.

38 *Correspondance*, Vol. V, p. 247, letter to George Sand, 12–14 November 1866.

39 *Ibid.*, p. 247, letter 25 October 1872.

40 Sand: *Correspondance*, Vol. VI, p. 377, letter to Flaubert, 12 January 1876.

41 *Ibid.*, p. 379, letter to Flaubert, 12 January 1876.

42 *Correspondance*, Vol. VII, p. 280, letter to George Sand, December 1875.

43 Sand: *Correspondance*, Vol. V, p. 177, letter to Flaubert, 8 February 1867.

44 *Ibid.*, Vol. VI, p. 367, letter to Flaubert, 18 and 19 December 1875.

45 *Correspondance*, Vol. VI, pp. 280 and 282, letter to George Sand, 8 September 1871.

46 For Flaubert's aesthetic doctrine see Starkie: *Flaubert: The Making of the Master*, pp. 334–9.

CHAPTER FIVE: THE MAN ABOUT TOWN

1 Goncourt: *Journal*, Vol. II, 24 March 1862.

2 *Correspondance*, Supp. Vol. II, p. 16, letter to Duplan, 12 November 1864.

3 LOV H 1355, letter from Prince Napoleon.

4 Auriant: *op. cit.*, p. 84, note 1.

5 LOV H 1355, letter from Prince Napoleon, 1863.

6 Mitchell and Fleury: *Un Demi-Siècle de Mémoires*, Vol. I, pp. 18–21.

7 *Correspondance*, Vol. V, p. 168, letter to Caroline, February 1865.

8 *Ibid.*, p. 162, letter to Caroline, 17 November 1862.

9 *Ibid.*, p. 140, letter to Duplan, April 1864.

10 Coppée: *Souvenirs d'un Parisien*, p. 111.

11 *Correspondance*, Vol. V, p. 28, letter to Caroline, June 1864.

12 *Ibid.*, p. 305, letter to Caroline, 7 June 1867.

13 *Ibid.*, p. 308, letter to George Sand, 15 June 1867.

14 *Ibid.*, p. 313, letter to Princesse Mathilde, June 1867.

15 LOV CII, fol. 1367, letter from Bouilhet.

16 Gérard-Gailly: *Le Grand Amour de Flaubert*, pp. 292, et seq.

17 *Correspondance*, Vol. V, p. 123, letter to Caroline, end of December 1863.
18 LOV BII, fol. 318, letter from Du Camp, 5 April 1864.
19 *Correspondance*, Vol. VI, p. 28, letter to Caroline, 19 June 1869.
20 *Ibid.*, Vol. V, p. 223, letter to Caroline, 11 August 1866.
21 Auriant: *Lettres Inédites*, pp. 74–9.
22 *Correspondance*, Supp. Vol. II, pp. 23 and 24, letter to Fovard, March 1865.
23 *Ibid.*, p. 70, letter to Duplan, 14 September 1866.
24 *Ibid.*, p. 113, letter to Commanville, May 1867.
25 *Ibid.*, pp. 238–9, note 2, to Duplan. This is not Flaubert's friend who died on 1 March 1870.

CHAPTER SIX: THE END OF AN ERA

1 *Correspondance*, Vol. IV, p. 126, letter to Mme Schlésinger, 26 October 1856, and p. 307, letter to Mme Schlésinger, 16 January 1859.
2 *Ibid.*, p. 351, letter to Amélie Bosquet, November or December 1859.
3 *Ibid.*, Supp. Vol. I, p. 280, letter to Schlésinger, 28 January 1862.
4 *Mercure de France*, 1 May 1952.
5 Bauchard: 'Sur les Traces de Flaubert et de Mme Schlésinger'; in *Revue d'Histoire Littéraire de la France*, January–March 1953.
6 LOV BII, letter from Du Camp, 20 August 1863.
7 *Mercure de France*, 1 May 1952.
8 Steinhardt-Leins: *Flauberts Grosse Liebe*.
9 Durry: *op. cit.*, pp. 137–200.
10 Bauchard: *op. cit.*
11 Gérard-Gailly: *Le Grand Amour de Flaubert*, p. 163.
12 *Correspondance*, Supp. Vol. p. 102, letter to Bouilhet, 27 March 1867.
13 Steinhardt-Leins: *op. cit.*, p. 13.
14 *Correspondance*, Vol. V, p. 256, letter to Mlle Leroyer de Chantepie, 13 December 1866.
15 Du Camp: *Les Forces Perdues*, pp. 212 and 301.
16 LOV, BII, letter to Flaubert, 7 December 1866.
17 *Correspondance*, Vol. V, p. 312, letter to Princesse Mathilde, June 1867, and p. 315, letter to Princesse Mathilde, 1 July 1867.
18 *Revue d'Histoire Littéraire de la France*, January–March 1964.
19 Troubat: *Souvenirs du Dernier Secrétaire de Sainte-Beuve*, pp. 350 et seq.
20 Goncourt: *Journal*, Monaco edition, Vol. VIII, pp. 161–5, 6 January 1869.

21 J. Richardson, in *Princess Mathilde*, has made this seem worse by rendering the French 'impotent' by the English 'impotent'.

22 Goncourt: *Journal*, Monaco edition, Vol. V, p. 143, 16 August, 1862.

23 *Ibid.*, Vol. XII, p. 40, 27 July 1879.

24 *Ibid.*, Vol. XI, p. 213, 25 September 1878.

25 Primoli: *Flaubert: Lettres à la Princesse Mathilde*, p. 365.

26 Richardson: *op. cit.*, p. 153.

27 *Ibid.*, p. 169.

28 *Ibid.*, p. 354.

29 Primoli: *op. cit.*, pp. 341 et seq.

30 *Correspondance*, Vol. VI, p. 5 and 7, letter to Princesse Mathilde, January 1869.

31 *Ibid.*, p. 7, letter to George Sand, 2 February 1869.

32 Richardson: *op. cit.*, p. 155.

33 Goncourt: *Journal*, Monaco edition, Vol. XII, p. 85, 25 September 1880.

34 *Correspondance*, Vol. V, p. 354, letter to Duplan, 24 January 1868.

35 *Ibid.*, Vol. VI, p. 31, letter to George Sand, June 1869.

36 LOV CII, letter from Bouilhet, 2 June 1869.

37 Georges Le Roy: *'Quelques Souvenirs Intimes sur Bouilhet'*, in *Mercure de France*, 16 August 1919.

38 *Correspondance*, Vol. VI, p. 43, letter to Du Camp, 23 July 1869.

39 *Ibid.*, p. 41, letter to Du Camp, 23 July 1869.

40 *Ibid.*, p. 102, letter to George Sand, 12 January 1870.

41 Du Camp: *Souvenirs Littéraires*, Vol. II, p. 194.

42 *Ibid.*, p. 461.

43 Bouilhet: *Poésies*, p. 415.

44 *Ibid.*, p. 383.

45 Du Camp: *op. cit.*, p. 470.

46 *Bulletin des Amis de Flaubert*, No. 13, 1958.

47 Published in *L'Éducation Sentimentale*, p. 702.

48 *Correspondance*, Vol. VI, p. 95, letter to George Sand, 3 December 1869.

49 *Ibid.*, Supp. Vol. II, p. 211, letter to George Sand, 17 December 1869.

50 *Ibid.*, Vol. VI, p. 115, letter to George Sand, May 1870.

51 *Ibid.*, Supp. Vol. II, p. 230, letter to Turgenev, 30 August 1870.

52 *Ibid.*, Vol. VI, p. 120, letter to Edmond de Goncourt, 26 June 1870.

53 *Ibid.*, Supp. Vol. II, p. 241, letter to Commanville, 18 August 1870.

Notes

CHAPTER SEVEN: L'ÉDUCATION SENTIMENTALE

1 *L'Éducation Sentimentale*, p. 635.
2 *Ibid.*, pp. 142–3.
3 *Ibid.*, p. 599.
4 *Correspondance*, Vol. V, p. 327, letter to Barbès, 8 October 1867.
5 *Ibid.*, Vol. II, p. 80, letter to Louise Colet, March 1848.
6 M. J. Durry: *Flaubert et ses Projets Inédits*, p. 137.
7 *Vide* Starkie: *The Making of the Master*.
8 *L'Éducation Sentimentale*, p. 351.
9 *Correspondance*, Vol. V, p. 158, letter to Mlle Leroyer de Chantepie, October 1864.
10 *L'Éducation Sentimentale*, p. 203.
11 *Ibid.*, pp. 540–1.
12 *Ibid.*, p. 178.
13 *Ibid.*, p. 97.
14 *Correspondance*, Vol. III, pp. 256–7, letter to Louise Colet, 28–29 June 1853.
15 *Mercure de France*, May 1952.
16 *L'Éducation Sentimentale*, pp. 205–6.
17 *Ibid.*, p. 296.
18 *Ibid.*, pp. 460–1.
19 *Ibid.*, pp. 588–9.
20 *Ibid.*, p. 229.
21 *Ibid.*, p. 536.
22 *Ibid.*, p. 76.
23 *Ibid.*, p. 200.
24 *Ibid.*, p. 195.
25 *Ibid.*, p. 284.
26 *Ibid.*, p. 571.
27 *Ibid.*, pp. 70–1.
28 *Ibid.*, p. 415.
29 *Ibid.*, p. 298.
30 *Ibid.*, pp. 414–6.
31 *Ibid.*, pp. 318–30.
32 *Ibid.*, p. 435.
33 *Ibid.*, p. 300.
34 *Ibid.*, pp. 603–6.
35 *Madame Bovary*, p. 265.
36 B.H.V.P. *Carnet 19*, p. 39.
37 *L'Éducation Sentimentale*, p. 612.
38 Descharmes and Dumesnil: *Autour de Flaubert*, Vol. II, p. 48, note.
39 James in *The House of Fiction* (edited by Leon Edel), p. 203.

371

Notes

Part Two: *The Third Republic*

CHAPTER EIGHT: THE WAR AND THE COMMUNE

1 *Correspondance*, Vol. VI, p. 132, letter to Mlle Leroyer de Chantepie, 8 July 1870.
2 *Ibid.*, pp. 133–5, letter to Caroline, 14 July 1870.
3 *Ibid.*, pp. 134–5, letter to George Sand, 20 July 1870.
4 *Ibid.*, Supp. Vol. II, p. 241, letter to Commanville, 18 August 1870.
5 *Ibid.*, Vol. VI, p. 137, letter to George Sand, 3 August 1870.
6 Du Camp: *Souvenirs Littéraires*, Vol. II, p. 448.
7 *Correspondance*, Vol. VI, p. 145, letter to Caroline, 31 August 1870.
8 *Ibid.*, p. 146, letter to Goncourt, beginning of September 1870.
9 *Ibid.*, p. 157, letter to Caroline, 27 September 1870.
10 *Ibid.*, p. 148, letter to George Sand, 10 September 1870.
11 *Ibid.*, p. 153, letter to Caroline, 22 September 1870.
12 *Ibid.*, p. 175, letter to Caroline, 24 October 1870.
13 *Ibid.*, p. 184, letter to George Sand, 30 October 1870.
14 *Ibid.*, p. 151, letter to George Sand, September 1870.
15 *Ibid.*, p. 159, letter to Du Camp, 29 September 1870.
16 *Ibid.*, p. 165, letter to George Sand, 17 October 1870.
17 *Ibid.*, p. 172, letter to Princesse Mathilde, 23 October 1870.
18 *Ibid.*, p. 193, letter to Caroline, 24 December 1870.
19 Horne: *The Fall of Paris*, p. 241.
20 *Correspondance*, Supp. Vol. II, p. 256, note.
21 Horne: *op. cit.*, p. 262.
22 *Correspondance*, Vol. VI, p. 206, letter to Princesse Mathilde, 4 March 1871.
23 *Ibid.*, p. 202, letter to George Sand, 11 March 1871.
24 *Ibid.*, p. 224, letter to George Sand, 24 April 1871.
25 *Ibid.*, p. 226, letter to Mme Roger des Genettes, 27 April 1871.
26 *Ibid.*, p. 248, letter to George Sand, 11 June 1871.
27 Horne: *op. cit.*, p. 392.
28 *Ibid.*, p. 160.
29 *Ibid.*, p. 416.
30 *Ibid.*, p. 418.
31 *Correspondance*, Vol. VI, p. 241 note.
32 *Ibid.*, p. 251 et seq., letter to Lapierre, 27 May 1871.
33 *Ibid.*, p. 248, letter to Sand, 1 June 1871.
34 *Ibid.*, Vol. VI. The arrangement of the order of the letters gives the impression that she went back to Saint-Gratien in March or April 1871. This cannot be correct. It is virtually proved by J. Richardson, in *Princess Mathilde*, p. 213, that she left for France only in early June 1871.

35 *Correspondance*, Vol. VI, p. 236, letter to Caroline, 10 May 1871.
36 George Sand: *Correspondance*, Vol. VI, p. 169, letter to Flaubert, 16 September 1871.
37 LOV AIV, letter to George Sand, 18 October 1871.
38 Richardson: *op. cit.*, pp. 213–4.
39 *Correspondance*, Vol. VI, p. 259, letter to Feydeau, 29 June 1871.
40 Goncourt: *Journal*, Monaco edition, Vol. X, pp. 22–3, 1 July 1871.

CHAPTER NINE: THE GHOST OF THE DEAD YEARS

1 *Correspondance*, Vol. VI, p. 237, letter to Mme Schlésinger, 22 May 1871.
2 *Ibid.*, p. 381, letter to Mme Schlésinger, 27 May 1872.
3 *Ibid.*, p. 427, letter to Mme Schlésinger, 5 October 1872.
4 *Ibid.*, p. 424, letter to Mme Roger des Genettes, 5 October 1872.
5 Du Camp: *Souvenirs Littéraires*, Vol. II, pp. 477–9.
6 LOV AII, letter from Mme Flaubert to Caroline, 28 March 1872.
7 *Correspondance*, Supp. Vol. III, p. 25, letter to George Sand, 6 April 1872.
8 *Ibid.*, Vol. VI, p. 367, letter to George Sand, 16 April 1872.
9 Maurice Barrès: *Cahiers*, Vol. I, p. 229.
10 *Correspondance*, Supp. Vol. III, p. 63, letter to Caroline, 19 November 1873.
11 *Ibid.*, Vol. VII, p. 122, letter to George Sand, 28 February 1874.
12 Sand: *Correspondance*, Vol. VI, p. 52, letter to Flaubert, 26 October 1872.
13 *Correspondance*, Vol. VI, p. 441, letter to George Sand, 28 October 1872.
14 *Ibid.*, p. 300, letter to Caroline, 26 October.
15 Goncourt: *Journal*, Monaco edition, Vol. X, p. 77, 5 March 1872 and p. 163, 10 February 1874.
16 *Correspondance*, Vol. VII, p. 12, letter to George Sand, 20 March 1873.
17 Maurois: *op. cit.*, p. 456.
18 *Correspondance*, Supp. Vol. II, p. 281, letter to Mayor of Rouen, 2 August 1871.
19 *Ibid.*, Vol. VI, pp. 463–72, letter to Mayor of Rouen, January 1872.
20 *Ibid.*, Vol. VI, p. 487, Preface to *Dernières Chansons* by Bouilhet.
21 *Ibid.*, Vol. VI, p. 349, letter to Mme Roger des Genettes, February 1872.
22 *Ibid.*, Vol. VII, p. 220, letter to Leparfait, November 1873.
23 *Ibid.*, p. 46, letter to Mme Roger des Genettes, 4 August 1873.
24 *Ibid.*, p. 50, letter to Caroline, 15 August 1873.
25 *Ibid.*, p. 94, letter to Caroline, 2 December 1873.

26 *Ibid.*, p. 100, letter to Caroline, 11 December 1873.
27 Letters 5 and 12 March, communicated by J. Richardson, from the Popelin papers.
28 Goncourt: *Journal*, Monaco edition, Vol. X, pp. 168–9, 12 March 1874.
29 *Correspondance*, Vol. VII, p. 127, letter to George Sand, 15 March.
30 Goncourt: *Journal*, Monaco edition, Vol. VI, p. 207, 11 January 1860.
31 *Correspondance*, Vol. VI, p. 228, letter to George Sand, 29 April 1871.
32 *Ibid.*, Vol. VII, p. 126, letter to George Sand, 12 March 1874.
33 *Oeuvres*, Vol. XV, letter from George Sand, 14 March and 3 April 1874.
34 Published in Flaubert: *Théâtre*, p. 518.

CHAPTER TEN: LA TENTATION DE SAINT ANTOINE

1 B.N. N.A.F. 23,666–23,671.
2 G. Dubosc: *Trois Normands*, p. 139.
3 *La Tentation de Saint Antoine*, pp. 1–2.
4 *Correspondance*, Vol. IV, p. 169, letter to Mlle Leroyer de Chantepie, 30 March 1857.
5 Leconte de Lisle: *La Paix des Dieux* (*Derniers Poèmes*).
6 B.N. N.A.F. 23,668. It has not been given in the notes to the Conard edition.
7 Leconte de Lisle: *Le Nazaréen* (*Poèmes Barbares*).
8 B.N. N.A.F. 23,668, fol. 234. This is the fair copy never published by Flaubert, and there are differences between the seven copies.
9 *La Tentation de Saint Antoine*, p. 166.
10 *Ibid.*, p. 174.
11 *Ibid.*, p. 176.
12 *Ibid.*, p. 181.
13 *Ibid.*, p. 187.
14 *Ibid.*, p. 197.
15 *Ibid.*, p. 200.
16 B.N. N.A.F. 23,666, fol. 134, unpublished.
17 *Correspondance*, Vol. VII, p. 22, letter to George Sand, end of May 1873.
18 *La Tentation de Saint Antoine*, p. 201.
19 LOV AIV, letter to George Sand, 28 June 1869.
20 Seznec: *op. cit.*, is important for the sources of the fabulous animals in *La Tentation de Saint Antoine*.
21 Seznec: *op. cit.*
22 Du Camp: *Souvenirs Littéraires*, Vol. II, pp. 329–30.

Notes

23 Anatole France: *La Vie Littéraire*, Vol. II, p. 221.
24 Letter from Taine to Flaubert, 1 April 1874, published in *La Tentation de Saint Antoine*, p. 683.
25 B.N. N.A.F. 23,670, fol. 54.
26 *La Tentation de Saint Antoine*, p. 30.
27 *Ibid.*, p. 147.

CHAPTER ELEVEN: BANKRUPTCY

1 *Correspondance*, Vol. VII, p. 163, letter to George Sand, 3 July 1874.
2 *Ibid.*, p. 166, letter to Princesse Mathilde, 10 July 1874.
3 Durry: *op. cit.*, p. 258.
4 *Correspondance*, Vol. VII, p. 184, letter to Caroline, 6 August 1874.
5 *Ibid.*, p. 189, letter to Caroline, 28 August 1874.
6 Zola: *Les Romanciers Naturalistes*, p. 149.
7 *Correspondance*, Supp. Vol. II, p. 302, letter to Commanville, 27 December 1871.
8 Edizioni di Storia e Letteratura, Rome 1960.
9 Spaziani: *op. cit.*, p. 85.
10 *Ibid.*, pp. 85–7.
11 *Ibid.*, p. 88.
12 *Correspondance*, Vol. VII, p. 245, letter to Caroline, 9 July 1875.
13 *Ibid.*, p. 256, letter to Princesse Mathilde, 3 September 1875.
14 *Ibid.*, Supp. Vol. III, p. 212, letter to Turgenev, 3 October 1875.
15 Goncourt: *Journal*, Monaco edition, Vol. XI, 8 November 1875.
16 *Correspondance*, Supp. Vol. III, p. 214, letter to George Sand, 3 October 1875.
17 *Ibid.*, Vol. VII, p. 272, letter to Caroline, 11 October 1875.
18 *Ibid.*, Supp. Vol. III, p. 197, p. 205, letters to Bardoux, 29 August and 13 September 1875.
19 *Ibid.*, Vol. VII, p. 276, letter 21 October 1875.
20 *Ibid.*, p. 262, letter to Caroline, 25 September 1875.
21 Sand: *Correspondance*, Vol. VI, p. 367, letter to Flaubert, December 1875.
22 *Correspondance*, Vol. VII, p. 280, letter to George Sand, end of December 1875.
23 *Ibid.*, p. 307, letter to Mme Roger des Genettes, 19 June 1876.
24 *Ibid.*, Vol. VIII, p. 65, letter to Maurice Sand, 29 August 1877.
25 *Ibid.*, Vol. VII, p. 299, letters to Mme Maurice Sand, 25 May and 3 June 1876.
26 Sand: *Correspondance*, Vol. VI, p. 380, letter to Flaubert, 12 January 1876.

27 *Ibid.*, p. 403, letter to Favre, 28 May 1876.
28 *Correspondance*, Vol. VII, p. 304, letter to Mlle Leroyer de Chantepie, 17 June 1876.
29 *Ibid.*, p. 380, letter to Caroline, Christmas Day 1876.
30 *Ibid.*, Supp. Vol. III, p. 335, note.
31 *Trois Contes*, p. 234.

CHAPTER TWELVE: TROIS CONTES

1 B.N. N.A.F. 23,663–665.
2 Du Camp: *Souvenirs Littéraires*, Vol. I, p. 525.
3 Lille le Beffroi: *Le Saint Julien de Flaubert*, 1903.
4 A. Raitt: 'The Composition of Flaubert's *Saint Julien l'Hospitalier*' in *French Studies*, October 1965.
5 *Correspondance*, Vol. I, p. 16, letter to Chevalier, 18 June 1835.
6 Raitt: *op. cit.*
7 Hugo: *Le Rhin* (Nelson edition), p. 345.
8 Raitt: *op. cit.*
9 *Trois Contes*, p. 85.
10 *Ibid.*, p. 79.
11 *Ibid.*, pp. 80–81.
12 *Ibid.*, pp. 90–91 et seq.
13 *Ibid.*, pp. 106–7 et seq.
14 *Notes de Voyages*, Vol. I, p. 15.
15 *Trois Contes*, pp. 111 et seq.
16 *Ibid.*, p. 121.
17 *Ibid.*, pp. 124–125.
18 *Correspondance*, Vol. VII, p. 352, letter to Gertrude Tennant, 19 October 1876.
19 *Ibid.*, Vol. VIII, p. 20, letter to Gertrude Tennant, February–March 1877.
20 *Ibid.*, Vol. VII, p. 378, letter to Gertrude Tennant, Christmas Day, 1876.
21 Bibliothèque Municipale de Rouen, g 226[8], fol. 195.
22 *Trois Contes*, p. 40.
23 *Ibid.*, p. 54.
24 *Ibid.*, pp. 19 et seq.
25 *Ibid.*, pp. 61–4.
26 *Ibid.*, p. 41.
27 *Ibid.*, p. 12.
28 *Correspondance*, Vol. VII, p. 296, letter to Mme Roger des Genettes, end of April 1876.
29 *Ibid.*, Vol. IV, p. 170, letter to Mlle Leroyer de Chantepie, 30 March 1857.

30 *Ibid.*, Vol. VII, p. 309, letter to Mme Roger des Genettes, 19 June 1876.
31 *Trois Contes*, p. 167.
32 *Ibid.*, p. 184.
33 *Vide* Starkie: *The Making of the Master*, p. 174.
34 *Trois Contes*, pp. 184 et seq.
35 *Ibid.*, p. 188.
36 *Ibid.*, p. 189.
37 *Ibid.*, p. 138.
38 *Ibid.*, p. 161.
39 *Ibid.*, pp. 226–7.

CHAPTER THIRTEEN: THE FINAL YEARS

1 R. Baldick: *Pages from the Goncourt Journal*, p. 231, note.
2 *Correspondance*, Vol. VIII, p. 60, letter to Caroline, 21 August 1877.
3 *Fortnightly Review*, 1 April 1878.
4 Goncourt: *Journal*, Monaco edition, Vol. XI, p. 231.
5 *Correspondance*, Supp. Vol. IV, p. 160, letter to Turgenev, 10 February 1879.
6 *Ibid.*, p. 117, letter to Caroline, 13 September 1877.
7 Bart: *op. cit.*, p. 724.
8 LOV AIII, fol. 214, 11 January 1879.
9 *Correspondance*, Vol. VIII, p. 117, letter to Caroline, 15 September 1878.
10 *Ibid.*, p. 191, letter to Caroline, 21 January 1879.
11 *Ibid.*, p. 205, letter to Caroline, February 1879.
12 *Correspondance*, Supp. Vol. IV, p. 176, letter to Caroline, 1 March 1879.
13 *Ibid.*, p. 186, letter to Caroline, 9 March 1879.
14 *Ibid.*, p. 229, letter to Caroline, 16 May 1879.
15 *Ibid.*, Vol. VIII, p. 171, letter to Princesse Mathilde, December 1878.
16 *Ibid.*, p. 172, letter to Princesse Mathilde, 21 December 1878.
17 *Ibid.*, Supp. Vol. IV, p. 146, letter to Goncourt, 3 January 1879.
18 *Ibid.*, Vol. VIII, p. 185, letter to Mme Brainne, January 1879.
19 LOV BVI, fol. 139, letter from Zola, February 1879. It is a long letter of which only a small portion is quoted here.
20 Flaubert: *Lettres Inédites à Raoul-Duval*, p. 225–7.
21 *Correspondance*, Vol. VIII, p. 261, letter to Caroline, 25 April 1879.
22 LOV BIV, fol. 357, letter from Maupassant, March 1879.
23 *Correspondance*, Vol. VIII, p. 267, letter beginning of June 1879.
24 *Ibid.*, p. 305, letter to Caroline, 8 October 1879.
25 *Ibid.*, p. 283, letter to Princesse Mathilde, 15 July 1879.

26 *Ibid.*, p. 308, letter to Comtesse de Loynes, 8 October 1879.
27 Primoli Diary, p. 10, 15 September 1879, communicated by J. Richardson.
28 *Correspondance*, Supp. Vol. IV, pp. 266–8, letter to Laporte, 28 September 1879.
29 *Ibid.*, p. 267 note.
30 *Ibid.*, Vol. VIII, p. 305, letter to Caroline, 8 October 1879.
31 *Ibid.*, p. 331, letter to Caroline, 6–7 December 1879.
32 LOV AIII, fol. 451, unpublished copy of a letter from Laporte to Flaubert.
33 *Correspondance*, Supp. Vol. IV, p. 297, letter to Caroline, 2 January 1880.
34 LOV AIII, fol. 451, letter to Caroline, 6 February 1880.
35 Flaubert: *Lettres Inédites à Raoul-Duval*, p. 231.
36 Goncourt: *Journal*, Monaco edition, Vol. XI, p. 145, 31 May 1877.
37 Digeon: *Le Dernier Visage de Flaubert*, pp. 66–7.
38 Durry: *op. cit.*, pp. 258 et seq.
39 Flaubert: *Lettres à Maupassant*, pp. 211 et seq.
40 LOV BIV, fol. 130, letter from Mme Lapierre, probably after 1870.
41 *Correspondance*, Supp. Vol. III, p. 24, letter to Mme Brainne, 31 March 1872.
42 *Ibid.*, p. 220, letter to Mme Brainne, 28 July 1876.
43 *Ibid.*, p. 300, letter to Mme Brainne, 31 December 1876.
44 *Ibid.*, p. 187, letter to Mme Brainne, 27 July 1875.
45 LOV BI, 1876, letter from Mme Brainne.
46 *Correspondance*, Vol. VII, p. 352, letter to Mme Tennant, 19 October 1876.
47 *Ibid.*, p. 376, letter to Mme Tennant, 25 December 1876.
48 *Ibid.*, Vol. VIII, p. 18, letter to Mme Tennant, 16 February 1877.
49 *Ibid.*, p. 20, letter to Mme Tennant, February-March 1877.
50 *Ibid.*, p. 116, letter to Mme Tennant, 4 May 1878.
51 *Ibid.*, p. 138, letter to Mme Tennant, 1 September 1878.
52 *Ibid.*, p. 347, letter to Mme Tennant, 13 January 1880.
53 *Les Romanciers Naturalistes*, p. 149.
54 LOV BIII. letter from Heredia, 1878.
55 *Correspondance*, Vol. VIII, p. 165, letter to Toudouze, 29 November 1878.
56 Flaubert: *Lettres Inédites à Raoul-Duval*, pp. 255–6.
57 *Correspondance*, Vol. IX, pp. 4 et seq., letter to Caroline, 14 March 1880.
58 *Ibid.*, p. 8, letter to Caroline, 15–16 March 1880.
59 Goncourt: *Journal*, Vol. VI, p. 109, 28 March 1880.
60 *Correspondance*, Vol. IX, p. 30, letter to Caroline, 28 April 1880.
61 Published by J. Richardson from the Popelin papers, in *The Times*

Literary Supplement, 13 June 1968 (hitherto unpublished).

62 Descharmes and Dumesnil: *Autour de Flaubert*, Vol. II, p. 100.

63 Dumesnil: *Gustave Flaubert, L'Homme et l'oeuvre*, p. 491.

64 M. Renault in *Le Concours Médical*, 22 January 1939.

65 Quoted in Flaubert: *Lettres Inédites à Raoul-Duval*, pp. 262–5.

66 *Correspondance*, Vol. IV, p. 341, letter to Feydeau, October–November 1859.

67 *Ibid.*, Vol. IX, p. 5, letter to Caroline, 14 March 1880.

68 LOV BVI, fol. 399, letter from Du Camp to Caroline, 17 May 1880.

69 Goncourt: *Journal*, Monaco edition, Vol. XII, pp. 75–8.

70 Zola: *op. cit.*, p. 137.

71 LOV BVI, letter 11 June 1881 to unknown correspondent.

72 Émile-Blanche: *La Pêche aux Souvenirs*, p. 63.

73 Barrès, *Mes Cahiers*, Vol. VII, p. 16.

CHAPTER FOURTEEN: BOUVARD ET PÉCUCHET

1 Bibliothèque Municipale de Rouen, g224; g225 1–3; g226 1–8; g227; gg10.

2 *Correspondance*, Vol. I, p. xliii.

3 Descharmes and Dumesnil: *op. cit.*, Vol. II, *Les Ancêtres de Bouvard et Pécuchet*.

4 Durry: *op. cit.*, Carnet 19.

5 *Correspondance*, Vol. VII, p. 171, letter to Mme Roger des Genettes, 14 July 1874.

6 *Ibid.*, Vol. VIII, p. 336, letter to Mme Tennant 16 December 1879.

7 Bibliothèque Municipale de Rouen, Plan gg10, not dated but certainly after the 1863 plan.

8 Durry: *op. cit.*, p. 96.

9 *Correspondance*, Vol. VIII, p. 356, letter to Mme Roger des Genettes, 25 January 1880.

10 Bibliothèque Municipale de Rouen, g226 1–8.

11 *Ibid.*, g225 1–3.

12 *Ibid.*, g224.

13 *Ibid.*, g227 and gg10.

14 *Ibid.*, g265, fol. 142–7 and 150.

15 *Correspondance*, Vol. VIII, p. 102, letter to Caroline, 9 December 1877.

16 *Ibid.*, p. 82, letter to Zola, 5 October, 1877.

17 Alberto Cento: *Bouvard et Pécuchet*, édition critique, 1964.

18 Bibliothèque Municipale de Rouen, gg10 fol. 32.

19 A. Cento: *op. cit.*, G. Bollème: *op. cit.*, D. L. Demorest: *À travers les plans, messages et dossiers de Bouvard et Pécuchet*.

20 It has been published in Bollème: *op. cit.*, pp. 98 and 192.

21 *Correspondance*, Vol. II, p. 237, letter to Bouilhet, 4 September 1850.
22 Bibliothèque Municipale de Rouen, gg10, fol. 68.
23 Bollème: *op. cit.*, pp. 73, 79, 110 and 135.
24 Bibliothèque Municipale de Rouen, g2264.
25 *Correspondance*, Vol. VI, p. 425, letter to Mme Roger des Genettes, 5 October 1872: p. 437, letter to Feydeau 28 October 1872; and Supp. Vol. III, p. 56, letter to Mme Brainne, 5 October 1872.
26 *Ibid.*, Vol. VIII, p. 336, letter to Mme Tennant, 16 December 1879.
27 *Bouvard et Pécuchet*, p. 66.
28 *Ibid.*, p. 96.
29 *Correspondance*, Vol. VI, p. 215, letter to George Sand, 31 March 1871.
30 Taine, *loc. cit.*
31 *Bouvard et Pécuchet*, p. 66.
32 Bibliothèque Municipale de Rouen, gg10, fol. 42.
33 *Bouvard et Pécuchet*, p. 292.
34 *Ibid.*, pp. 296 et seq.
35 *Ibid.*, pp. 299–300.
36 *Correspondance*, Vol. VIII, p. 353, letter to Maupassant, 23 January 1880.
37 *Bouvard et Pécuchet*, p. 390.
38 Brombert: *The Novels of Flaubert*, p. 262.
39 *Bouvard et Pécuchet*, p. 218.
40 *Ibid.*, p. 207.
41 *Ibid.*, p. 215.
42 *Ibid.*, p. 217.
43 *Ibid.*, p. 366.
44 *Ibid.*, p. 354.
45 Bibliothèque Municipale de Rouen, gg10.
46 *Bouvard et Pécuchet*, pp. 94–5.
47 *Ibid.*, pp. 293–4.
48 Thorlby: *Gustave Flaubert and the Art of Realism*, p. 56.
49 Baudelaire: *Une Charogne*, Pléiade edition, p. 103.
50 *Bouvard et Pécuchet*, pp. 326–7.
51 *Ibid.*, pp. 365–6.
52 *Correspondance*, Vol. VIII, p. 378, letter to Charpentier, 3 February 1880.
53 Brombert, *op. cit.*, p. 258.

CONCLUSION

1 *Correspondance*, Vol. VIII, pp. 61–2, letter to Louise Colet, 9 December 1852.

2 James: *French Poets and Novelists*, p. 209.

3 James: *Notes on Novelists*, p. 67.

4 James, in *The House of Fiction*, (edited by Leon Edel), p. 189.

5 Goncourt: *Journal*, Monaco edition, Vol. V, p. 67, 3 March 1862.

6 *Nouvelle Revue*, January 1881.

7 Preface to *Pierre et Jean* (Garnier edition), p. 21.

8 *L'Éducation Sentimentale*, pp. 92–3.

9 *Correspondance*, Vol. VI, p. 356, letter to George Sand, March 1872.

10 Brombert: *The Novels of Flaubert*, p. 159.

11 LOV BV, letter from Mme Régnier, 21 November 1869.

12 *Correspondance*, Supp. Vol. II, p. 245, letter to Dr Cloquet, 17 October 1870.

13 *Ibid.*, Supp. Vol. III, p. 46, letter to Raoul-Duval, August 1872.

14 *Ibid.*, Supp. Vol. IV, p. 226, letter to Caroline, 10 May 1879.

15 Zola: *op. cit.*, p. 151.

16 Mme Alphonse Daudet: *Souvenirs autour d'un Groupe Littéraire*, p. 18.

17 France: *La Vie Littéraire*, Vol. II, p. 19.

18 Goncourt: *Journal*, Monaco edition, Vol. X, p. 123, 26 February 1874.

19 Du Camp: *Souvenirs Littéraires*, Vol. I, p. 225.

20 Letter 24 May 1880, quoted in Albalat: *Gustave Flaubert et ses Amis*, p. 228.

21 *Correspondance*, Vol. VIII, p. 225, letter to Caroline, 16 April 1879.

22 *Ibid.*, Vol. VII, p. 370, letter to Turgenev, 14 December 1876.

23 Goncourt: *Journal*, Monaco edition, Vol. XI, p. 92, 5 May 1876.

24 *The House of Fiction*, (edited by Leon Edel), p. 189.

25 Goncourt: *Journal*, Monaco edition, Vol. III, p. 178, 9 April 1859.

26 *Ibid.*, Vol. VI, p. 144, 1 November 1853.

27 *Correspondance*, Vol. V, p. 371, letter to Caroline, May 1868.

28 L. Bertrand: *Gustave Flaubert*, p. 193, note 2.

29 Mauriac: *Trois Grands Hommes devant Dieu*, pp. 166–8.

30 *Correspondance*, Vol. VIII, p. 335, letter to Caroline, 16 December 1879.

31 *Ibid.*, Vol. IV, p. 278, letter to Feydeau, October 1858.

32 *Ibid.*, Vol. V, p. 275, letter to George Sand, 30 January 1867.

33 *Ibid.*, Vol. VIII, p. 239, letter to Caroline, 21 March 1879.

34 *Ibid.*, Vol. IV, p. 341, letter to Feydeau, October–November 1859.

35 *Ibid.*, Vol. II, p. 394, letter to Louise Colet, 24 April 1852.

36 LOV BIII, fol. 209, letter from France, undated.

37 *Correspondance*, Vol. VIII, p. 209, letter to Frankline Sabatier, February 1879.

INDEX

Index